DESIGN FOR EARTHQUAKES

DESIGN FOR EARTHQUAKES

JAMES AMBROSE
DIMITRY VERGUN

JOHN WILEY & SONS, INC.
New   York • Chichester • Weinheim • Brisbane • Singapore • Toronto

This publication is designed to provide accurate and authoritative information in regard to the subject matter covered. It is sold with the understanding that the publisher is not engaged in rendering professional services. If professional advice or other expert assistance is required, the services of a competent professional person should be sought.

Library of Congress Cataloging in Publication Data:
Ambrose, James E.
    Design for earthquake / James Ambrose, Dimitry Vergun.
      p. cm.
    Includes bibliographical references and index.
    ISBN 0-471-24188-1 (alk. paper)
    1. Earthquake resistant design.   I. Vergun, Dimitry, 1933–
  II. Title.
    TA658.44.A43   1999
    693.8'52—dc21   98-29972

Printed in the United States of America

10 9 8 7 6 5 4 3 2 1

CONTENTS

PREFACE

This book provides a general introduction to the topic of design of buildings for resistance to the effects of earthquakes. It is intended for a general readership, especially persons with an interest in the design and construction of buildings.

A major part of design for earthquake resistance involves the building structure, which has a primary role in preventing serious damage or actual structural collapse. Much of the material in this book examines building structures and, specifically, their resistance to lateral forces. Some sample structural computations are presented, although, for the most part, they are quite simple in form.

When an earthquake strikes, it shakes the whole building and its contents. Full design for earthquakes therefore, must, include considerations for the complete building construction, for the contents of the building, and for the building occupants. Many issues along these lines are addressed in this book.

The work of designing for earthquake effects is informed by a steady stream of studies, research, new technologies, and the cumulative knowledge gained from forensic studies of earthquake-damaged buildings. Design and construction practices, regulating codes, and industry and professional standards are continuously upgraded as a result of the flow of this information.

We developed the materials in this book from current information, but this knowledge base is growing so fast that by the time this book reaches the hands of readers much new knowledge will be available. While it is important to try to keep abreast of this expanding body of knowledge, first attention should be given to fundamental issues and principles, which, for the most part, remain unchanged, even as experience grows. We have chosen to focus here on fundamentals.

Although this book may appear to present a daunting amount of material, it is, nevertheless, just a toe in the door of the vast library of knowledge that exists to support the work of design for earthquake effects. Readers may use this book to gain a general awareness of the field or to launch a much more exhaustive program of study. For the working designer, that program will extend throughout an active career.

Both of us bring long experience in professional design practice and in teaching and writing to the task of creating this book. We are grateful to many people who helped us share our experience with you. Continuing a long tradition of academic excellence, the University of Southern California and its School of Architecture have been sources of consistent support and encouragement. Continuing to lead the field in publishing, the people at John Wiley & Sons inspire us to strive for a quality level that is the highest in the field of professional publications. Finally, our many design clients and students have given us enriching feedback that helps us continue to refine our information-delivery skills.

JAMES AMBROSE
DIMITRY VERGUN

INTRODUCTION

Over the years, earthquakes have been the cause of great disasters in the form of destruction of property and of injury and loss of life to the population. The unpredictability and sudden occurrence and of earthquakes makes them somewhat mysterious, both to the general public and to professional building designers. Until quite recently, design for earthquakes—if consciously considered at all—was done with simplistic methods and a small data base. Extensive study and research and a great international effort of cooperation have vastly improved design theories and procedures. Accordingly, most buildings in earthquake-prone areas today are designed in considerable detail for seismic resistance.

Despite the best efforts of scientists and designers, most truly effective design methods are those reinforced by experience. This experience, unfortunaely, grows by leaps when a major earthquake occurs and strongly affects regions of considerable development—notably urban areas. Observation of damaged buildings by experts in forensic engineering add immeasurably to our knowledge base. While extensive research studies are ongoing in many testing laboratories, the biggest laboratory remains the real world and real earthquakes.

Following a major earthquake that affects an urban area, there is a short period of time during which the general public has an intensified awareness of and a concern for the need for better design and control of construction for seismic resistance. Typically, in these times, information and recommendations pour forth from various sources. Eventually some changes are effected in design codes, and the art of design and the craft of building are nudged slightly upward.

The essential aim of this book is to provide designers with an overview of the problems of seismic design for buildings and the solutions available for design use in the form of information, design criteria and procedures, design aids, and construction technology. The focus of the book is on design, rather than on analytical investigation or scientific inquiry. Design—in architecture and in engineering—requires practical solutions to problems, whatever the present state of scientific knowledge or the reliability of analytical methods. Design work should be well informed and done with thorough consideration of eventualities.

Design decisions that affect the seismic response of buildings range from broad to highly specific ones. While much of this design work may be performed by structural engineers, many decisions are made by, or are strongly affected by, others. Building codes and industry standards establish restrictions on the use of procedures for analysis of structural behavior and for the selection of materials and basic systems for construction. Decisions about site development, buildings placement on sites, building form and dimensions, and the selection of materials and details for construction are often made by building owners and architects, among others.

It is necessary, of course, for a qualified structural designer to perform essential design tasks. However, it is equally important for someone to see that all of the decisions made by others are done with an understanding of their consequences for seismic performance of the building and of the developed building site. This book addresses the broad audience of people involved in controlling the design of buildings and their sites.

While ultimate collapse of the building structure is a principal concern, the building's performance during an earthquake must be considered in many other ways as well. If the structure remains intact, but nonstructural parts of the building sustain critical damage, occupants are traumatized or injured, and it is infeasible to restore the building for continued use, the design work may not be viewed as a success.

Since the work of designing structures is affected by many people besides the structural designer, we have presented the design problems in a manner intended to illustrate the full scope of influence. And while adequate structural performance under seismic loading conditions is a principal concern, we also consider the effects of seismic movements on the rest of the building and its occupants is.

The work in this book should be accessible to the broad range of people in the building design and construction fields. This calls for some compromise since all are trained highly in some areas and less—or not at all—in others. We assume that readers have general knowledge of building codes, current construction technology, principal problems of planning buildings, and at least an introduction to design of simple structures for buildings. Most of all, readers, need some real motivation for learning about making buildings safer during earthquakes.

Readers less prepared may wish to strengthen their backgrounds in order to get the most from the work in this book. We give a list of references at the back of this book, including many titles that can be useful for this purpose.

UNITS OF MEASUREMENT

Table 1 lists the standard units of measurement in the U.S. system with the abbreviations used in this work and a description of common usage in structural design work. Table 2 gives the corresponding units in the metric system. Conversion factors to be used for shifting from one unit system to the other are given in Table 3. Direct use of the conversion factors will produce what is called a *hard conversion* of a reasonably precise form.

Accuracy of Computations

Structures for buildings are seldom produced with a high degree of dimensional precision. Exact dimensions are difficult to achieve, even for the most diligent of workers and builders. Add this to considerations for the lack of precision in predicting loads for any

Table 1.   Units of Measurements: U.S. System

Name of Unit	Abbreviation	Use in Building Design
Length		
Foot	ft	Large dimensions, building plans, beam spans
Inch	in.	Small dimensions, size of member cross sections
Area		
Square feet	ft^2	Large areas
Square inches	$in.^2$	Small areas, properties of cross sections
Volume		
Cubic yards	yd^3	Large volumes, soil or concrete (commonly called "yards")
Cubic feet	ft^3	Quantities of materials
Cubic inches	$in.^3$	Small volumes
Force, Mass		
Pound	lb	Specific weight, force, load
Kip	kip, k	1000 pounds
Ton	Ton	2000 pounds
Pounds per foot	lb/ft, plf	Linear load (as on a beam)
Kips per foot	kips/ft, klf	Linear load (as on a beam)
Pounds per square foot	lb/ft^2, psf	Distributed load on a surface, pressure
Kips per square foot	k/ft^2, ksf	Distributed load on a surface, pressure
Pounds per cubic foot	lb/ft^3	Relative density, unit weight
Moment		
Foot-pounds	ft-lb	Rotational or bending moment
inch-pounds	in.-lb	Rotational or bending moment
Kip-feet	kip-ft	Rotational or bending moment
Kip-inches	kip-in.	Rotational or bending moment
Stress		
Pounds per square foot	lb/ft^2, psf	Soil pressure
Pounds per square inch	lb/in^2, psi	Stresses in structures
Kips per square foot	$kips/ft^2$, ksf	Soil pressure
Kips per square inch	$kips/in.^2$, ksi	Stresses in structures
Temperature		
Degree Fahrenheit	^oF	Temperature

structure, and the significance of highly precise structural computations is moot. This is not an argument to justify sloppy mathematical work, overly sloppy construction, or use of vague theories of investigation of behaviors. Nevertheless, it is a case for not being highly concerned with any numbers beyond about the second digit (103 or 104—who cares?).

While most professional design work these days is likely to be done with computer support, most of the work illustrated here is quite simple and was actually performed with a hand calculator (the 8-digit, scientific type is adequate). Even these primitive computations are rounded off occasionally.

Table 2.   Units of Measurements: SI. System

Name of Unit	Abbreviation	Use in Building Design
Length		
Meter	m	Large dimensions, building plans, beam spans
Millimeter	mm	Small dimensions, size of member cross sections
Area		
Square meters	m^2	Large areas
Square millimeters	mm^2	Small areas, properties of member cross sections
Volume		
Cubic meters	m^3	Large volumes
Cubic millimeters	mm^3	Small volumes
Mass		
Kilogram	kg	Mass of material (equivalent to weight in U.S. Units)
Kilograms per cubic meter	kg/m^3	Density (unit weight)
Force, Load		
Newton	N	Force or load on structure
Kilonewton	kN	1,000 Newtons
Stress		
Pascal	Pa	Stress or pressure (1 pascal $= 1\ N/m^2$)
Kilopascal	kPa	1,000 pascals
Megapascal	MPa	1,000,000 pascals
Gigapascal	GPa	1,000,000,000 pascals
Temperature		
Degree Celsius	°C	Temperature

Nomenclature

Notation used in this book complies generally with that used in the building design field. A general attempt has been made to conform to usage in the 1997 edition of the *Uniform Building Code* (Ref. 1). The following list includes all of the notation used in this book that is general and is related to the topic of the book. Specialized notation used by various professional groups, especially as related to individual materials (wood, steel, masonry, concrete, and so on) can be found in basic references for notation in these fields.

Building codes, including the *UBC*, use special notation that is generally carefully defined by the code, and the reader is referred to the source for interpretation of these definitions. When used in demonstrations of computations, such notation is explained in the text.

Ag   Ggross area of section, defined by the outer dimensions
An   Net area
C   Compressive force
E   Modulus of elasticity (general)

Table 3. Factors for Conversion of Units

To Convert from U.S. Units, to SI Units, Multiply by	U.S. Unit	SI Unit	To Convert from SI Units to U.S. Units, Multiply by
25.4	in.	mm	0.03937
0.3048	ft	m	3.281
645.2	in.^{2}	mm^2	1.550×10^{-3}
16.39×10^3	in^3	mm^3	61.02×10^{-6}
416.2×10^3	in.^{4}	mm^4	2.403×10^{-6}
0.09290	ft^2	m^2	10.76
0.02832	ft^3	m^3	35.31
0.4536	lb (mass)	kg	2.205
4.448	lb (force)	N	0.2248
4.448	kip (force)	kN	0.2248
1.356	ft-lb (moment)	N-m	0.7376
1.356	kip-ft (moment)	kN-m	0.7376
16.0185	lb/ft^3 (density)	kg/m^3	0.06243
14.59	lb/ft (load)	N/m	0.06853
14.59	kip/ft (load)	kN/m	0.06853
6.895	psi (stress)	kPa	0.1450
6.895	ksi (stress)	MPa	0.1450
0.04788	psf (load or pressure)	kPa	20.93
47.88	ksf (load or pressure)	kPa	0.02093
$0.566 \times (^\circ F - 32)$	$^\circ F$	$^\circ C$	$(1.8 \times {}^\circ C) + 32$

I   Moment of inertia

L   Length (usually of a span)

M   Bending moment

P   Concentrated load

S   Section modulus

T   Tension force

W   (1) Total gravity load; (2) weight, or dead load of an object; (3) total wind load force; (4) total of a uniformly distributed load or pressure due to gravity

a   Unit area compression face

e   Eccentricity of a nonaxial load, from point of application of the load to the centroid of the section

f   Computed stress

h   Effective height (usually meaning unbraced height) of a wall or column

l   Length, usually of a span

s   Spacing, center to center

PART 1

Basic Considerations

In this part we introduce the basic issues relating to the nature of earthquakes, the effects on buildings and building sites of earthquakes, and the general responses that designers have made in developing earthquake-resistant construction. The discussions in this part are mostly limited to general cases. This information is useful on its own and it also serves as a background and general reference for the several building and site cases presented in Part Two. These provide particular situations for application of the general information presented in this part. Readers with significant background in the general material presented in this part may prefer to skip to Part Two, using this part only as necessary for review or reference.

1

Earthquakes and Their Effects

Essentially, earthquakes are vibrations of the earth's crust caused by sudden and violent subterranean movements. They occur several times a day in various parts of the earth, although only a few each year are of sufficient magnitude to cause significant damage to buildings. Major earthquakes occur most frequently in regions called zones of high seismic risk but, theoretically, it is possible to have a major earthquake anywhere on the earth.

During an earthquake, the ground surface moves in all directions. The most damaging effects on stationary structures are generally caused by the movements parallel to the ground surface (that is, horizontally) because structures are ordinarily designed to support vertical gravity loads (Figure 1.1). In this regard, the effects of wind and earthquakes, are similar. Horizontal force effects are also described as *lateral*, as they are at right angles to the more commonly experienced load source—gravity.

If this book were a general study of earthquakes it would include considerations of ground faults, the propagation of seismic shock waves, the means of measuring and recording earthquakes, and so on. Instead, we concentrate on the influence of earthquakes on the design of buildings and of the sites on which buildings are placed.

1.1 HOW EARTHQUAKES WORK

An earthquake (also called a *seismic event*) is the vibration of the earth's surface that follows a sudden release of energy in the crust. This energy release can be caused by a sudden dislocation or fracture of a part of the earth's crust, or a volcanic eruption, or a man-made explosion of great magnitude. Vibrations, called *seismic waves*, emanate from the location of the energy release and travel through the earth's mass. On the surface of the earth, the wave action of these traveling vibrations causes motions of a typical harmonic nature, which can be plotted as a displacement/time or acceleration/time graph (Figure 1.2). These graphs can establish the frequency and amplitude of ground movements and the duration of the seismic event.

FIGURE 1.1 The steel post and beam frame, mostly comprising single-span beams, is highly unstable. Bracing is needed just for safety of assembly, but more so for resistance of lateral forces due to wind and earthquakes. Classic forms of bracing were developed for the earliest frames and many are still in use.

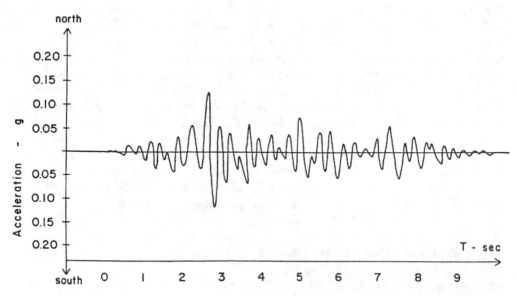

FIGURE 1.2 General form of the ground acceleration graph for a short-duration earthquake.

Large earthquakes can cause a number of hazardous actions. First is the simple motion of the ground surface—up and down and sideways. But beyond that, some of the most disastrous effects are caused by tidal waves and avalanches and by secondary actions of the ground surface that result in cracks, subsidence, vertical slip, horizontal slip, soil liquefaction, and earth slides on slopes (Figure 1.3).

FIGURE 1.3 Parts of many steep slopes are lost in every major earthquake. These are mostly failures that are ongoing or are waiting to happen, and the earthquake is just the final downhill push.

There is little that can be done to protect buildings and their sites from the secondary effects of earthquakes, other than to avoid locating buildings in areas with predictable vulnerability to these actions. For building designers, the major focus is on the effects induced in a building by the vibratory movements of its site.

Of course, it is possible to move a building purposely without causing significant damage to the construction. Many buildings, including multistory ones, have been picked up from their foundations and moved to new locations. What is harmful about movements caused by earthquakes is the speed with which the movements occur, plus the rapid reversals of direction that cause a violent shaking effect. The dynamic force effect of the rapid, jolting movement, plus the destabilizing effects of the shaking, can be disastrous for the building and its occupants and can dislodge furniture, building equipment, and loosely-attached fixtures.

To investige the potential for damage to a particular building from an earthquake, it is first necessary to establish the precise nature and magnitude of the movements that could be induced in the building. Once in motion, a building will respond in terms of its own particular dynamic response nature, with different buildings responding differently, even on the same site.

1.2   DYNAMIC PROPERTIES OF EARTHQUAKES

To determine the potential for building damage, the following aspects of ground motion must be considered:

1. The *direction* of the motion. Movement in different directions produces varying effects on a building. Since the ground can move in all directions, all possible movements must be considered for a single building.
2. The *displacement* from the neutral position.
3. The *acceleration* of the motion, as this relates directly to the magnitude of force on the building.
4. The general form of the cyclic motion in terms of its *duration* and the *frequency* or *period* of the motion.

Alone, dimensional displacements during seismic motions are not often critical. Typically, the displacement/time relationship is more critical, especially in terms of maximum accelerations. This is evident from the simple equation for dynamic force: $F = m \times a$ (or force equals mass times acceleration). Thus the potential force effect created by the building's movement is represented by its momentum, measured as the product of its *mass* (weight) and the acceleration of its motion.

It takes a number of coincident factors to produce a damaging earthquake. A primary consideration is the magnitude of the earthquake. Magnitude may be measured by the level of actual observed damage, which is the basis for the *Mercalli method*. This consists of identifying levels of damage and drawing a contour map around the epicenter, typically describing concentric zones outward with descending levels of damage.

The earthquake itself is commonly measured by the numerical scale first developed by Richter. This is a log-based scale that assigns a number that earthquake watchers have come to recognize as minor (2), moderate (4), or severe (6 or higher). Because of the log base, the magnitude rises much more rapidly than the simple numbers indicate. Thus a level 6 earthquake is not three times as violent as a level 2 earthquake, but instead is several hundred times as violent. Every earthquake detected by scientific monitors is assigned a number for its maximum shock level, and becomes part of the information base for identifying areas of risk for seismic events.

1.3   SEISMIC RISK

The general issue of risk begins with consideration of the likelihood of occurrence of a major earthquake at a given site. Historic records of location, frequency of occurrence, and magnitudes of earthquakes, as well as the knowledge of existence of geological faults, provide this identification. Building codes use these sources to establish criteria for building design recognizing site-specific seismic effects.

A condition of risk involves two other major concerns as well. The first concern regards the existing conditions of the building site. This may involve detecting the presence of conditions that could result in *soil liquefaction,* in which otherwise reasonably solid soil becomes as mobile as thick soup in a bowl and can result in exaggerated back and forth movements.Under such conditions, even a moderate earthquake can produce severe motion of a building on the site. Other site conditions may involve unconsolidated fill, potential slip of slopes, crumbling of cliff edges, and so on. Flooding from the failure of a poorly constructed dam that could be damaged by an earthquake is another consideration.

The second concern regards the risk presented by a building improperly constructed for the required level of resistance to earthquakes. This is not an unexpected condition for older buildings, but it is unfortunately true of some recently built ones. Every major earthquake reduces the stock of older buildings, but it also gives us hard lessons about the way we build now.

Clear identification of risk is a necessary first step toward planning new construction for better earthquake resistance. Otherwise, we are limited to shooting in the dark or to simply repeating past mistakes. Forensic studies of earthquake-damaged buildings—most notably, recently built ones—is a major source of data for informed design of future buildings.

Acceptable Response

The meaning of safety and acceptable response is quite complex when disastrous force actions are considered. Few buildings can be expected to endure violent windstorms or earthquakes with no damage whatsoever or no discomfort on the part of occupants. Designers must define a building's particular level of qualified response (minor damage up to total collapse), and then quantify the magnitude of force that relates to that response.

For earthquakes, this translates into determining just how big a shock (dynamic effect) should be used in establishing specific levels for the building's response. Economic considerations make it unlikely that designers would use the biggest earthquake imaginable as the quantified effect relating to a response of minor damage.

Engineers are likely to be more aware of this aspect of design, as it is often quite basic to design work relating to disastrous effects. Bomb shelters, for example, are always designed for a specific proximity to a particular size of bomb. Bank vaults are rated on this basis and their structures are designed accordingly.

Translating the concept of acceptable response into specific data and practical criteria for design use is not so easy, however. Frequently forgotten in the design effort is the construction detailing for various *nonstructural* items: glazing details for windows, supports for signs, and various elements of the HVAC, wiring, and piping systems, for example. Comparatively, it is relatively easy to design the major lateral resistive structure against full collapse under a specific size of seismic shock. All of this gets more complicated when the value system for design goals puts life safety as the top concern. Rightly so, of course, but often building owners may not be aware that the building code minimum requirements are focused on life safety and are not necessarily providing protection for their property investment.

1.4   LIFE SAFETY

A primary concern with regard to design for earthquake resistance—and *the* primary concern of regulatory building codes—is life safety: protecting building occupants and others from injury or death. For designers, this means contending with the potential for structural failures, nonstructural construction failures, and such secondary failures as gas explosions, shorts in electrical power systems and release of toxic sewer gases.

Structural Failures

Failure of the building structure may occur from any of several loadings, including that of the seismic effect. Usually, however, the failure involves a combination of loads—with gravity always involved, regardless of other loads. For earthquakes, the major load-resisting system is the *lateral load-resisting structure*. This system may be a separate entity that provides the singular function of bracing the rest of the building, including the gravity load-resisting structure. Often, the bracing system does double duty, however, with some or all of its components also utilized for other load-resisting functions.

We treat the general considerations for design of the earthquake-resisting structure in Chapter 3. Resistance is both qualified and quantified. *Qualification* provides for the nature of the loading; *quantification* relates to the degree of severity of the earthquake. That is to say, you need the right *kind* of structure, and you need a certain magnitude of load resistance for a desired level of safety beyond the demand of the loading. Safety is measured in relative terms by a percentage of reserve strength. A reserve capacity of 50% means the structure is twice as strong as it needs to be to barely survive the earthquake.

Nonstructural Failures

Much of building construction is not essentially involved in load resistance. The structural designer views this as nonstructural and it involves the rest of the people on the building design team. It may be true that failure of these elements will not result in the building falling down. Nevertheless, a suspended ceiling, overhead lighting fixtures, sprinkler piping, or HVAC ducts falling on the heads of the occupants below is definitely a safety problem. Successful design of this construction must include concern for its own forms of earthquake resistance.

A particularly ticklish problem is that of the potential for damage to nonstructural construction due to load-generated deformations of the earthquake bracing structure. When badly handled, this results in a lot of lost window glass, cracked stucco, and fallen masonry veneers (Figure 1.4). It may also cause stuck elevators, collapsed stairs, ruptured piping, and dislodged building equipment. Flying glass, equipment, and bricks; gas leaks; and unusable stairs, are all safety hazards.

Another concern is the relation between the bracing structure and the nonstructural construction. Structural designers usually consider the structure to be free to deform independently under loading. When stiff elements of the nonstructural construction restrict this deformation, the behavior of the structure may be critically altered from that assumed by structural designers.

Secondary Failures

Just as an earthquake may trigger secondary effects such as tidal waves and avalanches, the movement of a building during an earthquake may result in secondary failures. These actions may cause major damage, even when the structure and the rest of the construction resist the direct effects of the earthquake. For example, broken water piping may cause

FIGURE 1.4   A common form of failure is the loss of heavy wall finishes; masonry veneer being especially vulnerable.

flooding of roofs or floors or other forms of damage that may be both life threatening and costly to repair.

Two sources of this form of action account for many disasters following an earthquake: the electrical power system and the pressurized gas piping system. If the power does not immediately go off, fractured wiring and fixtures may spark fires or electrocute occupants. Gas leaks may be lethal to occupants trapped in confined spaces. But the greater danger is a gas explosion, usually ignited by an electrical spark.

Another type of secondary effect is the possibility of failure from one of the many significant aftershocks that follow a major earthquake. A building may survive the major earthquake in a weakened condition, only to collapse when hit by a smaller shock. Since major aftershocks commonly follow large earthquakes—sometimes only minutes later—this is a common form of failure.

1.5   DAMAGE TO STATIONARY STRUCTURES

Although buildings actually move in all directions during an earthquake, it is useful to consider the effects of two distinct movements: vertical and horizontal. Horizontal motion is most significant in that it tends to disturb the stability of the building, causing it to topple or to collapse sideways. Since buildings are basically constructed to resist gravity, many traditional systems of construction are not inherently resistive to horizontal forces. Thus design for earthquakes consists largely of solving the problem of bracing a building against sideways movement.

Vertical movements may also cause problems. When the ground supporting a building moves rapidly downward and then suddenly stops and starts upward, the momentum of the building produces a downward jolting force that adds to the effect of gravity. The result is a sudden, dynamic increase in gravity-induced stress. Nevertheless, since well-designed structures are designed for a margin of reserve capacity for gravity resistance, this is not often a critical problem for them.

When the ground moves up and then reverses direction downward, the upward momentum causes a sudden reversal of the normal gravity effects. This may lift the building from its supports or cause some stress reversals. This is the source of one form of failure with structures that employ large, heavy elements of construction—large precast concrete girders, for example (see Figure 1.5). In one failure scenario, the repeated up and down movements cause supported elements to bounce off their supports, an action described as *dancing*.

A building's response to an earthquake is related to various properties of the building itself. For dynamic response, the most notable properties are its *mass*, its *fundamental period* of free vibration (time to sway back and forth once), and the presence or absence of various factors that cause *damping* (reduction) or *resonance* (magnification) of the vibration.

The forces sustained by a building, as well as its ability to absorb forces without experiencing critical damage, are affected by these dynamic properties. In addition, the structure of the building—more specifically the elements of the structure involved in bracing the building—must resist these forces while performing within some acceptable limits of development of stresses (force resistance) and strains (deformation or deflection resistance).

Derived structural theories, laboratory experimental studies, forensic studies of damaged buildings, and general experience provide a basis for planning new buildings with some confidence in their resistance to earthquakes. Frankly, this confidence is based mostly on experience, rather than on general theories and their applications in theoretical investigations. Examining buildings that have endured various effects over time without experiencing significant failure provides the most assurance about the proper way to build. And, conversely, examining failures indicates most convincingly how *not* to build. This applies to the effects of gravity, climate, fire, wind, and building use, as well as to earthquakes.

FIGURE 1.5 Precast concrete structures with long-span, heavy girders are highly vulnerable to earthquake forces. Excessive movements often simply dislodge girders from their seat connections and the structure collapses under gravity forces.

It is likely that no building ever built could sustain the hardest jolt of a nearby major earthquake without some kind of damage. Thus, it becomes necessary to define various kinds of damage and to establish the tolerable levels of damage for them. The worst form of damage, of course, is the total collapse of a building, or even of some significant part of it. Short of this is the kind of damage that renders a significant portion of the building unusable, but does not result in its collapse or injury to occupants. Finally, is the relatively minor, although still undesirable, damage, such as cracked plaster, jammed doors, or broken window glass.

Typically, much of the damage from earthquakes consists of damage to nonstructural construction. While the basic structure remains intact, the rest of the building is reduced to trash. Complete earthquake-resistant design must involve the whole building, not just the structure as a whole or the bracing structure.

Earthquake damage may result primarily in restoration costs or in personal injury. Ideally, a building should respond to an earthquake of predictable magnitude with a minimal risk of repairable damage and with the lowest possible risk of injury to the occupants.

1.6   POST-EVENT RECOVERY

Typically, the performance of a building during an earthquake is the primary focus of designers and is of major concern to the building owners and users. But soon, of equal concern to the owners and occupants is the ability to use the building after the earthquake. Then these concerns must be addressed:

1. *Post-Event Usage and Occupancy.* Is the building able to be occupied and used immediately following the earthquake? If not, at least can it be safely entered to remove injured occupants or valuable building contents?

2. *Extent of and Time for Restoration.* If rendered temporarily unusable, how much work is required to get it back into shape and how long will it take? Is damage readily visible?

3. *Feasibility of Restoration.* Is the total cost of restoration, including help from insurance or government grants, a feasible investment for the owners? Damage to nonstructural construction may be "minor" in a structural sense, but can add up to great expense. Is the structural damage easily repaired? For example, is concrete or masonry heavily cracked or are steel members pushed into the ductile yield range.

4. *Localized Versus General Damage.* Is damage and unusable space a minor part of the whole building or is it spread through the building?

Designers should consider these issues. These are of great interest to building investors and users, but they may also be of major concern for the public if the building is of critical importance in the post-earthquake period. Hospitals, fire stations, and power plants, if rendered unusable, can seriously hamper rescue and repair efforts.

2

Seismic Response of Buildings and Sites

During an earthquake individual buildings and sites respond to ground movements transmitted to them through the ground. The movements are of a dynamic nature, and the response of an individual site or building depends on its own dynamic properties. This chapter introduces some of the issues involved in visualizing and evaluating the dynamic actions of sites and buildings during an earthquake.

2.1 DYNAMIC PROPERTIES OF BUILDINGS AND SITES

The force effect caused by motion is directly proportional to the dead weight of the structure—or more precisely, to the dead weight borne by the structure. This weight also partly determines the character of the dynamic response the structure will make. Other major influences on the structure's response are its fundamental period of vibration and its efficiency of energy absorption. Basically, the vibration period is determined by the mass, stiffness, and size of the structure. Energy efficiency is determined by the elasticity of the structure and by such factors as the stiffness of supports, the number of independently moving parts, the rigidity of connections, and so on.

A relationship of major concern is that which occurs between the period of the structure and that of the earthquake. Figure 2.1 shows a set of curves, called *spectrum response curves*, that represent this relationship as derived from a large number of earthquake "playbacks" on structures with different periods. The vertical plot on the graph indicates the intensity of the earthquake effect on the structure. The horizontal plot indicates the magnitude of the fundamental period of the structure. The upper curve represents the major effect on a structure with no damping. Damping (essentially interference) of the free movement of the structure occurs as some energy is used up due to inefficiencies of the structure (loose connections, complex form, large number of parts) or restraints on the free motion of the structure (due to attached construction, for example). Damping lowers the magnitude of the effects, but the basic form of the response remains.

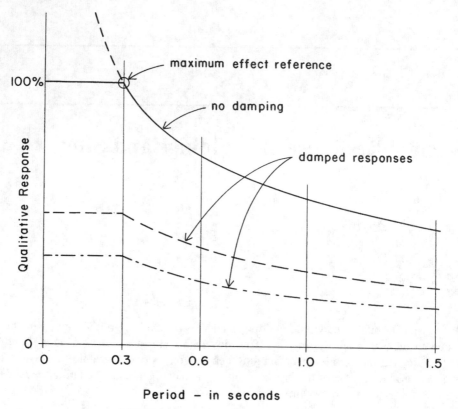

FIGURE 2.1   Spectrum response graph.

The general interpretation of the spectrum effect is that the earthquake has its major direct force effect on buildings with short periods. These tend to be buildings with stiff lateral bracing, such as shear walls and X-braced frames, and buildings that are small in size and/or squat in profile.

For very large flexible structures, such as tall towers and high-rise buildings, the fundamental period may be so long that the structure develops a whiplash effect, with different parts of the structure moving in opposite directions at the same time, as shown in Figure 2.2. Analysis of this behavior requires the use of dynamic methods that are beyond the scope of this book.

The three general cases of structural response are shown in Figure 2.3. The spectrum curves for buildings with a period below that representing the upper cutoff of the curves (approximately 0.3 sec), are for a rigid structure, with virtually no flexing. For buildings with a period slightly higher, there is some reduction in the force effect caused by the slight "giving" of the building and by its using up some of the energy of the motion-induced force in its own motion. As the building period increases, the behavior approaches that of the slender tower, as shown in Figure 2.2.

In addition to the movement of the structure as a whole, there are independent movements of individual parts. Each of these has their own periods of vibration, and the total motion occurring in the structure can thus be quite complex if it comprises a number of relatively flexible parts.

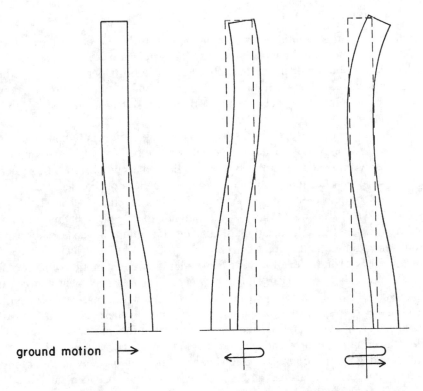

ground motion

FIGURE 2.2 Motion of a tall building during an earthquake.

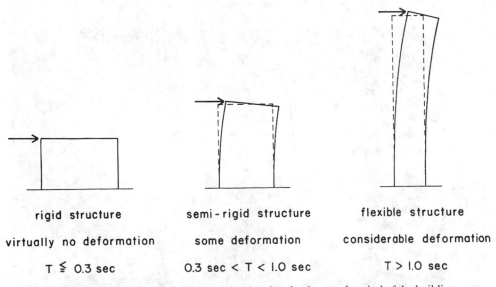

rigid structure

virtually no deformation

T ≦ 0.3 sec

semi-rigid structure

some deformation

0.3 sec < T < 1.0 sec

flexible structure

considerable deformation

T > 1.0 sec

FIGURE 2.3 Form of seismic response related to fundamental period of the building.

15

Earthquake Effects on Buildings

The principal concern in structural design for earthquake forces is for the lateral force-resisting system of the building. In most buildings, this system consists of some combination of horizontal distribution elements (usually roof and floor diaphragms) and vertical bracing elements (shear walls, rigid frames, trussed bents, and so on). Failure of any part of this system, or of connections between the parts, can result in major damage to the building, including the possibility of total collapse.

It is well to remember, however, that an earthquake shakes the whole building. If the building is to remain completely intact, the potential movement of all its parts must be considered. The survival of the structural system is a limited accomplishment if suspended ceilings fall, windows shatter, plumbing pipes burst, and elevators are derailed.

A major design consideration is that of tying the building together so that—quite literally—it is not shaken apart. This means that the various separate elements must be positively secured to one another. The detailing of construction connections is a major part of the structural design for earthquake resistance.

In some cases, it is desirable to allow for a degree of independent motion of parts of the building. This is especially critical in situations where a secure attachment between the structure and various nonstructural elements, such as window glazing, can result in the undesirable transfer of force to the nonstructural elements. In these cases, use must be made of connecting materials and details that allow for the holding of the elements in place while still permitting relative independence of motion.

When the building form is complex, various parts of the building may move differently, which can produce critical stresses at the points of connection between parts (see Figure 2.4). Sometimes, the best solution to this is to provide connections (actually, in some cases, nonconnections) that allow for a degree of independent movement of the parts. This type of connection is called a *seismic separation joint*, and its use is discussed in Sec. 3.8.

FIGURE 2.4   This tower tried to move independently, resulting in damage to the tower, the building, and the connection between them.

Except for the computation and application of the loads, the design for lateral load resistance from earthquakes is similar to that for the horizontal forces that result from wind. In some cases, the code requirements are the same for the two loading conditions. There are many special requirements for seismic design in the *Uniform Building Code (UBC)*, however, and the discussion that follows, together with the examples in Part Two, deal with the use of the code for analysis and design for earthquake effects.

2.2   BUILDING CODE REQUIREMENTS FOR EARTHQUAKE EFFECTS

The *UBC* presents the most up-to-date, complete guidelines for design for earthquake effects. Reissued every three years, its section on seismic design requirements is continually revised to reflect developments in the field.

Following is a brief digest of *UBC* requirements. Application of some of this material is illustrated in the building design examples in Part Two.

The basic requirements for investigation of seismic effects are presented in Chapter 16 of the *UBC*. That chapter contains definitions of many of the special terms that are used. For a clear understanding of the terminology, these should be studied. Further considerations—such as requirements for foundations, reinforced concrete, and so on—are covered in other chapters.

A critical determination for seismic design is the *base shear*—essentially, the total lateral force assumed to be delivered to the building at its base. For structural design, the force is assumed to be distributed vertically in the building, but the total force thus distributed is visualized as the base shear. As an equivalent static force effect, the base shear is expressed as a percentage of the building weight. In the earliest codes, this took the simple form of

$$V = 0.1W$$

or 10% of the building weight. This simple formula was embellished over the years to incorporate variables that reflected such issues as potential risk, building construction, dynamic response of the building, potential building/site interaction, and relative importance of the building's safety.

The changes in the 1988 *UBC* included considerations for an increased number of variations of the building form and the dynamic characteristics of the building. The formula for base shear took the form

$$V = \frac{ZIC}{R_w} W$$

where

Z is a factor that adjusts for probability of risk; values are given in a *UBC* table for geographic zones established by a map.

I is an *importance factor*; an acknowledgment that some buildings are more critical to the community than others. In this view, such buildings include those that house a large number of people, or essential emergency facilities (police and fire stations, hospitals, etc.), or potentially hazardous materials (toxic, explosive, etc.). I factors are given in a *UBC* table and the occupancy categories are described in detail.

C is a general factor that accounts for the specific, fundamental character of the building's dynamic response, as related to major recorded seismic events (big earthquakes).

R_W was a new factor, introduced in the 1988 *UBC*, encompassing issues dealt with previously by other factors. It takes into account the building's materials, type of construction, and type of lateral bracing system. A considerable amount of code data goes into establishing this factor.

W is the weight (or the *mass* for dynamics) of the building. This is the dead load of the building construction, but may also include considerations for the weight of some contents of the building, notably, heavy equipment, furnishings, stored materials, and so on.

The 1997 *UBC* presented yet another modification of the criteria for seismic design, based on experiences with several major earthquakes and extensive research. The basic formula for base shear is now expressed as

$$V = \frac{C_v I}{RT} W$$

The new factor, C_v, incorporates considerations for the defined risk zone (accounting for the omission of *Z* in the formula) and for the *soil profile type* for the building site. Six cases of soil profile type are defined by the code. Other factors are essentially the same as in previous codes. *T* identifies the fundamental period of the building.

In addition, for sites in the highest risk zone—Zone 4—the base shear cannot be less than

$$V = \frac{0.8ZN_v I}{R} W$$

The factor N_v, the *near-source factor*, relates to the proximity of the building site to known faults. As given in a *UBC* table, N_v depends on the actual distance to the fault, on the maximum size of earthquake that the fault is capable of producing, and on the established slip rate for the fault which generally indicates the predictable frequency of earthquakes on the fault.

Another change in the 1997 *UBC* deals with *redundancy*. A process is described in the code for determination of the degree of redundancy in the bracing system. If redundancy is low, a magnification factor must be used for the base shear. As defined by the code, redundancy refers to the presence of, or lack of, any backup capabilities in the bracing system. That is, if a primary, highly stressed element fails, is there any other bracing to share the load that was being carried by the failed element? If not, the system is vulnerable due to a lack of redundancy.

The effect of code changes results in a more complex problem for determining design force values, with more factors and more differentiation of conditions. For ordinary construction in common situations, with buildings of relatively simple form, however, certain simplifications of the criteria result in relatively simple computations for design.

It should be noted that building code criteria in general are developed with a particular concern in mind: life safety—the protection of the public from injury or death. This concern does not include the preservation of the building's appearance, the protection of the general security of the property as a financial investment, or the assurance that the building will remain functional after the big earthquake. Designers or building owners with concerns beyond life safety should consider the building code criteria to be minimal.

Although it is of major importance, the determination of the base shear is only the first step in the process of structural design or investigation for seismic effects. Many other factors must be dealt with, some of which are discussed in later sections of this chapter. However, the process of design goes beyond merely responding to commands of the codes. Many of these issues are discussed in Chapters 4 through 9.

Although the basic considerations for seismic effects are dealt with in *UBC* Sec. 1626, numerous requirements are scattered throughout the code. We discuss these in relation to the design of specific types of structures, use of particular materials, and development of various forms of construction.

Specific Dynamic Properties

The predictable response of a building to an earthquake can be generalized by type of building. These general considerations are largely dealt with when deriving the R_w factor for the base shear.

Still, each building also has individual properties. The actual building weight (the value for W in the equation for base shear), for example, is such a property. Additional specific properties include the fundamental period (T) of the building; the fundamental period of the building site; and the interaction of the building and site, matching their individual periods and their linkage during seismic movements.

Although the derivation of several code factors incorporates many considerations for dynamic effects, their use is still limited to producing shear force (V) for the equivalent *static* investigation. As much as this process may be refined, it is still not a real dynamic analysis using work and energy instead of static force. A dynamic analysis would also deal with the dynamic response of materials, since the repeated, rapidly reversing, cyclic effects on materials produce much different responses than single-direction static effects.

A further adjustment required for the equivalent static method involves the distribution of the total lateral force effect to the various levels of multilevel lateral bracing systems. The various types of lateral force-resisting systems are examined in Chapter 3, and applications are illustrated in Part Two.

For all the clumsiness of the various adjustments needed to make the static analysis method simulate dynamic behavior, it is still the most widely used analysis method for seismic design of building structures. The *UBC* does not provide any guidance about how to perform a true dynamic analysis; it only describes situations where it is indicated or actually required. For ordinary structures, complying with the concept of not being irregular in nature, the equivalent static method has been successfully applied in the past. However, the limits for its use steadily shrink as the new editions of the code increasingly restrict and encumber its use.

General Categories for Dynamic Response

Many aspects of a building's response to an earthquake can be predicted on the basis of the general character of the building in terms of form, materials, and general construction. In previous editions of the *UBC*, this was accounted for by use of a *K* factor, with data differentiating six basic forms of construction. A major change in the 1988 *UBC* was the use of the R_w factor, generally replacing the *K* factor and providing for 14 categories of construction of the lateral load-resisting system.

Another major change in the 1988 *UBC* was the identification of several cases of *structural irregularity*, which can limit the use of the equivalent static method and require a more rigorous, dynamic investigation. Two types of irregularity are defined: Those that are related to vertical form and relationships and those that are related to plan (horizontal) form and relationships. These issues are discussed in relation to building form more fully in Chapter 4.

Early editions of the *UBC* had been somewhat vague about what specifically constitutes a building that cannot be reliably investigated or designed by the equivalent static method. The 1988 edition defined the categories of buildings that require a true dynamic investigation for design. These requirements include considerations of the risk zone, building size or number of stories, bracing system, and degree of either vertical or plan irregularity.

A general effect of the 1988 edition of the *UBC* was to cause a much greater concern for general architectural features of the building. While the real concern in many cases is for the response of the lateral load-resisting system, the form of that system often is substantially defined by the form of the building in general. The various forms of irregularity are usually derived from architectural features of the building plans and vertical profile. Beyond this are many special requirements based on concerns over damage to various nonstructural elements, such as ceilings, parapets and cornices; signs; heavy suspended light fixtures or equipment; and freestanding partitions, shelving, or other items subject to lateral movement, overturning, or detachment during an earthquake.

In concern for life safety, building collapse is the principal worry, but flying or falling elements of the construction or furnishings also represent major hazards. The design of the structure may be modified, partly out of concern for nonstructural damage. Restrictions on lateral deflection of the bracing structure (*drift*) are based on this concern.

Distribution of Seismic Base Shear

The total horizontal force, computed as the base shear (*V*), must be distributed vertically and horizontally to the elements of the lateral load-resisting system. This process begins with a consideration of the actual distribution of the building mass, which essentially develops the actual inertial forces. However, for the purpose of simulating dynamic response, the distribution of forces for the actual investigation of the structure may be modified.

The *UBC* requires a redistribution of the lateral forces at the various levels of multistory buildings. These forces are assumed to be applied at the levels of the horizontal diaphragms, although the redistribution is intended to modify the form of the loading to the vertical bracing system. A principal effect of this modification is to move some of the lateral load to upper levels of the building, more realistically simulating the nature of the response of the vertical cantilever to the dynamic loads. Use of this criterion is illustrated in the multistory building examples in Part Two.

In a horizontal direction, the total shear at any level of the building is generally assumed to be distributed to the vertical elements of the system in proportion to their stiffnesses (resistance to lateral deflection). If the lateral bracing elements are placed symmetrically, and their collective centroid (center of resistance or center of stiffness) corresponds to the center of gravity of the building mass, this simple assumption may be adequate. Two considerations may alter this simple distribution, however. The first concerns the coincidence of location of the centroid of the bracing system and the center of gravity of the building mass. If there is a major discrepancy in the alignment of these, a horizontal torsional effect will produce shears that must be added to those produced by the direct shear force. Even when no actual theoretical eccentricity of this type occurs, the code may require the inclusion of an *accidental eccentricity* as a safety measure.

The second modification of horizontal distribution concerns the relative stiffness of the horizontal diaphragm (in effect, its deflection resistance in the diaphragm/beam action). The two major considerations that affect this are the aspect ratio of the diaphragm in plan (length-to-width ratio), and the basic construction of the diaphragm. Wood and formed steel deck diaphragms are flexible, while concrete decks are stiff. The actions of diaphragms in this respect are discussed in Section 3.4.

In some cases it may be possible to manipulate the distribution of forces by alterations of the construction. Seismic separation joints represent one such alteration (see discussion in Section 3.8). Another technique is to modify the stiffness of various vertical bracing elements to cause them to resist more or less of the total lateral load; thus, a building may have several vertical bracing elements, but a few may take most of the load if they are made very stiff.

2.3 FORMS OF SEISMIC RESPONSE

The results of seismic actions may be evaluated in various ways. What constitutes an acceptable response must be conditioned by a definition of the level (magnitude) and type of response. Do the forces induce only minor cracks or total collapse? Is it only some cosmetic damage that is easily repaired or a major structural failure? Were the building occupants only mildly disturbed or were they severely traumatized?

Before defining design goals and establishing design limits for responses, all the forms and types of responses are defined and individually considered. Determining success or failure of the design is a very complex analysis of many considerations.

Levels of Response

Several stages of response of a structure to seismic forces may be visualized in design. Consider the following as degrees of response to various levels (or magnitudes) of seismic force.

Minor Effect.   Under this effect, movements occur; stresses and strains develop in the structure; some minor cosmetic damage may occur (small plaster cracks, etc.); and occupants know there was an earthquake, but have no major anxiety or injury. All buildings should be capable of resisting this level of seismic action with only minor nonstructural damage, if any. This is generally acceptable for the many minor earthquakes that occur annually in high-risk zones.

Significant Response.   At this level, the structure is significantly stressed, but suffers no unrecoverable damage; nonstructural damage is limited to easily repaired items; and occupants may be emotionally upset, but suffer no serious injury. This is a response that may be expected from a reasonably strong earthquake, such as those that may occur every few years in a high-risk zone. The building structure and site respond well within their outer limits of capability.

Major Response. This level pushes the structure to its first-stage limits, possibly suffering some minor damage; significant nonstructural damage occurs, but is still feasible for restoration; and occupants may have some severe trauma, but only minor injuries occur, if any. This might be the response to a major earthquake, in the range of the maximum to be expected for the region, on the basis of local history and proximity to known faults. This would generally be the major experience visualized in design, with the site and structure basically still intact after the earthquake.

Severe Response. This level pushes the structure into its limiting form of response, suffering some major cracking, yield-level deformations, and other unrecoverable damage, but no collapse; major nonstructural damage occurs, but may be recoverable if the structure is repairable; and occupants may experience some injury, but, hopefully, no loss of life. In this case, the site and building may be damaged beyond a level that is feasible for restoration. However, structural failures are limited to something less than total collapse, and there is little or no loss of life. This is a form of damage that may be acceptable for an earthquake larger than has ever been known to occur locally, but still within the predictable capability based on nearby faults.

Extreme Response. At this level, the structure collapses; the site has major damage in the form of surface slides and subsidence; and basically, all is lost. This should only occur with an earthquake larger than ever known (or at least ever actually measured). Any site or building ever built could be destroyed by such an earthquake.

Design for specific levels of response are keyed to selected levels of earthquake intensity when true dynamic analysis is used.

Types of Failure

For development of design goals and criteria, all effects of structural failures and other forms of loss that may occur must be evaluated. Failure is a concern for design engineers, but it is not always a focus of attention for architects and builders.

Structural Failure. This usually refers to the lateral bracing system. Total failure is usually represented by a general collapse of the building, but minor failure may involve excessive movement, some permanent deformations, or some cracking of concrete or masonry. Qualified as structural, the failure has no general reference to overall damage to the building or its contents or to injury of occupants.

Nonstructural Failure. In general, this refers to everything beside the bracing structure, starting with the general construction, but including service systems and equipment. The structure may be perfectly sound after the earthquake, but a lot of nonstructural loss can make for infeasible restoration of the building or cause major injury of occupants. A ruptured fire sprinkler system or fractured gas piping can cause major secondary damage.

Trauma for Occupants.   Occupants of a building will move with the building. If the site and building magnify the earthquake's movements, the experience of the occupants may be severe, even in a moderate earthquake. If this is critical (as for patients in hospitals), success or failure may be measured by the amount of reduction of the seismic effect achieved by the site and/or the building.

Downtime for the Building or Site.   Even minor damage may make a building inaccessible or generally unusable after an earthquake. If the building is critical for emergency use (fire station or hospital), or essential for post-earthquake stability and recovery (bank, government administration building, telephone equipment building), success may be measured by the ease and speed of restoration to usage.

2.4   STRUCTURAL RESPONSE

The typical building exists as a vertical projection from the ground surface, to which it is reasonably securely attached. As such, its general response to horizontal forces is analogous to that of a vertically cantilevered beam (Figure 2.5). The direct responses of such a structure may be visualized in the form of the typical shear, moment, and deflected shape diagrams, as shown in the illustration.

The shear and moment effects require the development of internal resistance similar to that required for the beam at its various cross sections. Both of these effects, when considered as equivalent static forces, are most critical in magnitude at the base of the building. However, failure may occur at any point in the structure, wherever a lack of sufficient resistance exists.

Horizontal deflection (*"drift"* for the building as a whole) must be considered for a number of reasons. Excessive drift is likely to be objectionable to the building occupants and it could cause damage to the building contents and to nonstructural portions of the construction. On the other hand, structural deformation is a means for dissipating some of the energy of the seismic force action and thus, in many cases, is a positive consideration for the structure.

The direct action of the horizontal forces may result in a building sliding off its foundation, as shown in Figure 2.6*a*. If the building is adequately anchored to the foundation,

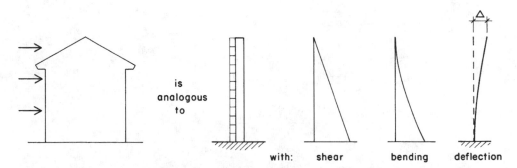

FIGURE 2.5   Cantilever functions of the vertical bracing system.

though, the next concern is for adequate resistance of the foundation itself, in the form of some combination of horizontal sliding friction and lateral earth pressure (Figure 2.6*b*). Sliding failure can also occur within the building structure, a classic case being the dislocation of a lightly attached roof, as shown in Figure 2.6*c*.

One form of the bending effect is that of the *overturning moment*. This may result in the building tipping over—with or without its foundation—as shown in Figure 2.7*a*. For this effect, the building mass has a dual role, being at once the source of the horizontal momentum force and a stabilizing resistance to the overturn tipping failure. The critical nature of the overturning effect has much to do with the form of the building's vertical profile. Buildings that are relatively squat in form (Figure 2.7*b*) are quite unlikely to fail in this manner, while those with tall, slender forms (Figure 2.7*c*) are highly vulnerable.

Bear in mind that the resistance to the horizontal forces is, in many cases, not developed by the building as a whole, but rather by discrete elements of the building structure. Thus, certain of the concerns illustrated in Figures 2.6 and 2.7 may have to do with the response of discrete elements.

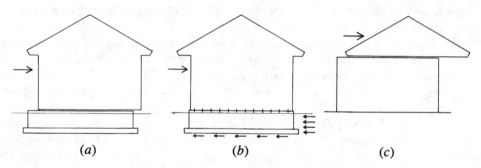

(a)   *(b)*   *(c)*

FIGURE 2.6 Lateral displacement.

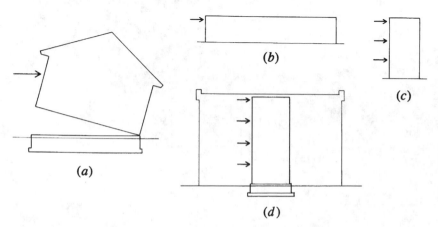

(a)   *(b)*   *(c)*   *(d)*

FIGURE 2.7 Overturning effect of horizontal loads.

Figure 2.7*d* shows a building in which lateral resistance is developed by a shear wall that is considerably narrower than the building's total width. The sliding and overturn effects must be investigated for this shear wall, considering it as a freestanding structure. In this case, while the building itself is relatively squat in profile, the shear wall is actually more slender, and overturning may be a critical concern.

Seismic action produces more than a single loading of the structure, as in the case of a gravity-loaded beam. The shear, bending, and deflection effects are actually rapidly reversed and then repeated. This reversal and repetition can result in a number of effects, including a loosening of connections, progressive cracking of brittle materials, or simply shaking the building apart. One type of effect of the repeated force action is shown in Figure 2.8. In this case, the rocking back and forth of the tall structure produces permanent deformations of the soil and a progressive loss of resistance to the structure's motion.

The actions illustrated in Figure 2.9*a* and *b* demonstrate combinations of the vertical gravity effects with the horizontal seismic effects. Since seismic activity also induces up-and-down motion, it is necessary to consider the possible combinations of gravity and seismic forces when both operate in a vertical direction. When the building mass moves downward and then suddenly reverses direction, the effect is as shown in Figure 2.9*c*, in which the downward gravity effect *W* is added to the inertial force *G*. Thus, the normal static dead load forces and stresses are increased by some magnitude. For this action, it is essential to consider all of the gravity load. When the building moves in the opposite direction (upward), the two force actions are opposite in direction, and the critical concern is whether the *G* force may be greater than the *W* force, producing uplift or internal stress reversals. For the latter situation, the worst case occurs when only the permanent gravity load (dead load) is present.

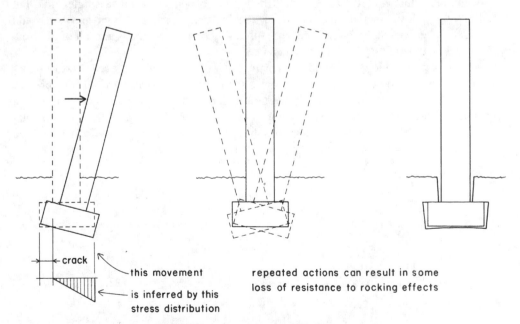

FIGURE 2.8   Loosening effect of cyclic motion.

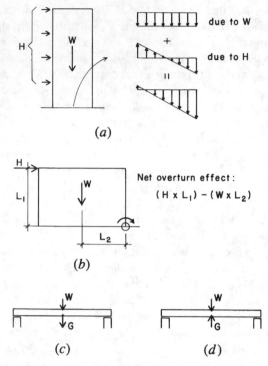

FIGURE 2.9   Effects of combined horizontal and vertical loads.

Remember that the effects illustrated in Figure 2.9 do not occur a single time, but rather in rapidly reversing succession, as the building is shaken back and forth and bounced up and down. Failure may occur with a single major jolt or as a result of progressive weakening effects due to the repeated actions.

Most of our techniques of building construction—accumulated over centuries of experience—focus on direct resistance of gravity forces. This is a natural result of our own experience with gravity acting on our bodies and of our handling the elements with which we build. We tend to produce constructions that are vulnerable to the effects of horizontal forces. Figure 2.10a illustrates such a structure, well oriented to gravity load resistance but vulnerable to the horizontal load conditions shown in Figure 2.10b.

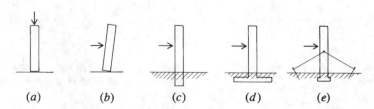

FIGURE 2.10   Resistance to overturning.

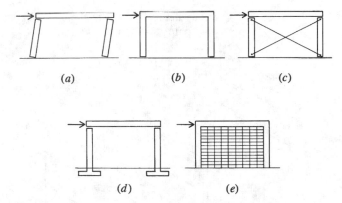

FIGURE 2.11   Bracing the laterally unstable post and beam structure.

We develop external stability for the gravity-resistant structure by modifying the existing (gravity-resisting) supports or by adding a separate bracing system. Figure 2.10c shows the simple solution used for fence posts and utility poles—burying them a sufficient distance into the ground to develop the required overturning moment. A solution for structures more complicated than simple posts is shown in Figure 2.10d, where the base is spread in order to increase the moment arm for the gravity-developed stabilizing moment (see Figure 2.9b). External bracing may be directly applied to individual structures, as shown in Figure 2.10e, or it may consist of linking unbraced parts of a complex structure to other parts that have bracing.

When they consist of discrete elements, as shown in Figure 2.11a, building frames of the traditional post and beam system lack lateral force resistance. For a single planar bay of such a system, stability may be achieved by:

1. making moment-resistive connections between the elements of the frame (Figure 2.11b)
2. trussing or X bracing to achieve triangulation (Figure 2.11c)
3. independently stabilizing the columns (Figure 2.11d)
4. using rigid infill wall surfaces (Figure 2.11e)

Which of these bracing techniques is chosen depends on the scale and complexity of the framework, on the materials and form of the frame elements, and on architectural planning and construction detailing.

Propagation of Lateral Loads

Seismic loads are generated by the dead weight of the building construction. In visualizing the application of seismic forces, we look at each part of the building and consider its weight as a horizontal force. The flow (or propagation) of these forces through the structure is demonstrated in Figure 2.12.

In most buildings, the initial loaded element of the lateral resistive system is the horizontal structure consisting of the spanning elements of the roof and framed floor systems.

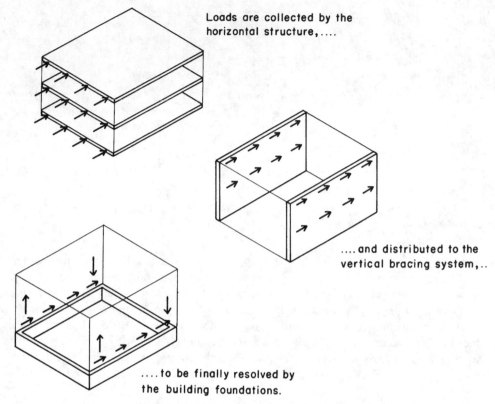

FIGURE 2.12   Load propagation in the box system.

These elements are loaded by their own weight and the weight of objects resting on or hung from them. Most vertical elements of the construction (primarily walls) will deliver the loads generated by their weight to one or more of the horizontal structures.

The horizontal structures (above ground level) must be braced by vertical bracing elements. In Figure 2.12, the exterior walls are parallel to the lateral load direction. In resisting the lateral loads, the horizontal structures span between these bracing elements and transfer the loads to them.

The vertical bracing elements in turn transfer the loads to the building foundation. This is the end of the line for the internal force transfers: The foundation transfers the forces externally to the supporting ground.

Actions of individual elements of such a system are shown in Figure 2.13. Vertical walls perpendicular to the direction of the lateral loads deliver part of their load to the structure below and part to that above. The horizontal structure spans between vertical bracing elements, delivering its loads as concentrated forces to the supporting structure. The vertical bracing elements are loaded by a combination of the gravity loads and the horizontal forces delivered by the horizontal structure.

These actions occur in rapidly reversing directions (back and forth) and in all possible separate directions (north-south, east-west, etc.). In large, complex buildings, different parts of the building are likely to be moving in opposite directions at the same instant.

Because of their relative stiffness in different directions, solid walls may function differently, depending on the direction of the lateral load with respect to the plane of their surface. Perpendicular to their planes, walls are usually relatively flexible. In their own planes, however, they tend to be quite stiff. In this case, the actions of the vertical walls in a one-story building may be assumed to be as shown in Figure 2.14.

2.5 STRUCTURAL FAILURES

Structural design involves a process of elimination of all reasonably considered possibilities for its failure. We concentrate here on the possible ways a structure can fail under the action of an earthquake.

Stability Failures

Stability is the first response factor that should be considered for any structure. Lateral forces and shaking actions are essentially destabilizing in nature; that is, they tend to cause failures that are not necessarily related to strength or stiffness, but to the general ability to resist the form of action. The simple post and beam structure is *inherently unstable* with regard to horizontal forces, regardless of the strength or stiffness of the beams and columns. For many structures not consciously designed to resist earthquake effects, this lack of basic inherent stability is a major flaw.

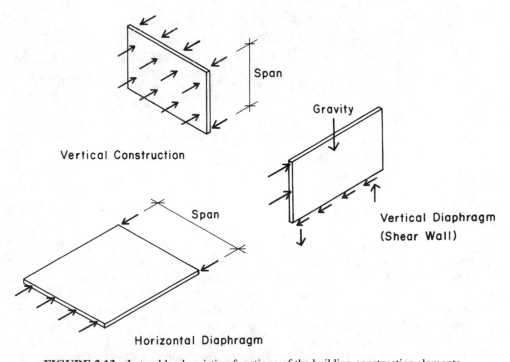

FIGURE 2.13 Lateral load-resisting functions of the building construction elements.

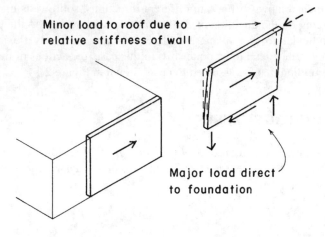

Minor load to roof due to
relative stiffness of wall

Major load direct
to foundation

(*a*)   Load in Plane of Wall

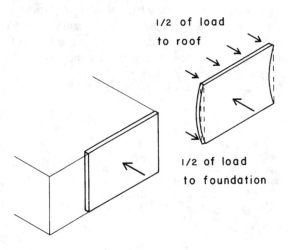

1/2 of load
to roof

1/2 of load
to foundation

(*b*)   Load Perpendicular to Plane of Wall

FIGURE 2.14   Resolution of the lateral load caused by the wall weight.

Stress Failure

A primary concern is the accumulation of stresses beyond the resistance capability of the materials of the structure, so many design formulas are based on stress responses.

Every individual building material has limitations. The structural natures of wood, steel, concrete, and masonry structures all derive both from the basic structural properties of the material and from the usual processes of production based on those general properties. Obtaining wood elements from trees, casting concrete, processing steel, and assembling masonry units affect the end forms of structures made from them. Thus, the behavior of wood structures relates to considerations of the orientation of the wood grain and the behavior of concrete involves considerations for shrinkage of the wet cast material. Steel elements are typically thin and subject to localized buckling, tearing, and other problems. Masonry is limited by the mortar joints and by the arrangement of units.

Stresses are typically complex in their development, occurring in various combinations, operating in three dimensions, and seldom uniformly dispersed in a structure. Failure is often highly localized at inception, occurring at critical locations, such as at points of maximum bending or at locations of abrupt change in the mass or form of the structure.

For seismic resistance, designers must consider how materials respond to dynamic effects. Two major factors are involved in these considerations.

Energy Capacity.   This is more important than simple static strength, as traditionally measured by stress limits. For example, compare a sheet of glass and a sheet of aluminum. Although their static force resistance may be similar, an impact load will shatter the glass due to its low energy-absorbing capability.

Stress Reversal.   A structural element or connection may have a specific limit of resistance to a single force, but subject it to rapidly reversing force and the cycles of rapid reversing stresses produced, and its response may differ.

Various other considerations also affect the value of materials for seismic resistance. A major concern is the sudden failure of brittle materials, a critical consideration for concrete and masonry. A favored approach is to use a ductile material, with its high tolerance for inelastic deformation without fracture. Another approach is to use materials with a degree of toughness, such as that displayed by plywood, laminated glazing, and fiber-reinforced concrete.

The behavior of typical construction materials and the forms of construction derived from them are discussed further in Section 2.7.

Deformation Failures

Any loading on a structure produces some amount of deformation. Although a structure may resist full collapse, excessive deformation may be a source of concern. Of particular concern is the effect on supported elements of the construction that must deform with the structure. Especially vulnerable are generally nondeformable materials such as window glazing, plaster, and masonry veneers. Deformations may also disturb the integrity of rigid piping or water seals in the building exterior. As a bracing system, the structure's relative stiffness may be reflected elsewhere. Other elements of the construction (other bracing. some nonstructural elements) may receive an undesirable share of the lateral forces if the intended bracing structure is not stiff enough.

Much of the nonstructural damage (cosmetic damage and service element failures) experienced in earthquakes can be attributed to the deformation of a structure, rather than to its strength failure. This is a major design issue that calls for a lot of cooperation between all the people involved in the building design. Deformation is typically a combination of stress development in the materials plus overall reconfiguration of the structure. Thus, both material choice and structural form are involved. Use of a very stiff material such as steel is not necessarily effective, for example, if the structure consists of slender elements subjected to bending.

Secondary Failures

Many structural failures occur in sequence. Ultimately, there may be several stages of sequential response actions before complete failure occurs. Or the failure of one structure may simply precipitate the failure of another, which in turn precipitates the failure of another, and so on.

One example of this is the three-sided building, in which the lack of symmetry and alignment of the load and resistances causes major twisting of the building. However, actual collapse may be due to the deformation failure of a single joint or the unstable condition of a wall, or some other condition not directly related to the actual torsional effect. Torsion of a whole building is a three-dimensional action that causes force interactions not always considered in design for ordinary responses.

Figure 2.15a shows a section with a portion of the edge of a building and a nearby retaining wall. The series of illustrations show a sequence of failures that begins with the drop of the supporting soil at the toe of the retaining wall (Figure 2.15b). With this loss of support, the wall rotates outward from the retained soil behind it (Figure 2.15c), causing a slope failure of the now unretained soil (Figure 2.15d). This leaves an unstable slope at the building edge, aggravated by the surcharge load of the building foundation, which causes a second slope failure (Figure 2.15e) that undermines the edge foundation of the building. Failure of this portion of the building (Figure 2.15f) may well cause more failure sequences—conceivably causing building collapse. All of this failure proceeds for the want of a more stable soil condition at the toe of the retaining wall.

In some cases, secondary failures may occur even when the initial precipitating condition is not a failure. This is the situation when flexible bracing systems are deformed, for example. The bracing structure itself may respond well within tolerable limits, but what is being braced fails because it cannot sustain the degree of deformation.

Connection Failures

The joints between elements of the structure are another major source of failure in buildings that are not designed for earthquake resistance. Failures of roof-to-wall, floor-to-wall, wall corner, and building-to-foundation connections account for many building collapses. Many forms of basic construction have inherent resistance to earthquake forces (as discussed in Section 2.7), but a potential floor diaphragm cannot interact with a potential shear wall, unless the forces can be transferred between the members. Design of these connections is a major part of the engineering design for seismic response.

Connections are also a major concern within the bracing systems developed as trusses and rigid frames. Due to recent experiences in major earthquakes, intensive research is being done on column-to-beam connections in both welded steel and reinforced concrete frames.

2.6   NONSTRUCTURAL DAMAGE

Typically, the majority of the building construction is not considered to provide lateral bracing. Instead, it is there to anchor the building for wind effects and to add to the seismic force by its mass. But this simplistic view is coming into increasing conflict with reality.

While the basic lateral-resistive structure is the first line of defense, and justifiably the prime concern for seismic resistance, *everything* in the building construction should be

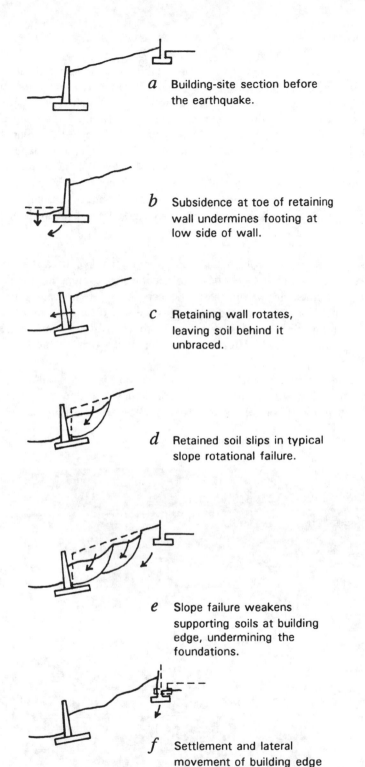

a Building-site section before the earthquake.

b Subsidence at toe of retaining wall undermines footing at low side of wall.

c Retaining wall rotates, leaving soil behind it unbraced.

d Retained soil slips in typical slope rotational failure.

e Slope failure weakens supporting soils at building edge, undermining the foundations.

f Settlement and lateral movement of building edge causes additional distress to building construction.

FIGURE 2.15 Major sequential failures triggered by a minor site failure.

resistive to seismic forces (Figure 2.16). Nonstructural walls, suspended ceilings, window frames, curtain walls, and decorative elements should be secure against movement during the shaking actions. Failure here may not lead to building collapse, but it still constitutes danger for occupants and requires costly replacement or repair. Loss of stucco, masonry veneer, window glass, and suspended ceilings is classed as "cosmetic" failure by structural engineers, but it still adds to the bill for getting the building back in shape.

A stiff wall is a stiff wall, whether it is labeled a shear wall or not. Thus many curtain walls and interior partitions provide major shear wall effects, even though there is theoretically a whole separate system assumed to provide independent bracing. This situation results in two potential problems that have been the source of much damage in recent earthquakes.

1. Due to its stiffness, the nonstructural construction may receive a share of the lateral force for which it does not have sufficient resistive strength. This is a primary source of cracks in exterior plaster (stucco) and a primary reason for window glass breakage. Possible remedies for this are to isolate the stiff nonstructural elements from the acting force, stiffen the true bracing system, or use control joints or other means to affect the behavior of the nonstructural construction (Figure 2.17).

2. Coincident structural action of nonstructural elements may modify the behavior of the lateral bracing structure. A common situation of this type is a soft story effect due to nonstructural bracing existing in some stories and not others in a

FIGURE 2.16   The suspended ceiling in this library fell, rupturing fire sprinklers and dousing books and carpet.

multistory building. Another situation is the inadvertent stiffening of columns in a rigid frame system that was designed based on flexible columns. The remedies here include those mentioned above, but more than that, the careful development of the structural attachments between the nonstructural elements and the bracing structure.

FIGURE 2.17   Rigid wall finishes on flexible support structures will move in an earthquake. This produces thousands of stucco cracks in familiar patterns (*a*). Some of this cracking can be prevented by use of reinforcement. However, a better solution is to precrack the stucco with control joints (*b*).

Nonstructural construction also includes all the building service systems for electric power, water, ventilation, and so on. These must be developed to have their own independent bracing and to be isolated from actions of the structural bracing system. Basic planning of these systems should be coordinated with the general planning of the lateral bracing system to avoid interference.

Common failures include flush-tank toilets that are dislodged from their rusted-out anchor bolts and from the water tanks that sometimes just sit atop them. Suspended lighting can fail by swinging or by being dropped. Furnaces, air conditioners, and water heaters that are not firmly braced can tilt over or slide sideways. Particularly dangerous are the various gas appliances that get dislodged, leaving broken gas lines.

A common scenario involves the combination of power loss and gas leaks. Electric power is often lost during an earthquake, and if it comes back on quickly, sparks from various equipment can ignite collected gas. Many fires are started by this series of events.

Water-sealing membranes and flashing may be ruptured or pulled loose as the building rocks and rolls. If everything else works, but the roof leaks or the curtain wall leaks Figure 2.18), the building owner will not be happy. Violent back-and-forth jerking of any building is likely to produce tearing fractures of sealed and flashed joints. The greater the number of such joints (due, for example to complex roof geometries), the higher the statistical likelihood of leaks, whether caused by an earthquake or only aggravated by it. For the highly vulnerable flat roof, a major earthquake jolt is almost certain to produce some leaks, and the next rainstorm will prove it.

In all regions, older residences often have masonry chimneys and fireplaces. This refers to *real* masonry, not something applied to make it appear to be a masonry structure. For a modest wood frame residence, a large masonry fireplace with a tall masonry chimney and a heavy masonry or concrete foundation may well represent a total weight greater

FIGURE 2.18   Flat roofs can also be wracked like the stucco walls. Here is a major crack in the rigid covering that quite likely relates to a corresponding one in the waterproofing membrane it is protecting.

than that of the whole rest of the residence construction. It is also a monolithic unit and will respond quite independently during an earthquake (Figure 2.19).

Although a masonry chimney or fireplace may be attached to the rest of the construction, a problem arises regarding code-required fire separation, which may result in a true condition of virtual seismic separation between the two units—the masonry structure and the rest of the building. As a result, an independent set of responses is quite likely. There are three common failures in this situation:

1. The masonry structure may fully detach from the house and, if not independently stable, topple over or fail in the general manner of an unreinforced masonry structure. This is more likely if it is actually on the outside edge of the house, which is quite common (Figure 2.20).

2. The independent movements of the house structure and the masonry structure may result in major detachment and fracture of their interface, not necessarily resulting in the collapse of either, but causing loss of many sealed joints.

3. The two structures may actually work together reasonably, but the portion of the chimney that extends above the house (required by code) constitutes a vertically cantilevered, unreinforced masonry structure, and it collapses on its own, dump-

FIGURE 2.19   This chimney pulled out of the wall and might have toppled outward with one more good jolt.

FIGURE 2.20   The heavy chimney on the outside edge of a building may separate and become dependent on its own stability. This chimney was evidently well built and reinforced, as it remained intact in spite of its fall onto a concrete fence. It is tough to keep the chimney and the house structure well connected while satisfying fire separation requirements.

ing its remains on the roof and/or the building site. Falling chunks of masonry are never a good thing (Figure 2.21).

Much of this undesirable action can also occur with masonry veneer construction, even though it is attached to a lighter structure. The fire separation, weight of the masonry elements, and vertically cantilevered chimney top can still occur, and falling bricks from a veneer are just as undesirable as ones falling from a real masonry structure.

2.7   BEHAVIOR OF ORDINARY CONSTRUCTION

The nature of the response of building structures to various force actions has much to do with the materials of construction. This has partly to do with various properties of the materials themselves and partly to do with the products and assemblages that are made from them. In the case of seismic actions, it has also to do with the density of the materials and the weight of the structures made from them.

As with any force action, seismic action generates responses that relate to the fundamental stress and strain behaviors of materials. These are basic concerns:

Stress Resistance. Of various types (tension, compression, shear, combined stress, two- and three-dimensional stresses, etc.) at various levels of magnitude

Strain Resistance. Related to other materials; related to stress magnitudes; affected by temperature, moisture, age, previous loadings, and so on

Special Behaviors. Effects of stress direction, reversal, repetition, and such qualitative responses as ductility, brittle fracture, strain hardening, and so on

FIGURE 2.21   Also a familiar sight—the cantilevered top of a masonry chimney gone. Protruding steel bars indicate an attempt to develop a reinforced masonry structure, but there was evidently little bond between the bars and the mortar or grout.

The dynamic response properties of materials are also important in seismic analysis. These include:

Energy Absorption.   Whereas resistance to static force is basically limited by stress magnitude, energy-absorbing capacity is essentially indicated by the area under the stress-strain graph (Figure 2.22). This results in a concern for the form of the graph, with special concern for various inelastic behaviors.

Resilience.   This is the limit of the energy absorption capacity which will not result in significant permanent deformation or nonrepairable damage. It is important in determining the potential for reuse of the structure after the loading.

Toughness.   This is essentially the ultimate limit of energy absorption, which usually infers some permanent damage in the form of ductile yielding, brittle fracture, splitting, shredding, delamination, and so on.

Response to Cyclic Loading.   This involves the repetition and reversal effects of seismic actions that may result in progressive failure, fatigue, grinding, and so on.

Effect of Load Duration.   The short duration, rapid peaking, impact or shock effect produces effects that differ for various materials. Materials with a yield character have more tolerance; those with a brittle nature are vulnerable.

We consider now the common materials of building construction and the products and assemblages ordinarily produced from them.

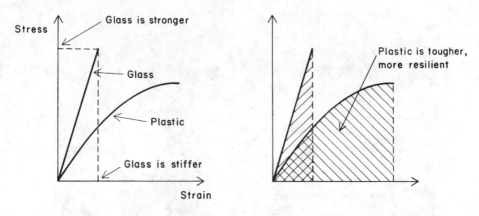

(a) Evaluation for Static Response   (b) Evaluation for Dynamic Response

FIGURE 2.22   Static versus dynamic response.

Wood

For structural purposes, wood is used primarily in the form of boards, structural lumber, glued-laminated products such as plywood and laminated timbers, built-up wood-plus-plywood elements, and fiber products. For solid wood elements, grain orientation and flaws such as knots, pitch pockets, and splits are important but lamination and building up multiple-piece elements may reduce their effects.

Wood structures ordinarily consist of assemblages of many individual elements that must be fastened together (Figure 2.23). The response of wood structures to force actions, therefore, often has as much to do with the methods of fastening as with basic properties of the materials. Connections that rely on nails or bolts in loose holes may experience excessive deformation or loosening during seismic actions. It is generally desirable that connections remain *tight* and resist the force magnitudes required of them (Figure 2.24).

Cross-grain bending, as shown in Figure 2.25, is a critical stress condition that should be avoided for seismic response. The construction of structures that utilize plywood (or other surfacing) on light wood framing to develop horizontal and vertical diaphragms must be careful to avoid this situation. Although they are utilized to develop sliding resistance of walls, wood sills are not used for vertical force resistance. Resistance to uplift and overturn are developed by end anchorage of the walls (see the discussion in Section 3.8).

The low modulus of elasticity of wood generally means that wood structures experience considerable deformation. This is partly accounted for by the high energy-absorbing character of wood structures. The actual amount of deflections, or the relative stiffness of the structure as compared to other parts of the construction, may present some problems. Stiff surfacing materials, such as tile or plaster, are likely to be damaged if the wood structure deflects fully. In buildings with mixes of wood and masonry or concrete, the stiffer elements are likely to absorb dynamic loadings, or to fail if they must rely on bracing from the wood structure. In these situations, careful analysis of deflections and conservative design are important.

The low density of wood (one-fifth that of concrete, one-fifteenth that of steel) is an asset in reducing the building mass for seismic load. Wood elements are usually bulky,

FIGURE 2.23   The classic wood frame structure for low-rise construction: two-by framing, panel sheathing, and an applied exterior finish. Lateral bracing is commonly achieved by the rigid panel sheathing, developed as planar diaphragms.

however, so that wood structures are generally about the same in total weight as steel structures because steel elements are typically made of thin parts. More dramatic comparisons can be made between wood structures and structures of masonry or concrete, both of which have greater density and bulkiness.

For many years, plywood panels made with plies of softwood have been the most effective material for use in both vertical and horizontal diaphragms on wood frame structures. The 4-ft x 8-ft panel is the most common size (despite the onset of metric conversion). For walls, the common thickness choices are $3/8$ in. and $1/2$ in. The thinner $3/8$ in. plywood usually consists of three plies, which puts a lot of responsibility on the single, middle ply (Figure 2.26).

Steel

Steel is the most versatile structural material, used in some form for almost every type of construction. It is essential for the assemblage of wood structures: for nails, screws, bolts, framing devices, and anchor bolts. It is also essential as wire or rods for reinforcement for structures of masonry and concrete. Steel structures themselves range from those of light sheet metal elements to the heaviest of rolled and built-up elements.

(a)

(b)

(c)

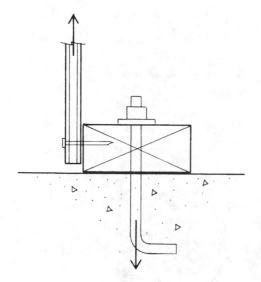

FIGURE 2.25   Development of cross-grain bending in a wood sill.

An advantage of steel is its strength in resisting stresses of various type, direction, reversal, or combinations. Its relative stiffness permits it to absorb a high percentage of total force when it is used with other materials. In concrete structures, the steel reinforcement usually takes major parts of the internal forces, while ordinarily occupying only about 2% of the total volume.

Steel's ductility, a highly significant property, is especially important in most ordinary rolled sections and in concrete reinforcing rods. These are useful in developing energy-absorbing resistance, providing a means for partially overcoming the brittle nature of structures of masonry and concrete.

A principal concern in steel structures—due to the typical thin form of steel parts—is the chance of buckling. At upper limits of extreme thinness, resistance is primarily a function of the stiffness of the material rather than its stress-absorbing capabilities. This limits the potential for utilization of higher grades of steel, since the stiffness (modulus of elasticity) remains constant.

As with wood, steel structures are assembled from many elements so jointing methods and the detailing of connections is a major part of the design work. Under seismic actions, loosening of bolts, brittle fracture in welds, tearing at locations of stress concentration, and twisting in eccentrically loaded joints are problematic. Many joint details that are sufficient for gravity or wind load situations are not acceptable for the rapid cyclic actions during earthquakes.

Although the modulus of elasticity of the material is very high, the use of thin and slender parts means that steel structures are ordinarily quite deformable. While adding to energy absorption, these deformations may be critical of themselves if the structure moves too much.

FIGURE 2.24   The light wood frame structure is commonly assembled with use of a lot of steel connectors: nails, screws, bolts, and now—sheet metal fastening devices of all sorts. Simple devices are used for routine assembly of the stud wall (*a*) and the platform floor and roof structures (*b*). However, the proper installation requires complete nailing, and lack of it can leave the structure vulnerable to movements (*c*).

FIGURE 2.26 Plywood has a high level of toughness and doesn't often fail in a brittle manner. However, with only three plies, flaws become more critical and major flaws or gaps in the center ply leave a very thin outer ply to take shear stresses (*a*). A continuous gap in the center ply (*b*) is a fatal flaw.

Concrete

The principal limitation of concrete as a structural material is its relatively low resistance to tensile stress—often as low as 10% of its resistance to compressive stress. For most structural tasks, steel reinforcement must be used to absorb internal tension forces, or pre-stressing must be utilized to counteract load-developed tensile stresses (Figure 2.27).

While wood and steel can be used for small elements, concrete is ordinarily used in bulky form, resulting in structures with considerable dead weight. Due both to the large mass and the typically high relative stiffness of the structures, concrete structures absorb considerable force during seismic movement.

Concrete structures ordinarily experience a great deal of cracking. Some of this is due to the shrinkage of the material during the drying process and to uneven expansion and contraction during changes in temperature. Shrinkage is more extensive when more water is used for mixing or when the wet mix is allowed to dry too rapidly after casting. Temperature stresses are more severe for exposed structures and where the climate range is greater.

Cracking is also inherent in the normal structural functioning of ordinary reinforced concrete. Tension induced by bending, torsion, and shear actions—although ultimately resisted by steel reinforcing—will often be at some level of strain beyond the fracture limit for the concrete. Thus, the concrete must crack to permit the necessary level of stress to develop in the steel reinforcement.

FIGURE 2.27   Without reinforcement, concrete has low tensile resistance and low resistance to energy loadings. Many residential foundations are unreinforced and failures are common.

When a concrete structure is subjected to the oscillatory actions of an earthquake, the rapid reversal of stresses will tend to exaggerate existing cracks. This action may cause progression of the cracking and a grinding effect along the planes of the cracks. While this may be a principal means of energy absorption, it can also produce considerable nonrepairable damage, especially when reinforcing is not adequate.

In many cases, the useful strength limit of a reinforced concrete structure is that which is developed at the point of plastic yielding of the reinforcement. If this is an early stage of failure of the structure, it tends to give the structure a form of ductile behavior, in contrast to the normal brittle nature of the stiff, tension-weak concrete. So, for both static and dynamic loading, the design is usually carried out to develop this yielding mode as the initial failure condition.

In large concrete structures, a considerable number of "cold joints" ordinarily occur at points where the continuous pouring has been halted during the construction process. Provision must be made for structural continuity of both the steel and concrete through these joints. Doweling of the steel bars usually assures that the joint will not pull apart. However, the concrete-to-concrete relationship is essentially the same as at a crack, and grinding during seismic action must be considered.

Because concrete structures are so heavy and generally quite stiff, seismic actions typically produce major forces in them. Therefore, they must be proportionately stronger than framed structures of wood or steel. However, ordinary techniques of construction will often result in major natural resistance to seismic effects, so that little need be done in many cases to provide anything extra for seismic resistance.

Structures requiring especially careful study for seismic response are those employing elements of precast concrete, as opposed to concrete that is site poured into forms. These structures are similar to wood and steel structures in their vulnerablity to the integrity of the jointing methods. In contrast to wood and steel, however, the structural elements are heavy so that dynamic behavior is even more critical (Figure 1.5).

Masonry

Down through the ages, masonry has been popular for its fire resistance, its thermal storage, and its endurance under attacks of rot, aging, weather, and siege-breaking enemy armies. Whenever a major earthquake occurs, though, there is typically a considerable loss of the existing stock of old masonry structures. The combination of the weight, stiffness, and tension weakness of the material makes it highly vulnerable to earthquakes (Figure 2.28). In regions of high seismic risk it is now generally required to use a form of masonry construction that employs considerable steel reinforcement and special forms of anchorage between masonry walls and horizontal floor and roof structures (Figure 2.29).

Most structural masonry for seismic-resistive buildings is now produced with units of hollow, precast concrete and is reinforced both horizontally and vertically. Steel rods are inserted in vertically aligned voids, which are then filled with concrete to produce small reinforced concrete columns inside the wall. Rods are typically placed in horizontal rows of U-shaped blocks, which are filled with concrete to produce tie beams.

Reinforced brick construction and various combinations of bricks and concrete units may also be used, but the all-concrete structure is used most widely in regions of high seismic risk. Brick and stone finishes are most commonly used as facings, applied as veneers over some substructure, which may be wood, steel, concrete, or reinforced concrete block construction. Adequately fastening these veneers is critical in seismic design.

FIGURE 2.28 The unreinforced brick masonry structure is highly vulnerable to shock from the earthquake. (*a*) The front portion of this side wall pulled loose, taking the parapet over the front wall with it, and dumping a lot of bricks at the entrance to the store (*b*).

FIGURE 2.28 (*Continued*)   Wall piers and corners are subject to concentrated effects (*c*) and easily fractured if unreinforced. Even when walls are sufficiently strong, the cantilevered parapets above them are often vulnerable (*d*) and are subject to accelerated decay due to their exposure.

The integrity of any masonry construction depends on the quality of the mortar joints and the structural character of the masonry units. It also depends a lot on the skill and care of the masons, on the control of the moisture content of the units during laying, on protection against rapid drying of the mortar, and on the prevention of shock to the laid-up units prior to hardening of the mortar. The less the amount of reinforcing, the more the skill and care of the workers becomes critical.

With the wall of reinforced hollow units, the concrete-filled voids with their steel rods constitute a sort of reinforced concrete rigid frame inside the wall. This frame interacts in

FIGURE 2.29   Reinforced masonry construction with hollow concrete blocks.

a composite manner with the infill of masonry units that are bonded to it. Theoretical analysis of this construction is quite complex, but its behavior has been demonstrated by tests, as well as by the response of many buildings to earthquakes.

There are many similarities between reinforced masonry and ordinary reinforced concrete. Stiffness and excessive weight is a liability for both in seismic action. Nevertheless, the reinforced concrete unit masonry shear wall is widely used to brace low-rise buildings of various types of construction.

Effects of Joints

Buildings ordinarily consist of a great number of individual elements that are then joined together to create the whole construction. Elements of the structure (decks, beams, columns, etc.) are connected, roof and floor planes intersect, and the building proper is anchored to its foundation. The structural response of the building as a whole involves the actions of a vast number of joints.

Joints exist in endless variety, varying with the size, shape, and material of the connected elements, with the loads being transferred, and with the need for various nonstructural functions. The latter may include concerns for weather seal, water tightness, expansion and contraction, demountability, and so on. Of major concern is the need for the use of jointing methods that are technically and economically feasible, with emphasis on those that use standard, tested products and permit relatively simple and rapid assemblage.

With regard to seismic response, there are a number of particular concerns for joints. Of prime concern is reliance on a quantified load capacity for a specific joint function. For ordinary jointing methods such as nailing, welding, and bolting, this capacity is generally determinable by engineering computations. For special fasteners, capacities are mostly established by testing, using methods that are acceptable to the building codes.

For dynamic effects of jolting and shaking due to earthquakes, joints need resistances beyond those usually required for gravity and wind loads. Fracture due to stress concentrations, progressive deformations, and loosening of joints are of particular concern.

Reliance on nail withdrawal in wood, unfinished bolts in steel, and simple doweling alone for anchorage in concrete is usually unacceptable in seismic design.

The complete and successful design and construction detailing of joints is a major part of the seismic design for a building. The most accurate and complete computations for the investigation of structural behavior and careful design of the major elements of the bracing system will be for naught if the load transfers through the system are not thoroughly developed by study of the jointing along the load paths.

While jointing of the lateral bracing system is a prime concern, the complete seismic design must also consider the connection of the many nonstructural elements. Proper attachment of wall finish elements, light fixtures, doors, and so on is essential to prevent the objects from becoming flying missiles during an earthquake.

In many situations, jointing techniques must allow for movement while simultaneously providing support or attachment. Window glass must be securely held in a metal frame, but must have a degree of freedom to allow for thermal changes and to prevent structural deformations of the frame from transferring load to the glass. Sometimes structural joints need to allow for a similar condition. For example, a seismic control joint may provide for vertical support but allow horizontal movement. The specific requirements for any joint must be fully studied for a successful design.

Dead Weight of Construction

The weight of the building must be determined for gravity and for seismic design. For most buildings, this requires considerable approximation due to the number of elements composing the complete construction. Since hair-splitting accuracy is not expected, the results of any investigation using the dead weight of the building should not be considered to have an unrealistic level of precision.

To determine the weight of the building construction the following information is required:

1. Exact details and dimensions of the construction. This is known at the *end* of the building design process but is usually somewhat sketchy during the early stages of design, when a major portion of the structural design is usually done.

2. Properties of the materials and elements of the construction. This includes the densities of the materials and the usual sizes, thicknesses, and so on. For simple, ordinary elements, such as concrete slabs or plywood panels, this may be relatively easy. For complex or custom-designed elements, such as glass and metal curtain wall systems, it may involve a lot of guesswork.

3. Allowance for construction elements that typically are not precisely defined in early stages of the building design. This usually includes items such as electrical fixtures and air ducts. These are typically accounted for by adding some general amount to the live or dead load. This is sometimes specified by building codes.

For the final structural design, the dead load of the construction should be as accurately accounted for as is possible. By this time, the final details of the construction are sufficiently developed to make such a determination possible. For preliminary design, however, it is usually necessary to use some very approximate values based on past experience with similar construction.

Rehabilitation, Repair, and Upgrade

It is sometimes necessary to consider repairing or upgrading an existing building to improve its seismic resistance. One such situation occurs when a building has sustained a severe earthquake shock. It can still be safe for ordinary conditions, but unsafe if it were to suffer another major seismic shock.

Work of this type is generally more feasible for structures with frames of wood or steel than for those with construction of concrete or masonry. Where extensive cracking and yielding of steel reinforcement has occurred in masonry or concrete structures, repair often is not economically feasible. However, when the damage is isolated, it may be possible to remove the damaged parts of the structure and either replace them with new construction or simply use the remaining, undamaged part of the structure.

A problem sometimes encountered in such design work is that the design of the entire structure must often be brought into compliance with present codes, whereas the original design would likely have been done under less stringent code requirements. This is especially true for seismic design, as the codes have been evolving toward increasingly severe requirements. In extreme cases, this might rule against the feasibility of restoration or rehabilitation.

Upgrading may be necessary because of a proposed remodeling or change of occupancy. It may also be required, or simply desired, to improve the seismic resistance of a building that has a type of construction that has been shown to be unsafe. A classic situation of the latter type is that of the thousands of existing older buildings in regions of high seismic risk that have structures of unreinforced masonry. Due both to its weight and its lack of shock resistance, this type of construction has been responsible for a great amount of earthquake-generated property loss and injury. Its use has been generally outlawed in high-risk areas with some building code jurisdiction.

While unreinforced masonry is a major culprit, there are many other undesirable types of construction for earthquake-prone areas. These continue to exist primarily because they have not yet sustained a major shock, although the potential risk may be high. They are *permitted* to exist mainly because new requirements of building codes normally apply only to new construction or to remodeling or changes in occupancy. In unusual circumstances, the government body that administers a code may pass regulations requiring upgrades of particularly hazardous construction.

Most buildings tend to age less than gracefully with regard to their seismic resistance. As we learn more, we tend to require more and *do* more about seismic design. Yesterday's designs rapidly become obsolete by today's standards. This is certainly a matter of degree for any specific building, but it is nevertheless a general trend. Thus, just about *any* existing building more than a few years old may be viewed as a candidate for some rehabilitation, if the most stringent seismic resistance, as we are presently able to determine it and design for it, is desirable.

2.8   SITE FAILURES

Figure 2.30 shows five common forms of site failure that may occur during an earthquake. If significant in dimension of movement, all can produce undesirable effects on a carefully developed site or on an original, undisturbed one. Often worse, however, are the effects on site structures. Fences, freestanding walls, retaining walls, pavements, structured drain

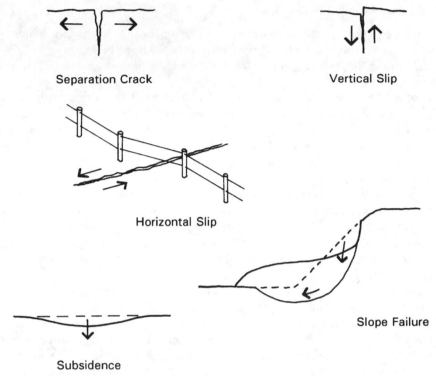

FIGURE 2.30   Common forms of failure of the ground surface.

channels, and buried items such as vaults, piping, and tunnels may be significantly damaged if the supporting ground moves extensively.

Movement of surface soils may also occur as a secondary failure, triggered by the failure of a constructed retaining structure. A wall can be toppled by lateral seismic force generated by the weight of the structure plus the weight of the retained soils, added to the existing gravity-induced lateral soil pressures due to the change in grade. If the wall is tall enough, this may produce a considerable lateral soil movement behind the wall.

Worst of all, can be the effect of site movements on supported buildings and various site structures. Hardly any form of construction can sustain a movement of the dimension illustrated in Figure 2.30. For stiff concrete and masonry construction, the tolerance for such movements is close to zero.

Movements of the surface ground mass may be part of a general regional fault of the surface soil, larger in scope than a single building site (Figure 2.31). Design and preparation of an individual site for this type of failure is pretty much impossible, although some such movements may be predictable in certain situations. Sloping sites, sites on massive fills, and sites with long histories of slope failures are good candidates for problems—with or without an earthquake. As with the preconditioned building, a site failure event may be already underway or just waiting to happen, and the earthquake is the trigger for the event.

Another site consideration is the potential for building-site interaction during the earthquake. Fundamental dynamic properties of the building may combine badly with funda-

FIGURE 2.31   Minor surface crack in a pavement—except that it extended more than 800 ft through several properties and under several houses in a development built over a buried stream bed.

mental dynamic properties of the site in an earthquake. Worst cases include resonant effects between the site and building and other negative modifications by the site of the seismic action to the detriment of the building.

Resonance in the site-building interaction may produce a magnification of the dynamic effects on the building, beyond the level produced directly by the earthquake. To anticipate this, the dynamic character of the building and the site must be investigated separately and then matched up for possible interaction.

In general, any site does some modification of the earthquake vibrations that pass through it on the way to a supported structure. This may include lessening or increasing the effects, changing the frequency or period of the vibration, or channeling the effect in a particular direction. Lessening, or damping, of the vibrations is usually good, and most sites do some of this. The other effects all offer some possible increased distress for supported structures.

A widespread and treacherous soil condition is that of the soil mass subject to liquefaction. This generally occurs in relatively soft, loose soil masses with high ground water levels (thus, mostly found in low-lying areas with extensive fills—both natural and manmade). During an earthquake of any extended duration, the continuing vibration turns this soil mass into something like a massive bowl of gelatin. It shakes in a slow, exaggerated manner and continues to quiver after the forced movements induced by the earthquake. The result is usually a magnification of the dimension of movements and a modification to a much slower frequency. For supported structures with a low tolerance for either extensive movement or slow movement (or both), this produces something much worse than the direct seismic effect.

The most common site failures are small cracks and subsidence due to minor shifting or consolidation of fills (Figure 2.31). These may disrupt site drainage and crack up pavements, but often pose no serious threat to buildings, unless they occur beneath a building that is exceptionally sensitive to vertical movements (sitecast concrete and masonry structures, for example). The point to note is that a building site—both within the legal site boundary and beyond—needs just as careful investigation for seismic response as any structure designed for support by the site.

2.9   BUILDING FOUNDATION FAILURES

Building foundations are transitional elements between the building and the ground. As such, they must work as parts of the building structural system, but they also have direct relationships with the supporting ground. Failures can occur for various reasons and may be difficult to fully anticipate in design of the foundations. A primary need is for a full discovery process regarding geotechnical conditions and the properties of the site materials.

Site Failures Affecting Foundations

What happens to the building site in terms of failures usually will have ramifications for the building foundations; if the supporting ground moves, the foundations will move. Thus, a major source of building foundation failure has nothing directly to do with the design of the foundation itself—it is just in the wrong place at the wrong time, or the building was ill suited for the site.

A common vulnerable site is one with major amounts of unconsolidated materials at surface and near-surface levels. These may be natural deposits, but frequently they consist of recently placed materials, mostly constituted as fill for construction. Movement in these soils is common in earthquakes, and affected structures will certainly experience some distress.

An especially hazardous situation occurs when foundations are placed on soils of varying compressibility, as may occur on a hillside site that transitions to a flat condition. Other situations of this type occur with foundations at different levels and sites that have been leveled out over original conditions that were not flat. Movements during an earthquake may include vertical settlement (subsidence) and lateral movements.

Tying of Foundations

It is essential that the building foundation system move in unison during an earthquake. When supports consist largely of isolated column footings, it may be necessary to add ties to achieve this, as shown in Figure 2.32. Where extensive below-grade construction for

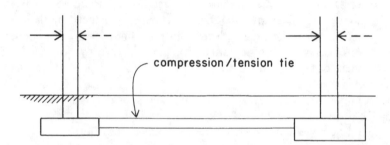

FIGURE 2.32   Tying of isolated foundations to ensure common lateral movement.

basements occurs, elements of this construction may achieve some or all of this tying function.

Another reason for tying isolated footings may involve the sharing of lateral loads. Individual footings that receive large lateral loads may need to share this loading with other parts of the foundation system. This may extend to the use of grade walls or basement walls as the primary resisting elements for lateral load that is transferred to the ground.

Individual tie elements between footings may consist of reinforced concrete elements designed for both tension and compression. Tension is achieved by the steel reinforcement, which must be adequately developed in the footings for anchorage. Compression requires the usual considerations for a concrete column, including concerns for thinness.

Whenever possible, a shallow bearing foundation is used, simply because of its easier construction and lower cost. However, when the necessary criteria for safety and lack of settlement cannot be assured, the usual solution is a deep foundation; that is, one that reaches down farther into the ground mass. The two general types of deep foundations are driven piles and drilled or excavated piers (caissons).

When computed lateral loads are transferred to footings, ties may be designed for these loads. The *UBC* requires that ties for piles and caissons be designed for 10% of the vertical load on the heaviest loaded foundation. For isolated footings that are not supports for parts of the lateral bracing system, there is no easily quantified basis for design of ties. For this situation, it is common to design ties on the basis of minimum requirements for columns.

A problem with shallow bearing foundations is that they often bear on relatively compressible soils. Figure 2.8 illustrates the effect that can occur with a large lateral load and a strong overturning moment. With repeated applications and reversals of such a load, the soil beneath the footing edges becomes compressed, resulting in an increased tendency for the structure to be easily rocked. This represents a certain loss of stability for the structure

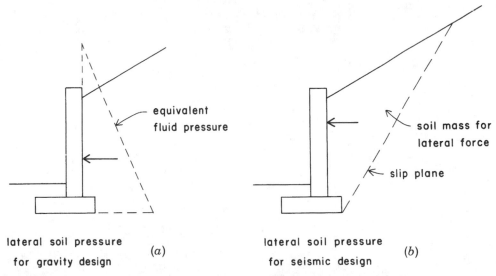

FIGURE 2.33   Tall retaining wall with assumed distribution of lateral soil pressure due to (*a*) gravity force (*b*) seismic force.

and some reduction of its resistance to dynamic effects. The only reasonable solution for this is to reduce the edge stress to a low value—most effectively by widening the footing.

When deep foundation elements are used the building foundation is essentially bypassing the surface-level soils. However, the upper soil levels still constitute the site surface and must be dealt with in the full site development. Usually, they must also provide lateral support for the tops of the deep foundation system.

A frequently used site structure is the cantilever retaining wall (Figure 2.33). This structure is ordinarily designed to resist lateral force, pressure generated from the soil on the high side of the wall. A common design procedure is one where the lateral soil pressure is considered to be developed by an equivalent fluid with a unit density of some percentage of the soil weight (Figure 2.33*a*).

For a relatively tall retaining wall (6 ft or more from the low-side surface level) the lateral action of an earthquake will impel the retained soil mass against the back side of the wall. Significant movement of the wall permits the development of a typical slip plane failure (see Section 8.2), providing a basis for defining of the soil mass that should be considered for lateral seismic force. For a tall wall, with an inclined soil surface behind the wall, as shown in Figure 2.33*b*, this may constitute a considerable lateral force.

Failure of a retaining wall may also cause the secondary failure of some major portion of the site behind the wall. If this failure in turn results in loss of supported structures (paving, site walls, buildings), the resulting domino effect may be disastrous (Figure 2.15). This all makes the very careful design of tall retaining walls a serious matter.

3

Design for Structural Response

The potential for damage to buildings in earthquakes was the subject of Chapters 1 & 2. In this chapter we consider enhancement of a building's structure to respond to the effects of earthquakes. The primary concern here is developing the building's lateral force-resisting structure (that combination of structural elements that braces the building for seismic effects). (Note: Although the building codes use the term *lateral force-resisting structure*, we prefer the shorter term *lateral bracing structure*, or simply the *bracing structure*.) The discussion in this chapter focuses on the bracing structure; general design concerns for the building as a whole are addressed in Chapter 4.

3.1 GENERAL DESIGN CONSIDERATIONS

The relative importance of design for seismic effects as an influence on general building design varies greatly among buildings. The location of the building is a major consideration, with the basic issue of seismic risk varying over a considerable range. Other important variations include the weight of the construction, the building size, and the general nature of the building's responses to dynamic loading effects of an earthquake.

The materials and form of the building construction are also a concern, as these may strongly affect the choice of bracing system. For the bracing system itself, a major consideration is choice of the basic form, or type; these are discussed in the next section. This choice is related to the generation of seismic effects, as the type of bracing structure helps determine load magnitudes.

Influence of Dead Load

Dead weight of the building construction is a consideration in wind-resistant design, because it is a stabilizing factor against uplift, overturn, and sliding. As heavy construction also usually implies considerable stiffness, there are also less likely to be problems with vibration and flutter. Dead weight also can be advantagious for the stabilizing or restoring effect during an earthquake, but it is mostly *disadvantagious*, as the actual seismic force is proportional to the weight (mass) of the building.

Anchorage for Uplift, Sliding, and Overturn

Connection methods ordinarily used for various forms of construction may provide for adequate transfer of seismic-generated forces. For structural design, the first consideration is to determine the capacity of ordinary connections as required by codes for minimum construction or as typical construction practice. If these are determined to be inadequate, then additional measures must be taken to develop enhanced anchorage and load transfer capabilities. Developing of adequate connections is a major part of structural design. In addition, careful inspection should be made of the finished construction work, as workers may be asked to do things that are out of the ordinary and consequently, unpracticed. Forensic studies of wind-damaged and earthquake-damaged buildings have revealed many cases where special connections have been omitted, even though they were carefully specified.

Forms of connections relate to the type of forces being transferred as well as to the general materials and forms of the construction. Commonly used connections are usually rated for capacity by the building codes on the basis of research studies. Examples of connections are illustrated in the building design cases in Part Two.

Considerations for Building Shape

Buildings with relatively simple forms and some degree of symmetry usually have the lowest requirements for elaborate or extensive bracing or for complex connections for lateral loads. The building form in general should be designed with a clear understanding of ramifications in terms of structural requirements when wind or seismic forces are high. When a complex form is deemed necessary, the structural cost must be acknowledged.

Relative Stiffness of Structural Elements

In most buildings, the lateral bracing structure contains two basic types of elements: the horizontal distribution elements and the vertical cantilevered elements. The manner in which the horizontal elements distribute forces and the manner in which the vertical elements share forces are critical considerations for analysis of structural behavior due to lateral force effects. The relative stiffness of individual vertical elements is a major property that affects these relationships. This issue is discussed for the basic types of bracing systems in the next section and is illustrated in Part Two.

Stiffness of Nonstructural Elements

When the vertical elements of the lateral resistive structure are relatively flexible, as with rigid frames with slender members or wood-framed shear walls short in plan length, considerable lateral force may be transferred to nonstructural elements of the building construction. Wall finishes of masonry veneer, ceramic tile, and plaster or stucco can produce relatively rigid planes whose stiffnesses exceed those of the structures by which they are supported and braced. When this is the case, the finish materials may take the lateral load initially, with the bracing structure going to work only when the finish materials or their attachment connections fail.

This situation is not entirely a matter of relative stiffness, however, because the propagation of lateral load through the building also depends on the attachments between elements of the construction. Thus, structural behavior may be at least partly controlled by careful detailing of the connections between building parts. Nevertheless, when stiff forms of construction are intended for use for nonstructural elements, relative stiffness and load sharing must be carefully considered. A particular problem is the use of nonstructural walls of rigid construction, especially when they are tightly connected to the bracing structure.

Allowance for Movement of the Structure

All structures deform when loaded. The actual dimension of movement may be insignificant, as in the case of a sitecast concrete shear wall, or it may be considerable, as in the case of a steel rigid frame with slender members. The effect of these movements on other parts of the building construction must be considered. The case of load transfer to nonstructural finish elements, as just described, is one example of this problem. Additional critical examples are windows and doors. Window glazing must be installed to allow for some movement of the glass with respect to the frame. Window and door frames should be installed with some allowance for movement of the structure without load being transferred to the frames.

3.2   TYPES OF LATERAL FORCE-RESISTING SYSTEMS

Box, or Panelized, System

The box system is usually of the form shown in Figure 3.1, consisting of some combination of horizontal and vertical planar elements (*diaphragms*). Actually, most buildings use horizontal diaphragms because roof and floor construction provide them as a matter of course. The other types of systems consist primarily of variations of the vertical bracing elements. An occasional exception is a roof or floor structure with many openings or a form of construction that prevents it from functioning as a diaphragm; in which case, some other form of horizontal structure must be used. In reality, the box is classified as such due to the extreme stiffness of its elements; thus a very stiff truss or rigid frame may be substituted for a shear wall and still preserve the nature of the box system.

Internally Braced Frames

The typical assemblage of separate post and beam elements is not inherently stable under lateral loading unless the frame is braced in some manner. Shear walls may be used to achieve this bracing, so the system functions as a box even though there is a frame structure. Many frame structures are braced in this manner. It is possible, however, to use diagonal members, X bracing, knee braces, and so on, to achieve the necessary lateral stability of the frame. When some form of trussing is employed for bracing, the term *braced frame* describes the structure.

Rigid Frames

In general, trussing refers to the retaining of pinned joints between members, relying on triangulated arrangements of members for stability. When bending and shear are created

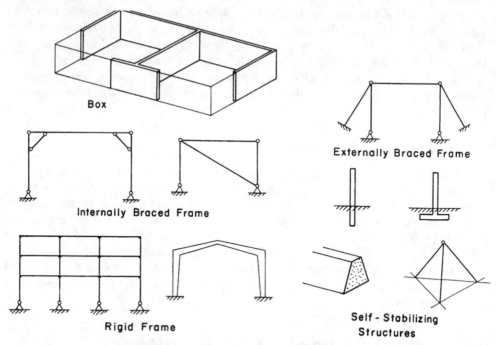

Box

Internally Braced Frame

Rigid Frame

Externally Braced Frame

Self - Stabilizing
Structures

FIGURE 3.1   Types of lateral load-resisting systems.

in the members due to lateral forces, the action is usually described as *rigid frame* behavior. This is usually achieved with joints that are capable of transferring moments between members (thus it actually takes *rigid joints* to make a rigid frame). However, some trussing arrangements may also serve to develop forms of rigid frame behavior, as is the case of the knee-braced frame. Unfortunately the term rigid frame is often a misnomer, as this type of structure is frequently the *least* resistive to lateral deflections—that is, it is not more rigid but rather more flexible than most shear walls or truss-braced frames.

Externally Braced Frames

Using guys, struts, buttresses, and so on, externally frees interior spaces in the building from intrusive bracing elements.

Self-Stabilizing Structures

Self-stabilizing elements such as cantilever retaining walls, gravity dams, flagpoles, pyramids, and tripods provide stability by basic form and orientation. In most cases, these structures are developed to optimize resistance to lateral effects.

3.3   LATERAL BRACING SYSTEMS

For both structural design and architectural planning concerns, complex buildings might employ a variety of bracing elements. Walls with a frame structure, although not necessarily used for gravity load resistance, can be used to brace the frame for lateral loads. Shear walls may be used to brace a building in one direction, whereas a braced frame (truss) or a rigid frame can be used in the perpendicular direction. Multistory buildings occasionally have one type of system, such as a rigid frame, for the upper stories and a different system, such as a box or braced frame, for the lower stories. Each of the lateral bracing systems described in Section 3.2 is available in a number of variations in terms of materials, forms of the parts, details of the construction, and relation to the rest of the building con-

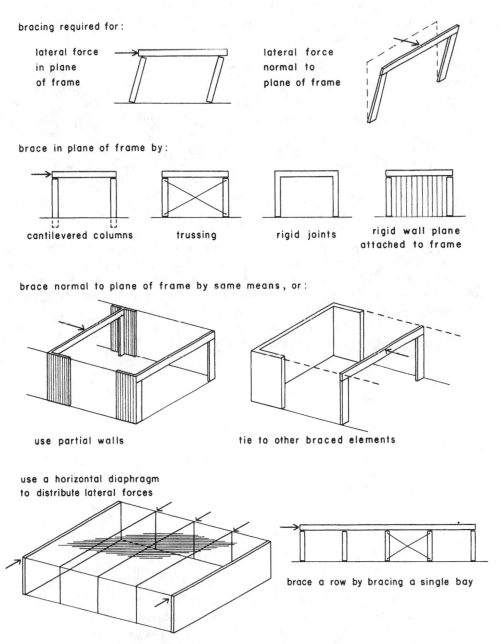

bracing required for:

lateral force in plane of frame

lateral force normal to plane of frame

brace in plane of frame by:

cantilevered columns   trussing   rigid joints   rigid wall plane attached to frame

brace normal to plane of frame by same means, or:

use partial walls   tie to other braced elements

use a horizontal diaphragm to distribute lateral forces

brace a row by bracing a single bay

FIGURE 3.2   Bracing of framed structures.

struction. These variations may result in different behavior characteristics, although each of the basic types has its own particular properties (type of stresses developed in members, forms of deformation, etc.). Various design considerations for the basic types of bracing are described in the following sections.

Elements of the general building structure, designed for gravity loads, are often employed in developing the lateral bracing structure. Similarly, basic construction elements developed for architectural planning may be employed in planning the bracing structure.

Walls of the proper size and in appropriate locations may be used as shear walls, depending on their construction details, on the materials used, on their height-to-width ratio, and on the manner in which they are attached to the other elements of the system for load transfer.

In many cases, it is neither necessary nor desirable to use every wall as a shear wall or to brace every bay of the building frame. Figure 3.2 shows various situations in which the lateral bracing of the building is achieved by partial bracing of the whole structure. This procedure requires that there be some load-distributing elements, such as the roof and floor diaphragms, horizontal ties and struts, and so on, that serve to connect the unstabilized portions of the building to the lateral resistive elements.

The effect of lateral movement on all the building construction, not just the bracing structure, is important. Much of the overall building damage resulting from windstorms and earthquakes occurs with the nonstructural parts of the building. Keeping them attached to the bracing structure, while avoiding effects of excessive lateral structural deformation, is no mean trick.

The choice of the lateral bracing system must be related to the lateral loading conditions. It must also, however, be coordinated with the design for gravity loads, with considerations for other loads (seismic, thermal, soil pressure), and with architectural planning requirements. Most buildings permit consideration of alternative bracing methods, although the choices may be limited by size of the building, building code or zoning restrictions, magnitude of lateral forces, desire for enhanced life safety, or a need to protect investment by limiting damage to construction.

3.4 HORIZONTAL BRACING

Lateral resistive structural systems generally comprise combinations of vertical elements and horizontal elements. The most common horizontal elements used are roofs and floors, with the continuous planar deck the primary component that functions for lateral force resistance. When this deck is of sufficient strength and stiffness to be a rigid plane, it is called a *horizontal diaphragm*.

General Behavior of Horizontal Diaphragms

A horizontal diaphragm typically functions by collecting the lateral forces at a particular level of the building and then distributing them to the vertical elements of the lateral bracing system. For wind forces, the lateral loading of the horizontal diaphragm is principally done by attaching the exterior walls to its edges. Wind pressures on exterior walls are transferred to the diaphragm edges as pushing effects (on the windward side) or pulling effects (on the side opposite the wind). For seismic forces, the load to a horizontal diaphragm is due to the weight of the diaphragm construction plus the weights of items resting on or connected to the diaphragm. A "zone" of load periphery is thus defined for an individual diaphragm, depending to some extent on the nature of vertical structural elements.

The particular structural behavior of the horizontal diaphragm and the manner in which loads are distributed to vertical bracing elements depend on a number of considerations. Specific cases are best described in the examples in Part Two. Some of the general issues of concern are treated below.

Relative Stiffness of the Horizontal Diaphragm.   If the horizontal diaphragm is relatively flexible, it may deflect so much that its continuity is negligible and the distribution of loads to the relatively stiff vertical elements essentially is on a peripheral basis. If the deck is quite rigid, on the other hand, the distribution to vertical elements essentially is on the basis of their relative stiffness with respect to each other. These two situations are illustrated for a simple box system in Figure 3.3.

Torsional Effects.   If the centroid of the lateral forces in the horizontal diaphragm does not coincide with the center of stiffness of the vertical elements, there will be a twisting action (called both *rotation effect* and *torsional effect*) on the structure. This effect is in addition to the direct shear effect of the forces. An asymmetrical condition with regard to the bracing structure or with the general building form may generate this effect. Figure 3.4 shows a situation in which this effect occurs because of a lack of symmetry of the vertical bracing elements of the lateral resistive system. Usually, this effect is significant only if the horizontal diaphragm is relatively stiff. Diaphragm stiffness is a matter of construction materials and the ratio of dimensions of the diaphragm. In general, wood and metal deck diaphragms are quite flexible, whereas sitecast concrete decks are very stiff (as are metal decks with cast concrete fill). A long, narrow diaphragm of any material may be quite flexible, however.

Relative Stiffness of the Vertical Elements.   When vertical elements share load from a rigid horizontal diaphragm, as shown in Figure 3.3, their relative stiffness must be determined in order to establish the distribution. This determination is relatively simple when the elements are of a similar type, such as all plywood shear walls. When the vertical elements are of different construction, such as a mix of plywood and masonry walls or of shear walls and braced frames, their actual deflections must be calculated in order to establish the distribution.

Use of Control Joints.   The general approach in design for lateral loads is to tie the whole structure together to assure its overall continuity of deformation. Sometimes, however, because of the irregular form or large size of the building, it may be desirable to use structural separation joints to control the building's behavior under lateral loads. In some cases, these joints may function to create total separation, allowing for completely independent motion of the separate parts of the building. In other cases, the joints may control movements in a single direction while achieving connection for load transfer in other directions. A general discussion of the use of separation joints is given in Section 3.8. Building forms that might need separation joints are discussed Section 4.2.

Design and Usage Conditions

In performing their basic tasks, horizontal diaphragms present a number of potential stress problems. A major consideration is that of the shear stress in the plane of the diaphragm

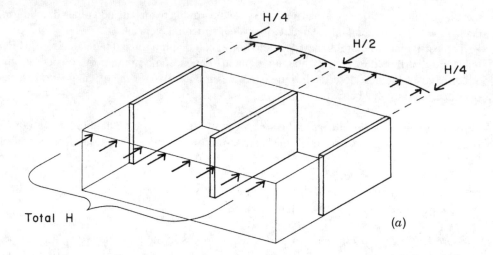

Peripheral distribution – flexible horizontal diaphragm

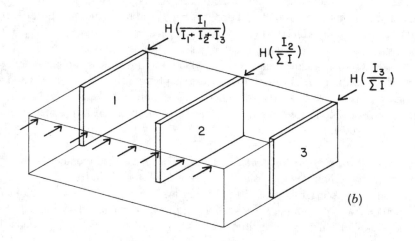

Proportionate stiffness distribution – rigid horizontal diaphragm

FIGURE 3.3 Distribution of load from a horizontal diaphragm to vertical bracing elements by (*a*) peripheral distribution from a flexible horizontal diaphragm and (*b*) proportionate stiffness distribution from a rigid horizontal diaphragm.

caused by the of the spanning action, as shown in Figure 3.5. This span results in shear stress in the material as well as a force that must be transferred across any joints in the deck when it is composed of separate elements such as plywood panels or units of formed sheet steel. Figure 3.6 shows a typical detail at the joint between two plywood panels. The stress in the diaphragm here must be passed from one plywood panel through the edge nails to the framing member and then back out through the other nails to the adjacent panel.

As is the usual case with shear stress, both diagonal tension and compression are induced simultaneously. The diagonal tension is critical in tension-weak materials such as concrete. The diagonal compression is a potential source of buckling in decks composed

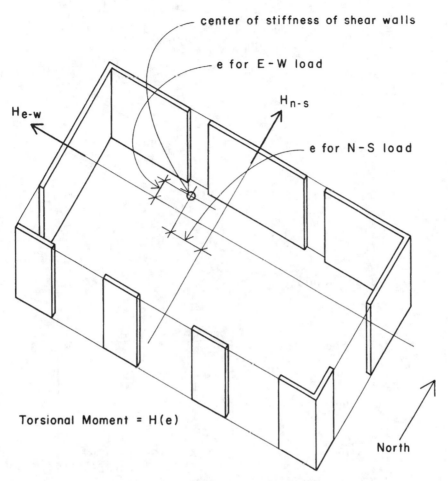

center of stiffness of shear walls

e for E-W load

H_{n-s}

H_{e-w}

e for N-S load

Torsional Moment = H(e)

North

FIGURE 3.4   Torsional effect of a lateral load.

of thin sheets of plywood or steel. In plywood decks, the thickness of the plywood relative to the spacing of the framing members must be considered, and it is also the reason plywood panels must be nailed to intermediate framing members (not at the panel edges) as well as to edge framing. In metal decks, the gauge of the sheet metal and the spacing of stiffening ribs must be considered. Tables of allowable diaphragm shear values for various decks usually incorporate limits relating to these considerations.

Diaphragms with continuous decks are designed in a manner similar to that for formed steel beams with thin webs and edge flanges. The deck (*web*) is designed primarily to resist shear, and the diaphragm edge framing members (*flanges*) are designed to resist bending moment. This analogy is illustrated in Figure 3.7. The diaphragm edge members are commonly referred to as *chords*, using an analogy to a spanning truss. With the reversible direction of lateral loads, the chords must be designed for both tension and compression.

With diaphragm edges of some length, it is frequently necessary to design splices for the chords to develop the continuity of the chord tension forces. In many cases, framing members, which may be employed for chord functions, occur normally at the diaphragm

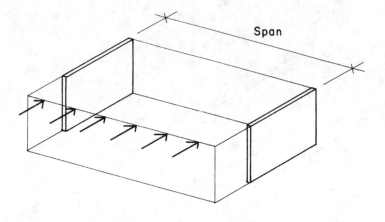

Beam Analogy

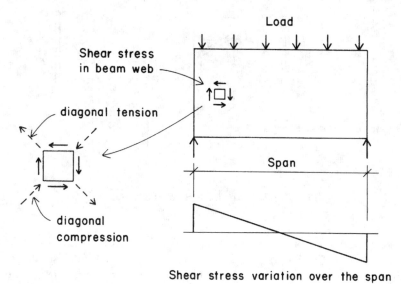

FIGURE 3.5 Beam functions of a horizontal diaphragm.

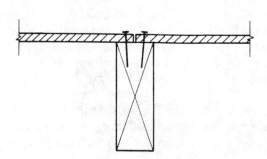

FIGURE 3.6 Continuity of a plywood diaphragm through nailed edges of the plywood panels.

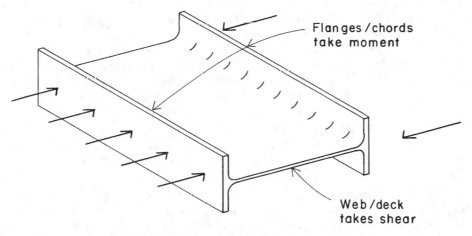

Flanges/chords
take moment

Web/deck
takes shear

FIGURE 3.7   The beam analogy for a horizontal diaphragm.

edges. Edge beams, top plates of stud walls, and continuous wall-face ledgers frequently fulfill these functions.

In some cases, the collection of forces into the diaphragm or the distribution of loads to vertical elements may induce a stress level beyond the capacity of the deck. Figure 3.8 shows a building in which a continuous roof diaphragm is connected to a series of shear walls. Load collection and force transfers require that some force be dragged along the dotted lines shown in the figure. For the outside walls, the edge framing used for chords can do double service for this purpose. For the interior shear wall, and possibly for the

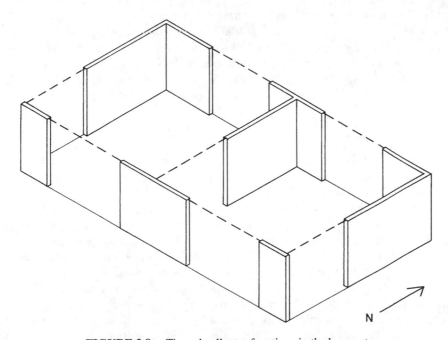

N

FIGURE 3.8   Tie and collector functions in the box system.

edges when the roof is cantilevered past the walls, some other framing members may be necessary to reinforce the deck.

The diaphragm shear capacities for commonly used decks of various materials are available from manufacturers and may be approved by building code authorities. Tabulated load capacities for wood-framed decks with sheathing of plywood and other products are provided in the *UBC*. Selections of deck materials made from these tables must be coordinated with the other requirements for decks, including design for gravity loads and attachment of supported materials such as roofing.

Openings for stairs, elevators, ducts, and skylights are common in roof and floor decks. Small openings may not significantly reduce the deck capacity, mostly requiring some reinforcement of the edges of the opening. However, large openings—or a profusion of small openings—may require other solutions for horizontal bracing. One solution is to develop the large deck as a series of *subdiaphragms* within the larger deck form. Another common solution is to replace the deck entirely with a horizontal truss system, as explained in Sec. 3.6. In some ways, the pierced deck is similar in nature to the pierced shear wall, which is discussed in the next section.

The horizontal deflection of flexible diaphragms, especially those with high span-to-depth ratios, may be critical with regard to other elements of the building construction. This is not a common situation, since most diaphragms have very low span-to-depth ratios. The critical condition often involves a building that is very long and narrow in plan and has no interior vertical bracing elements.

Typical Construction

A wood-framed structure with plywood sheathings is a common horizontal diaphragm. For high-slope roofs, plywood may be as thin as $3/8$ in. However, flat roofs with membrane roofing usually require a minimum of $1/2$-in. plywood for attachment of roofing materials. Floor decks are commonly a minimum of $3/4$ in.

Attaching decking to wood frames was traditionally done by nailing—by hand, with a hammer—and rated shear capacities are still mostly based on hand nailing. Most attachment is now done with powered equipment, however. Nailing variables include the size of nail and the center-to-center spacing of nails. In some cases, with larger nails and close spacings, the framing is required to be wider than the common 1.5-in.-wide, nominal 2-in. lumber.

In general, wood-framed diaphragms are flexible, with deflection affected by the low modulus of elasticity of the wood materials, crushing of the plywood by the nails, and bending in the nails. Therefore, it is desirable to restrict ratios of span-to-depth. This is not so much a problem for the diaphragm itself as it is an issue with regard to major deformations for the rest of the building construction.

Decks of boards or timber planks, usually with tongue-and-groove joints, were once widely used and the underside exposed appearance of this construction is still popular. The construction has very low diaphragm capacity, however, unless the units are placed diagonally to the framing. This appearance is now often achieved with thick plywood panels with grooves cut in the exposed underside. If actual boards or plank are used, a thin sheet of plywood can be attached to the top surface to develop diaphragm capability.

Formed sheet steel decks can be used as diaphragms for either roofs or floors. Stiffnesses are generally comparable with those of plywood decks. Concrete fill is ordinarily used in floor decks, significantly increasing the diaphragm stiffness and stabilizing the deck against buckling. As with nailing plywood, attaching of steel decks to the steel framing is a critical concern; for roofs, the problem of uplift is an additional consideration.

Sitecast concrete decks usually provide the strongest and stiffest diaphragms. Precast deck systems, as well as the cast slab portion of precast systems, can also be used for diaphragms.

Many other types of roof deck construction may offer capability for diaphragm action, although shear capacities may be low. Local code agencies should be consulted if anything other than ordinary construction is anticipated.

Stiffness and Deflection

As spanning elements, the relative stiffness and actual dimensions of deformation of horizontal diaphragms depend on a number of factors:

Materials of the construction; the modulus of elasticity for shear deformation being a major property

Continuity of the diaphragm span over a number of vertical bracing supports

The span-to-depth ratio of the diaphragm

Special conditions, such as chord-length change, yielding of connections, and effects of openings

In general, wood and metal decks tend to produce quite flexible diaphragms, whereas sitecast concrete decks tend to produce the most rigid diaphragms. Ranging between these extremes are decks of lightweight concrete, gypsum concrete, and composite construction with lightweight concrete fill on top of wood or metal decks. For true dynamic analysis, the variations are more complex because the weight and degree of elasticity of the materials must also be considered.

With respect to their span-to-depth ratios, most horizontal diaphragms tend to be in the classification of deep beams. As shown in Figure 3.9, even the shallowest of diaphragms, such as the maximum 4-to-1 case allowed for a plywood deck by the *UBC*, tends to present a fairly stiff flexural member. As the span-to-depth ratio falls below about 4, the deformation characteristic of the diaphragm approaches that of a deep beam, in which deflection is primarily caused by shear strain rather than flexural strain.

3.5   SHEAR WALLS

Usually, vertical diaphragms (more commonly called *shear walls*) are also building walls, employed for architectural planning purposes. As such, in addition to their shear wall functions, they fulfill various architectural functions and may also serve as bearing walls for gravity loads. The location of walls, the materials used, and the details of their construction must be designed with all of these functions in mind. Various cases involving these combined concerns are illustrated in the examples in Part Two.

The most common shear wall constructions are those of sitecast concrete, masonry with concrete blocks (CMUs), and stud frames with studs of wood or light gauge steel and surfacing elements of various materials. Framed wall construction can be made rigid in the wall plane by use of diagonal members that create a trussing effect; however, the more common method is to utilize the planar rigidity of the surfacing materials.

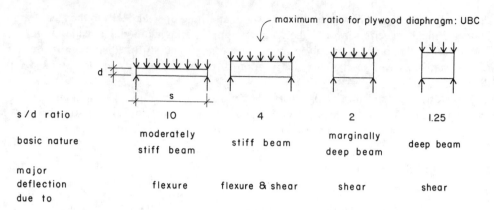

maximum ratio for plywood diaphragm: UBC

s/d ratio	10	4	2	1.25
basic nature	moderately stiff beam	stiff beam	marginally deep beam	deep beam
major deflection due to	flexure	flexure & shear	shear	shear

FIGURE 3.9   Beam action behavior of a horizontal diaphragm related to span-to- depth ratio.

Choice of shear wall construction may be limited by the magnitude of lateral shear that must be resisted. Although capacities range downward from heavily reinforced concrete walls to light frames with gypsum drywall, other wall functions or general fire-resisting requirements often affect choices for construction.

General Behavior

Primary shear wall action involves resolution of a lateral force delivered to the top of the wall and resisted at the bottom by a combination of horizontal force and moment. For the wall and its supports, three structural actions are involved (Figure 3.10).

Direct Shear Resistance.   This involves the transfer of the lateral load from the top to the bottom of the wall. Stress in the wall consists of the usual direct shear plus the resultant diagonal tension and diagonal compression.

Cantilever Moment Resistance.   All vertical elements of the lateral bracing system tend to work like vertically cantilevered beams, with a primary need for a resistance to the toppling, overturning effect at their base. This is usually visualized as being resisted by tension and compression in the wall edges (flanges, chords) and by the net rotational moment transferred from the wall to its support.

Horizontal Sliding Resistance.   This is the direct horizontal reaction to the lateral load and must be developed as a sliding resistance at the wall base.

The shear stress function is usually considered independently of other structural functions of the wall. The maximum shear stress that derives from lateral loads is compared to a rated capacity for the wall construction. This may require an actual stress investigation for the wall, but it is often a matter of using data from reference sources for the particular kind of construction.

Investigation and design of various forms of wall construction must be done with the latest, code-acceptable procedures and data. Although there are many illustrations of wall

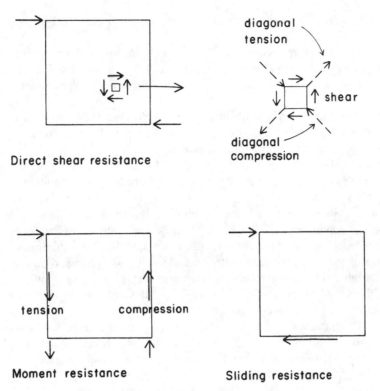

Direct shear resistance

diagonal
tension

shear

diagonal
compression

tension   compression

Moment resistance

Sliding resistance

FIGURE 3.10   Functions of a shear wall.

construction in this book, this is not a complete text on design and construction of all possible forms of wall construction. The presentation here is limited to general discussion and the cases in Part Two.

Although it is possibile for walls to buckle as a result of the diagonal compression effect, this is usually not a critical problem because other limitations constrain wall thinness. The thickness of masonry walls is limited by maximum values for the ratio of unsupported wall height or length-to-wall thickness. Sitecast concrete wall thickness is usually limited by forming and casting considerations and by reinforcement requirements. Precast concrete walls may be made quite thin but are typically stiffened to allow handling for erection.

Stud-framed walls are usually limited in thickness by limitations on the stud size relative to the wall height. Furthermore, stud-framed walls typically have surfacing on both sides which produces a sandwich-panel effect that stiffens the wall. Where surfacing occurs on one side only, it may be desirable to add blocking between studs to stabilize them for shear wall action.

As in the case of horizontal diaphragms, the moment effect on a shear wall is usually considered to be resisted by the two vertical edges of the wall, acting like the flanges of a beam or the chords of a truss. For concrete and masonry construction, the wall ends are usually designed as columns within the wall construction. In some cases, concrete or masonry walls may have enlarged ends developed as pilasters for additional strength.

In wood-framed walls, the end framing members develop chord functions. Such end members should be investigated for combinations of lateral force effects plus required functions for gravity load resistance. Wall ends are frequently used to support lintels or headers over openings.

Overturn resistance at the base of concrete and masonry walls is typically resisted by the dowelling of the vertical reinforcement into the supports (the foundation or a wall below). Anchors for wood-framed walls are typically bolted to the end framing members (chords) for the wall.

Overturning effects must be investigated for individual shear walls as well as for the building as a whole. For these effects, the dead weight of the construction serves as a counteracting, stabilizing effect. This stabilizing moment is deducted from the total overturning effect in order to derive the requirements for anchorage of the structure. Generally, if the overturning moment does not exceed two-thirds of the stabilizing moment, no anchorage is required.

For an individual shear wall, the overturning investigation is summarized in Figure 3.11. Specific applications are illustrated in the design examples in Part Two.

Resistance to horizontal sliding at the base of a shear wall is partly resisted by friction at the base of the wall generated by the dead load. For concrete and masonry walls with relatively high dead loads, the friction resistance may be more than sufficient. However, ordinary dowelling of the vertical reinforcement adds considerably to this resistance, so nothing additional is required in most cases.

For wood-framed walls, the friction is usually ignored and the sill bolts are designed for the entire lateral load. For walls that are short in plan length, there may be a need for some increase in the size and/or number of bolts over the minimum required by codes.

Design and Usage Considerations

An important judgment that often must be made in designing for lateral loads is how to distribute lateral force between a number of shear walls that share the load from a single horizontal diaphragm. One factor is the relative stiffness of the horizontal diaphragm, which was discussed in Section 3.4 and illustrated in Figure 3.3. Symmetry, use of control joints, or other factors may make this a simple judgment in many cases. However, in some

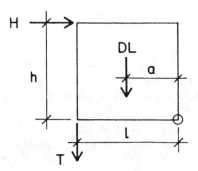

FIGURE 3.11   Determination of tie-down requirements for a shear wall.

To determine T:

for wind – $DL(a) + T(l) = 1.5\left[H(h)\right]$

for seismic – $0.85\left[DL(a)\right] + T(l) = H(h)$

cases it is necessary to determine the relative stiffness of the walls in order to perform a distribution on this basis.

If considered in terms of static force and elastic stress-strain conditions, the relative stiffness of a wall is inversely proportional to its deflection under a unit load. Figure 3.12 shows the manner of deflection of a shear wall for two assumed conditions. In Figure 3.12a the wall is considered to be fixed at its top and bottom, flexing in a double curve with an inflection at mid-height. This is the case usually assumed for concrete and masonry walls that occur in a continuous construction with a wide strip of wall above the individual wall piers. The continuous wall above and the continuous foundation below are assumed to provide the fixity shown.

When wall piers are essentially freestanding, they may function primarily as simple vertical cantilevers, as shown in Figure 3.12b. These may be linked by the wall construction between them, but not restrained in the form of their deflection.

A third possibility for wall deflection is shown in Figure 3.12c, in which a pier is reasonably fixed at its top but not at its bottom, thus also functioning as a simple cantilever— merely upside down from that in Figure 3.12b. This may be the case for wall piers that are supported on individual footings, rather than on a continuous foundation.

In some instances, the deflection of a wall may result largely from shear strain, rather than from flexural strain, perhaps because of the wall construction or the proportion of wall height to wall plan length. (See Figure 3.16a and the general discussion of stiffness and deflection later in this section.) Wall deflection may also be a problem strictly based on its magnitude, just as in the case of the flexible horizontal diaphragm. Furthermore, the deformation of any structure subjected to dynamic loading (seismic shock, wind gust) is

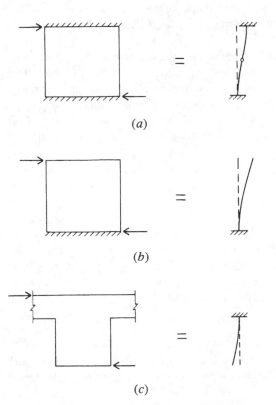

(a)

(b)

(c)

FIGURE 3.12   Function of a shear wall based on support conditions: (a) fixed top and bottom and (b) and (c) cantilevered.

not exactly the same as its response to static loading. Thus, precise calculations of wall deflections are somewhat academic.

The following are some general recommendations for one-story shear walls:

1. For wood-framed walls with a height-to-length ratio of 2 or less, assume the wall stiffness to be proportional to the plan length of the wall.

2. For wood-framed walls with a height-to-length ratio over 2 and for concrete and masonry walls, assume the wall stiffness to be a function of the height-to-length ratio and the manner of support (cantilevered or doubly fixed). Use the values for pier rigidity given in tables for concrete or masonry piers.

3. Avoid situations in which walls of significantly great differences in stiffness share loads in a single direction. Even if they are large in number, the less stiff walls will tend to receive a very small part of the load.

4. Avoid mixing shear walls of different construction (for example, wood-framed with masonry) when they share loads from a single direction.

Item 4 in the preceding list can be illustrated by the two situations shown in Figure 3.13. The first is a series of wall piers in a single row. If some of these piers are of concrete or masonry and others are wood-framed, the stiffer concrete or masonry piers will tend to absorb the major portion of the wall load. A conservative designer would assume the stiffer piers would take the entire load. Otherwise, load sharing is determined on the basis of actual calculated deflections.

In the second situation in Figure 3.13, the separated walls share load in a single direction from a horizontal diaphragm. If the horizontal diaphragm is sufficiently stiff, the distribution here will also be on the basis of proportional stiffness, and a deflection calculation of the individual walls is required.

In addition to the various considerations mentioned for the shear walls themselves, they must be attached to the horizontal diaphragms to effect the transfer of lateral forces. This largely involves careful study of the details of the construction, and, if necessary, development of special anchorage details to achieve what the ordinary construction does not.

A final consideration for shear walls is that they must be made an integral part of the whole building construction. In long buildings with large door or window openings or other gaps, shear walls are often considered as entities (that is, as isolated, independent piers) for their structural design. If the wall is built as a continuous construction, however, its behavior under lateral load must be studied to be sure that elements that are not parts of the bracing system do not suffer damage because of the wall distortions.

An example of this situation is shown in Figure 3.14. The long solid wall portion performs the bracing function for the entire wall and would be designed as an isolated pier. However, when the wall deflects, the effect of the movements on the shorter piers, on the headers over the openings, on the door or window framing, and on window glazing must be considered. The headers may be cracked loose from the solid wall portions or pulled off their supports, as shown in the lower illustration in Figure 3.14.

Typical Construction

The various types of common construction for shear walls are wood and steel frames with various surfacing, reinforced masonry, and sitecast or precast reinforced concrete. In the

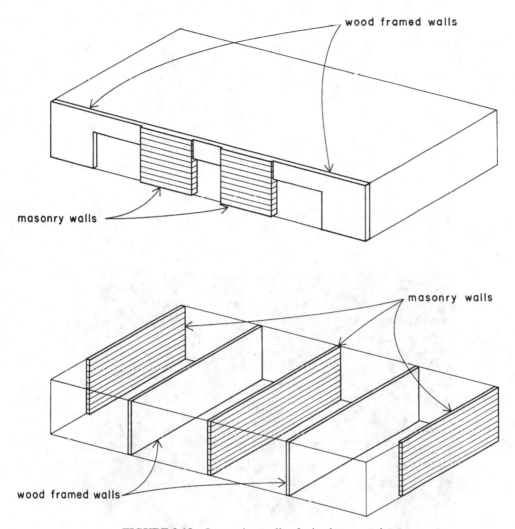

FIGURE 3.13   Interacting walls of mixed construction.

past, the most used wood frame walls had sheathing of diagonally placed boards or ply-wood. In some cases, to avoid consideration for surfacing, a form of trussed wall was produced with *let-in* bracing, consisting of 1-in. nominal boards (actually 3/4-in. thick) that were notched into the stud faces. This technique is still used in some cases, although it is more often achieved with thin steel straps. Experience and testing have established acceptable rated capacities for other surfacing, so that plywood is used somewhat less when shear loads are low (Figure 3.15).

For all types of walls there are various considerations (good carpentry and masonry practices, code requirements, product availability, etc.) that establish a certain minimum construction. In many situations, this "minimum" is really adequate for low levels of shear loading, and extra requirements are needed only for attachments and joint load transfers. Increasing basic wall strength beyond the minimum usually requires increasing the size or

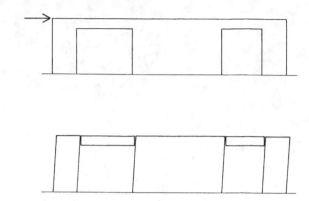

FIGURE 3.14   Effect of wall deformation on shallow headers over openings.

FIGURE 3.15   Wall diaphragm construction. Garage side wall with stucco fastened directly to studs without sheathing and end wall pier with plywood. Let-in bracing probably used here only to brace frame during construction.

quality of surfacing units, adding or strengthening attachments, developing elements to function as chords or collectors, and so on. Designers should be knowledgeable about the various ordinary forms of construction and what simple things can be done to modify them for enhanced seismic resistance.

Load Capacity

Load capacities for wood-framed diaphragms derived from various industry sources are given in the *UBC*. In addition to basic choices for plywood grade and thickness and nail type, size, and spacing, there are various considerations for arrangement of panels, size and spacing of framing, special nailing at diaphragm edges, and other special situations. *UBC* tables are complex and are appended with extensive footnotes.

Masonry design is largely achieved with design standards developed by industry organizations. Investigations for reinforced construction are made with procedures that emulate reinforced concrete design. For CMU construction variables include unit size and grade, mortar type, and the amount of filling of cores. Reinforcement begins with required minimum placement and percentages and can be increased considerably above this level. Although shortcuts are provided in the form of tables and other aids, design generally must be achieved with load and stress investigations.

The concrete shear wall is a relatively simple structure, but no concrete design can be viewed as simple these days. Codes are complex and design computations are exceedingly laborious. Design of concrete structures helped foster the need for computer-aided methods and is increasingly largely not achievable in real time otherwise. No simple load capacity tables here. Where it can be utilized, however, the heavily-reinforced concrete shear wall is the strongest and stiffest element for resistance to lateral forces. And where it exists for the general construction, minimum construction may function for bracing well within its capacity.

Stiffness and Deflection

As with the horizontal diaphragm, there are several potential factors to consider in the deflection of a shear wall. As shown in Figure 3.16a, shear walls tend to be relatively stiff, approaching deep beams instead of ordinary flexural members.

The two general cases for a wall are the cantilever and the doubly fixed pier. The cantilever, fixed at its base, is the most common case, occurring mostly as a free-standing, one-story wall. Other cases were described previously in this section and are illustrated in Figure 3.12.

As shown in Figure 3.16b, if the doubly fixed pier has an inflection point at its mid-height, its deflection can be approximated by considering it to be the sum of the deflections of two half-height cantilevered piers. However, yielding at the supports and flexure in supporting elements may produce some support rotation and result in additional deflection.

For deflection of multistory walls, as shown in Figure 3.16c, separate deflections are found for the individual stories, to which is added the effects of rotations. In the illustration, this results in a deflection at the top that is the sum of multiple components.

Rotation caused by soil deformation at the base of the wall can also contribute to the deflection of shear walls, as shown in Figure 3.16d. This is especially true for tall walls supported by isolated footings and bearing on compressible soils such as loose sand or soft clay—a situation to be avoided if at all possible.

Masonry Shear Walls

Although many forms of masonry produce walls with sufficient strength for use as shear walls, the construction widely used in regions of severe windstorms or high risk of earthquakes is that using hollow units of precast concrete (concrete blocks), now referred to as CMU construction. This construction may be used with only minor reinforcing (technically qualified as *unreinforced masonry*), but it is usually developed as *reinforced masonry* for structural applications.

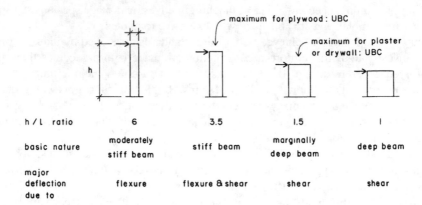

h/l ratio   6   3.5   1.5   1

basic nature   moderately   stiff beam   marginally   deep beam
                stiff beam   deep beam

major
deflection   flexure   flexure & shear   shear   shear
due to

(*a*)   Behavior of cantilvered elements related to height-to-length ratios

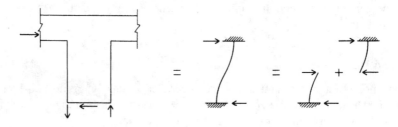

(*b*)   Deflection assumption for a fully fixed masonry pier

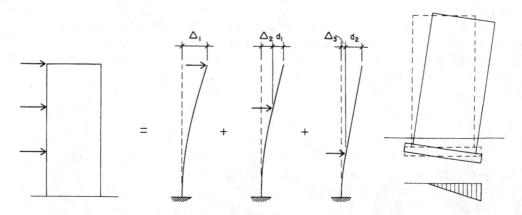

(*c*)   Deflection of a multistory shear wall

(*d*) Shear wall tilt caused by
       uneven soil pressure

FIGURE 3.16   Considerations for deflection of shear walls.

Reinforcement usually consists of small-diameter steel bars placed in continuous vertical and horizontal voids that are then filled with concrete. The filled voids and reinforcement literally form a planar rigid frame of reinforced concrete within the masonry wall (Figure 3.17).

Design codes require minimum amounts of reinforcement and maximum spacing of the filled and reinforced continuous voids. This, together with other minimum requirements, produces a minimal form of construction that typically has a rating equal to that at the high end for wood-framed walls. Above this minimum is a significant range of increase—up to a fully concrete-filled wall with major reinforcement and a capacity well above that of the minimal construction. The minimum wall (created with a single-block thickness) is a nominal 8-in. thick (usually 7.5 in. actually). A 10-in.-nominal thickness block is available, but for reasons of coordination of dimensions, the most used blocks are 8, 12, or 16 in. thick.

Code requirements also provide for the reinforcement of wall tops, ends, and intersections and the edges around wall openings. For anchorage and continuity of the vertical reinforcement, dowels are placed in concrete supports to match the bars in the wall above.

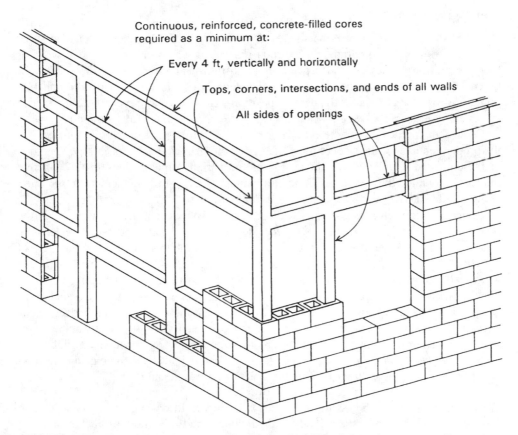

Continuous, reinforced, concrete-filled cores
required as a minimum at:

Every 4 ft, vertically and horizontally

Tops, corners, intersections, and ends of all walls

All sides of openings

FIGURE 3.17   The reinforced concrete frame created within reinforced masonry wall construction with hollow concrete blocks.

Unlike wood-framed shear walls, masonry walls are used frequently also as bearing walls for support of roof or floor structures or for walls above in multistory construction. Therefore, complete design must deal with the loading combinations that occur.

For alignment of vertical reinforced voids, a regimented order of placement of units is required. The face pattern of the wall is restricted on this basis. Blocks cannot be cut for a custom-dimensioned wall length, as is possible in other forms of masonry construction. For these reasons, the building plan must be carefully developed with the block modular dimensions in mind.

In general, the strength and stiffness of masonry walls approaches that of walls of precast or sitecast concrete. Masonry and concrete walls generally produce the stiffest bracing systems for low-rise buildings.

As discussed previously, a long wall may be constructed as continuous, despite the existence of some openings. When these occur, there is a range of behavior for the wall based on the frequency and size of openings and the net dimensions of solid wall elements. Figure 3.18 shows the general relationships and the range of character of the continuous structure, from solid wall to flexible rigid frame. A wood-framed wall may proceed through this range, but the rigid frame actions are mostly limited to masonry or concrete walls.

Concrete Shear Walls

Concrete shear walls represent the single strongest element for resistance to lateral shear force. When used for subgrade construction (basement walls) or for extensive walls in low-rise buildings, they indeed provide great stiffness and strength for the shear wall tasks. Their greatest strengths are generally developed with sitecast construction (concrete poured in forms at the site in the desired position). However, large precast walls are also capable of considerable bracing when properly developed with the total structure.

Of critical concern for concrete walls—and all reinforced concrete, for that matter—is the proper detailing of the steel reinforcement. Recommended details for this are specified in building codes and in the publications of the various organizations in the concrete industry, including the American Concrete Institute (ACI), Portland Cement Association (PCA), and Concrete Reinforcing Steel Institute (CRSI).

Concrete construction is generally similar to the masonry construction discussed in the preceding section. The structures produced are heavy and stiff and weak in tension. Required seismic shear forces for design are a maximum due to the combination of weight and overall stiffness of the structures. For earthquakes, concrete shear walls can work well, but proper detailing of the construction is very important. When used in combination with other structures (wood and steel framing, for example), adequate anchorage or effective separation must be used to provide for the differences in seismic movements. For wind, the heavy, solid, stiff structure (concrete or masonry) is often an advantage, providing an anchor for lighter elements of the construction. Indeed, excessive weight is of opposite concern generally for wind and seismic effects. Typically, concrete and masonry foundation walls are the direct anchors for structures of wood and steel.

An advantage with reinforced concrete over reinforced masonry (particularly concrete block construction), is the greater flexibility with regard to placement of the steel reinforcing bars. These can be placed only in the modular voids and mortar joints of masonry walls, but they can be placed with more freedom in the concrete mass. Furthermore, the steel rods must be vertical or horizontal in masonry, while the bars can take any direction in the concrete mass.

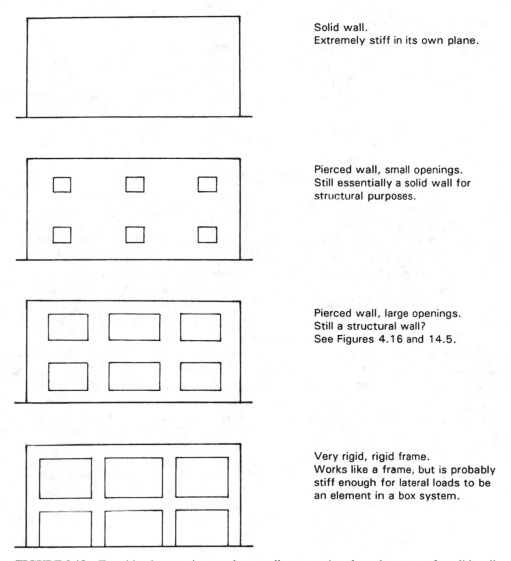

Solid wall.
Extremely stiff in its own plane.

Pierced wall, small openings.
Still essentially a solid wall for
structural purposes.

Pierced wall, large openings.
Still a structural wall?
See Figures 4.16 and 14.5.

Very rigid, rigid frame.
Works like a frame, but is probably
stiff enough for lateral loads to be
an element in a box system.

FIGURE 3.18   Transition in a continuous planar wall construction, from the nature of a solid wall to that of a flexible, moment-resisting frame (rigid frame).

3.6   TRUSSED FRAMES

Although there are several ways to brace a frame against lateral loads, the term *braced frame* refers to frames that utilize trussing, or triangular arrangements, as the primary bracing technique. In buildings, trussing is used mostly with vertical bracing elements, combined with the usual horizontal diaphragms for the lateral bracing system. It is possible, however, to use a horizontal truss either to replace a planar diaphragm or where no diaphragm actually exists (such as with a fully glazed roof). It is also possible to produce a fully three-dimensional trussed frame, as is mostly done for tower structures.

Use of Trussing for Bracing

Post and beam systems, consisting of separate vertical and horizontal members, may be generally stable for gravity loads, but they must be braced in some manner for lateral loads. The three common ways of bracing are with attached shear walls, moment-resisting joints between members, or with the addition of diagonal members to achieve trussing. If two of these are used in combination on the same frame, the frame is said to be *double braced* or *dual braced*. Dual bracing has special energy-absorbing implications for dynamic loading and is thus highly favored for seismic resistance; in the new code terminology, it has a high *redundancy*.

Trussing is usually formed by the insertion of diagonal members in the rectangular bays of the framing. If single diagonals are used, they must serve a dual function, acting in tension for lateral load in one direction and in compression when the load direction is reversed (Figure 3.19). Because of buckling, the long diagonals are much less effective in compression, so frames are sometimes braced with crisscrossed sets of diagonals, called *X bracing*. The symmetrical form of X bracing makes it an architectural form that designers sometimes choose for the building exterior or interior (Figure 3.20).

Ordinarily, trussing produces only axial forces in truss members, compared to the shear and bending caused by rigid frame action. It also results in a much stiffer brace, even with relatively light and slender members. Stiffness for the rigid frame can only be created with very thick (and usually much heavier) members.

Individual beam and column framed bays may be braced as shown in Figure 3.19. One-story, multibayed frames may be braced by bracing only a few bays; other bays being dragged along to the stiffened bays by the continuity of the frame construction (Figure 3.21*a*). Similarly, a single-bayed, multistoried tower may be fully braced, as shown in Figure 3.21*b*, while a multibayed, multistoried frame can function with a single braced

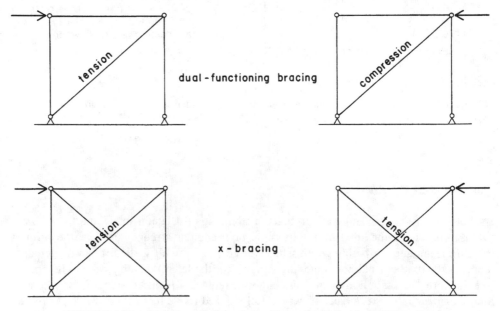

FIGURE 3.19 Dual-functioning, single-diagonal trussing versus X bracing.

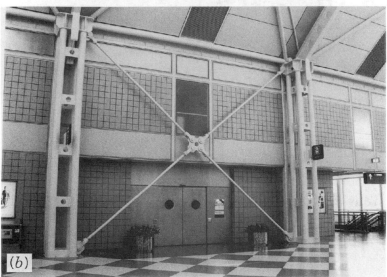

FIGURE 3.20 X bracing may be dramatically displayed on the building exterior (*a*) or sometimes on the interior (*b*), although it is tricky to avoid interference with traffic, viewing, or other necessary functions.

bay (see Figure 3.21c). Since diagonals often interfere with traffic or the placement of doors and windows, this technique of partial trussing has distinct advantages.

Just about any form of construction used for the upper floors of multistoried buildings should have significant diaphragm capacity. Roofs, however, often use lighter construction or are extensively perforated by openings, so that the basic construction is incapable of adequate development of diaphragm action. Roofs may also be sloped so steeply that action for horizontal forces is questionable. For such roofs, or for floors with many openings or elevation changes, an alternative may be to use a horizontal trussing system, developed in a manner similar to that for vertical bents.

Figure 3.22 shows a roof for a single-story building in which trussing has been developed in all of the edge bays of the roof framing. As with vertical framing bents, a satisfactory system can be developed without trussing all of the framework; load from one side of the building can be dragged through the framing to the truss on the opposite side, so that the two trusses share lateral loading.

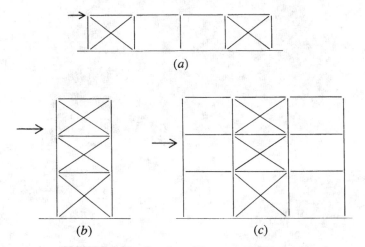

FIGURE 3.21   Bracing of frames with X-bracing.

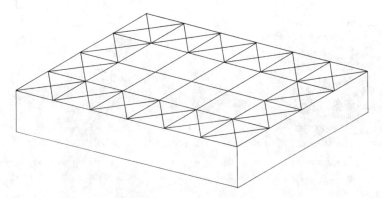

FIGURE 3.22   Horizontal bracing with X bracing. Basic unit created is an edge truss, generated by adding X braces to the framed bays of the horizontal structure.

For single-span structures, trussing may be utilized in a variety of forms for the combined gravity and lateral-load resistive structural system. Figure 3.23a shows a typical gable roof profile with the rafters tied at their bottom ends by a horizontal member. The horizontal tie achieves a single unit truss with the rafters, while resisting the outward thrust at the rafter ends. Once defined as a truss, the combined system will also function as such for lateral loads, whether from wind on the roof or horizontal seismic movements.

The horizontal tie shown in Figure 3.23a might interfere with interior building functions or be unsightly. Other solutions are possible, including arches and rigid frames, but the horizontal outward thrust must still be resolved. Two alternative truss forms are shown in Figures 3.23b and c. The truss form shown in Figure 3.23b is called a *scissors truss*, which produces an exposed interior form reflective of the roof surface form.

The structure shown in Figure 3.23c, although produced with two individual trusses, is in effect a rigid frame of a form called *three hinged*, for the hinge points at the two bases and at the peak of the gable. Between the hinge points, the structure has two scissor trusses. This structure, of course, has outward thrusts at the lower hinge points that are not resolved internally as they are for the structures in Figures 3.23a and b.

The structure shown in Figure 3.23d consists of a flat-spanning truss that rests on two columns at its ends. The truss top chord has a minor slope for roof drainage. If the columns are pin-jointed at their tops, then the structure lacks resistance to lateral loads and must be separately braced. On the other hand, if the columns are of a single piece to the top of the truss, a moment-resisting joint is effectively achieved at the ends of the truss span, and the combined truss+column structure becomes a rigid frame. If knee braces (diagonals between the truss bottom and the columns) are added, the moment connection is further spread, reducing the effect of the rigid frame forces on both the truss and the columns. The knee braces further shorten the columns for lateral buckling and for lateral deflections.

The knee braces shown in Figure 3.23d can be used with a simple post and beam structure, as shown in Figure 3.24, transforming it into a rigid frame. The advantage of the knee brace over other techniques that produce rigid frame action is that the frame jointing

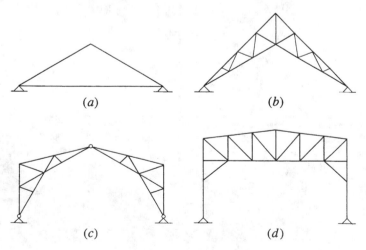

(a)   (b)

(c)   (d)

FIGURE 3.23 Forms of single-span trussed frames: (a) simple tied gable frame (b) scissors truss (c) three-hinged bent with two scissors trusses (d) rigid frame trussed bent created with knee-braced columns.

remains simple, avoiding the heavy moment-resisting connections usually required—an added expense in steel frames and generally infeasible in wood frames.

Eccentrically Braced Frames

The knee brace is one form of what is called *eccentric bracing* because one or more ends of the truss member does not connect at a truss joint, but rather within the length of a continuous member. The range of trussed bracing is shown in Figure 3.25. *Concentric bracing* (Figure 3.25*a*) connects to joints of the rectilinear frame, producing a conventional form of trussing. As used for lateral bracing this may be achieved with single diagonals, but it is also frequently used in the form of X bracing to avoid the problem of buckling of long compression members.

(a)

(b)

FIGURE 3.24 The knee-braced frame: (*a*) making a rigid column-to-beam joint with the eccentric bracing (*b*) form of deformation of the braced bent under lateral load (*c*) example of the use of knee bracing in a light steel frame.

As shown in Figure 3.25b, V bracing, and its inverted form, chevron bracing, connects to a beam/column joint at one end, but within the beam span at the other end. This results in a failure mode that involves developing of a plastic hinge in the beam, thus exploiting the dynamic energy-absorbing effect of plastic yield of the steel frame, while retaining the relative stiffness of a trussed structure. This is presently a highly favored form for seismic

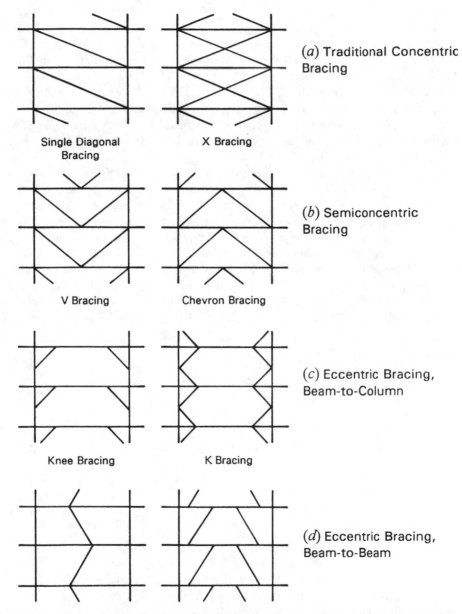

(*a*) Traditional Concentric Bracing

Single Diagonal Bracing   X Bracing

(*b*) Semiconcentric Bracing

V Bracing   Chevron Bracing

(*c*) Eccentric Bracing, Beam-to-Column

Knee Bracing   K Bracing

(*d*) Eccentric Bracing, Beam-to-Beam

FIGURE 3.25 Options for development of the braced frame: (*a*) ordinary joint-to-joint trussing (*b*) semiconcentric bracing (one end of the brace connected to a joint and the other end not (*c*) fully eccentric bracing, beam-to-column (*d*) fully eccentric bracing, beam-to-beam.

bracing. Since the braces are eccentric at only one end, it is sometimes referred to as *semi-concentric bracing*.

V bracing is popular for building exteriors, as it leaves the upper central portion of the framed bay open, permitting insertion of a window. Chevron bracing, on the other hand, is popular for interiors, where a corridor or door can be accommodated. The open center portion of the bay is also preserved with knee bracing and K bracing. Single diagonal and X bracing do not allow for this planning, which partly accounts for the development of the other forms.

Both knee bracing and K bracing (Figure 3.25*c*) are traditional forms of fully eccentric bracing, having been used for bracing frames for wind forces for many years. These are still often used for wind bracing, but they are not favored for seismic bracing due to the bending that is induced in the columns.

An unusual form of eccentric bracing developed recently is shown in Figure 3.25*d*, where tilted members are connected to beams at different levels. While quite a ways from conventional trussing, it nevertheless provides a trusslike action for the frame. Developed for use with a rigid frame system, it provides both stiffening and a dual-bracing redundant energy capacity.

Use of the various forms of trussed bracing depends on the dimensions of beam spans and column heights and the size of frame members. In high-rise buildings, for example, columns in lower stories are very large and stiff, and the effects of bracing in producing column bending are of little concern. For tall framed buildings and for open framed towers, it is not uncommon to change forms of bracing several times in the total frame height, as sizes and proportions of members change.

On the other hand, in low-rise buildings columns tend to be small, and if beam spans are long, the beams may be deep and stiff. Thus, V bracing and chevron bracing are favored for low-rise buildings. Figure 3.26 shows the use of V bracing for a two-story building with relatively small columns and deep, long-spanning beams.

Planning of Trussed Bracing

Using trussed bracing involves the following considerations to determine the form of the bracing system and elements:

1. Diagonal members must be placed so they do not interfere with the action of the gravity-resistive structure or with general use of the building. If bracing members are designed essentially as axial stress members, they must be placed in the frame and attached so they avoid loadings other than those required for their bracing functions. They must also be located so they do not interfere with placement of doors, windows, corridors, roof openings, or with elements of the building services, such as piping, ducts, light fixtures, and so on.

2. The reversibility of lateral loads must be considered. As shown in Figure 3.19, this requires either dual-functioning single diagonals or X-bracing.

3. Although diagonals may function only for lateral loads, columns and beams must function for gravity loads as well and must be designed for critical load combinations.

4. Diagonals placed in rectilinear frames are usually quite long. If designed for tension only (as with X bracing), they may be very slender and can sag under their own dead weight and so require some support.

FIGURE 3.26 Use of V-bracing for a perimeter bracing system in a low-rise office building.

5. The trussed structure should be tight; that is, it should be able to sustain reversible loads with little give in the connections. Connections should also resist loosening with repeated loading.

6. In order to avoid gravity loading on the diagonals, the connections of the diagonals are sometimes not completed until the rest of the frame is fully assembled and at least the major weight of construction is in place.

7. Lateral deflection of the truss must be considered. This may relate to load distributions or to relative stiffness in a mixed system of vertical bracing elements. For tall slender trusses, it may also relate to deformations that are critical for other parts of the building construction.

8. In most cases, the development of trussed bracing involves placing diagonals in a limited number of bays of the rectilinear framing (Figure 3.21). Location of the bracing must be coordinated with architectural planning and must reflect logical placement of vertical bracing elements for the building.

The braced frame may be used for an entire building's vertical bracing elements, but it can be mixed with other systems in a single building too. Figure 3.27 shows the use of braced frames for the vertical resistive structure in one direction and shear walls for the other direction. In this example, the two systems act essentially independently, except for torsion effects, and there is no need for a deflection analysis to determine load sharing.

Figure 3.28 shows a structure in which the end bays of the roof framing are truss braced. For loading in the direction shown, these trussed bays take the highest magnitude of shear in the horizontal structure, allowing the deck diaphragm to be designed for a lower shear stress.

Figure 3.29 shows a low-rise office building with a mixed wood and steel structure. X bracing is developed in some bays of the steel structure and may well function as the pri-

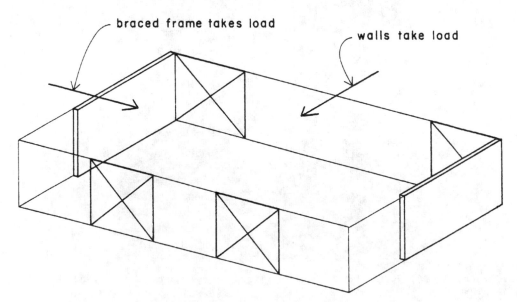

FIGURE 3.27   Mixed vertical elements for lateral resistance.

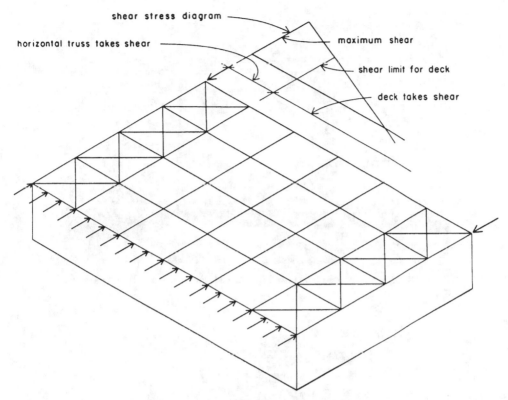

shear stress diagram

horizontal truss takes shear

maximum shear

shear limit for deck

deck takes shear

FIGURE 3.28   Horizontal bracing developed as a mixed system, with part braced frame and part diaphragm.

mary bracing system. However, the plywood covered wood frame is also capable of developing resistance, so this could be a mixed system in some situations. In this example, the diagonals consist of single steel channel sections turned back-to-back so that they can cross in the center without a joint (Figure 3.30).

While individual building elements and some subsystems are often composed of a single material, most buildings employ construction with many different materials. Figure 3.31*a* shows a single-story building under construction, with structural elements in view consisting of all the major structural materials: wood, steel, masonry, and concrete. Mixtures of construction are also common with lateral bracing systems, as shown in Figure 3.31*b*. Our discussion often focuses on single-component systems and single materials for simplicity, but whole buildings are often complex and diverse.

Although buildings and structures are often planned and constructed in two-dimensional components (horizontal floor and roof planes and vertical walls or framing bents), buildings are truly three dimensional. Generation of lateral forces and development of bracing is essentially a three-dimensional problem. Although an individual horizontal or vertical plane of the structure may be stable and adequately load resistive, the whole system must interact appropriately. While the single triangle is the basic stabilizing unit for a planar truss, the three-dimensional structure may not be truly stable just because its component planes are braced.

FIGURE 3.29   X-braced bents used in a mixed steel and wood frame structure.

FIGURE 3.30   Connection detail for the X-braced frame.

FIGURE 3.31 Buildings typically utilize a mixture of materials. (*a*) In this modest building all the major structural materials are in evidence: steel, wood, masonry, and concrete. Usage is often a practical matter of cost and availability. (*b*) Mixing also extends to lateral bracing systems. This building displays possible elements of trussing, rigid frame, and shear wall systems—only the designers know which are the real bracing elements.

In a purely geometric sense, the basic unit for a three-dimensional truss is the four-sided figure called a tetrahedron (Figure 3.32). However, since most buildings consist of spaces defined in rectilinear forms, the trussed structure is most often a box-shaped frame with planes of diagonals in the sides of the boxes. If the general stability of the frame depends on the trussing, the system must be carefully studied to be sure that stability is truly achieved. This is particularly critical for open trussed towers. For buildings, the whole system generally includes rigid planes of roof and floor framing, which somewhat reduces the problem for the trussing.

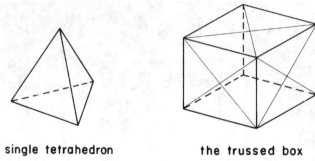

single tetrahedron   the trussed box

FIGURE 3.32   Development of three-dimensional trussing. Basic unit is the single four-sided tetrahedron. X bracing of the six-sided box forms multiple tetrahedron unit.

Typical Construction

Developing details of construction for trussed bracing is in many ways similar to designing spanning trusses. The materials used (generally wood or steel), the form of individual truss members, the type of jointing (nails, bolts, welds, etc.), and the determination of magnitudes of member forces are all major considerations. Since many of the members of the bracing truss serve dual roles for gravity and lateral loads, member selection is seldom based on truss action alone. Quite often trussed bracing is produced by simply adding diagonals or X bracing to a system already conceived for gravity loads and for the general development of the desired architectural forms and spaces.

Figure 3.33 shows some details for wood framing with added diagonals. Wood framing members are most often rectangular in cross section and metal connecting devices of various form are used in the assembly of frameworks. Figure 3.33a shows a typical beam and column assembly with diagonals consisting of pairs of wood members bolted to the frame. When X bracing is used, and members need take only tension forces, steel rods may be used, as shown in Figure 3.33b. For the wood diagonal an alternative to the bolted connection is the type of joint shown in Figure 3.33c, employing a gusset plate to attach single members in a single plane. If finished construction detailing makes the protruding members or connection elements undesirable, a bolted connection similar to that shown in Figure 3.33d may be used.

Frequently, the lateral deformation of braced structures is caused by movements within framing connections. Bolted connections are especially vulnerable, since both oversizing of the holes and shrinkage of the wood contribute to a lack of tightness in the joints. Special devices, such as steel split rings (Figure 3.34), may be inserted into bolted joints to add increased resistance to slippage.

Gusset plates ordinarily consist of plywood, sheet steel, or steel plates, depending mostly on the magnitude of the loads. Joints with plywood gussets should be fastened with screws or ring-shank nails for increased tightness. Steel plate gussets are usually attached with bolts or lag screws. Thin sheet metal gussets should be secured with screws.

Figure 3.35 shows some details for the incorporation of diagonal bracing in light steel frames. As with wood structures, bolt loosening is a potential problem. High strength bolts with calibrated tightening should be used for all structural connections. However, nuts on ordinary bolts can be kept in place by welding or by scarring of the bolt threads.

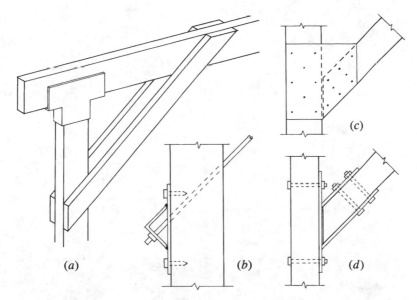

FIGURE 3.33   Details for wood frames with diagonal bracing.

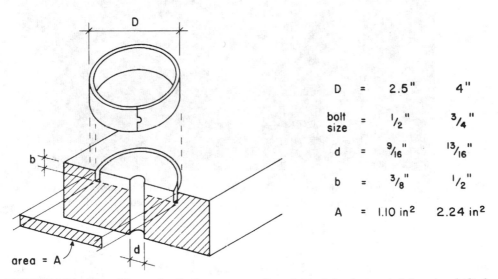

D	=	2.5"		4"
bolt size	=	$1/2$"		$3/4$"
d	=	$9/16$"		$13/16$"
b	=	$3/8$"		$1/2$"
A	=	1.10 in^2		2.24 in^2

area = A

FIGURE 3.34   Use of the steel split-ring connector for enhanced development of shear in a bolted joint.

Of course, welding produces the most rigid joints, but erectors often prefer field bolting over field welding, especially for diagonal bracing inserted after the frame is erected.

Various types of steel elements can be used for bracing members. The choice depends mostly on load magnitudes, but also on the details of connections for the frame. Figure 3.36 shows an interior view of a building in which a system of exposed trussed steel bents is used for a roof structure as well as for lateral bracing. The columns are round steel

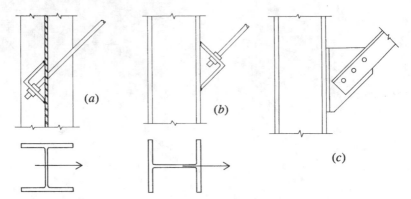

FIGURE 3.35   Details for steel frames with diagonal bracing.

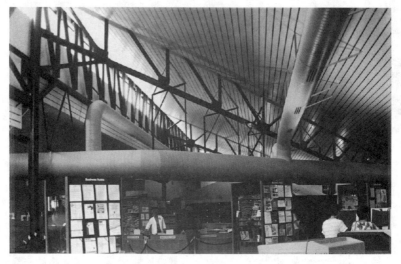

FIGURE 3.36   Building with an exposed steel structure consisting of a two-way trussed bent system. Public library for the City of Thousand Oaks, California. Architects: Albert Martin, Los Angeles.

pipes and most truss members are double angles with welded gusset plate joints (Figure 3.37).

Use of round steel pipe diagonals is shown in Figure 3.26. Steel channels can also used for X bracing, as shown in the building in Figure 3.30.

Stiffness and Deflection

Typically, the braced frame is a relatively stiff structure. This assumes that the major contribution to the overall deformation of the structure is the shortening and lengthening of the members of the frame. There are, however, two other potentially significant contributions to the movement of the braced frame.

FIGURE 3.37   Joint detail for the structure in Figure 3.36. Connection of double-angle diagonals to the round steel pipe column.

1. *Movement of the Supports.* This includes the possibilitiy of deformation of the foundations or supporting structural elements and yielding of the anchorage connections. Foundations on compressible soil will rotate when soil pressures are not of uniform magnitude. Deformation of anchorages may be caused by stretched anchor bolts, bent base plates, and other connection deformations.

2. *Deformation in the Frame Connections.* This has to do with the form of connection elements and the type of fastening used. Tighter connections may be produced by using welds instead of bolts, screws instead of nails, and so on.

It is good design practice to study the details for assembly of braced frames with an eye toward reducing deformation within the connections. This generally favors the choice of welding, high-strength bolts, screws, and other fastening techniques that tend to produce stiff, tight, joints that resist loosening. It also affects the choice of materials or form of the frame members, as these may affect deformations within the joints or the use of particular connecting methods.

Deflection of X-Braced Frames

At the maximum load condition, an X-braced frame is assumed to have its compression diagonals in a state of elastic buckling; resistance is developed entirely by the tension diagonals. The deflected condition of a single panel of such a frame is shown in Figure 3.38*a*, with the deflected condition represented by the parallelogram form. As shown, the exact geometric form of this parallelogram is defined by the dimension *d*, which is the frame's lateral deflection. The approximate value for this dimension, based on the elongation of the tension diagonal, can be derived as follows. Assuming the change in the angle of the diagonal, $\Delta \theta$ in Figure 3.38*b,* to be quite small, the change in length of the diagonal may be used to approximate one side of the triangle of which *d* is the hypotenuse. Thus

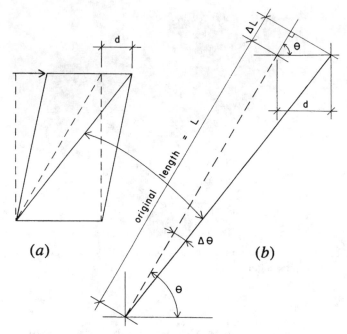

FIGURE 3.38   Horizontal deflection of a trussed structure.

$$d = \frac{\Delta L}{\cos\theta} = \frac{TL}{AE}\left(\frac{1}{\cos\theta}\right) = \frac{TL}{AE \cos\theta}$$

in which:

    T = the tension in the diagonal due to lateral load
    A = the cross-sectional area of the diagonal
    E = the elastic modulus of the diagonal
    θ = the angle of the diagonal from the horizontal

This computation is conservative in that it ignores the component of the lateral load required to cause buckling of the compression diagonal. Of course, this required force can be easily determined if necessary. However, there are also contributions to the deflection caused by deformation in the connections and yielding of the supports of the frame. If these addition and subtraction effects can be viewed as compensating for each other, the true deflection may indeed be close to that determined by tension elongation of the diagonal alone. In any event, it is probably as good as any computation for true deflection of a real structure.

The deflection of multistory X-braced frames has two components, both of which may be significant. As shown in Figure 3.39, the first effect is caused by the change in length of the vertical members (columns) of the frame as a result of the overturning moment effect on the frame. The second effect is caused by the elongation of the tension diagonals, as just demonstrated. These deflections occur in each story of the frame and can be calculated individually and summed up for the whole frame. Although the deflection due to the overturning moment exists in single-story frames, it becomes more significant as a frame gets taller and has a greater height-to-width ratio.

3.7 RIGID FRAMES

Beam and column framing systems for multistory buildings are typically configured in a three-dimensional (or general spatial) system. The building codes have adopted the term *space frame* for this system, although architects have generally used the term to describe spatial trussed structures.

One means of stabilizing the beam and column frame is by using moment-resistive joints for some or all of the connections between the beams and columns. This yields the term *moment-resistive space frame*. The two predominant forms for such a framework are:

1. Steel rolled sections with joints using welds or high-strength bolts for connections.
2. Sitecast concrete with the monolithic casting and the extension of reinforcement achieving the member continuity that creates the moment-resistive joints.

These systems require very thorough engineering design, due to their highly indeterminate force resolution and the general complexities of constructions using welded steel or reinforced concrete.

There is some confusion over the name to be used in referring to frames in which interactions between members include the transfer of moments through the connections. In the past, the term most frequently used was *rigid frame*. This term came primarily from the classification of the connections or joints of the frame as *fixed* (or rigid) versus *pinned*, the latter term implying an inability to transfer moment through the joint. Trusses are ordinar-

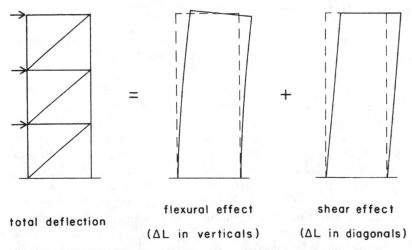

total deflection   flexural effect   shear effect
                        (ΔL in verticals)   (ΔL in diagonals)

FIGURE 3.39   Horizontal deflection of a multistory trussed frame.

ily assumed to have pinned joints, so the forces in members are typically only direct tension or compression.

As a general descriptive term, however, the name rigid frame is badly conceived, since many of the frames of this type are subject to considerable lateral deflection, as compared to shear walls or truss-braced frames. In the technical literature now the name commonly used is moment-resistive frame. For an even bigger mouthful, the particular nature of frames most used for seismic resistance is further qualified by the term *ductile moment-resistive space frame*. With apologies to the *UBC* and others, for simpler reference in this book we use the term rigid frame. Do not forget the problem of lateral deflections, though.

General Behavior of Rigid Frames

In the rigid frame, both gravity and lateral loadings produce interactive moments between members. The joints of the frame, other than at supports, will move under loading as they do in a trussed frame. However, although truss members remain straight, the members of a rigid frame flex or curve due to induced bending and shear stresses in the members. When frame members are relatively slender, the actual dimensions of deformations due to bending will be much greater than those due only to axial tension or compression; this accounts for the greater deformation of rigid frames.

For resistance to seismic loads, the flexural deformations of the rigid frame represent an advantage. This comes from the basic laws of mechanics, in which some of the energy of the dynamic loading is used up by the work accomplished in moving the frame—the more the frame moves, therefore, the less energy is required for direct force resistance by development of stresses in the material. Where this advantage truly exists, use of a rigid frame for seismic bracing results in less required design load. This has been one factor in its increasing popularity.

Recent experiences with rigid frames—most notably, steel frames with relatively slender members—has shown that the magnitudes of deflection involved in developing maximum resistance are in many cases so damaging to enclosed nonstructural construction that designing such bracing is questionable on an overall performance basis. The design issue is one of weighting of different values; those for life safety, property damage, economy, and so on.

Most rigid frames consist either of steel or sitecast concrete. Steel frames have either welded or bolted connections for the moment-transfer joints. Most steel frames employ rolled shapes for the frame members, the most common shape being that designated as a W shape; although the cross sections are actually I or H in form. For development of moment in a single plane of framing, this shape can be oriented for its greatest strength with its flanges perpendicular to the plane of the frame. With beams and columns both so oriented, the form of the typical moment-resistive joint is common.

Sitecast concrete frames achieve moment transfers through the continuous concrete material and the extension of steel reinforcing bars into adjacent members. The reinforcing becomes especially critical for seismic response for its ability to meet three conditions. The first is the most direct requirement for tension continuity through the joint and transfer of tension forces between members. The second concern is for development of enhanced shear resistance in the region of the joint. Finally, an increasingly desired effect is that of containment of the concrete in the region of the joint—thus elevating its stress capacity for resistance to three-dimensional joint stresses under high dynamic load.

As a bracing system, the rigid frame offers a distinct advantage for architectural planning. Absence of solid walls and truss diagonals frees up both the building exterior face and interior spaces, permitting the greatest freedom for placement of windows, doors, and corridors, and the general arrangement of interior rooms. For functioning as rigid frame bents, however, columns and beams must be aligned in planar sets. Offsets in column placement or the existence of large openings that displace beams may make the development of continuous planar bents difficult or impossible.

Lateral deflections are a major concern with rigid frames, whether they produce objectionable sensations for building occupants, cause damage to sensitive building contents, or damage to nonstructural construction. Excessive deflections can also be damaging to the rigid frames themselves. Although steel frame members may be flexible, heavily welded joints generally are not, and the movements of members may be damaging to rigid welds. For concrete frames, excessive deformation usually means extensive cracking of the concrete and possible dislodging of inadequately anchored reinforcement. Consequently, deformation analysis is increasingly important for rigid frame behavior.

Loading Conditions

Unlike plywood shear walls and X bracing, rigid frame bracing cannot be used for lateral loads alone. Structural actions induced by lateral loading always must be combined with gravity load effects. The individual loading conditions may be studied separately in order to simplify the work of visualizing and quantifying the structural behavior, but is must be borne in mind that they do not occur independently.

Figure 3.40a shows the form of deformation and the distribution of internal bending moments in a single-span rigid frame, as induced by vertical gravity loading. If the frame is not required to resist lateral loads, the singular forms of these responses can be assumed, and the various details of the structure can be developed in this context. Thus, the direction of rotation at the column base, the sign of the moment at the beam-to-column joints, the sign of the bending moment and distribution of stresses at midspan, and the location of inflection points in the beam may all relate to choices of the form of the members and the development of connections. If a frame is reasonably symmetrical, the only concerns for deflection are the outward bowing of the columns and the vertical sag of the beam.

Under lateral loading, the form of deformation and distribution of internal bending moment is as shown in Figure 3.40b. If the gravity and lateral loadings are combined, the net effect are as shown in Figure 3.40c. Note the effects of the combined loading:

1. Horizontal deflection (*drift*) at the top of the frame must now be considered, as well as the deflections mentioned previously for the gravity loading. With excessive drift, a critical condition for the columns may be the P-delta effect caused by the nonalignment of the column loading with the column axis.

2. The maximum value for the moment at the beam-to-column connection is increased on one side and reduced on the opposite side of the bent. This increased moment may require that the connection, the beam, and the column have to be increased in capacity.

3. If the lateral load is sufficient, the sign of the moment as induced by gravity load may be reversed. The form of the connection, and possibly the form of the members, may need to be changed to reflect this condition of reversal moment.

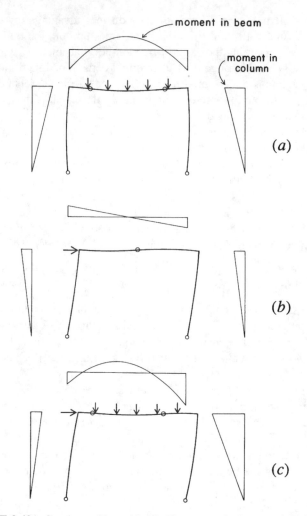

FIGURE 3.40   Gravity and lateral load effects on a single-span rigid frame.

4. The direction of the lateral load shown is rapidly reversed during an earthquake, typically more rapidly than the responding movements of the displaced structure. The slower the frame response movements, the more complex the actual dynamic effects on the structure.

While single-span rigid frames are often used for buildings, the multispan or multistory frame is more usual. Figure 3.41 shows the response of a two-bay, two-story frame to lateral loads and to a gravity load on a single beam. The response to lateral load is similar to that for the single bent in Figure 3.40*b*. For gravity loads, the multiunit frame must be analyzed for a more complex set of potential combinations, since the live load portion of the gravity loads is random and thus may or may not occur in any given beam span.

Lateral loads produced by winds generally will result in the loading condition shown in Figure 3.41*a*. Because of its relative flexibility and size, however, it is likely a multistory

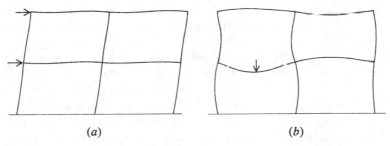

FIGURE 3.41 Frame deformations in a multiunit rigid frame: (*a*) under lateral load (*b*) under gravity load on a single beam.

building frame would respond so slowly to rapidly reversing seismic motions that upper levels of the frame experience a whip-like effect; thus separate levels may be moving in opposite directions at a single moment. Figure 3.42 illustrates the response that might occur if a two-story frame experiences this action. Only a true dynamic analysis can ascertain whether this action would occur and is of critical concern for a particular frame.

Approximate Analysis for Gravity Loads

Most rigid frames are statically indeterminate and their structural investigation requires the use of some method beyond simple statics. Simple frames of few members may be analyzed by *hand* methods, but for complex frames the analysis becomes very laborious. Computer-aided methods are readily available and are pretty much required for complex frames with multiple loading conditions.

For preliminary design, however, it is often useful to have some approximate analysis, which often can be fairly quickly performed. Internal forces, some member sizes, and even approximate deflections thus determined may be used for an early determination of the structural actions and some preliminary choices for member sizes. These approximate member sizes—and especially their relative stiffnesses—can be used to simplify a computer-aided analysis and design at a later stage. For early determination of approximate member sizes for planning, for early cost estimates, and for other preliminary design uses, the approximate analysis can be quite efficient.

For the simple, single-bay bent shown in Figure 3.42, the analysis for gravity loads is quite simple, since a single loading condition exists and the only necessary assumption is that of the relative stiffnesses of the beam and columns. The frame with pin-based

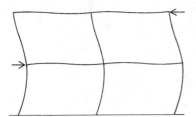

FIGURE 3.42 Effect of rapid reversal of lateral loads.

columns (Figure 3.43*a*) is analogous to a three-span beam on rotation-free supports. If the column bases are fixed (Figure 3.43*b*), the end supports of the analogous beam are assumed to be fixed.

For multibayed, multistory frames, an approximate analysis may be performed using techniques such as those described in Chapter 8 of the *ACI Code* (Ref. 14). This is more applicable to concrete frames, but can be used for quick approximation of welded steel frames as well. This method is illustrated in the design example in Section 13.4.

Even when using approximate methods, it is advisable to analyze separately for dead loads and live loads. The results then can be combined as required for the various critical combinations with wind loads and seismic loads.

Because of the reduced safety factors or higher allowable stresses permitted with load combinations that include wind or seismic loading, in some cases gravity loading may be the dominant consideration for structural design. This is often the case with long spanning beams and the lower columns in tall buildings. Even though wind or seismic load produce a greater load total, the difference may not exceed the increase permitted for the combination. Thus, the preliminary sizing of these large structural members can often be quite reasonably established from a relatively simple analysis for gravity load alone.

Approximate Analysis for Lateral Load

Various approximate methods may be used for the analysis of rigid frames under statically applied lateral loading. For ordinary frames, whether single-bay, multibay, or even multistory, approximate methods are commonly used for loading due to wind or as obtained

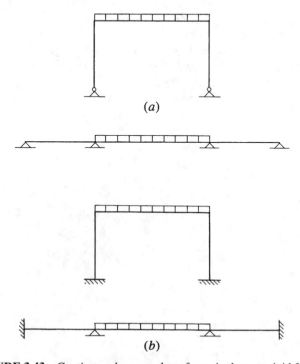

FIGURE 3.43   Continuous beam analogy for a single-span rigid frame.

from equivalent static load analysis for seismic effects. More exact analyses are possible, especially when computer aided.

For complex frames—due to irregularities of member lengths, lack of symmetry, tapered members, and so on—analysis is hardly feasible without the computer. Complexity is multiplied for seismic design, which may involve combined loadings and dynamic loading conditions. But quick approximations are still useful for preliminary design work.

For the simple framed bent shown in Figure 3.44, the effects of the single lateral force may be quite simply visualized in terms of the deflected frame shape, the support reaction forces, and the form of bending in the members and frame joints.

If the columns are pin based (no moment transferred at the connection) and of equal stiffness, it is reasonable to assume that the horizontal reactions at the base of the columns are equal, thus permitting an analysis by statics alone. If the column bases are fixed for rotation, the frame cannot be analyzed by statics alone, although formulas incorporating properties of the members may be used to find some forces and bypass a complete indeterminate analysis procedure. An approximation may be made by assuming a location for the column inflection points and also assuming the horizontal reactions to be equal.

Typically, the column bases are somewhere between the two extreme conditions of pinned or fixed, so member designs can be based on the worst case for each assumption. Then, when details of the final construction permit better informed design, adjustments are made.

For multibayed frames, such as that shown in Figure 3.45a, an approximate analysis may be done in a manner similar to that for the single-bay frame. If the columns are all of equal stiffness (in terms of lateral deflection resistance), the total load is simply divided by the number of columns. Assumptions for the column base conditions would be the same as for the single-bay frame. If the columns are not all of the same stiffness, an approximate distribution can be made on the basis of their relative stiffnesses.

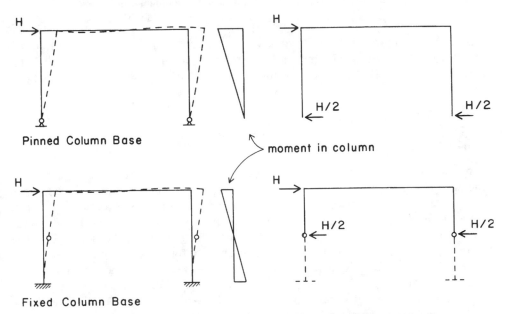

FIGURE 3.44   Effect of column base condition on a single-span rigid frame.

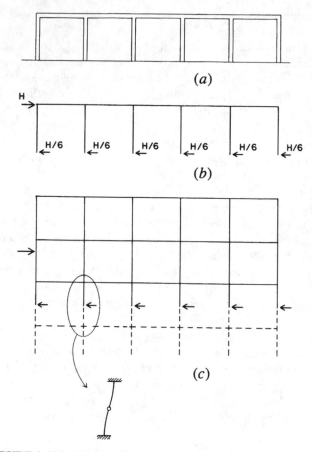

FIGURE 3.45   Distribution of lateral load in a multiunit rigid frame.

Figure 3.45*c* illustrates the basis for an approximation of the horizontal shear forces in the columns of a selected story in a multistory frame. Like the horizontal reactions in the single-story frame, individual column shears are distributed on the basis of the relative column stiffnesses. Use of such an approximation method is illustrated for the concrete frame in Chapter 13.

General Considerations for Frames

From a purely structural point of view, the rigid frame offers many advantages as a lateral bracing system for earthquake effects. Building codes tend to favor it over shear walls or braced (trussed) frames by requiring less design load. For multibayed and multistory frames, reaction time is usually quite slow (long period of vibration) and forces tend to disperse and dissipate rapidly through the multiple interactions in the frame. The rigid frame is a highly efficient, energy-absorbing mechanism for dynamic loads.

Architecturally, the rigid frame offers the least potential for interference with planning of open spaces within the building and in exterior walls. So it is highly favored where planning requires ordered rectangular grids, open spaces, and through passages. The essential advantage is the lack of structural need for solid wall surfaces and diagonal framing members.

Rigid frames present some disadvantages, too:

1. Lateral deflection, (*drift*) of the structure when loaded is often a problem. As a result, it is often necessary to stiffen the frame, mostly by increasing the number and/or size of members. Frames with slender members are likely to have more drift than the rest of the construction can tolerate.
2. Frame connections must be stronger, especially in steel frames. Development of adequate moment-resisting joints adds to the cost of all types of frames. Failures in recent earthquakes have increased this problem for both steel and reinforced concrete frames. Moment-resisting connections for frames of precast concrete are especially challenging.
3. Investigating dynamic behavior for frames of unusual or complex form may be questionable, even with computer-aided methods. Building codes now require true dynamic analyses for an increasing number of cases, many of which relate to form considerations.
4. Effective rigid frame action and efficiency of the load-resolving system require some continuity of members (continuous columns and beams), reasonably equal member lengths in adjacent spans and stories, and other geometric aspects that may inhibit free planning of building exteriors or interiors.

There must, of course, be a coordination between the designs for lateral and gravity loadings. If a rigid frame is used for bracing, its development often begins with a system conceptualized primarily for gravity loads. Horizontal frame members are roof and floor beams; vertical members are building columns. In many cases, however, some elements of the horizontal-spanning system may function only for gravity loading. If only some selected vertical beam/column bents are used for bracing, many of the building columns may not participate in the bracing function. For the *perimeter-bracing system*, only the bents in exterior wall planes are used, leaving the entire interior framing system free of involvement in bracing.

Selection of members and construction details for frames depends a great deal on the construction materials used. The following sections present some considerations for frames of the two most frequently used materials—steel and concrete.

Steel Frames. High-rise steel frames with moment-resisting connections designed for wind loads were used in the early days of skyscraper development. Rivets were the basic fastener, and the forms of connections that were developed related to the functions of placing the rivets, to the available steel products, to the usual form of the connected parts, and to the working situations—some of which involved daredevils hanging in space.

Connections today are either welded or are bolted with high-strength bolts used in connections mostly resembling those originally developed for rivets. For most small- to medium-size frames, members consist of single-piece, hot-rolled sections (W shapes mostly), and of connections formed by direct welding of the parts. Figure 3.46 shows the erected frame for a low-rise office building.

The *trussed bent* is a special form of rigid frame in which some or all of the frame members may be developed by trussing. See the discussion in Section 3.6 for variations of this form. Also discussed in Section 3.6 is the *eccentrically braced frame*, which uses a combination of rigid frame and truss actions.

For tall buildings, a popular system uses a perimeter bracing arrangement with closely spaced, stiff columns and heavy spandrel wall beams. This system offers a major advantage in its overall resistance to deflections. Figure 3.47 shows the erected frame for a steel perimeter bent for a multistory office building. Note that the bents are discontinuous at the corners, thus avoiding the problem of concentrated forces on the corner columns, espe-

FIGURE 3.46   Steel structure with a perimeter bracing system of rigid frame bents. (*a*) General form of the frame. (*b*) Form of the column splice and the beam column connections. Bolted connections are used for erection and alignment of the frame. The moment-resisting connections are achieved by welding the beam ends to the column flanges.

cially under torsional action of the building. The view of the finished building shows the expressed form of the bracing bents.

Concrete Frames. Sitecast concrete frames with continuous columns and beams constitute a natural rigid frame. For both lateral and gravity loads, member ends and connec-

FIGURE 3.47 Use of closely spaced columns and stiff spandrels to achieve a perimeter bracing rigid frame bent system. (*a*) General form of the steel structure. (*b*) Detail of the corner showing the separation of the bents on adjacent sides.

FIGURE 3.47 (Continued) (c) View of the finished building showing the expressed form of the bent system.

tions must be heavily reinforced for the frame actions. While all column-line beams form bents with their supporting columns, it is possible to manipulate the frame behavior so selected bents function as primary bracing bents for the building. The usual means for collecting forces into selected bents is to stiffen those bents with thicker members. Figure 3.48 shows two buildings with exposed concrete frames that have the potential for rigid frame action. It so happens, however, that both buildings are braced laterally by concrete shear walls, which is not an uncommon practice.

Precast concrete structures are often difficult to develop as rigid frames, unless the precast elements are multiple-element units that constitute individual bents. Developing moment-resisting joints for individual precast members is quite difficult. In most cases, buildings utilizing precast concrete structures for gravity loads are braced by separate concrete or masonry shear walls or by sitecast concrete frames that are connected to the precast construction.

3.8 CONSIDERATIONS FOR DEVELOPING BRACING SYSTEMS

Most buildings contain combinations of walls and a frame of wood, steel, or concrete. Planning and designing the lateral force-resisting structure requires determining the roles of the frames and walls. This and other factors in the full development of bracing systems are discussed in this section.

FIGURE 3.48 The exposed concrete frame structure. Although almost any concrete frame is a candidate for a rigid frame bracing system, many are instead actually braced by concrete or masonry shear walls, due to the relative stiffnesses of walls and frames. Such is the case for these buildings, both of which are braced by sitecast concrete walls around stairs and elevators.

In addition to the principal elements of bracing systems (diaphragms, braced bents, etc.), a number of special elements or devices are generally required for the complete functioning of the system.

Coexisting Independent Bracing Elements

Most buildings have some solid walls—that is, walls with continuous solid surfaces free of structural openings for windows or doors. When the gravity load-resisting structure of the building consists of a frame, the relationship between solid walls and the frame presents several possibilities regarding response to lateral loads.

The frame may be a braced (trussed) frame or a moment-resistive (rigid) frame designed for the total resistance of the lateral loads. In this case, attaching the walls must be done in a way that prevents the walls from absorbing lateral forces. Because walls tend to be quite stiff in their own planes, such attachment often requires special details that will allow the frame to deform as required by the loading without pushing on the walls.

Conversely, a frame can be designed for resistance of gravity loads only, and the walls become the primary bracing system—both for lateral loads and for stability of slender frame columns. Care must be taken to ensure that interaction of the two separate systems allows each of them to perform their individual functions. Deflection of beams must occur without transfer of gravity loads to walls beneath the beams. However, it is likely some beams and columns will be required to anchor the walls and to distribute loads to them from the roof or deck diaphragms.

Load Sharing

It is not uncommon to have both walls and frames perform bracing functions in the same building system. In some cases, walls and frames may be used for bracing at different locations or may be oriented to resist loads from different directions. Figure 3.49a shows a situation in which a shear wall is used at one end of a building and a parallel frame at the other end, sharing resistance to lateral load in one direction. In Figure 3.49b, walls are used for bracing in one direction and frames for bracing in the perpendicular direction. In both of these examples, the walls and frames interact quite simply; that is, essentially they act independently for force resistance.

The situations shown in Figures 3.49c and d represent cases in which walls and frames share loads in a way that requires some determination of distribution of single loads to the two different systems. In Figure 3.49c, the rigid diaphragm divides its load between the four bracing elements in proportion to their individual stiffnesses. Since the elements are not the same (don't all deflect equally), this distribution is quite difficult to analyze precisely; the more so for dynamic loading. Figure 3.49d shows two cases of relative stiffness interaction. In the long wall, the three separated elements will share load in that wall plane, the distribution being in relation to individual stiffnesses of the elements. In the short wall, assuming the wall and frame to be rigidly attached, the wall is quite likely to provide the major bracing effort, unless it is of very flexible construction (wood framed) and the frame is very stiff (thick concrete members).

Collectors, Ties, and Drag Struts

Collecting and distributing lateral forces within a bracing system and connecting system components often requires use of special elements. In many cases, ordinary elements of framed systems may perform these functions. However, it may also be that special framing elements and special connections are required.

Figure 3.50 shows a structure consisting of a horizontal diaphragm and a number of isolated exterior shear walls. For loading in the north-south direction, the framing members labeled A probably serve as chords for the roof diaphragm. In most cases, these members will be parts of the roof edge or the top of the wall. For the lateral load in the east-west direction they serve as *collectors*, gathering the load in a continuous manner

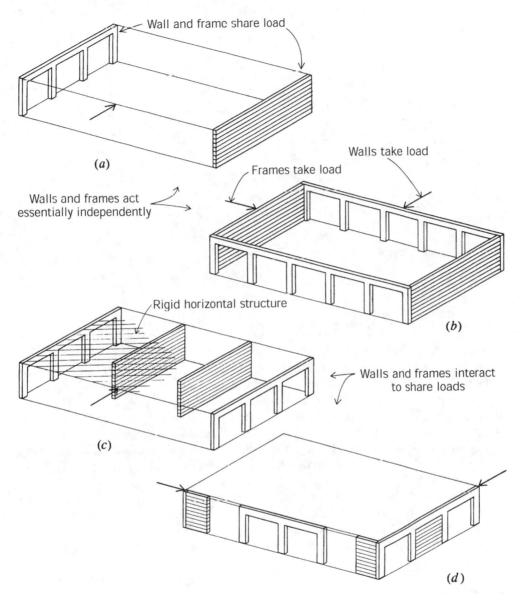

FIGURE 3.49 Response of mixed frame and wall structure to lateral loads. (*a*) Widely separated frame and wall share load without interaction related to their relative stiffnesses. (*b*) Oriented in different directions, frames and walls respond separately to loads in the direction parallel to their planes. (*c*) A rigid connecting structure that causes walls and frames to deflect the same amount will distribute in proportion to the individual stiffnesses of the bracing elements. Unless the frames have very stout members, the walls are likely to take most of the load. (*d*) When sharing load in a single plane, separate wall and frame elements (or different walls) also receive loads in proportion to their individual stiffnesses.

113

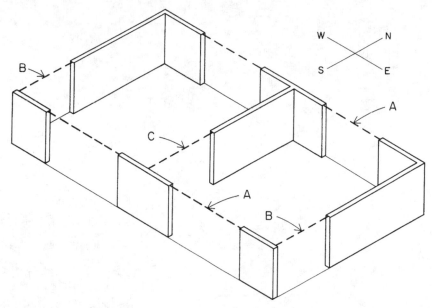

FIGURE 3.50   Collector functions in a box system.

from the diaphragm edge and distributing it to the isolated wall piers. For the collector/distribution function they act as both compression struts and tension drag members; now pushing and then pulling on the walls as the load direction reverses. The members must be designed for the dual compression and tension actions (yielding the name *drag strut*) and their attachment to the walls must also facilitate the reversible load direction. In a similar manner, members B and C serve to collect the diaphragm loads at the open spaces and push (in the north direction) or pull (in the south direction) the load into the bracing walls.

The complete functioning of a bracing system must be carefully studied to determine the need for such members. Ordinary members of the building construction—top plates of the stud walls, edge framing of roofs and floors, header beams over openings, and so on—often serve these bracing functions. If so used, such members must be investigated for the combined loading conditions.

Anchorage Elements

Functioning of a bracing system involves attaching bracing elements for the various required load transfers. There is a great variety of connecting methods and devices, encompassing the range of load-transfer conditions, magnitude of forces, and the choices of materials of the connected members. Some common types of connecting elements and needs are described in the following sections.

Tie-Downs.   A common connection need involves the resistance to vertical uplift. For concrete and masonry structures, such resistance is ordinarily achieved by dowels or by extension of the member's reinforcement through the joint. Steel columns may be anchored by the anchor bolts at their bases. As in other situations, connecting elements that occur "normally" in the construction should first be considered for their capacity, before special devices are added.

The illustrations in Figure 3.51 show some devices that are used for anchoring wood elements in various situations. Hardware manufacturers produce these devices in great variety, covering just about all imaginable situations. In most cases the devices are load tested and rated in conformance with the building codes.

The terms *tie-down* or *hold-down* describe the type of anchor shown in Figure 3.51*e*. Installation of such a device, commonly used for anchoring the ends of shear walls, is shown in Figure 3.52.

Horizontal Anchors. In addition to the transfer of gravity load (vertical) and lateral shear load (horizontal) at the edges of diaphragms, there is usually the need for resisting the pulling away of the diaphragm edge from its supports. Connections developed for other load functions may provide this function, but it is sometimes necessary to provide special attachment. Such a device is called a *horizontal anchor*. Figures 3.53*a* and *b* show a common method for support of a plywood deck at a masonry wall (*a*) and a wood stud wall (*b*). A wood ledger is attached to the wall and the deck is nailed to the ledger in the same way it is attached to the rest of the framing. This may be adequate for most load transfers, but a large force exerted to pull the deck away from the wall will induce cross-grain bending in the ledger, for which the wood member has very low resistance. Where such forces exist—or where codes specifically require it—an anchor device similar to that shown in Figure 3.53*c* can be used to more firmly attach the deck to the wall.

Shear Anchors. Tie-downs and horizontal anchors largely involve actions of pulling away. Another form of action in joints is that of shear, or resistance to slipping between

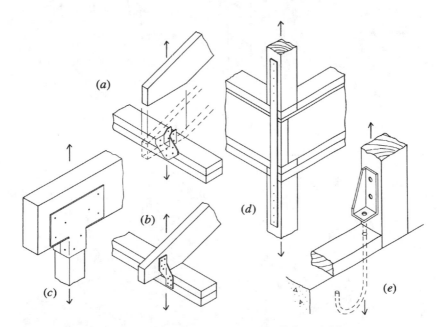

FIGURE 3.51 Metal anchoring devices for light wood frames.

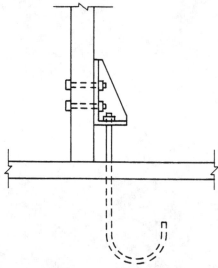

FIGURE 3.52 Tie-down anchor in a plywood shear wall.

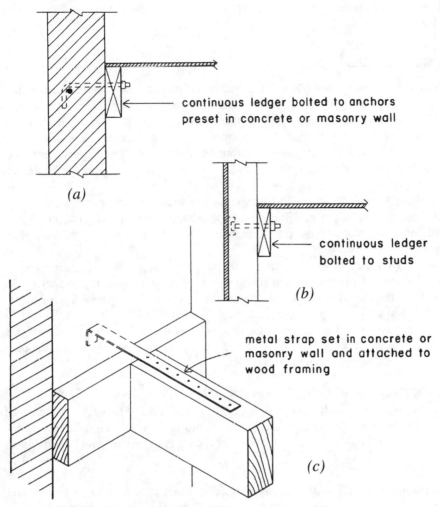

FIGURE 3.53 Horizontal anchors for wood framed diaphragms.

the members. Interaction of members of a bracing system involves various force transfers of this type.

In the situations shown in Figure 3.53*a* and *b*, the major transfer of force between the plywood deck diaphragm and the supporting shear wall is one of a horizontal sliding in a direction parallel to the wall face. This force is transferred from the plywood deck to the ledger by nails and from the ledger to the wall by bolts. While the nails do not resist any gravity forces, they will function for the horizontal pull. The loading conditions provided for by the bolts and the ledger are those of vertical gravity load transfer, plus the lateral sliding (shear) parallel to the wall, plus the pulling away force perpendicular to the wall.

Another form of shear is the sliding at the bottom of a shear wall. For wood framed walls, this force is ordinarily transferred through the attachment of the wall sill to its supports (for example, anchor bolts in a concrete supporting wall). Concrete and masonry walls are ordinarily anchored by the extended reinforcement or dowels at their bases. Where reinforcement is needed, the key-type anchor shown in Figure 3.54 can be used.

Separation Joints

During the swaying motions induced by earthquakes, different parts of a building tend to move independently because of the difference in their masses; their fundamental periods; and variations in damping, support constraint, and so on. It is usually desirable to tie the bracing structure, together so that it moves as a whole as much as possible. Sometimes, however, it is better to separate parts from one another in a manner that permits each reasonable freedom of motion. The joints between parts that facilitate this motion are called *separation joints*.

Figure 3.55 shows some building forms in which the extreme difference of period of adjacent masses of the building makes it preferable to cause separation. Design of the building connection at these intersections must account for the considerations that follow

Specific Direction of Movements.   For buildings with generally rectangular forms, such as those shown, primary movements occur with respect to the major axes of the forms. There are thus two distinct components of the motion at the separation joint: a shear parallel to the joint and together-apart motion perpendicular to the joint. For very tall buildings there may also be a vertical shear motion at the joint. With building forms of greater geometric complexity, the motions of the respective masses may be more random and the joint actions may be much more complex.

Actual Dimensions of Movement at the Joints.   If the joint is to be effective, so that the parts do not pound each other, some necessary dimension of movement must be safely tolerated at the joints. The more complex the motions of the building, the more difficult it is to predict the dimensions of movements, which makes this very much a judgment-based design situation.

Detailing the Joint for Effective Separation.   The joint is to both provide structural separation and still maintain the general connection of the adjacent building parts. Various design techniques use connections that employ sliding, rolling, rotating, swinging, or flexible ele-

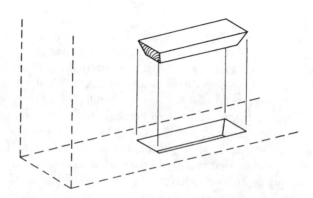

FIGURE 3.54   Forming of a shear key in a concrete base for a wall.

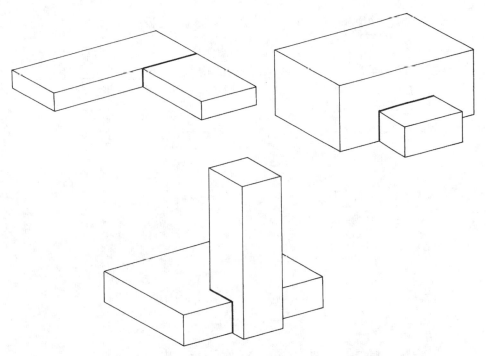

FIGURE 3.55   Potential situations requiring seismic separation joints.

ments. A major distinction is location of the joint—floor, roof, or wall. Other concerns involve the need for fire control, weather seals in exterior surfaces, and sound control.

Figure 3.56 shows the conceptual development of a separation joint for a roof or floor. Closure of the joint is achieved by either a flexible element or a sliding rigid element. In general, the flexible element works better for the weather-sealing continuity of the roofing, while the sliding plate works better for the traffic-bearing floor.

The drawings in Figure 3.57 show some means of achieving partial structural separation: That is, the freedom to move separately for some types of forces and the ability to transfer other forces through the joint. Figure 3.57a shows the classic form of paving joints in concrete slabs, in which horizontal movement is facilitated, while vertical separa-

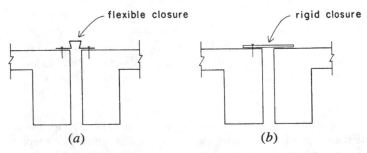

FIGURE 3.56   Closure of horizontal separation joints.

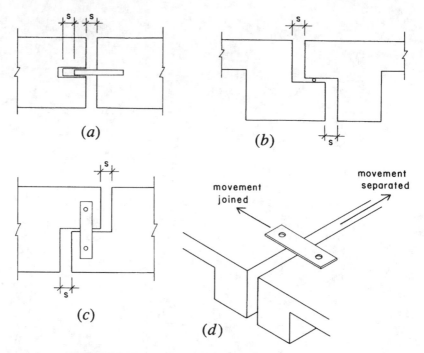

(a)   (b)

(c)   (d)

FIGURE 3.57   Means for achieving partial separation.

tion (creating a bump in the continuous pavement) is prevented. In Figures 3.57*b* and *c,* horizontal movement is again facilitated, while the structure at the left provides for vertical support of the structure at the right. Figure 3.57*d* shows a means for permitting differential horizontal movements in one direction while restraining them in the perpendicular direction.

Possible combinations of joint requirements—both structural and nonstructural—are endless. Lessons learned in the past from construction of thermal expansion joints for roofs, long building walls, and bridge supports give a headstart for this design task.

3.9   SITE AND FOUNDATION CONCERNS

Building sites provide support for buildings but they are also sources of concern for lateral forces. For wind, the site represents the ultimate resisting element that must anchor the building by absorbing the wind forces. For earthquakes, this function is the same for conceptual purposes, but in truth the ground is the *source* for the earthquake forces. This section presents some of the problems of dealing with earthquake effects at building sites.

Building-Site Relations

For buildings that sit on the ground, a design objective is to support the building so that it does not move after its initial construction. This is not possible—in a technical sense—since any stress developed in bearing pressure will produce some strain and deformation, even with bearing on solid rock. It becomes, therefore, a matter of relative magnitude of movement. Dropping vertically by a fraction of an inch is acceptable as insignificant; sinking out of site below the ground surface is obviously not acceptable.

In reality, what is required is a definition of acceptable safety in terms of both strength and deformation, just as it is with almost any structural design work. Foundation design begins by establishing the limits for strength and movements and proceeds to determine the interface structure (foundation) required to achieve the building-to-ground connection.

In a broad consideration of site problems it is necessary to consider two additional problems, besides that of the building foundation:

Site Surface Development. What is necessary to achieve the desired site profile, to achieve any site construction (pavements, walls, etc.), and to support any site planting.

Macrosite Considerations. Although legally defined by boundary lines, the site is also a continuous part of a larger geological formation.

For earthquakes there are some additional potential concerns, including the following:

Proximity to Existing Faults. This is a major factor in the definition of seismic risk. The *UBC* now includes a magnification factor for design regarding seismic force based on this.

Potential for Soil Liquefaction or Other Site Response Behavior. Specific hazardous conditions must be determined by geotechnical discovery. The *UBC* also has a magnification factor based on soil conditions.

Site Problems

Each building presents a unique situation in regard to the combination of true site conditions, design requirements for wind and earthquakes, and the specific form of the building. However, most cases fall into a few common situations. The following discussion covers these common design situations and frequently encountered problems.

General Case, Basic Considerations.   During an earthquake, the building's foundation has a dual role. Initially it is the origin point for the seismic effects on the building, as the ground grabs the structure by the foundation when shaking the building. For investigation, however, we also visualize the seismic forces on the building structure generated by the building's own mass and momentum. For analysis of the force effects, therefore, the objective is to resolve the seismic forces on the structure back into the ground through the foundation. The foundation is at once the starting point for seismic effects and the end point for resolution of the forces.

For this dual role, it is desirable that the building's foundation system act as a single unit while moving. If elements of the foundation system are isolated from one another, as in the case of individual column footings, some form of tie must be used to make them work together for horizontal movements. It may be possible to use already existing elements of the construction such as foundation walls, wall footings, grade beams, and so on, for this task. However, it is sometimes necessary to provide separate ties, especially for buildings without basements.

Recontoured Sites.   Sites are usually altered from their original condition when buildings are placed on them. This might be only a minimal alteration, consisting primarily of excavation for the foundation, with little change to the site outside the building. It is quite common, however, to make significant changes to raise, lower, or generally reform (called *recontouring*) the site surface. There are various possible problems that may be encountered in this work. Some of these problems are discussed later in this section. The special case of the sloping building site is discussed at length in Chapter 16.

Shallow Foundations.   Shallow foundations consist of simple bearing footings, placed a short distance (called *shallow* versus *deep*) below the surrounding ground surface. For buildings without basements, this may result in a relatively light foundation structure, which may not be adequate for resistance to major uplift or the overturning effects of wind or earthquakes. At shallow depths, the soil is usually quite compressible, which can produce various problems. Figure 2.7 illustrates the effect that can occur with a large lateral load and a strong overturning moment. With seismic force repeatedly applied back and forth, the confining soil becomes compressed at the footing edges, which results in the structure's progressive loss of resistance to rocking.

Shallow foundations are typically designed for the capacity of the soils on which they directly bear. The pressures they develop are transmitted to some extent to lower soils, which, in some cases, may be less stable than the upper layers. Additionally, the recontouring of sites may result in having some footings bear on fill material that is more compressible than undisturbed soil. Finally, for a large building, it is quite possible that footings at different locations simply bear on different soils. Figure 3.58 illustrates some problems of this type.

In Figure 3.58*a,* a flat building site is created on a general slope (called a *transition site*), which can result in part of the building supported by fill and part by firm ground produced by excavation. Even for gravity loads, this is not a good situation, but it is especially hazardous for earthquakes. Not only will the fill material be more compressed by vertical forces, it is likely to be generally consolidated and spread out—here, most likely downhill.

In Figure 3.58*b,* a building has footings at various depths below ground, and the progressive consolidation of upper soils will most likely pull the building down in an uneven manner. Again this is a gravity design problem, but can be aggravated by an earthquake that causes a general shaking and consolidation of the upper soils.

In Figure 3.58*c,* a situation similar to that in Figure 3.58*b* is created by a soil profile that is not flat, even though the building has all its footings at one level.

This is only a small sample of possible problems for shallow foundations in earthquakes. Individual cases need a lot of study for these and other basic concerns.

Site with Major Surface Level Changes.   Surface level changes may be made gradually by sloping or abruptly by a sudden drop. Problems for slopes vary greatly, primarily depending on the angle of the slope. As the angle increases, problems of retaining the soil surface and preventing downslope movements of foundations become more critical. Figure 3.59 illustrates a shallow footing in a sloped site. The dimension A, called the *daylight dimension*, must be sufficient to prevent the slope failure (slip-plane rotation) of the supporting soil. Lateral load on the footing will further aggravate this situation. A preferred solution is to tie the footing back to other construction. Otherwise, the footing should simply be lowered a conservative distance to eliminate the danger of the slope failure.

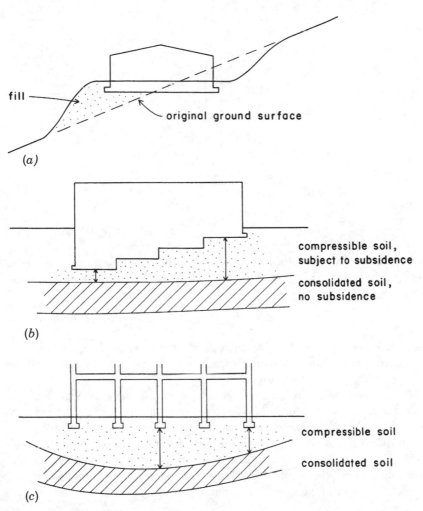

FIGURE 3.58 Potential foundation problems for both gravity and seismic effects. (*a*) Building bearing partly on fill and partly on excavated original soil. (*b*) Foundations placed at different depths in a compressible soil layer. (*c*) Level foundations bearing on a compressible soil of varying thickness. All of these will produce differential settlement of the foundations.

Abrupt changes in surface levels are often compensated for by some form of retaining structure. The vertical height of the change is the critical variable, requiring a range of structures from simple curbs to tall retaining walls. Of course, the surface level change may be braced by a building as a whole, using its basement walls for direct soil retaining and the whole building foundation for bracing the vertical cut.

Soil Liquefaction

Soil liquefaction sometimes occurs during an earthquake. Due to a combination of ground configuration, special soil properties, and a high ground-water level, the ground-level soil on a site may experience greatly exaggerated back-and-forth movement. This excessive

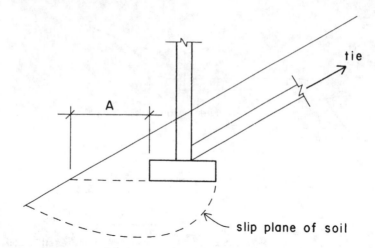

FIGURE 3.59   Critical dimension for a bearing footing in a sloped site for control of failure by pushing the supporting soil out into the slope face. Dimension A is called the *daylight dimension.*

motion may be applied to buildings that sit on or otherwise rely on the soil mass for lateral stability. The condition exists most frequently in areas with extensive fill—either man-made or natural but of recent origin.

Major concentrations of damaged buildings from strong earthquakes are often located in areas of high potential for soil liquefaction, even at considerable distances from the epicenter. Sites of old waterways, swamps, and lakes or reclaimed waterfront sites are areas at high risk. There is no real design solution for this situation, other than to recognize the potential for considerable magnification of ordinary seismic effects. The only defense against disaster is a thorough knowledge of the geology of the region in the vicinity of the site and the history of damage from previous earthquakes in the region.

Deep Foundations

With a deep foundation there are three separate elements that need consideration: the supported building, the deep foundations, and the in-between mass of the upper soil levels. The problem of lateral force resistance by deep foundations is discussed in Section 7.1.

3.10   LATERAL FORCES ON FOUNDATIONS

A major aspect of the design of foundations for earthquakes is that of the resolution of horizontal force effects. Consideration for this problem begins with an understanding of general lateral force effects in soils.

Lateral Force Resistance in Soils

The horizontal movement of an object buried in soil is usually resisted by some combination of friction and passive soil pressure.

Passive Soil Pressure.   Passive resistance in soil is visualized by considering the effect of pushing some solid object horizontally through the soil mass. If this is done in relation to a vertical cut, as shown in Figure 3.60a, the soil mass will tend to move inward and upward, causing a bulge in the ground surface behind the cut. If the slip-plane type of movement is assumed, the failure action is as shown in the illustration. In this situation—as opposed to one of failure of the retaining structure by moving outward—the gravity load of the soil is a useful resistive force.

If the analogy is made to development of fluid pressure, as shown in Figure 3.60b, the magnitude of passive pressure is assumed to vary with the depth below the ground surface. For a structure such as a retaining wall, whose top is near to the ground surface, the variation of pressure is a simple triangular form. For buried objects, however, there is a

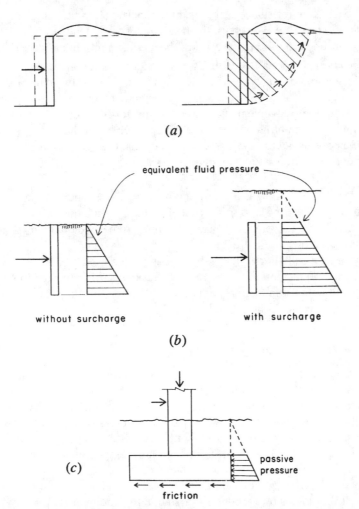

(a)

equivalent fluid pressure

without surcharge   with surcharge

(b)

(c)   passive pressure

friction

FIGURE 3.60 Aspects of the development of lateral (horizontal) soil pressure. (*a*) Passive resistance to horizontal movement of a solid object. (*b*) Pressure variation, without and with surcharge. (*c*) Resistance to horizontal movement of a footing by combined friction and passive pressure.

surcharge effect that increases the useable passive pressure; this is the case for the typical buried footing.

Soil Friction.   The potential force in resisting the slipping between some object and the soil depends on a number of factors:

Form of the Contact Surface. If a very smooth object is placed on soil, there will be a great tendency for it to slip. With concrete footings cast on top of rough, loose soil surfaces, there is a bit more of grab at the contact surface.

Type of Soil. The soil grain size, grain shape, relative density, and water content are all factors that can affect development of friction resistance. Well-graded, dense, angular sands and gravels will develop considerable friction. Loose, rounded, saturated, fine sand and soft clays will have low friction resistance. For sand and gravel, the friction resistance is reasonably proportional to the compressive bearing at the contact face. For clays, the friction resistance tends to be independent of the contact bearing force—except for the need of a minimum force.

Force Direction. Friction, as a force, always works in the opposite direction of the slip-inducing force. As with any stress, there is also some deformation that accompanies the force. Thus, a heavy development of friction implies some extent of slipping movement. For the back-and-forth actions of an earthquake, this can mean some progressive, cumulative movement if the total passive resistance of the soil is not the same for both directions. For this reason, many designers do not rely on friction for resistance of seismic actions.

Friction seldom exists alone as a horizontal resistive force. Foundations are ordinarily buried with their soil-bearing bottoms well below the ground surface. In this situation, resistance to horizontal movement typically involves some combination of friction and passive pressure, as shown in Figure 3.60c.

Enhancing resistance to horizontal slipping may be achieved by adding a *shear key*, a short projecting lug on the bottom of the footing. Basically, this helps the footing grab the soil mass with a little boost in the form of passive pressure. This device is commonly used with retaining walls, as we discuss in Section 8.2.

Development of Resistance to Overturning

Wind and earthquake effects, combined with gravity effects, produce various requirements for foundations. Typically involved is some combination of resistance to vertical pressure, horizontal sliding, and overturning (toppling) moment. Figure 3.61 shows a situation in which a simple column footing is subjected to forces that result in this combined effect. Resistance to downward movement (settlement) is developed by vertical soil pressure. Resistance to horizontal movement (sliding) is developed by a combination of pressures, mostly lateral passive pressure and contact face friction.

Resistance to overturn is somewhat more complex, as the dead weight of the structure becomes a contributing factor, producing a stabilizing moment that partly resists the overturn effect. For very shallow footings, the other primary resistance to overturn is developed by vertical pressure at the soil contact face (bottom of the footing). The force

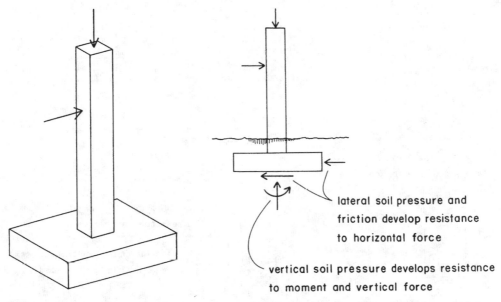

FIGURE 3.61   Development of resistance to combined vertical load and lateral load by an isolated bearing footing.

action visualized at this point is one involving a combined compression and bending effect.

Figure 3.62 illustrates a classical approach to the combined direct force and bending moment at a cross section. In this case, the cross section is the contact face of the footing bottom with the soil. However the combined force and moment originate, a common analytical technique is to make a transformation into an equivalent eccentric force that produces the same combined effect. The value for the hypothetical eccentricity e is established by dividing the moment by the force, as shown in the figure. The net, or combined, stress distribution at the section is visualized as the sum of separate stresses created by the force and the bending. For the limiting stresses at the edges of the section, the general equation for the combined stress is

$$P = \text{(direct stress)} \pm \text{(bending stress)}$$

or

$$P = \frac{N}{A} \pm \frac{Nec}{I}$$

Three cases for this combined stress are shown in the figure. The first case occurs when e is small, resulting in very little bending stress. The section is thus subjected to all compressive stress, varying from a maximum value at one edge to a minimum on the opposite edge.

The second case occurs when the two stress components are equal, so that the minimum stress becomes zero. This is the boundary condition between the first and third

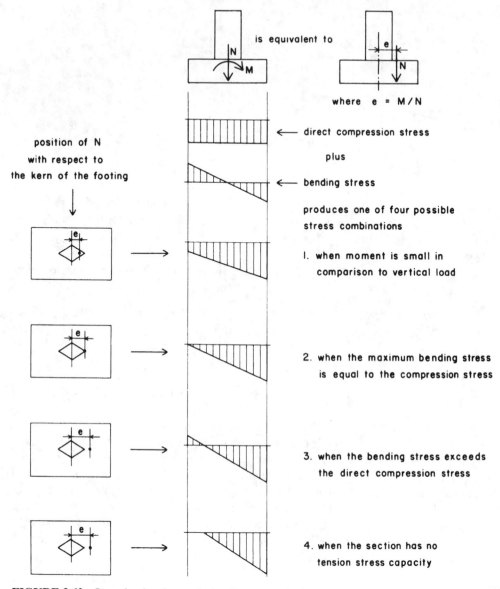

FIGURE 3.62 Investigation for vertical soil pressure due to combined compression and bending moment, using the equivalent eccentric load method.

cases, since any increase in e will tend to produce some reversal stress (in this situation, tension) on the section.

The second stress case is a significant one for the footing, since tension stress is not possible for the soil-to-footing interface. The third case is only possible for a beam or column or some other continuously solid element. The value for e that produces Case 2 can be derived by equating the two stress components as follows:

$$\frac{N}{A} = \frac{Nec}{I}, \quad e = \frac{I}{Ac}$$

This value for e establishes what is known as the *kern limit* of the section. The kern is defined as a zone around the centroid of the section within which an eccentric force will not cause reversal stress on the section. The form and dimensions of this zone may be established for any geometric shape by application of the derived formula for e. The kern limit zones for three common geometric shapes are shown in Figure 3.63.

When tension stress is not possible, larger eccentricities of the normal force will produce a so-called *cracked section*, which is shown as Case 4 in Figure 3.62. In this situation, some portion of the cross section becomes unstressed, or cracked, and the compressive stress on the remainder of the section must develop the entire resistance to the loading effects of the combined force and moment.

Figure 3.64 shows a technique for the analysis of a cracked section, called the *pressure wedge method*. The *wedge* is a volume that represents the total compressive force as developed by the soil pressure (stress times stressed area). Analysis of the static equilibrium of this wedge produces two relationships that may be used to establish the dimensions of the stress wedge. These relationships are:

1. The volume of the wedge is equal to the vertical force. (Sum of vertical forces equals zero.)
2. The centroid (center of gravity) of the wedge is located on a vertical line that coincides with the location of the hypothetical eccentric force. (Sum of moments equals zero.)

Referring to Figure 3.64, the three dimensions of the wedge are w (width of the footing), p (maximum soil pressure), and x (limiting dimension of the stressed portion of the cracked section). In this situation, the footing width is known, so the definition of the wedge requires only the determination of p and x.

For the rectangular section, the centroid of the wedge is at the third point of the triangle. Defining this distance from the edge as a, as shown in the figure, then x is equal to 3 times a. And it may be observed that a is equal to half the footing width minus e. Thus, once the eccentricity is computed, the value of a and x can be determined.

The volume of the stress wedge may be expressed in terms of its three dimensions as

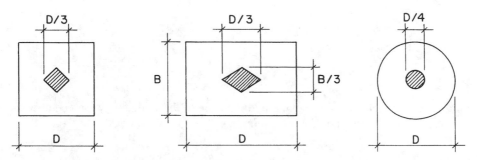

FIGURE 3.63 Kern limits for common shapes.

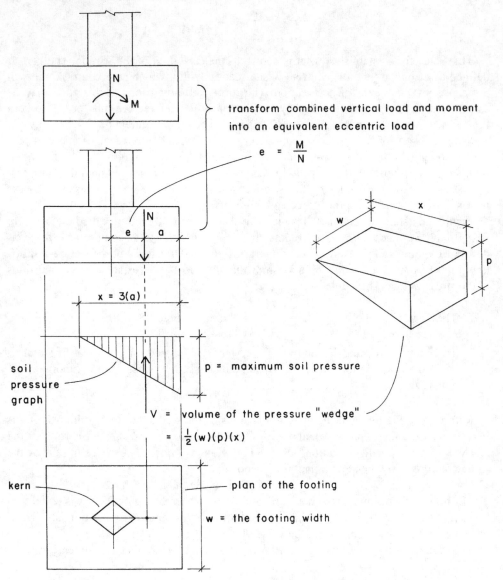

FIGURE 3.64   Investigation of the cracked section by the pressure wedge method.

$$V = \frac{1}{2} \, (wpx)$$

With w and x established, the remaining dimension of the wedge may then be established by transforming the equation for the volume to

$$p = \frac{2N}{wx}$$

All four cases of combined stress shown in Figure 3.62 will cause rotation (tilt) of the footing due to deformation of the compressible soil. The extent of this rotation and concern for its effect on the supported structure must be carefully considered in the design of the footing. Generally, it is not desirable for long-term loads (such as dead load) to develop uneven stress on the footing. Thus, the extreme situations of stress shown in Cases 2 and 4 in Figure 3.62 should be allowed only for short duration loads.

When foundations have significant depth below the surrounding ground surface, other forces will be developed to resist overturning moment, in addition to the vertical pressure shown in Figure 3.62. Figure 3.65a shows the general case for such a foundation. The moment effect and general horizontal force effect is visualized as causing a center of rotation for the foundation at some distance above the bottom of the footing. The position of the rotated structure is indicated by the dashed line figure in the illustration. Resistance to this movement is developed by several force components in the soil, possibly including some friction on the bottom of the footing.

When the footing is quite shallow, as shown in Figure 3.65b, the center of rotation moves down and toward the toe of the footing. It is common in this case to assume the rotation point to occur at the toe of the footing, and the overturning effect to be resisted only by the weights of the supported structure, the foundation, and any soil on top of the

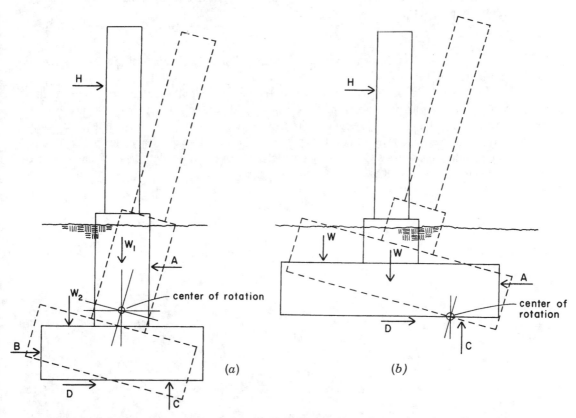

FIGURE 3.65 Force actions and movement of footings subjected to overturning effects. (a) Action of a deeply placed footing. (b) Action of a shallow footing.

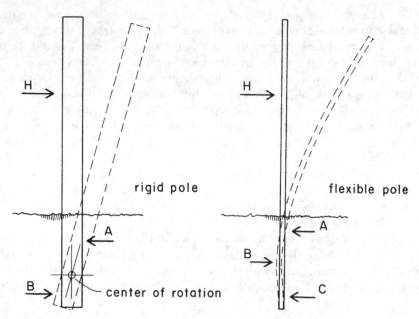

FIGURE 3.66   Force actions and movement under lateral load of poletype structures with varying degrees of pole stiffness.

foundation. Resisting force A in this case is considered to function only to resist horizontal movement.

When a foundation is very deep, it may function essentially like a buried pole. In this case, resistance to both horizontal movement and rotation are developed only by the forces A and B, as shown in Figure 3.66. However, if the pole is quite flexible, its bending may cause the two forces to develop quite close to the ground surface, generating a third force component—force C in the figure. Behavior of pole foundations is discussed more thoroughly in Section 8.5.

4

Design for General Building Response

The discussion in Chapter 3 focused on the structural design of the bracing for seismic effects. In order to visualize the structure within the whole building, it is common practice to illustrate it as a freestanding entity. However, designers must also deal with the response of the entire building during an earthquake. This adds concern for what is generally lumped together and referred to as *nonstructural damage*. In addition, many aspects of the design and construction of the nonstructural elements can contribute greatly to the structural response. The behavior of the bracing structure may well be influenced by what is supported by and attached to it. In this chapter we focus on a whole view of the building and especially on the considerations for seismic design that involve the nonstructural parts.

4.1 BASIC CONSIDERATIONS

When seismic design is an afterthought rather than a consideration in the earliest decisions on form and planning of the building, it is likely that optimal resistant conditions will not be developed. Some of the major issues the design should contend with in the early planning stages are:

1. *Need for a lateral bracing system.* In some cases, because of the building form or size or construction materials, the choice for lateral bracing may be limited. Commonly, however, there are options, with each having different required features (alignment of columns, incorporation of solid walls, etc.). The particular system to be used should be established early, although an informed decision requires some exploration and development of options.

2. *Implications of architectural design decisions.* When certain features are desired, it should be clearly understood that there are consequences in the form of potential problems with regard to seismic design. Some situations that commonly cause problems are the following:

- General complexity and lack of symmetry in the building form
- Random arrangement of vertical elements (walls and columns), resulting in a haphazard framing system in general
- Lack of planar continuity in the horizontal structure due to openings, multiplanar form, or split levels
- Continuous but multiunit or multimassed building form
- Special forms with curves, slopes, and other features that limit the performance of the structure for seismic actions
- Large spans, tall walls, or long openings that limit placement of bracing elements and result in high concentrations of load
- Proportional dimensions that limit structural behavior—especially deformations—or forms that are too thin, narrow, shallow in depth, and so on
- Use of highly vulnerable materials or forms of construction, especially ones affected by movements of supporting structures

3. *Reasonable allowance for seismic design work.* Consideration should be given to the time, cost, and scheduling for design investigations and study of alternative solutions. The more the potential complexity and difficulty of the design work (see item 2, above), the more time and cost are required.

4. *Using building shapes and forms of construction not developed with seismic effects in mind.* Many popular architectural forms have been developed in regions where earthquakes were not considered problems. When these forms are imported to areas of high seismic risk, a mismatch often occurs.

4.2   ARCHITECTURAL FORM AND SEISMIC RESPONSE

Most buildings are complex in form. They have walls arranged in complicated patterns. They are divided vertically by multilevel floors. Roofs are sloped, arched, or generally multiplanar. Walls are pierced by openings for doors and windows. Floors are pierced by stairs, elevators, ducts, and pipes. Roofs are pierced by skylights, vents, and chimneys. The general building form has cutbacks, protrusions, re-entrant corners, and other types of multimassing. Thus, the resulting dispersion of the building mass and its response to seismic effects can be complicated and difficult to visualize, let alone to analyze for quantitative evaluation of structural behaviors.

Despite this complexity, investigation for seismic response often can be simplified by the fact that primarily, what must be dealt with, are those elements of the building that are directly involved in the resistance of lateral forces. That is, to what we refer to as the *lateral bracing system*; or in *UBC* language, the *lateral force-resisting system*. In many cases, most of the building construction, including those parts of the structure that function only for gravity load resistance, may have only minimal involvement in seismic response. These elements contribute to the load generated by the building mass and may provide some damping effects on the motion of the bracing structure. But they do not really help to achieve resistance to seismic load effects.

For a complete consideration of building form, it is necessary to deal with two aspects: Overall building form and the form of the lateral bracing system. The overall building form is defined by the general construction. This, of course, contains the general building structure, but the bracing structure may be limited or may be defined somewhat differently. Figure 4.1a shows the exterior form for a simple one-story building. By comparison,

Figure 4.1*b* shows the same building with the parapet, canopy, window wall, and other elements removed, leaving the essential parts of the lateral bracing system. This system consists of the horizontal roof structure and selected exterior walls that function as shear walls. The whole building must be considered for determination of the building mass for seismic load, but the stripped down bracing structure must be visualized in order to investigate the effects of lateral loads.

Developing a reasonable lateral bracing system within a given building form may be easy or difficult, and, for some proposed plan arrangements, it may be next to impossible. Figure 4.2*a* shows a building plan for which the potential for developing of shear walls in the north-south direction is quite reasonable. The two long end shear walls are most likely more than adequate, assuming that the roof diaphragm can achieve the span between them. The interior walls may also be available, however, which would greatly reduce the necessary diaphragm functions of the roof.

In the east-west direction, however, the plan in Figure 4.2*a* shows a continuous construction without solid walls on the south side, leaving only the north wall for shear wall action in this direction. Seismic lateral forces will produce a considerable torsion on the building, and major distortion of the south wall is likely to occur. This is the classic *three-sided building*, which is common and accounts for a number of failures in every earthquake.

If the modification shown in Figure 4.2*b* is possible, there may be enough shear wall for the south wall to produce a reasonable seismic response. Some torsion will still occur, however, as the structure is still not symmetrical for lateral resistance in the east-west direction. The torsional effect will add some extra force to the south shear walls.

Another possibility for this situation, and one that preserves more of the open south wall, is shown in Figure 4.2*c*. This involves the introduction of a row of stiff columns in

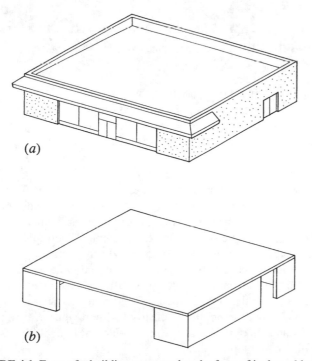

(*a*)

(*b*)

FIGURE 4.1 Form of a building compared to the form of its lateral bracing system.

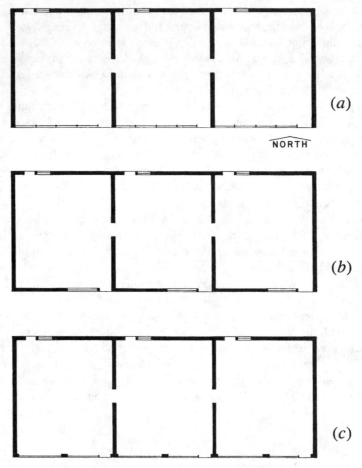

NORTH

FIGURE 4.2 Plan development of lateral bracing.

the south wall. These may be used in combination with a beam to produce a rigid frame or with a truss for a trussed bent. In this case, the stiffness of the south wall structure must be increased enough so that it is closer in deflection resistance to the very stiff shear walls on the north side. Torsion is produced by differences in stiffness, not strength, so any solution must deal with the stiffness differentials of the combined resisting elements.

In the plan shown in Figure 4.3a, the column layout results in a limited number of possible bracing bents that can be developed as rigid beam/column frames. In the north-south direction, the interior columns are either offset from the exterior columns or the beams are interrupted by the floor opening; thus, the two exterior bents at the building ends are the only ones usable. In the east-west direction, the large opening interrupts two of the bents, leaving only three continuous bents that are not disposed symmetrically.

The plan modification shown in Figure 4.3b results in only one unusable column line in each direction, with the remaining usable rows disposed symmetrically for force in each direction. For a structure that uses all the available bents in each direction and all the usable columns for rigid frame action, this is clearly an improvement. However, there are more interior columns and shorter clear spans in the plan in Figure 4.3b, which may present difficulties for planning interior spaces.

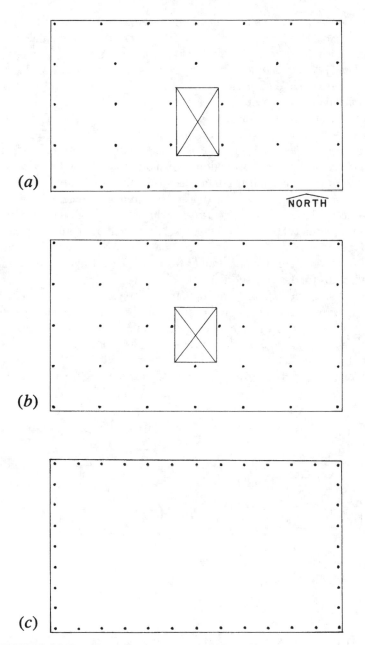

FIGURE 4.3 Development of column layouts for planning of lateral bracing.

A different solution for the plan in Figure 4.3a, referred to as a *perimeter bracing system,* is one in which only the four exterior column rows are used in combination with the spandrel beams. This produces a structural advantage of enhanced resistance to torsion, which makes the system a favorite for seismic designers. An architectural advantage is the freedom of placement of interior columns, which may be considered only for gravity loads. Thus, the plan in Figure 4.3a is perfectly fine with the perimeter bent system.

A further improvement of the perimeter bent system is that shown in the plan in Figure 4.3c, in which the column spacing is cut in half on the exterior column lines. The structural advantages gained are a reduction in lateral shear for each column, plus a substantial reduction of lateral deflection due to the very short, stiff spandrels as well as to the additional columns. Located at the exterior wall, the extra columns are not likely to be a problem for architectural planning of the building interior.

In addition to planning concerns, the vertical massing of a building has various implications for its seismic response. The three building profiles shown in Figures 4.4a, b, and c represent a range of potential response with regard to the fundamental period of the building and concerns for lateral deflection. The short, very stiff building shown in Figure 4.4a tends to absorb a larger jolt from an earthquake because of its very short period of vibration. As the building gets taller—and possibly also more slender in profile (height-to-width ratio)—its fundamental period increases, with a corresponding reduction in dynamic effect from an earthquake jolt. (See Figures 2.1 through 2.3 and the discussion of the fundamental period in Chapter 2.) By the time the profile shown in Figure 4.4c is achieved—a building of considerable height—the total lateral force may be reduced to a fraction of what it is for the very short and stiff building.

Of course, although the lateral shear force may be reduced, potential problems for lateral deflection increase as the building becomes taller and more slender in profile. Thus, while a relatively flexible structure may be adequate for the short building, stiffness becomes an increasingly significant factor for the tall structure.

The overall inherent stability of a building may be evident in its vertical massing or profile. With regard to lateral forces, the structure shown in Figure 4.4d has considerable

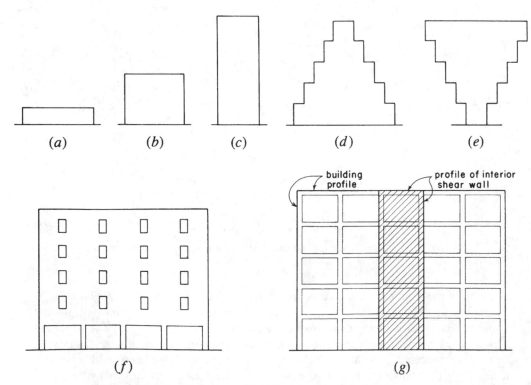

FIGURE 4.4   Considerations of building profile and lateral load resistance.

potential for stability, whereas that shown in Figure 4.4*e* would be highly questionable. This is to say that the lateral bracing structure for the building in Figure 4.4*d* can be quite easily achieved, while that for the building in Figure 4.4*e* could be possible if it was developed basically as a single-masted tower, but it would certainly work a lot harder for the same total building volume.

Of special concern are abrupt changes in stiffness that occur between levels in multi-level buildings. These commonly occur because of setbacks, such as those shown in Figure 4.4*d*. However, an especially bad condition might occur with no general change in the building profile, but with a change in stiffness due to other causes. Figure 4.4*f* shows a building with relatively solid walls in the upper levels, but an open form at the ground level, with vertical construction consisting only of columns. This building might develop a *soft story*, which occurs when there is an abrupt change in total story stiffness between adjacent levels. While this condition might affect only the lateral bracing structure, it also might occur under dynamic loading even though the form is only architectural. That is, the existence of solid nonstructural walls may actually achieve the dynamic response, even though the walls are not supposed to be part of the bracing system. Indeed, the bracing structure may be a five-story frame similar to that exposed at the ground level, with no apparent basis for critical differential stiffness at the various levels. Still, if the nonstructural walls constrain movements of the structure, the soft story effect can occur.

Another case where the form of the building and the form of the bracing structure are separately considered is shown in Figure 4.4*g*. Here the building has an overall profile that is relatively squat with no apparent vertically slender problem. However, it is proposed to brace the building with interior shear walls with the profile shown as shaded in the figure. These shear walls are indeed quite tall and slender, and will behave as tower-like structures.

Investigating the dynamic response of a complex building is, in the best of circumstances, a difficult problem. Anything done to simplify the investigation will not only make the analysis easier to perform, but will tend to make its reliability more certain. Thus, for seismic design, there is an advantage in obtaining regularity and symmetry in the building plan and general massing and in the disposition of the elements of the lateral bracing system.

When no symmetry exists, a building tends to experience twisting as well as the usual rocking back and forth. The twisting action often has its greatest effect on the joints between elements of the bracing system and on connections between the structure and supported elements of the building. Thorough investigation and careful detailing of these joints for construction are necessary for a successful seismic design. The more complex the seismic response and the more complicated and unusual the details of the construction, the more difficult it is to assure a thorough and reliable design.

Most buildings are not symmetrical—sometimes being on one or even no axis. However, real architectural symmetry is not necessarily the true issue in seismic response. The alignment of the net effect of the building mass (or the centroid of the lateral force) with the center of stiffness of the bracing system is of critical concern. When these are not aligned, there is a torsional moment in a horizontal plane. The greater the eccentricity, the greater the torsional moment and the increased effect on the bracing system. Because such buildings are common, bracing systems with enhanced resistance to the torsional effects are popular.

Figure 4.5 shows a common example—the three-sided building. In this situation, the lack of resistive vertical elements on one side of the building requires that the opposite wall take all of the direct effect of the lateral force that is parallel to it. Assuming the center of gravity of the building mass to be approximately at the center of the plan, the lateral seismic force has a large eccentricity from the center of stiffness of the resisting system—in this case, the single resisting wall. Since this wall has virtually no resistance to torsion on its own, the two walls perpendicular to the load must act to resist the torsion. While this is theoretically possible, there will nevertheless be a lot of twisting deformation of the building and considerable in-plane distortion in the window wall.

Construction of three-sided buildings is highly restricted in regions with high seismic risk. Torsion can exist even when there are shear walls on all sides, so the critical consideration is the alignment—or lack of it—between the load and the center of resistance of the resisting elements. And, the real concern is for what the form of distortion is for the building and what possibly gets damaged during excessive movements-as the structurally-open, glazed wall in Figure 4.5 surely would. For seismic action, this is not a single twisting deformation, but rather a back-and-forth, rapidly reversed one (Figure 4.6.).

There are, of course, worse possible cases than the three-sided building. Figure 4.7 shows, for example, a two-sided building with adjacent open sides. Or consider a building with no potential for bracing in one direction.

Most buildings are of more complex form than the simple box in Figure 4.5. If several distinct geometric forms are combined in a single building, the building is described as

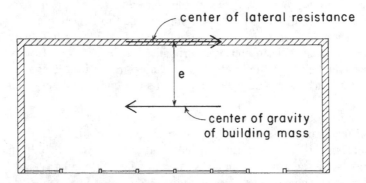

FIGURE 4.5   Classic form of the three-sided building.

FIGURE 4.6   A classic case of the three-sided building—the commercial building with an open front. Movement in this building was extreme, resulting in a total loss of the front glazing and a lot of interior damage. Movement of the roof caused the roof framing to pull loose from the ledger at the wall, dumping the whole end bay of the roof.

FIGURE 4.7   Think three sided is bad? Try two sided. This carport didn't have a chance.

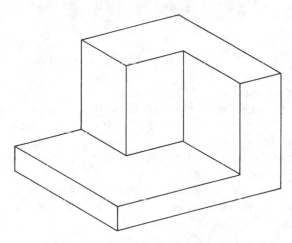

FIGURE 4.8   Example of multimassed building.

being *multimassed*. Generally, the structural deformation of such buildings during lateral loading is complex, involving combinations of flexure and torsion. The building shown in Figure 4.8 consists of an L-shaped tower that is joined to an extended lower portion. Under lateral seismic action, the various parts of this building will have different responses and deformation. If the construction of the building is developed as a continuous system, the combined movement will be quite complex, with extreme twisting effects and considerable stress at the points of connection between the discrete parts of the building.

If the two parts of the tower in Figure 4.9 are separated, as shown in Figure 4.9*a* and *c*, the independent deformation actions of the separated elements will differ due to their difference in stiffness. It may be possible to permit these independent movements by providing seismic separation joints, which tolerate them, thus preventing the complex movements of the multimassed structure and relieving the stresses at the joints.

There is also the potential for difference in response of the tower and the lower portion of the building, as shown in Figure 4.9*e*. Separation may be created here in order to elim-

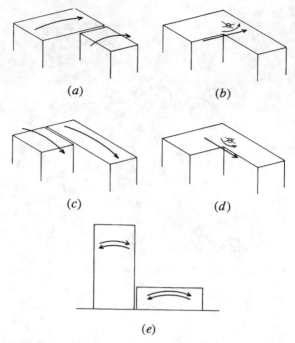

FIGURE 4.9   Seismic movements in multimassed building.

inate the need to investigate the dynamic interaction of the separate parts. However, it may not be feasible or architecturally desirable to make the provisions necessary to achieve effective separation. The other option is to design for the twisting and the dynamic interface actions on the bracing structure. A full design of alternative solutions will probably be required for an informed design decision. This double design effort is part of the price paid for creating a multimassed building.

Figure 4.10a shows an L-shaped building in which the architectural separation of the separate masses is accentuated. The linking element, although contiguous with the two tower parts, is unlikely to be capable of holding them together under seismic movements. To consider the linkage, the two types of movement shown in Figures 4.10b and c must be provided for. In addition, the lateral bracing of the linkage itself must be achieved.

There are four options for the linkage construction shown in Figure 4.10.

1. Somehow, it may be made strong enough to achieve the linkage during seismic movements and with the two parts, developed as a continuous structure.
2. It may be totally separated (at least seismically) from the two parts and braced independently for its own lateral seismic actions.
3. It may be separated on one side and attached on the other side; thus, simply going along for the ride with the part on the attached side.
4. The attached and separated sides in (3) may be reversed.

For structural behaviors, stress concentrations generally occur at points of geometric discontinuity. These include openings for doors or windows in shear walls and changes in shape in continuous construction—whether in two or three dimensions. These concentrations can cause problems for static force response, but the problems are much exaggerated with the dynamic, rapidly reversing actions caused by earthquakes (Figure 4.11).

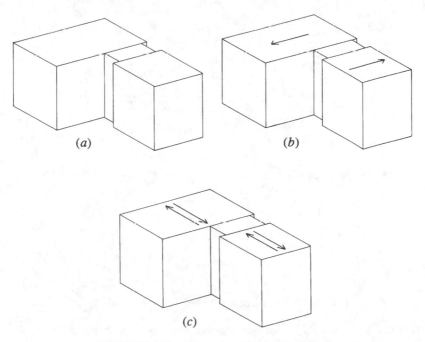

FIGURE 4.10 Movement of linked buildings.

FIGURE 4.11 Movement of the separate large masses of this apartment building caused major fracture of the light stair construction between the masses.

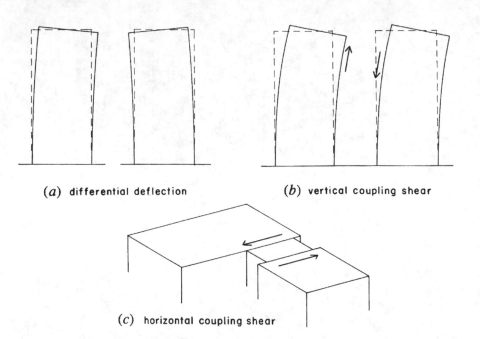

(*a*) differential deflection (*b*) vertical coupling shear

(*c*) horizontal coupling shear

FIGURE 4.12 Movements of separated masses that may develop stress for linking construction.

(*a*)

FIGURE 4.13 (a) These two tall walls ground up the connecting links as they moved in an earthquake.

FIGURE 4.13   *(Continued)*

Figure 4.12 shows the three basic forms of potential movement that must be dealt with at the joints between parts in a multimassed building. When moving as shown in Figure 4.12*a*, the separate elements may be torn apart or may bump each other (the latter is called *pounding*, *battering*, or *hammering*). A rigid connection must sustain the forces that can produce the magnitudes of deflection involved in the actions, or a separation joint must accommodate the actual dimensions of potential deflections (Figure 4.13).

Pounding actions may also occur when one part is quite flexible, and so moves considerably, while an attached part is quite rigid, and so tends to have little movement (Figure 4.14).

Another type of differential movement between parts is that shown in Figure 4.12*b*. This involves a vertical shearing action similar to that which occurs between parts in laminated elements subjected to bending. For the vertically cantilevered parts shown, both the shear and the lateral deflection vary from zero at the base to a maximum at the top. The taller the structure, the greater the dimension of critical movement near the top.

A third type of action is the horizontal shearing effect shown in Figure 4.12*c*. This is a common problem due to the fact that it occurs in very short, as well as tall, buildings.

The actions shown in Figure 4.12 can occur individually and may be handled by individual solutions. They often also occur simultaneously, however, as they would for the

FIGURE 4.14   Although no collapse occurred, the movement of the tall bell tower for this church caused distress for the connected, stiffer building roof structure (*a*) as well as for interior rigid partition construction of concrete block construction (*b*).

linkage shown in Figure 4.10, and the problem becomes one of dealing with a complex set of movements. For various reasons, a single form of movement may be more critical, prompting a solution that provides rigid attachment for some effects and separation for others.

Individual joined masses are sometimes so different in size or stiffness that the indicated solution is clearly to attach the smaller part to the larger and let it tag along. Such is the case for the situations shown in Figure 4.15*a* and *b*, in which the smaller lower portion or

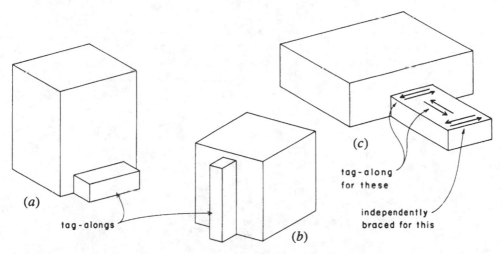

FIGURE 4.15   Exterior building elements linked to the larger building mass for lateral bracing.

the narrow stair tower would be treated as attachments, designed to hang on rather than developed with their own bracing.

In other cases, the tag-along relationship may be a conditioned one, as shown in Figure 4.15c, where the smaller element extends some distance from the larger. In this situation, the movement of the smaller part at the point of attachment may be resisted by the attachment connection, thus preventing the two forms of movement shown. However, some bracing could be provided at the outer end of the smaller part to share the resistance to movements parallel to the larger part.

The tag-along technique is often used for stairs, chimneys, entries, and other elements that are part of a building but are generally outside the main mass. It is also possible, of course, to consider the total separation of such elements in some cases.

Another classic problem of joined elements is that of coupled shear walls. These are walls that occur in sets in a single wall plane and are connected by the continuous construction of the wall. Figure 4.16 illustrates such a situation in a multistory building. The elements that serve to link such walls—in this example, the spandrel panels beneath the windows—can be wracked severely by the vertical shearing effect as illustrated in Figure 4.12b. As the building rocks back and forth, this effect is rapidly reversed, progressively developing the diagonal cracking shown in Figures 4.16b and c. This results in the X-shaped crack patterns shown in Figure 4.14d, which may be observed on the walls of many masonry-, concrete-, and stucco-surfaced buildings in regions of seismic activity. If the horizontal distance between the vertical window strips is relatively short, these cracks may extend into these areas as well (Figure 4.17).

Forces applied to buildings must flow with a direct continuity through the elements of the structure, be transferred effectively from element to element, and eventually be resolved into the supporting ground. Problems occur where the flow of the forces are interrupted. For example, in a multistory building, the resolution of gravity forces requires a smooth, vertical path; thus, columns and bearing walls are normally stacked on top of each other. If a column is removed in a lower story, a major problem is created, requiring the use of a heavy transfer structure—a girder or truss.

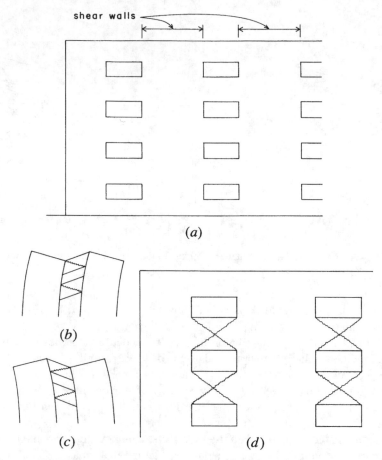

FIGURE 4.16   Actions that develop X cracking in walls.

A common type of discontinuity that occurs is that of openings in diaphragms. These can be a problem because of their location, size, arrangement, or shape. Figure 4.18 shows a horizontal diaphragm with an opening. The diaphragm is braced by four shear walls, and if it is considered to be continuous (a three-span beam), it will distribute its load to the walls in proportion to their stiffnesses. For a hole the size of that in Figure 4.18a, this is a reasonable assumption. The only special requirement here is to reinforce the edges and corners around the opening for the concentrations of stress.

If the opening is as large as that shown in Figure 4.18b, it is generally impossible to maintain the continuity of the diaphragm as a whole. In the example, the best solution would be to consider there to be four increments of the diaphragm, each collecting and transferring some portion of the total lateral force to the shear walls. Distribution to the shear walls would thus be on a peripheral basis, rather than on a proportional stiffness basis, as discussed in Section. 3.4.

Exactly what size of opening defines the transition between these behaviors is conjectural. In some cases, it may be advisable to assume both forms of behavior and to produce a design that effectively achieves either behavior.

Another difficulty that must be dealt with sometimes is that of the interrupted multistory shear wall. Figure 4.19a shows such a situation, with a wall that is not vertically contin-

FIGURE 4.17   Example of severe X cracking in a pierced concrete wall. In this case, the cracking is continuous through wall piers and spandrel panels.

uous down to its foundation. In this example, it may be possible to utilize the horizontal structure at the second level to redistribute the horizontal shear force to other walls in the first story in the same wall plane. The overturn effect, however, cannot be so redirected, thus requiring that the columns at the ends of the upper shear wall continue down to the foundation.

It is sometimes possible to redistribute the shear force from an interrupted wall, as shown in Figure 4.19b, into walls that are parallel but not in the same plane. Again, however, the overturn from the upper wall must be accommodated by continuing the structure at the ends of the walls down to the foundation.

Figure 4.20 shows an X-braced frame structure with a situation similar to that for the shear wall in Figure 4.19a. In this case, the continuous vertical columns and the beams at the second level are used to sidestep the X bracing. However, the problem of transferring overturn from the upper levels remains the same.

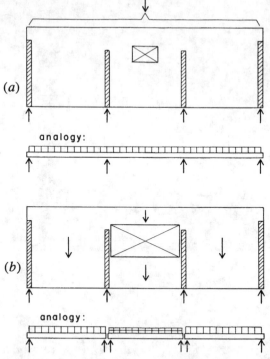

FIGURE 4.18 Effects of openings on the character of distribution by a horizontal diaphragm. (*a*) A minor opening does not essentially change the rigid, continuous nature of the horizontal diaphragm. (*b*) A major opening can interrupt the continuity of the diaphragm and reduce it locally to a set of subdiaphragms.

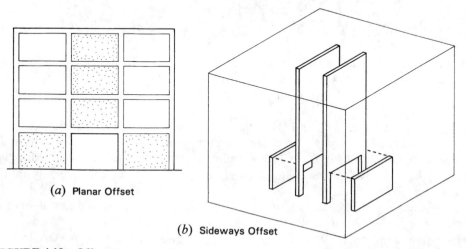

(*a*) Planar Offset

(*b*) Sideways Offset

FIGURE 4.19 Offsets in the lateral bracing system. (*a*) Vertical offset in a single plane. (*b*) Sideways offset, usually between levels in a multistory structure.

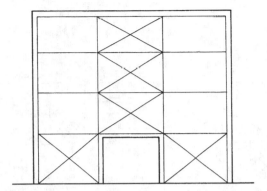

FIGURE 4.20   Vertical offset in a braced-frame system.

Sidestepping, offsetting, and other changes in the bracing system throughout the height of a multilevel building may work for a static force investigation. However, there are many opportunities for creation of irregularities that require a dynamic analysis, and the possible creation of soft or weak stories.

4.3   BUILDING FORM AND THE UBC

The 1988 edition of the *UBC* emphasized the idea of seismic design as an architectural design concern. Although this was not a new idea, it was given greater attention in this edition. Subsequent editions of the *UBC* in 1991, 1994, and 1997 reinforced and refined the idea.

There is a considerable body of evidence, obtained mostly from postquake inspections of buildings, that indicates that building form and major construction materials have considerable influence on the response of buildings to earthquakes. The *UBC* recognized the importance of building form by defining the *regular structure* (and, by corollary, the *irregular structure*). The conditions producing irregularity are specified in code tables. Although the code reference is to structures, it is ordinarily assumed that the general building form is a major influence on the form of the buildings structural system.

Figure 4.21 illustrates a number of form irregularities. Descriptions in Figure 4.21 include several types mentioned in discussions in this book, such as the soft story, the diaphragm with openings, the interrupted vertical structure, and the multimassed building.

Concern for the conditions shown in Figure 4.21 is not presented as an argument against diversity in architectural form, but merely to make designers conscious of implications for seismic response. Unusual forms sometimes come strictly from the minds of architectural designers, but they also frequently derive from functional requirements. Simplicity, symmetry, and regularity are all desirable for seismic response, but circumstances sometimes make them difficult to achieve.

A solution of sorts is to divorce the issue of form as *architectural* from form as *structural*. Figure 4.22 shows two cases where this is partly achieved. In the plan view, the exterior wall is seen to meander, albeit in a symmetrical manner. If this is accepted as a *structural* definition of the perimeter, the result is a complex, multimassed, irregularly perimetered structure. Forget about continuity of shear walls, wall tops, or diaphragm

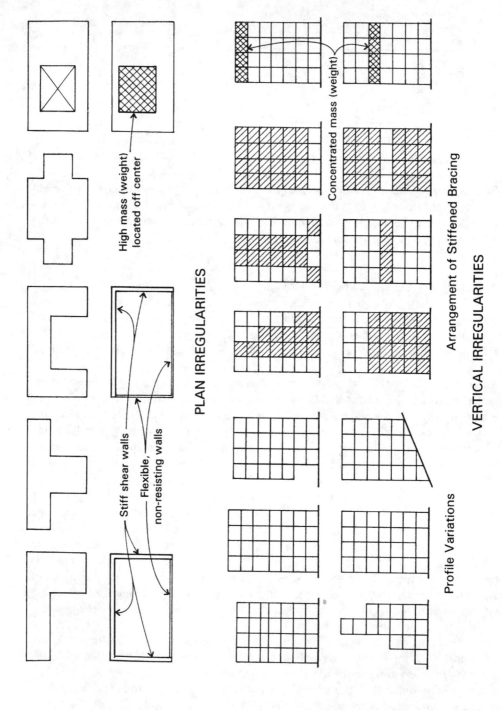

PLAN IRREGULARITIES

High mass (weight) located off center

Stiff shear walls

Flexible, non-resisting walls

Profile Variations

Arrangement of Stiffened Bracing

Concentrated mass (weight)

VERTICAL IRREGULARITIES

FIGURE 4.21 Examples of building forms with irregular seismic response.

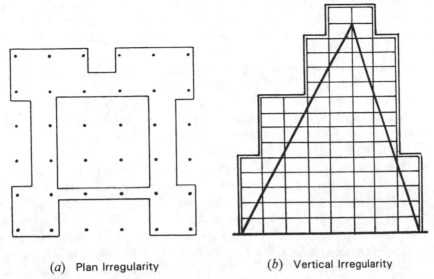

(a) Plan Irregularity   (b) Vertical Irregularity

FIGURE 4.22   Irregular building forms with regular bracing structures. (a) A highly irregular building wall plan with an orderly column system that can be used for a trussed or rigid-frame bracing system. (b) Vertical irregularity with multiple setbacks, but a gradually tapered bracing system that may be regular in nature.

chords. As defined by the columns, however, the structure is quite orderly and—if developed as the bracing system—neatly eliminates all structural irregularities in the plan. The seismic load generated by the meandering walls is simply grabbed by the horizontal structure and distributed to the highly regular bracing structure.

The example in Figure 4.22b shows a vertical section through a multistory building with a series of setbacks—also bad for structural irregularity; especially when as asymmetrical and abruptly occurring, as shown here. The bracing is achieved with a truss system, though, that graduates in strength and stiffness in a very smooth transition from top to bottom.

For plan irregularities, a successful solution is often a seismic separation joint. These can work for low-rise buildings, as has been demonstrated in many recent earthquakes. However, the joints must be carefully designed, not only for the seismic actions, but for all the other linkages that occur at the location of the joint. Roof water seals, fire containment, gravity support of construction, or continued facilitation of traffic may be involved.

Vertical Irregularity

For towers and multistory buildings, irregularity may occur because of vertical arrangements of the construction or the building form. The code defines the following cases of this condition:

1. *Soft Story.* As we described in Section 4.3, this situation occurs when an abrupt change in lateral stiffness is created in adjacent stories of a multistory building. A classic case is the building with an open ground-level plan and with solid wall construction—possibly both exterior and interior—above the first story.

2. *Weight Irregularity.* This often occurs in conjunction with other irregularities, such as setbacks or interior open spaces. However, a more common condition is that of heavy roof construction or heavy HVAC equipment on the roof of a light-weight framed building.

3. *Vertical Geometric Irregularity.* A common example of this is the abrupt setback of upper levels. This irregular condition may be affected by relationships between the general building form and the form of the lateral bracing structure. This can go either way: An irregular building form may be alleviated by a regular bracing system (Figure 4.22*b*), or a regular building form may be braced by a structure with major vertical discontinuities.

4. *In-Plane Discontinuities in Vertical Bracing.* This refers to offsets of the form illustrated in Figure 4.19*a*, limiting them to specified distances. This tends to be less of a problem on the building exterior than on the interior, where changes in space usage on different levels requires reorganization of structural arrangements.

5. *Weak Story.* This is a corollary to the soft story; in this case, the difference of concern in adjacent stories is one of strength. As with differences in stiffness, the problem may be caused by what at first was considered to be nonstructural construction, notably for interior walls or curtain walls. Minimum code-required construction frequently has considerable seismic resistance, and it can upset the assumed distributions used for the design of the bracing structure.

These conditions may occur alone or in combination. For example, a soft story can also be a weak story, although the two conditions are essentially different—one based on stiffness and the other on force resistance or simple strength. Vertical irregularity may be combined with horizontal—or plan—irregularity, which is defined in the following discussion.

Plan Irregularities

These conditions may affect buildings of any height, although bad seismic responses will usually be magnified for multistory buildings. A really bad case results from a combination of plan and vertical irregularity, for which different plan irregularities may occur at different levels, producing unbelievably complex seismic movements. Plan irregularities include:

1. *Torsional Irregularity.* This occurs when the plan location of the center of gravity of the building does not align with the center of resistance of the bracing structure. Since very few buildings are perfectly symmetrical, the concern is one of degree of eccentricity, not perfect alignment. To resist this, the bracing structure should be widely dispersed, offering maximum torsional resistance. The perimeter bracing system offers an ideal case of such bracing.

2. *Reentrant Corners.* This has to do with situations such as those represented by the L-shaped or T-shaped plan (Figure 4.23). Minor corner conditions, such as those shown in Figures 4.23*c* and *d*, are excepted from concern. This relates to the forms of behavior for multimassed buildings (Figures 4.9 and 4.10) discussed in Section 4.2.

3. *Diaphragm Discontinuity* In most cases, a roof or floor diaphragm is considered a contiguous, rigid planar element. However, plan form discrepancies or changes

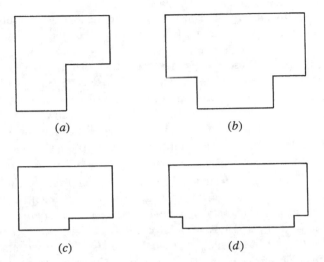

FIGURE 4.23   Reentrant corners in the building plan may be major, as in (*a*) and (*b*), or minor, as in (*c*) or (*d*).

in construction may modify the behavior of the diaphragm. Large openings for skylights or enclosed atrium spaces, changes in levels, or the existence of a zig-zag building edge may cause this.

4. *Out-of-Plane Offsets.* This refers to the situation illustrated in Figure 4.19*b*, which is considered to be an irregularity without qualification.

5. *Nonparallel Systems.* This refers to shear walls or bracing bents that are curved or angled in plan, rather than aligned in parallel sets.

All of these irregularities have possible solutions. Their existence, however, indicates less than ideal design choices regarding seismic response. If seismic risk is high, the collection of a large number of them in a building ought to call for serious consideration of different planning.

4.4   REDUCTION OF VULNERABILITY

Much of the building damage that occurs in an earthquake is highly predictable from even a casual inspection of the building or its design. With minor training, people with little experience can be equipped to spot obvious problematic cases. For design professionals, a few hours of training will prepare them to spot most of the potential vulnerabilities of buildings. This section considers some of these common and easily detectable vulnerabilities. Most of these situations cannot be controlled by decisions of the expert seismically trained engineering designers.

Vulnerable Nonstructural Elements

Many commonly used elements of building construction are especially vulnerable to earthquake damage. Most of these are nonstructural—that is, not parts of the structure used for seismic bracing. Due to their nonstructural character, they often do not receive thorough design study by the structural designer; thus, in regions of high seismic risk they often constitute major areas of vulnerability. Some typical situations include:

1. *Suspended Ceilings.* These are often subject to horizontal movement. If not restrained at their edges, or if they are hung with elements that resist horizontal movement, they can swing and bump other parts of the construction. Another common failure is that due to an upward acceleration followed by a downward jolt that snaps suspending structural elements. Exaggerated horizontal movement or dropping failure often causes additional damage to other elements, such as lighting, HVAC components, and fire sprinklers (Figure 2.16).

2. *Cantilevered Elements.* Projecting balconies, canopies, parapets, chimneys, and large cornices should be designed for seismic forces in all directions perpendicular to the cantilever. Horizontally projected elements are often developed for resistance only to gravity; thus seismic or wind effects in other directions can have a critical effect. Freestanding site walls are also highly vulnerable in this regard, often being supported on shallow footings placed on fill or soft soils (Figure 8.4).

3. *Miscellaneous Suspended Objects.* Lighting fixtures, signs, HVAC equipment, audio speakers, catwalks, and other items that are hanging should be studied for the effects of pendulumlike movements. As with suspended ceilings, supports should resist both horizontal movements and vertical jolts.

4. *Piping.* Building movements during seismic activity can rupture rigid piping, generally installed with no tolerance for movements. Damage to piping with pressurized contents is most dangerous. Gas lines pose additional threats of explosion or fire.

5. *Heavy Objects.* Anything that is heavy represents a major lateral force, whether a part of the construction, a piece of building equipment, or items of the building furnishings. Furnishings are pretty much out of the designer's control, but construction and equipment should be carefully studied for individual response. This includes heavy nonstructural walls, heavy wall surfacing (masonry, tile, etc.), water heaters, water tanks, boilers, fans, and, especially, anything heavy on the roof (Figure 11.6).

6. *Stiff, Weak Elements.* Any item of the construction that is installed in a manner to restrict lateral movement of the building will try to do so. This includes window glazing rigidly installed in its framing as well as plastered (or stuccoed) wall surfacing, wall or floor tiling, masonry veneers, and even the ubiquitous gypsum drywall partition. Because of their stiffness, these are often the first line of resistance. But stiffness and strength do not always go hand in hand, which accounts for the massive amount of broken glass and cracked stucco, plaster, concrete, masonry, and even gypsum drywall in buildings with no significant *structural* damage. Safe, maybe; undamaged, no. Feasible for restoration? Maybe not.

Soft Story

As created by building form, the soft story potential is easy to spot. Two cases are common: The open story vertically adjacent to stories with considerable solid wall construction and the tall story adjacent to shorter ones. Combine them (as often occurs with open ground-floor plans), and the potential is doubled. More subtly, the condition may be an interior one that is not visible on the building exterior—as with a hotel with an open ground floor and rooms with many interior walls above.

The soft story sometimes occurs at an upper story, but the most common situation is the open ground-level story (Figure 4.24). Although there is a lot of historical architectural design precedent for this building form, it is frequently only a functional consideration. While it is an undesirable condition, there are some structural remedies that may permit its use, but its necessity from an architectural design point of view should be carefully considered.

The reference to *story* is only figurative, as the condition is essentially one of change of stiffness at different vertical levels. A common instance of this is a one-story building in which a tall wall has extensive openings at ground level and a solid, continuous wall surface above, extending over the openings (Figure 4.25).

The classic case, however, remains the ground floor—often literally open with little lateral bracing (Figure 4.26). Several things can conspire to aggravate this condition. For a multistory building, lateral shear is greatest at the base. Many cases involve both an open plan and a taller story height, yielding a double dose of vulnerability. Often, much of what creates the major difference in stiffness is nonstructural construction (mostly curtain and partition walls), and would not have been considered real bracing by the structural designer.

If the tall, relatively open ground-level story is necessary, Figure 4.27 presents some possibilities for reducing the soft-story effect.

1. Open form bracing (single diagonal or X) to stiffen an open frame (Figure 4.27*a*). Trussed bracing is in the same class of stiffness of most shear wall construction, especially if it is not constructed of solid concrete or masonry walls.

2. Keep the open periphery, but provide a stiffened interior bracing system (Figure 4.27*b*).

3. Increase the stiffness of the ground floor story of a rigid frame if it is taller. One means is to add columns (Figure 4.27*c*). Another is to make columns larger or stiffen them by tapering (Figure 4.27*d*).

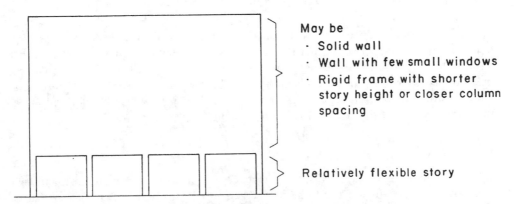

May be
- Solid wall
- Wall with few small windows
- Rigid frame with shorter story height or closer column spacing

Relatively flexible story

FIGURE 4.24   The most common case of the soft story.

FIGURE 4.25   A classic example of a soft story, with a rigid upper wall made continuous with a more flexible lower portion. Failure did not occur in the wood frame itself, but the movement could not be tolerated by the stiff stucco finish. An often effective simple solution is to provide relief joints in the stucco at the logical point of failure.

    4. Develop the ground-level story as an upward extension of the foundations, moving the supported structure up above the ground (Figure 4.27e). Figure 4.28 shows a building with a potential for this type of structure.

    The soft story actually can be used as an energy-absorbing device in special cases. This deliberate use requires a very extensive dynamic analysis, but the codes are stressing that anyway for any building with significant irregularities. To a certain degree, the current methods used for mitigation of seismic effects (base isolators, in-line shock absorbers, etc.) constitute deliberate irregularities in the siesmic load path, which is technically what the soft story is. (See the discussion of mitigation in Chapter 6.)

Weak Story

It is essential to understand the distinction between a soft story and a weak story, although it is possible for a single story to be both. The soft story is based on stiffness—that is, resistance to deformation. The weak story is based on load capacity, which might be con-

FIGURE 4.26   A soft-story failure in a large apartment complex. Individual units extended at the rear of the complex had open parking at ground level with only steel pipe column supports for the rigid box of the upper levels. These extended units were wagged like the tail of a dog until collapse at the rear end occurred, the ends of the units dropped, and the units tore loose from the complex.

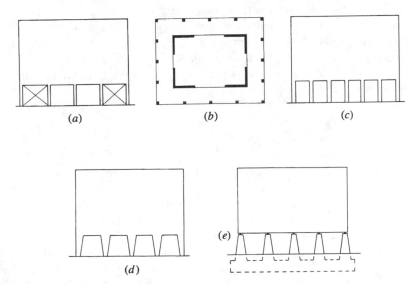

FIGURE 4.27   Some possible remedies for the open ground-floor soft story, essentially preserving the openness as an architectural feature.

sidered for static force, but for seismic action must be considered for dynamic (energy) resistance.

The weak story condition may actually be created by the over-stiffening or over-strengthening of a lower floor. Correction for the soft story at the ground level—including methods shown in Figure 4.27—must be very carefully investigated, as they can result in

FIGURE 4.28   Possible development of the scheme in Figure 4.27*e*.

a weak story in the second story (Figure 4.29). This is indicative of the complexities of structural investigation and design that are created by the building irregularities described by the *UBC*, and the reason why they have emerged as code concerns.

Although it doesn't always qualify as a weak-story condition by the code definition, a commonly vulnerable building is one in which the first story bracing is simply not strong enough. This situation accounts for a large number of bracing failures in low-rise buildings. Often the same form of bracing is used in all stories, and simply fails in the most heavily loaded story at the building base (Figure 4.30).

4.5   SITE DESIGN FOR SEISMIC RESPONSE

"Should this building be built on this site?" This is the first design question to be asked about a building site. Maybe the question should be asked of *any building*, for that matter, but always it should be considered for a building like the one anticipated. Once it is established that the site *will* be used, an extremely thorough investigation should be made before starting any building design. The site, in both the tight consideration of its legal boundaries and the larger concern for its involvement in the general geological area, should be entirely understood with regard to seismic risk and potential behavior during an earthquake. That understanding is essential in order to define the problem the building design has to deal with when responding to earthquakes.

For most sites, the building code with jurisdiction will provide a base in terms of risk assigned by region. This may serve as a starting point, but it does not pinpoint the exact nature of a site. For example, all of Los Angeles may be defined by the code as being in a single zone for seismic risk. But there are dozens of known faults in the area, and close proximity to one of these is definitely an increased hazard. The 1997 *UBC* now provides for modification of design forces on this basis. In addition, there are many regions of high probability for soil liquefaction, which offers additional risk. Again, the 1997 *UBC* pro-

FIGURE 4.29   The upper portion of this five-story building dropped vertically when the second-story columns collapsed. The massive end shear walls of CMU construction failed when the connecting structure collapsed. The tall open first story offered a potential for a soft-story condition at that level, but it was highly stiffened and remained intact. The abrupt change in strength and/or stiffness at the second story thus created a soft or weak story—or both—at that level.

vides for this hazard. What the risk is for a particular building on a particular site is a highly qualified judgment call, but one that designers should carefully consider.

Aside from specific, seismic risk there are other site conditions that may present risk. Precariously unstable slopes, fragile soil structures, and ongoing downhill slippage of large soil masses may hover on the verge of a disastrous event for a long time, only to be triggered by an exceptionally large rainfall or an earthquake.

Designers should aim for the ability to define a specific degree of risk that begins with the conditions for the site. This ability may yield ways to improve the site in order to

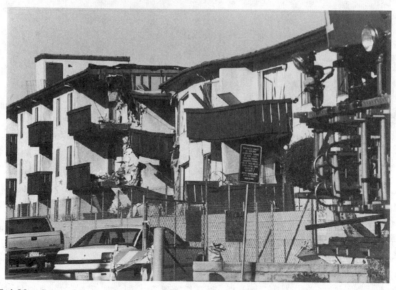

FIGURE 4.30   Several parts of this large apartment complex collapsed due to failure of the first-story bracing. The unit on the right here was originally the same height as the one on the left. One possible cause was the open ground-floor parking, although use of weak shear wall materials in the first story may have been a contributing factor as well.

reduce the risk of various forms of failure. For example, treacherous slopes might be stabilized, reshaped, or braced and unstable soils might be preconsolidated, chemically stabilized, or removed and replaced.

Although the site presents a specific defined risk condition, not everything can be blamed on the site. Design decisions may create a building that would be at risk anywhere because of bad seismic response properties (soft story, three-sided, etc.). Too, the building-site, dynamic interaction might be a bad match. Such interactive responses might be predictable, and so should inform the site design or the building design, or both.

Major risks presented by a site tend to be those that are beyond control by the site designer or building designer. Proximity to faults, liquefiable soil under the whole region, and other gross conditions cannot be changed by clever design of a single site or building. What remains, however, is for the designers to *know about* these conditions and respond as best they can to the degree of risk presented by them.

What can be dealt with for a specific site are the various aspects of ordinary site development: regrading, cuts and fills, reshaping of surface drainage, excavation, and site construction. These should all be undertaken with a goal of not making conditions worse, and maybe even effecting some improvements (removing bad soils, preconsolidation of unstable soils, reshaping treacherous slopes, etc.). Design should not create new treacherous slopes, overirrigate or use extensive tile field drains to create a new liquefiable soil condition, build up extensive and scarcely compacted fills and then build structures on them. Regarding seismic response, site design should leave things in better shape. And try not to build the dumbest possible building for this particular site.

5

Retrofit and Repair

Getting it right the first time is always the aim of design for a new building or site. However, for various reasons, it is often necessary to improve or restore the seismic resistance of an existing building. A retrofit (strengthening) of a building might be urged by the building owner, as new information indicates the vulnerability of the building. Although rare, new legislation might require that certain forms of construction be strengthened. And, of course, many buildings suffer damage from an earthquake, but remain feasible to repair. This chapter examines these options.

5.1 NEED FOR STRENGTHENING

The need for strengthening may be generated in many ways. In some cases, it is legally mandated by ordinances that require owners to strengthen older buildings or have their buildings demolished. Such has been the case in regard to old unreinforced masonry buildings, because of their undisputed vulnerability to seismic shocks. However, building owners may act on their own to provide reassurance or enhance the property value of their buildings. Whenever a major windstorm or earthquake occurs, affecting a significant number of buildings, many observers will inspect the damage. One direct benefit from this forensic study is the steady improvement of our collective judgment about correct design and construction practices; a secondary benefit is an improved ability to predict weaknesses of existing buildings.

Thus, each major windstorm and earthquake typically brings some changes in regulations and practices. Some of the lessons learned are simply reaffirmations of old lessons. How many times do we need to be shown, for example, that ordinarily connected, light wood frames can be easily pulled apart by high winds? Yet, for various reasons, we still have large existing stocks of these highly vulnerable buildings in high risk areas.

For real advancement of knowledge, however, the more significant lessons from each disaster have to do with the performance of recently constructed buildings. When structures that have been designed and built in accordance with the latest standards and codes fail, they get considerable study. These occurrences most affect development of new practices, while observations of more of the older types of failures simply strengthen our convictions and resolve.

Failures, of course, are not always due to flaws in our theories or our judgments regarding structural behaviors. A major factor—seemingly on the increase—has to do with the gaps that can routinely occur between design and construction. What designers determine to be required must go through several stages of communication and development before construction occurs. Here is a typical scenario:

1. A structural designer does the necessary computations for the members of a reinforced concrete frame structure, determining member dimension, required amounts of reinforcement, and other essential properties for the structure.

2. A graphic specialist (drafter)—probably not the structural designer who did the computations—translates the designer's notes into construction plans and details.

3. A specifications writer—probably neither the designer nor the drafter—prepares the specifications that largely define the specific materials and other factors that control the quality of the construction.

4. Various persons on behalf of, or in the employ of, a builder interpret the contract documents (drawings and specifications) and prepare derivative drawings and instructions for the fabricators, suppliers, and workers who will do the actual construction. The workers may thus never really see the original design documents.

5. Construction proceeds with various forms of inspection (or with none) and often is highly vulnerable to the skill and/or integrity of the workers and contractors. The original designer is infrequently directly involved in any inspection activity.

The opportunities for inadequate construction in this situation are obviously many. If the original designer does not thoroughly review the drawings and specifications and the contractor's drawings and instructions (typically called *shop drawings*), and then has no part in inspection of the construction, the chances of the final construction exactly agreeing with the designer's conception are slim.

Major lessons from disasters often have to do with flaws in the process and not merely the theoretically regulated practices of design and construction. Changes in standards and codes may do little to correct these situations.

Nevertheless, it is to be expected that all parties in the scenario above can learn better ways of designing and building from the damaged structures in any major windstorm or earthquake and, consequently, have a basis for determining what might need strengthening in existing buildings. As time goes on, the behavior of supposedly strengthened buildings may reveal more lessons.

The cumulative experience, continuous research, and refinement of design and construction practices provide a basis for assessing existing construction for vulnerability. A model is provided by the acceptable design work proposed by current design regulations and practices and by the current level of available technology and building construction craft. Existing construction can be measured against this standard and remedies proposed for improving seismic resistance.

5.2   ASSESSING DAMAGE

A critical task that must be done immediately following a major earthquake is assessing the condition of damaged buildings. The haste stems from the need to tell building occupants and the public how hazardous the building is. Is further damage and possible total collapse imminent? Or should persons be allowed back into the building to retrieve belongings or restore their homes or businesses? Major aftershocks typically follow every major earthquake, and additional damage is to be expected for many buildings.

Assessment for safety is a critical recovery task. Usually, another kind of assessment must also be done. What needs to be done to make the building able to be occupied again and certified for safety with regard to future earthquakes? This assessment requires a much more detailed and deliberate inspection of the building than that for safety. Eventually, it may be used as a basis for design work for general repairs and to strengthen the building structure.

Typically, much repair work is of a cosmetic nature, involving replacement of glazing, plaster, masonry veneers, and other nonstructural items. This may add up to a significant cost, and the total cost may make structural repairs infeasible—not on their own, but as part of the total cost. Thus, while a careful assessment of structural damage is critical, and a well-informed design for structural repairs must be performed, the work frequently may not be undertaken.

In some cases, structural damage may be quite evident, especially when the structure itself is exposed to view. However, many structures are covered by other construction, and thus may have damage that is not made evident by visual inspection, unless the covering materials have been damaged and removed. After the discovery of failure of many welded steel frames in the 1994 Northridge, California, earthquake, undamaged covering construction was removed from several steel frames and damaged welds were discovered. Certainly many such situations remain undiscovered today.

Building foundations present particularly difficult cases. These are almost always obscured from view and not easily inspected by any means. For larger buildings, inspection may be more feasible, but then these foundations are more likely to be of substantial, reinforced concrete construction. Smaller buildings—including most single family houses—are likely to have weaker concrete or masonry construction with little or no reinforcement. As is also possible for the rest of the bracing structure, cracked foundations may have resisted the earthquake's major blow but spent an energy capacity that can no longer be tapped. Another earthquake—even a smaller one—may cause significant failure.

Another insidious damage condition, and one not easy to assess by simple means, is that of the general nature of supporting soils. The violent movements that shake buildings must go through the ground to get to the building. Surely, this has the potential for reforming of soil structures, with resulting major changes in structural responses for support of structures above. For buildings supported on shallow bearing foundations, a post-event discovery process for new geotechnical data is a good idea. Settlement and general reconfiguration of the supporting soil materials can occur slowly over many years following a major earthquake.

Of course, assessment is only a first step, providing for a well-informed design for repairs. A major second step is to decide on the level of repairs that should be made to bring the reconditioned building back into use.

5.3   ASSESSING VULNERABILITY

Another kind of assessment that must often be made is that of the potential vulnerability of an existing building or site. This vulnerability may be a result of seismic design never having been considered, or it may be due to knowledge gained since construction was completed.

When any major disaster causes significant damage to buildings, the general vulnerability of similar buildings is effectively demonstrated. With time and the accumulation of evidence, this eventually leads to the conclusion that a particular kind of building—of a certain age and type of construction—has potential, identifiable vulnerabilities for various risks, including windstorms and earthquakes.

The nature and degree of predictable, potential damage for a building depends on the following:

1. The materials of construction and the date of construction. Based on the available technology, on the building code in force at the time of construction, and on the typical construction practices of the period, some reasonable expectations can be forecast.

2. The exact location of the building. This relates to risk for the general region, but also very specifically to the site conditions for an individual building. Of special concern are general problems of instability at the site and specifics such as a potential for soil liquefaction in an earthquake. There may also be building-site interaction potential that was not considered in the original structural design.

3. The general condition of the structure. Rusted steel, rotted timbers, cracked masonry or concrete, or other forms of deterioration may exist, so that the structure is not as good as when it was built.

4. The general effects of winds or earthquakes on other similar structures of approximately the same age in the immediate area. This is probably the most reliable indicator of potential problems.

With all of this information, plus a review of the original structural design and construction drawings (if they are available), a reasonable projection of potential damage can be made. The work to be done to reduce the hazard will depend on circumstances we discuss in the remaining sections of this chapter.

5.4   CONSTRUCTION TIMELINE AND VULNERABILITY

Building codes tend to reflect a consensus of necessary standards. To be enforced, they must be enacted as ordinances by a governmental body (usually at city or county level). As such, they must display an interest in the public welfare, but they must respond to all the usual pressures of previously enacted ordinances, as well. Nobody who understands the process expects a building code to be on the leading edge of developments in any area.

Still, advances are made, often in response to public pressure brought on by major disasters—particularly disastrous fires, floods, windstorms, and earthquakes. These events are usually necessary to overcome a general lethargy and inertia that resists changes, as well as the pressure of various groups that have vested interests (building owners, building trade unions, developers, building product manufacturers).

When significant changes are made in building codes, they usually apply only to future construction. Making owners of existing buildings do something to improve their properties is usually very difficult. Thus, older buildings are mostly affected by changes in the codes only when some significant remodeling or change of occupancy (building use) is proposed; then the construction generally must be brought up to the standards of the current codes.

In this situation, the status of any existing building is such that it stands in some particular condition with regard to potential shortcomings. For any changes in the building code that require higher seismic design standards, the existing stock of buildings is date-stamped with some form of compliance failure. As time goes on, the list of shortcomings grows with each change in the code.

Considering the situation for code requirements for wind and earthquakes, an example may be made using the *UBC*. This model code has been regularly issued in a new edition—lately, every three years.

The 1997 edition followed editions published in 1994, 1991, 1988, 1985, 1982, 1979, 1976, 1973, 1971, and so on. That means that a particular building constructed in 1972, for example, was probably built in conformance with the requirements of the 1971 *UBC*, if that was the code of jurisdiction. In 1999, therefore, the building cannot be expected to have any of the features that were required by the nine upgrades of the code since 1971.

Positioning a building in time with regard to code changes may be used to anticipate what might be required for a code retrofit. If a retrofit is required for a remodeling, as an example, the building must be made to comply to the present code. However, if upgrading is desired simply for its benefits, the needs may be more specifically identified by determining the construction and its design at the time that work was done.

Since codes are clearly documented, the significant changes for a particular building can be relatively easily determined. However, code changes are not the whole picture, and other factors may be of equal or greater significance. All the points raised in Section 5.3 should be considered, if real improvement—not just getting a permit for remodeling—is the goal.

Of course, not all code changes have necessarily resulted in improved resistances to wind or earthquakes. Adjustments in structural requirements also reflect evidence from research and changes in the availability and use of building materials and products over time. Some examples follow:

1. The commonly used grade of steel prior to World War II was A7 steel, with the basic allowable bending stress of 20,000 pounds per square inch (psi). Shortly after the war, the common grade became A36 steel, with a basic allowable bending stress of 24,000 psi. This resulted in a general increase of tolerable bending moments some 20% higher, the resulting use of smaller members, and some accompanying increased flexibility (reduced stiffness) of structures in general. As a result, steel structures built after about 1945 can be expected to have slightly bouncier floors, skinnier columns, and possibly more sidesway (drift) from lateral loads. And potentially, some increased possibilities for buckling failures, which are part of the load limit conditions for many steel frames.

2. Starting with the 1963 edition of the ACI Code, most reinforced concrete structures were increasingly designed by what is now called the *strength method*; versus the older *working stress method*. In some ways, the strength method permits smaller concrete dimensions and the use of more steel and higher grades of steel (with higher usable stress). Thus, as with steel structures, some increased flexibility is a possibility. Also, since concrete remains essentially a brittle (tension-crack developing) material, some increased amount of cracking in structural actions can be expected.

3. In the 1960s, increasing pressures from the building industry, unions, and others resulted in building code acknowledgments of the usable diaphragm capacities of wood frame surfacing materials other than plywood. Thus, gypsum drywall, plaster, stucco, and wood fiber panels were permitted for shear walls. Eventually, wood fiber panels were also permitted for roof and floor diaphragms by some codes. This is now viewed as highly questionable by many engineers on the basis of the performance of buildings in windstorms and earthquakes in the past two decades—notably, buildings built since the early 1960s.

Knowing a building's date of construction is important if real improvement is desired in any structural modifications. Changes in the way buildings get constructed should be done cautiously, so as not to lose earlier significant advantages in favor of perceived improvements.

5.5   DESIGN FOR REDUCING VULNERABILITY

In general, reducing the potential for damage in existing buildings involves improving the effectiveness of the building's lateral resistive structure.

Loss of Original Construction

In some cases, a building's lack of strength may be due to deterioration or misuse. Wear of exposed structural elements or the usual ravages of time, moisture, or other effects can reduce the physical capacity of many structures. Strengthening, in these cases, means essentially repair, although other reasons for strengthening may also be present. Steel bolts or ties may be rusted, masonry may be heavily cracked, essential wood framing may be rotted, and some major structural members may have been altered or even removed in remodeling. These possibilities should be investigated first in any efforts to improve the structure of an older building.

Quality of Original Construction

When first built, strength may have been restricted by omissions or poor construction. Recent studies of buildings under construction, as well as forensic examinations of damaged buildings, have indicated that this problem is quite widespread. The potential for this is inherent in typical design and construction processes. Before proceeding with plans to *improve on* the existing structure as designed, it should be determined that the existing construction conforms with the original design. In some cases, especially where structural elements are exposed to view, this can be done fairly easily. However, it is not so easy in other situations; for example, determining whether reinforcement is placed properly inside reinforced concrete or masonry construction.

Reducing the Forces

It may be possible to make alterations of the building that partially relieve the forces on the structure. Two examples involve removing elements that protrude from the building surface or that otherwise result in added wind forces and replacing heavy nonstructural elements with lighter ones to reduce the building mass for seismic forces. Thus, the structure is essentially strengthened with regard to its task, with no change of the structure itself.

After all of these considerations, if real strengthening is still required, it will probably involve the potential shortcomings of a particular structure. These shortcomings can be discovered by theoretical studies, by laboratory experiments, or by forensic examinations of damaged buildings. The damage may be actual structural failure of some form, or it may be related to extensive nonstructural loss, such as broken glass, dropped ceilings, burst piping, and so on.

The term *strengthening* may not best describe the need to improve the behavior of a lateral resistive structure. Extensive nonstructural damage often occurs where no significant damage to the structure is involved. *Cosmetic damage,* often due to the excessive movement of the building, can be caused by the structure's lack of stiffness. This relates, of course, to how success or failure of the structure is defined, which is an issue we discussed in Chapter 2. However, where potential nonstructural damage is of great concern, the stiffness of the structure may be as important for design as its strength. It may even be a concern for life safety, if the nonstructural damage is especially hazardous, as with glass falling from upper-story windows, gas piping breaking, ceilings dropping, and so on.

Adding Strength to the Lateral Bracing Structure

When real additional strength (basically, more force resistance) is needed, the process for developing it involves the following considerations:

1. Which form of strengthening is particular to the materials and form of construction of the structure?
2. How much additional strength is required, and what is the basis for its quantification?
3. Should the existing structure be improved or reinforced or should it be replaced?
4. What available technology or means in general can be used to strengthen a particular type of structure?

A partial answer to question number 2 simply may be to bring an existing building up to the level of current building code requirements. This issue is examined in the next section. Of more significance, however, may be to observe the success of previous strengthening efforts on buildings that were subsequently subjected to major windstorms or earthquakes.

Modifications of Stiffness

When a number of structural elements share the task of resisting a single force, the initial share taken by each individual element is determined by the relative stiffness of the elements. A problem arises when the stiffer elements are not necessarily the stronger ones. Such may be the case when the bracing system is a relatively light rigid frame connected to an extensive solid wall system. Even though the walls are not supposed to take the lateral forces, their relative stiffness will result in their taking the load—up to the point where they might fail before any significant part of the load is taken by the frame.

A common cause for nonstructural damage occurs when the walls are rigid but not strong, as in the case of stucco or brick veneer applied to a frame or even to a plywood shear wall. Possible solutions include reducing the stiffness of the walls or restricting load transfers through the connections between the walls and the support structure. In so doing, the intended bracing system may be made to do its job as designed.

Some situations involving soft story failures occur because of this relationship between a frame and the building wall construction. In the illustration in Figure 4.24, the building may actually have a rigid frame for its full height, but a rigidly attached upper-wall construction may achieve the actual bracing of the upper levels, particularly in dynamic response to seismic forces. This may result in extensive damage to the nonstructural walls or a soft story failure at the open story or both.

Another type of element that frequently attracts unintended lateral force is window glass. In its own plane, a large sheet of glass has the same stiffness character as a wall surface of plaster, stucco, or masonry veneer. In addition, most types of glass have the same low capacity for tension, shock, and deformation as concrete, masonry, and plaster. Glass breakage in windstorms usually occurs due to out-of-plane wind pressures, but in earthquakes it is usually due to in-plane lateral forces.

Improvement of the lateral resisting structure—considered strengthening or not—can be achieved partly by improving the relationships between the bracing structure and the rest of the building construction. The building thus becomes more resistive in general to the load conditions, with possibly no actual increase in the strength of the bracing system.

For remedial purposes, this improved relationship between the bracing and the rest of the building may be achieved in one of two basic ways:

1. Reducing the proportionate stiffness and potential for attraction of loads by the nonstructural elements
2. Increasing the stiffness of the bracing system

Improving the lateral resistive structure is considered in the next section.

5.6   STRENGTHENING FOR SEISMIC RESISTANCE

The idea of increasing strength begins with a structure already existing or designed and involves a form of quantified improvement of the structure's resistance. Some means for achieving this include:

1. Increasing the strength of individual elements of the structure by making them larger or otherwise better for the necessary structural performances (bending,

compression, shear, etc.). If this is done for all the elements, some collective gain for the whole structure is inevitable.

2. Redeveloping the general structural system for better overall performance. Examples include aligning columns to produce bents; adding columns to stiffen a bent; rearranging members of a trussed system for better force distribution; using separation joints to control internal distributions in the whole system; planning for less rotation effect in a complex, unsymmetrical plan.

3. Improving details for the load-transferring connections between elements in the system, such as using positive connections.

4. Adding secondary elements for better performance of a system, such as adding shear walls or eccentric trussed bracing to a rigid frame.

Means for Improving Seismic Resistance

The best means for achieving any improvements depends first on whether the building already exists or is still being designed. In the design stages, it may still be possible to reconsider factors relating to the general building size and form, the exact placement of individual elements of the lateral resistive system, and choices for basic construction materials. Gains in these areas might result in a better structure by improving the actual loading conditions or form of structural responses. For retrofit work, means may well relate to changes being made for other purposes.

A second major consideration is for the materials and form of the lateral resistive system. Is the basic structural material wood, steel, concrete, or masonry? Is the system a box type, trussed, rigid frame, or some other basic form? Changing materials, basic structural type, and various details of the system may bring improvements before any considerations are made for the strength of individual members or connections.

Finally is the consideration for achieving more strength from individual members of the system. Based on their individual tasks, what constitutes the most significant type of strength gain? Adding more mass of material may not be the issue, but rather improvement of buckling resistance by bracing, increasing of frame member relative stiffness, or rearranging of internal elements (such as reinforcement in concrete or masonry elements).

Strengthening of Concrete and Masonry Structures

Repair and strengthening of existing concrete and masonry structures have always been difficult tasks. The rigid, brittle materials and the solid form of the construction makes damage repair that consists of lost surface materials or major cracks challenging. Wood and steel structures are usually much easier to fix up, although getting to them may be a problem because they are frequently buried under other construction. On the other hand, concrete and masonry structures are frequently exposed to view, due to their typical high resistance to fire or weather. Cost effectiveness for repair of wood and steel structures often hinges on the cost of removal and replacement of finish materials. For concrete and masonry structures the structural repairs themselves may be costly—if they are technically feasible to achieve in the first place.

In spite of difficulties, the need to repair damaged structures or reinforce existing ones has generated a lot of activity in this area. Earthquake–damaged concrete and masonry structures abound after a major earthquake. Damage often effects large structures, monumental buildings, and major bridges for thoroughfares which represents large investments of money and effort to replace or repair. Add damage due to corrosive environmental conditions (sea air, for example), effects of foundation settlements, and other ground movements, and a major industry is created for the task of saving these structures.

Following major earthquakes in dense urban areas in recent decades (in Mexico City, Los Angeles, San Francisco, Kobe, etc.) major effects have been expended to develop means for repairing and retrofitting concrete and masonry structures. New methods have been discovered from the efforts of researchers, inventors, designers, and the developers of new materials and products.

One new method of considerable interest to those seeking to repair or strengthen concrete and masonry structures involves the use of structural laminates which are applied to the exterior of the structures. This method addresses a longstanding problem; how to repair or strengthen solid structures of concrete or masonry that can't be taken apart and put back together? Laminates consist of built up layers of plastic and reinforcement of glass or carbon fiber. Some forms of application are:

Strips.   Used to give linear flexural strength to beams, one-way slabs, and walls subjected to out-of-plane bending.

Wraps.   Used to provide both reinforcement and confinement for columns, beams, and beam-column joints. A full wrap may also provide protection from surface loss due to exposure to corrosive conditions.

Sheet.   Used on wall surfaces to provide in-plane shear strength. May be used on both sides of a wall to provide out-of-plane flexural reinforcement. May also be used on sides of beams for shear reinforcement. Adds flexural strength and reduces deflection for two-way slabs.

These methods are important for repair and retrofit of reinforced construction where other means of enhancing the buried steel bars are not possible. The surface–applied reinforcement is in an optimal position for developing flexural resistance by interaction with the compression in the concrete and masonry.

The most dramatic aid is for unreinforced masonry (URM). Existing walls, columns, and vaults of URM can be developed with tensile reinforcement—a boon to the saving of many historical landmarks. For additional reinforcement and aesthetics, a virtually invisible clear laminate with glass fiber reinforcement can be used on surfaces exposed to view, retaining almost entirely the original form, color, and texture of the viewed surfaces.

Lessons from Repair and Retrofit Work

Work for repair of damage and for retrofit to reduce vulnerability is still largely experimental in nature and awaits the critical evaluation and validation of nature's full scale testing over time. Lessons are being learned with each new major earthquake, but there are still many mysteries.

As methods for repair and retrofit become validated, we can use the feedback to modify work for original construction. Some of the innovative materials and methods used may eventually become stock parts of the inventory for selection for new construction.

For longer range survival we may eventually learn how to make structures—and indeed whole buildings as well—that can withstand the force of many earthquakes (and windstorms, firestorms, floods, etc.) and bounce back quickly with easy repairs or replacements of damaged parts. Like the demolition derby race car, they can be quickly and easily patched up and put back into the race, almost as good as new.

Adjusting the Safety Factor

Although it is an oversimplification, the basic means of adding strength to a building structure is to increase the safety factor. A simple definition of the safety factor is as follows:

$$\text{S.F.} = \frac{\text{The actual capacity of the structure}}{\text{The required capacity of the structure}}$$

Improvement of safety may be achieved by using higher safety factors (directly in the strength method or by reducing design allowable stresses in the stress method) or by increasing the design loads. For an example of the latter, the base shear as determined by the *UBC* formulas might be increased by 50%.

A common procedure in the design process for a building is to offer alternatives to the design client. These alternatives come with a price tag, and the basic question posed by the designer is "How much do you want and how much are you willing to pay?" More expensive carpet? More space in the building entry? A more lush landscape?

Suppose, in a similar way, that the opportunity could be offered to the client to choose the safety factor or performance level for various physical responses and behaviors. Who says it should be left to the architect, the structual engineer, or the writers and publishers of building codes to decide what the safety factor for design should be?

Although the data needed may be incomplete, speculative, or even flawed, the design of the structure will be done with considerable precision. A component of the mathematics involved is the setting of a specific value (say X) for a level of safety that represents a margin of reserve strength. But who sets the value for X? Who says the structure should be twice, three times, or 1.47 times as strong as the failure model? Why not let the design clients set the value? Give them the same kind of choices they get for carpet, interior space, and landscaping. Give them alternatives with a lateral force-resisting system designed for safety factors of 2 (the all-time historical average), 3, 4, 5. Let them buy the safety they want. And enjoy the carpet, space, and nice site with a level of peace of mind they feel good about.

Satisfying the building code requirements—which is what is routinely done by designers—means acceptance of a *minimal* design, the *minimum* safety factor. If that level of safety is assumed to be represented by an average safety factor of 2, then using one of 3 means giving 50% greater safety. How much more would it cost for a structure with 50% more resistance? Probably not much for the average building.

For most buildings, the structure is usually not more than about 15% of the total building cost. Not all of the cost is for the lateral-resistive structural elements. With most of the gravity-resistive system remaining unchanged, increasing only the lateral-resistive system by 50% should not raise the cost of the average building structure by more than a few percent.

If these cost increases are used with respect to the whole building project cost, the cost of increased safety becomes even less significant. In areas with high land values (most urban areas, in other words) the building cost may be half or less of the whole cost for the land and its development.

Thus, strengthening could be viewed as an increase in safety simply achieved by providing something more than the minimum resistance required by legally enforced codes. But a more intelligent view of strengthening would relate to the demonstrated major weaknesses of particular materials and systems. For this kind of strengthening, particular behaviors of a specific structure would be given special attention and some higher degree of strengthening. This focused or concentrated strengthening is most useful for existing buildings, whose similarities to structures that have failed are observable.

6

Mitigation of Seismic Effects

Until recently, most design efforts for earthquake resistance have been aimed at strengthening structures or controlling their behavior in some way. A different approach is that of trying to reduce the impact of the earthquake itself by mitigation (reduction) of the seismic effects applied to the building. Various ways of achieving this include:

Use of seismic separation joints
Use of base isolation
Use of motion- and shock-absorbing devices within the building structure
Architectural design to reduce vulnerability and unwanted responses
Modification of ground materials to improve seismic response

The general objective of these efforts is to modify the form and/or magnitude of the energy load on the building and its bracing structure; that is, to reduce the demand for seismic resistance. A second objective, which may be quite important for some buildings, is the reduction of actual movement of the building.

6.1 USE OF SEPARATION JOINTS

Means of achieving seismic separation are discussed in Section 3.8. Reasons for separation include a desire to isolate individual components of a multimassed building, or to eliminate the structural connection between parts of a continuous building or building group. Situations of this type are illustrated in Section 4.1.

When successfully achieved, seismic separation permits the separate parts to function individually for seismic response. This may eliminate some undesirable action—such as severe torsion—that would otherwise occur if the connected parts functioned as a unit. In other cases, the purpose may be to disconnect a part that would individually experience little movement from one that is likely to experience considerable movement.

175

Whatever their basic structural purpose may be, a usual constraint for seismic separation joints is the necessity to fulfill other functions of the connection, such as supporting gravity loads or maintaining a water seal for a roof. Thus the complete construction detailing for the connection may be quite complex, if all these purposes are to be served.

A difficult design decision pertaining to any separation joint (seismic, temperature expansion, shrinkage control, settlement differential, etc.) regards the actual dimension of separation, usually represented by the tolerable dimension of movement within the joint. This involves judging how much each part can be allowed to move, which can only be determined by a deformation investigation of the two separate structures. Usually, deformation of even the simplest of structures can only be approximated, and the more complex the structure or the loading, the more approximate the computed dimension of movement. For a building (including consideration for the effects of nonstructural construction) under dynamic loading from an earthquake, modified by ground conditions, computation of an actual dimension of movement is hypothetical. This needs to be understood when estimating how useful any separation joint might be.

In fact, separation may be only partly achieved by design. This is how the base isolator and the in-line shock absorber function, as we discuss in the following sections. These devices also achieve a form of separation, while still maintaining some force-transfer capabilities. In a way, they are a form of measured separation devices. The traditional separation joint, on the other hand, is generally visualized as achieving full separation—successfully or not.

6.2   BASE ISOLATION

One way to achieve what amounts to a form of shock absorbtion between the ground and a building is by use of *base isolators*. Since seismic force is induced in a building by movement of the supporting ground, the isolation consists of absorbing some of this motion in the building-to-ground connection.

It should be noted that this does not represent a total elimination of the effects of the earthquake, merely a reduction of the horizontal movements and the dynamic energy load that is delivered to the lateral bracing system. So all the efforts to produce good seismic response of the building should still be undertaken. A comprehensive functioning bracing system is still needed and all efforts to reduce nonstructural damage should still be considered.

This is not just a matter of seismic resistance by the building, however. Of possibly greater significance in some situations is reducing the effects of movement on the building's occupants and contents. Consider how valuable the mitigation effort can be in reducing the earthquake trauma for bed-ridden patients in a hospital, for valuable and sensitive equipment or machinery, for priceless objects in a museum, or for the fragile and irreplaceable construction elements of highly valued historic buildings.

Typically, base isolation is achieved by placing isolation devices between the bottoms of building supports and their foundations (Figure 6.1.). The base refers to that of the building; specifically, the base defined in the seismic design codes—the location where the major earthquake force is delivered to the building's lateral bracing system. This is, in many ways, the right spot for the shock-absorbing system—the exact location of the delivery of the punch. Isolation means eliminating the building contact with the ground, at least for the horizontal blow from the earthquake. This is only a partial isolation, but if significant in magnitude, it may reduce the movement of the building and the dynamic energy load on the bracing by a useful amount.

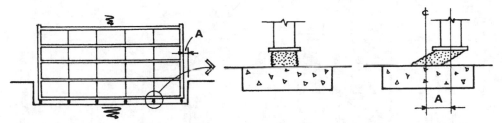

FIGURE 6.1 Base isolation is usually achieved with two basic elements: a buffering support device (isolator) and a horizontal restraint system. Horizontal restraint is commonly provided by a "moat" spaced some controlled distance from the building edge (it may be the exterior basement wall construction). Isolators have a maximum displacement capacity (dimension A in the figure), which is matched to the spaced edge separation.

More accumulation of full-scale test results (by actual earthquakes) is necessary before we can wholeheartedly embrace this method. It does, nevertheless, seem to offer a possibility of great value for all buildings in general and for those with highly vulnerable occupants or contents in particular. Highly vulnerable older buildings of great value, incapable of being strengthened, can also benefit. Old masonry buildings are one such example, and several old buildings with cultural value have been preserved by this method.

A problem with most base isolation methods so far developed is that they deal primarily only with horizontal movements. While the horizontal movements for most earthquakes in the past have been found to be considerably stronger than vertical movements, some major vertical movements have been recorded in recent events—notably in the 1994 Northridge, California, earthquake. While it is theoretically possible to buffer these actions as well, current base isolation continues to focus on applications where the horizontal effects are of major concern.

Techniques for achieving base isolation have been developed experimentally and are increasingly used where appropriate. At present, the methods available work best for limited forms and sizes of building. As these limitations restrict the planning of buildings to a degree, they are not yet widely used.

6.3   SHOCK ABSORBERS AND MOTION MODIFICATION

One form of mitigation is that involving the use of some energy-absorbing elements (shock absorbers) within the bracing system. These may be used mainly for their damping effects on dynamic vibrations of the structure, and, instead of swinging back and forth repeatedly, the structure quickly comes to a stop, eliminating some of the effects of rapid stress reversal. However, another benefit may be that of actual energy absorption—something now achieved by the extensive cracking of stucco and masonry, for example.

Piston-type shock absorbers have been used in both new construction and as parts of the systems for protecting existing vulnerable buildings. Three methods for using in-line shock absorbers are shown in Figure 6.2.

1. A simple bracing system, such as a truss, can be developed as shown in (*a*), with dampers replacing the truss diagonals. The truss thus works directly as a truss, but with a major additional shock-absorbing, motion-damping capability. This

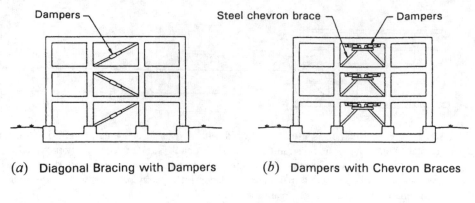

(*a*) **Diagonal Bracing with Dampers**   (*b*) **Dampers with Chevron Braces**

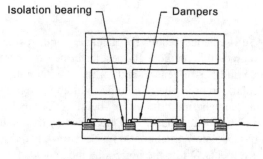

(*c*) **Dampers with Base Isolation**

FIGURE 6.2   Use of in-line shock absorbers for reduction of energy loading and damping of seismic movements. Illustration provided courtesy of Taylor Devices, Inc.

method has been used for historic buildings with little intrusion, as the system can be incorporated in interior walls in many cases.

2. A second method involves the buffering of the critical connection in a chevron bracing system as shown in (*b*). This reduces the need for reliance on plastic yielding of the girders as the major energy-absorbing element. Thus, not only is a major improvement in damping and motion reduction achieved, but the building's primary structure is protected.

3. A special application involves the use of a base control system using the combination of ordinary base isolators and piston dampers. Since each has different dynamic behaviors, they work together in a manner described as *out of phase*, with each exhibiting its own behavior to provide a double energy-absorbing function. The result is a net reduction of seismic force and motion beyond what either element is capable of alone. This method was used recently as part of a complex seismic resistance system designed for a major medical facility in Colton, California, with the design goal of keeping the emergency facility operational even after a "big one" on the infamous San Andreas fault—only nine miles away.

Figure 6.3 shows the installation of an in-line shock absorber as an ordinary diagonal member in a steel frame. The structure illustrated is being developed for laboratory testing. Simple raw force absorption is a major feature of this device, but its actual effect on

FIGURE 6.3   Testing of an in-line device installed as a diagonal member in a steel frame. Photo provided courtesy of Taylor Devices, Inc.

movement is possibly of greater significance. The graphs in Figure 6.4, show the general nature of this effect. In Figure 6.4*a,* the characteristic of an unmodified structure is shown, with the structure swaying significantly through several back-and-forth cycles (up and down in the graph). Natural damping causes this swaying to diminish with time, but often not without several discernable cycles of vibration.

The curve in Figure 6.4*b* shows the nature of the modification achieved by base isolation. Two effects should be noted: the reduction of the amplitude (actual magnitude of movement) and the more rapid damping (faster stopping of discernable movement). As shown in Figure 6.4*c,* the in-line shock absorber does somewhat the same thing as the base isolator. However, the shock absorber is designed to stop the movement faster—essentially before the completion of a full cycle, and ideally pretty much after only a half cycle. Finally, in Figure 6.4*d,* the coupled base isolator and in-line shock absorber can be seen to effect a significant stop to swaying and a major reduction of the amplitude.

Energy-damping and shock-absorbing functions are ordinarily performed by the failures of various elements of the building construction. Every fractured pane of window glazing, buckled partition wall, and dropped ceiling absorbs some energy and relieves the dynamic effect on the bracing structure. In the structure itself, yielding of reinforcing

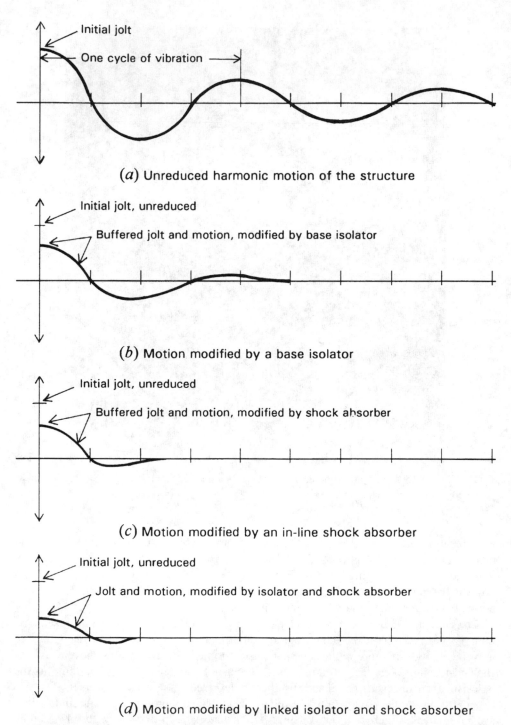

(a) Unreduced harmonic motion of the structure

(b) Motion modified by a base isolator

(c) Motion modified by an in-line shock absorber

(d) Motion modified by linked isolator and shock absorber

FIGURE 6.4 Harmonic vibration of a structure due to an initial horizontally displacing dynamic jolt: (a) unmodified, (b) modified by base isolation, (c) modified by a dynamic shock absorber, (d) modified by both base isolation and a shock absorber.

steel is assumed to occur in conjunction with major cracking of the brittle concrete or masonry, thus giving those otherwise brittle structures a yield character. The yielding of the steel gives a nature of toughness to a structure that is otherwise subject to sudden failure by brittle fracture. The combination of the cracking of the mass of concrete or masonry and the development of inelastic strain in the steel absorbs a lot of energy from the earthquake.

For the concrete or masonry structure that has been designed to develop yield in the steel reinforcement, the effective limit is likely to occur with major cracking and nonrecoverable, major deformations. This state of plastic deformation is also true for a steel structure allowed to develop yield-level stresses and plastic hinging. Yielding of the structure may prevent full collapse, but the structure is likely to be unusable and not feasibly repaired after the earthquake. The purpose of shock absorbers is to *reduce* the need for yield of the steel in the main bracing elements and, therefore, to reduce damage of nonstructural construction.

In general, design for mitigation of seismic forces is developed with the aim of both softening the blow and keeping the structure useable. Some energy-absorbing elements might be lost, but the structure is essentially unharmed or, at worst, slightly damaged but easily repairable. And the building occupants, the nonstructural construction, and the building contents have all experienced a softer ride than the earthquake promised. In the case of essential emergency facilities (hospitals, fire stations, communication centers, power plants), a critical goal is to have the facility continue in operation immediately following the earthquake.

6.4 ARCHITECTURAL DESIGN FOR MITIGATION

Any effect that functions to reduce the impact of an earthquake in terms of the resistance required by the bracing system for a building can be classified as mitigation. In this regard, the general architectural design of the building offers the greatest potential for mitigation efforts.

Decisions involving the building form, dimensions, use of materials, and particular construction details have great influence on how the building responds to an earthquake. Add the extended considerations for site design, and many of the factors affecting the way the building and its site respond to an earthquake are set in place, and the design requirements for the bracing system of the building are established. If mitigation (reduction) of seismic effects is added to other architectural and site design goals, the resulting design will surely contain fewer inherent vulnerabilities and bad seismic effects in general.

The potential for problems generated from this area of design is discussed in Chapter 4. For a given situation—as defined by the site conditions, seismic risk, required building size, limitations on material use, and other specific factors—it is relatively easy to derive a short list of the least desirable conditions that could be developed in the design. If seismic mitigation is really important, make avoiding them a priority in the design. This is a negative approach—defining what *not* to do—but it will nevertheless have a positive effect on the seismic response.

Another approach is to establish positive goals, such as reduction of seismic movements. Most mitigation efforts and the design of the structural system in general use this approach. But what they need to deal with can be established initially by numerous architectural and site design decisions.

The importance of this effort can hardly be overemphasized. In strictly economic terms, for example, emphasizing architectural and site design decisions that result in an optimal situation for seismic response might cost nothing. If that is the case, and a significant reduction in seismic effects is accomplished, the gain may be equal in significance to the addition of a costly base isolation or in-line shock absorber system. This is a benefit/cost value that is hard to pass up. And it is hard to justify a design that produces the opposite result—a worst-case seismic design problem.

6.5   GROUND MODIFICATION

Many engineers and most architects are not aware of what can be done these days to modify existing ground conditions that affect the structural performance of sites. Use of methods such as dynamic compaction, jet grouting, soil nailing, and slurry cut-off walls can modify or stabilize site conditions that once were insurmountably bad. The state of the art of geotechnical engineering has grown immensely in the past few decades, and building and site designers are well advised to become aware of current technologies.

These exotic techniques do not come cheaply in many cases, but the trade-off is to have to later compensate for uncorrected situations. For example, if a serious soil liquefaction situation can be significantly reduced by a certain technique, it may reduce design requirements for the seismic-resistive structure. More important, it may effectively reduce the possibility for exaggerated movements during an earthquake—a positive gain in terms of reduced trauma to building occupants or sensitive contents. This is the kind of gain that can be obtained with base isolation, for example, but the expensive base isolators may not be required if the site is sufficiently modified.

It would seem that this is the first place to consider for reduction of seismic effects. But as in many situations, the logical sequences often get inverted, and a lot of effort can go into designing superresistive structural systems before the full potential for mitigation is sufficiently explored.

6.6   THE WHOLE MITIGATION EFFORT

Mitigation is steadily growing as a first stage of design for seismic response. It has as its base the positive aspect of reducing the effects of the earthquake before considering the necessary defensive actions. That is, first doing all that is possible in order to make the situation one where the *least* needs to be done for the building, its occupants, and its contents in order to survive the earthquake.

For a comprehensive mitigation effort, it is necessary to consider all the areas of activity described in this chapter. In addition, they ought to be considered in a logical sequence. Don't jump into consideration of base isolation until all possibilities for ground modification and alternatives for the architectural and site designs have been explored. You might not *need* seismic separation joints, if the architectural design is carefully considered.

Look seriously into benefit/cost factors for any mitigation effort. Benefits are not all economic, although that is an inescapable concern. Peace of mind should be worth something, and it might derive from the stabilization of a site, for example, in addition to any measurable structural gain. Base isolation may significantly reduce the cost of the structural bracing, but it might have even greater value in terms of reduced motion trauma for the occupants of the building.

7

Special Problems

7.1 LATERAL AND UPLIFT FORCES ON DEEP FOUNDATIONS

Developing of resistance to horizontal forces, vertically directed upward forces, and over-turning moments presents special situations and problems for deep foundations. Whereas a bearing footing has no potential for development of tension between the supported structure and the ground, both piles and piers have considerable resistance to uplift. On the other hand, the sliding friction resistance of footings is absent at the top of deep foundation elements. These basic considerations constitute a starting point for design of deep foundations for lateral force effects.

Lateral Force Resistance

Resistance to horizontal force at the top of piles and piers is very poor in most cases. Their relatively narrow profile offers little potential for development of passive soil pressure. In addition, the process of installation often causes considerable disturbance of the soil around the top of the foundation elements. For these reasons, designers rarely count on this form of lateral resistance for deep foundations.

The most common method for resolving horizontal forces with deep foundations is to transfer the forces to other parts of the building construction. Often, existing foundation walls, paving slabs, or grade beams can be utilized for this purpose. Where the deep foundation elements are isolated, it may be necessary to add ties to transfer the forces. Essentially, this is the same process used to tie isolated footings together into a single system for horizontal ground movements.

For large freestanding structures without significant subgrade construction, the horizontal resistance of pile groups is usually developed through the use of piles driven at an angle. These *battered piles* may be utilized for both compression and tension. This is a widely used practice for isolated towers and bridge piers, but is not often necessary for buildings where subgrade construction is more common.

Uplift Resistance

Friction piles and large piers with belled bottoms have considerable resistance to uplift. Exceptions are the friction pile with a tapered form and concrete piles without reinforcement. End-bearing piles may have less resistance, although if they are quite long, they will develop considerable uplift resistance as well.

The combined weight of the shaft and the bell of a belled pier constitutes a considerable dead load for resistance to uplift. In addition, if the bell is large, considerable soil resistance will be developed to restrict its upward movement. Finally, if the shaft is long and constructed without a permanent casing, some soil friction similar to that for the pile will be developed. These effects can be combined to offer major resistance to upward movement. However, the concrete shaft must be reinforced or prestressed in order to develop the tension force.

Uplift resistance of piles must usually be established by field tests. For large piers, and even for very large piles, this may not be feasible due to the large magnitude of loads. However, in many cases uplift forces are considerably smaller than the downward design forces, and a conservative design estimate of uplift capacity may be sufficient.

Moment Resistance

Piles ordinarily exist in groups, tied together by a common sitecast concrete cap. If overturning moment is applied to this structure, the resistance will be developed by the group, similar to the response of a group of rivets or bolts. Figure 7.1 shows the case of a moment on a pile group, represented by an eccentric vertical load. Just as for the bearing footing described in Section 3.10, the pile group has a kern limit. If the vertical load is outside this limit, uplift resistance will be required from some piles. If the load stays inside the limit, the problem is reduced simply to finding the maximum load on the piles at the edge of the group.

While individual piles have some resistance to bending moments at their tops, it is seldom relied on by designers. In any event, it seldom matters, since piles are mostly installed in connected groups. Piers, on the other hand, are typically installed singly. The thick concrete top of the pier has a potential for considerable bending resistance, although it must be reinforced adequately for the effect of tension and shear stresses.

A special case for piles or piers occurs when they are used in the manner of buried poles. This case is illustrated in Section 8.5.

7.2   GROUND TENSION ANCHORS

Foundations developed especially for tension resistance (uplift) are a special, although not unusual, case. Some of the situations that require this type of foundation are the following:

1. Anchorage of very lightweight structures, such as tents, pneumatic structures, and some light metal buildings—all of which can blow away in a windstorm
2. Anchorage of cables for tension structures or for guyed towers
3. Anchorage for uplift resistance as part of the development of overturn resistance

Figure 7.2 shows a number of elements that may be used for tension anchorage. The simple tent stake (Figure 7.2a) probably is the most widely used tension anchor, and it is

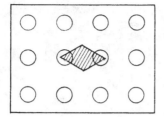

Plan of the pile group showing the form of the kern limit

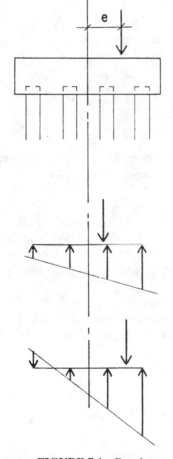

Transformation of a combined compression and overturning moment into an equivalent eccentric load

Case 1: minor eccentricity producing uneven compression loads on the individual piles

Case 2: large eccentricity, outside the kern limit, producing uplift on some piles

FIGURE 7.1 Development of moment resistance by pile groups.

used in sizes ranging from large nails to huge stakes for circus tents. Also commonly used is the screw-ended stake, which offers the advantages of being somewhat more easily inserted and withdrawn and having less tendency to loosen. Of course, stakes are used only for temporary structures.

Ordinary concrete footings (Figure 7.2b) offer some resistance to tension in the form of their own dead weight, enhanced by covering soil when the footing is deeply placed. The *dead-man anchor* typically consists of a buried block of concrete. Column and wall foot-

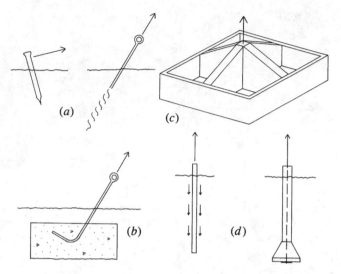

FIGURE 7.2   Forms of ground tension anchors.

ings, concrete and masonry piers (above and below ground), and entire basement structures may be used in this manner. Indeed, most lightweight buildings are anchored in this
way by their foundations.

Resistance to exceptionally high uplift force can require special anchoring foundations
that develop resistance through a combination of their own dead weight plus the ballast
effect of soil fill placed in or on them (Figure 7.2c). In some situations, these foundations
may do double service, for example, serving in tension for forces on a supported structure
in one direction and in compression when the forces reverse (as both wind and earthquakes produce).

As we discussed in Section 7.1, deep foundation elements may be used for tension
resistance as well (Figure 7.2d). Since these foundation elements ordinarily exist in conjunction with additional foundation construction, the whole system may be utilized for its
tension resistance.

The nature of tension forces must be considered as well as their magnitude. Forces
caused by wind or earthquakes have a jarring effect that can progressively loosen tension
connections. Additionally, where soil pressures are relied on for passive resistance, the
progressive deformation of soft soils can cause buried elements to become "loose" with
respect to the confining soils.

7.3   SITE DEVELOPMENT FOR SEISMIC RESPONSE

Site development for seismic response begins with all of the general concerns for site
development for other factors. Everything that must be considered for the soil materials at
the site surface, at the recontoured surface, and for some distance beneath the surface
(subgrade conditions) must be discovered by investigation and analyzed for relationship
to the proposed construction. Construction for the recontoured, finished site surface must
be considered, including moving and processing soil materials.

For response to earthquakes, what gets added to the usual considerations depends on many of the same factors that affect the usual design work. The site surface must be stabilized as much as possible—for both the usual reasons and the effects of the ground vibrations and hard jolts during an earthquake. Settlement of the ground surface (called *subsidence*) can occur for various reasons, including the lack of adequate consolidation of fill materials, and often it can be caused by dynamic vibrations during an earthquake. Where naturally occurring surface soils are not densely compacted, contain considerable organic material, are subject to frequent freeze/thaw cycles, or are for other reasons unstable, subsidence must be expected as a natural event. Subsidence of finished site surfaces, however, occurs most often due to settlement of fill materials deposited during construction.

Soils on sloped surfaces are subject to down-slope movement from many causes. Loose, erodible surface materials may be steadily lost from the natural actions of precipitation during wet periods and from wind during dry periods. This is what gives hills consisting of soil masses their characteristic rounded forms. Steep slopes and sharply cut cliffs are always subject to potential large mass movements due simply to the gravity forces on the soil materials. Stabilizing sloped sites begins with recognition of all of these concerns, most of which can be aggravated by the jolting and vibrations during an earthquake. If something is on the verge of moving down a slope, it will get an extra push from an earthquake.

In addition to aggravating the natural effects of gravity, an earthquake also introduces dynamic horizontal, back-and-forth actions and vertical, up-and-down action. These actions of lateral shaking and vertical bouncing will be added to natural effects of gravity for a combined experience that can cause many forms of failure for the site and for structures resting on the site.

Design for Site Responses

Design for seismic response of a site must incorporate the limitations for changes of the natural characteristics of the site. Site surfaces may be relatively easily changed to some degree, but alterations of the subgrade conditions are more difficult and often more costly to achieve. In any event, some specific achievable condition for the finished site must be accepted and the expectations for its seismic response must be defined. Realistic possibilities for subsidence, down-slope movements, lateral shifts, and other forms of failure must be acknowledged and their relations to life safety and/or post-event restoration should be dealt with in the design process.

Requirements for the building to be placed on the site may impact significantly on the general site design (such as the need for a basement). Conversely, a realistic view of site conditions may affect the building design (for example, eliminating the basement if excavation is difficult or the ground water level is very high).

For the site itself, anything done for seismic response must be done in the full context of other concerns for the site development. This is much too broad a topic to be fully discussed here, although some specific situations are presented in the examples in Part Two. Some general considerations for seismic response include:

1. Recognize the potential instability of the site surface and do what is possible within that context. Where failures may trigger major damage to structures, some design action is required to reduce the potential for the failure. Otherwise, find another site.

2. In addition to other concerns, add the actions of an earthquake to the consideration of the need for deep foundations. If site surface stability is unpreventably at risk, there may at least be a means for stabilizing the building by anchoring it to deeper, more stable soils.

3. Design critical site structures as well as possible to avoid seismic failure, especially where their stability can affect other major construction, such as that for principal roads, buildings, dams, and so on.

4. For site construction that is unavoidably along for the ride with the site surface (pavements, small curbs, etc.), consider the use of construction that is most easily replaced, such as loose-laid stone works versus cast concrete structures. Minor site movements may be tolerated by such construction—or restoration might be possible without full replacement of the original work.

8

Special Design Cases

This chapter treats a number of special situations and types of structures that generate unique considerations for seismic design.

8.1 HILLSIDE CONSTRUCTION

Whether out of necessity or for reasons of prestige or scenic views, buildings are frequently placed on sites with significant slopes. Sample cases of this condition are discussed in Chapter 16. This discussion deals with the general problem of the steeply sloped site.

Seismic effects aside, gravity alone will work to try to roll something down a steep slope. In fact, the site itself—that is, the soil materials at surface levels—may be subject to slipping down the slope. The degree of the problem is usually established primarily by the angle of the slope, as shown in Figure 8.1a. This may be a simple matter of erosion due to runoff of precipitation, or an actual structural soil failure in the form of a rotational slope fault, as shown in Figure 8.1b.

While simple erosion and rotational slips account for most slope losses, there are various other unstable situations that can precipitate down-slope movements. The existence of sloping soil strata is one such case, which is aggravated when a softer soil is perched on top of a dense soil or rock layer (Figure 8.1c).

Stabilizing the site itself should be a first concern. This starts with the effects of erosion and slope rotational failure just described. Most slope failures during an earthquake are ones that were impending from other causes or vulnerabilities. Add a little jolting push from an earthquake and the natural gravity effects take over to cause the ordinary failure.

During an earthquake, two force effects are added to the sloping site to encourage a slope failure. The first is a vertical thrust, serving to bounce the soil mass and add to the normal vertical downward pull of gravity. The second effect is a lateral, horizontal thrust—which, when directed down the slope, will help the down-slope slide occur. The combination of these adds considerably to the general development of the rotational slope failure in a loose soil mass.

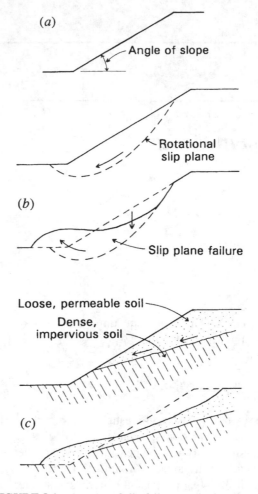

FIGURE 8.1   Aspects of slip failure on sloping sites.

All of the efforts that can be made to discourage general slope failures can also be utilized for seismic resistance. It is largely a matter of increasing the design loads, basically by considering the soil to have a greater weight (increased downward force) and greater active horizontal pressure (in this case, down-slope force). If a retaining structure is used (cantilever retaining wall, piles, etc.), the ordinary horizontal forces as considered for gravity are simply increased for lateral seismic effect. In other words, the basic means for slope retention are not essentially changed, they are just made stronger.

Effective design for the steep slope has to be informed by a thorough geological discovery of the subgrade conditions and the overall formation and stability of the sloped site. Issues may well extend beyond the borders of a single site. Any alterations of the site —including putting a building on it—will surely affect neighboring properties. At particular risk are the down-slope neighbors, for whom general surface drainage will surely be altered and some new instability conditions may be created.

What happens to a sloping site is affected considerably by any buildings placed on it. Heavy construction will add vertical gravity load, which is one component of what promotes a rotational or general down-slope slide failure. Stabilizing the raw site may not be enough; the whole problem of site plus building must be considered.

A special problem is that of the *transition site*, typically formed by a combination of up-slope cut and down-slope fill, as shown in Figure 8.2. This is commonly used to establish roads, but it is also used to create flat sites for buildings. The cut may undermine the slope itself, while the fill materials create a new problem in terms of their own stability and differential settlements caused by consolidation over time. This case is discussed as the first example in Chapter 16.

A stable building platform (a *downhill frame*) can be created for either a mass of fill or a structure placed on a sloping site. This may consist of a foundation system that is simply laid on the sloped surface and anchored by some minor penetrations that grab into subgrade materials, as shown in Figure 8.3a. For a more certain anchorage, it may be necessary to use deep foundation elements consisting of driven piles or drilled piers. For a still more secure foundation for a building, the tops of the piles or piers may be joined to the surface structure for a rigid frame effect in resistance to lateral or down-slope forces, as shown in Figure 8.3b.

8.2   SITE STRUCTURES

Whatever the foundation system for a building (basically, whether shallow footings or deep piles or piers), site structures are mostly supported by the site surface and shallow subgrade materials. Ordinary site structures may include pavements, curbs, freestanding walls, cantilever retaining walls, and bases for signs or large lighting elements.

Tall elements, such as site edge walls or tall retaining walls, must be designed to withstand lateral seismic forces due to their own weight and to any extra soil pressures developed by seismic effects. Bases for signs or large lighting elements must be designed to withstand the overturning effect generated by the supported elements.

In general, the fate of site structures is joined with that of the general site surface. Large soil mass movements will surely take supported structures along, whether in the

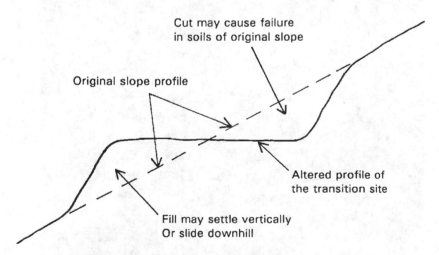

FIGURE 8.2   Potential failures of a transition site in a general slope.

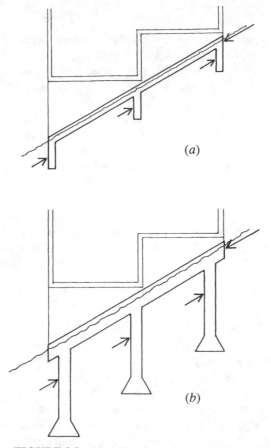

(a)

(b)

FIGURE 8.3 Methods of securing a transition site.

(a)

form of settlement, lateral cracks, vertical slips, or slope failures. If soil movement is considered inevitable, and movement of structures must be prevented, the only solution is that used for buildings in the same situation—deep foundations. This may involve considerations for both vertical and lateral resistance by the deep foundations.

A special problem to be considered is that of the potential for the failure of one site structure to precipitate a sequence of failures of larger magnitude. Such is the case illustrated in Figure 2.15, in which a minor site failure has the potential for triggering a sequence of failures that could bring down a large building. This is not common, but the potential for such scenarios must be studied for any building and site design.

A common site structure is the site edge wall consisting of a single thickness of masonry units, usually concrete blocks (CMUs). These are typically placed on narrow footings and minimally designed for overturning effects of wind or seismic force. Typically, miles of them topple in part or whole in major earthquakes (Figure 8.4*a*). In earthquake country,

FIGURE 8.4   A highly vulnerable structure—the CMU property-line fence—is, typically, 6 ft above grade with a minimal footing. Here the wall simply failed in flexure (*a*) and a closer look (*b*) shows that the vertical reinforcement was there but mostly was not grouted into the voids. Even when properly constructed, however, overturn is common with soft soils, very shallow footings, and a minimal footing width.

they are usually constructed as *reinforced masonry*. They have both vertical and horizontal reinforcement, with the vertical bars spliced to matching dowels from the footing. Whether this construction is completed as specified is sometimes a gamble, as it is not the major kind of structure usually deserving close inspection. In the case of the collapsed wall in Figure 8.4*a*, vertical bars were indeed inserted in the block voids. But there is little evidence that they were solidly grouted into the voids, which pretty much makes them useless (Figure 8.4*b*).

Cantilevered Retaining Walls

Cantilevered retaining walls are often critical site structures, since their success may be quite important to the general stability of the site. Failure of a large retaining wall—or of one very strategically placed (Figure 2.15)—can trigger a major general site failure. Design of retaining walls for earthquakes begins with the basic design for gravity forces and the development of the construction as related to the general site role for the structure. In most cases, design for earthquakes consists of simply adding some extra horizontal force to that already generated by soil pressures.

Strictly speaking, any wall that sustains significant lateral soil pressure is a retaining wall. However, the term is usually used with reference to a cantilever retaining wall, which is a freestanding wall without lateral support at its top. The major design consideration for such a wall is how tall it needs to be. The range of this height establishes the following categories:

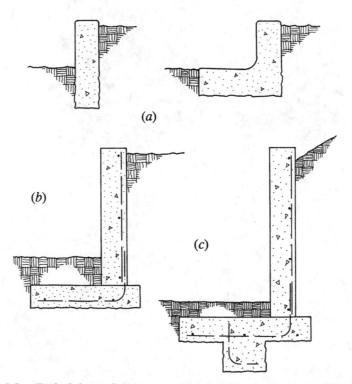

FIGURE 8.5   Typical forms for short concrete retaining structures. (*a*) Simple curb and curb with gutter. (*b*) Short cantilever retaining wall with separate footing. (*c*) Variation of (*b*), enhanced for resistance to sliding with a shear key on the bottom of the footing.

Curbs. Curbs are the lowest freestanding retaining structures. The two most common forms are shown in Figure 8.5a. The selection between the two is made on whether a gutter is needed on the low side of the curb. Use of these structures is typically limited to grade-level changes of about 2 ft or less.

Short Retaining Walls. Vertical walls up to about 10 ft in height are usually built as shown in Fig. 8.5b. These are a concrete or masonry wall of uniform thickness. The wall thickness, footing width and thickness, vertical wall reinforcing, and transverse footing reinforcing are all designed for the lateral shear and cantilever bending moment plus the weights of the wall, footing, and earth fill.

Of course, with any retaining wall, care should be taken to assure adequate drainage to prevent buildup of wet soil and a hydrostatic pressure behind it.

When the bottom of the footing is a short distance below grade on the low side of the wall and/or the lateral pressure resistance of the soil is low, it may be necessary to use an extension below the footing—a shear key—to increase the resistance to sliding. The form of such a key is shown in Fig. 8.5c.

Tall Retaining Walls. As the wall height increases, it grows less feasible to use the simple construction shown in Figure 8.5. The overturning moment increases sharply with the increase in height. For very tall walls, one modification used is to taper the wall thickness. This permits the development of a reasonable cross section for the high bending stress at the base without an excessive amount of concrete. However, as the wall becomes very tall, it is often necessary to consider the use of various bracing techniques, as shown in Figure 8.6.

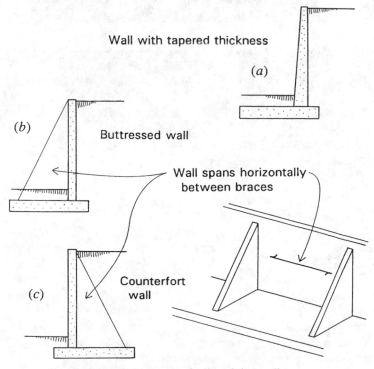

FIGURE 8.6 Forms of tall retaining walls.

The design of tall retaining walls should be done after a more rigorous analysis of the active soil pressure than that represented by the simplified equivalent fluid stress method. Considerations also must be given to any surcharge load or to downslope conditions behind the wall (upper side).

Soft Retaining Structures

Slopes and grade changes can be protected by various devices, including the rigidly built retaining wall. However, there are many other types of structure that have much greater tolerance for adjustment to minor movements. If these are adequately constructed for their

FIGURE 8.7   Rigid concrete and masonry walls are highly likely to crack up with even minor site movements. One solution is to use "loose" structures of stone (*a*) or flat elements of stone or broken concrete (*b*), which can adjust to minor movements.

retention purposes, they may survive an earthquake with very little damage, even after some significant movement of supporting soils.

A historic solution of this type is the simple pile of rocks (Figure 8.7*a*), which can be effective indeed if the pile is made to lean into the slope behind it. Fairly flat pieces with layers slanted slightly away from the wall face would make for an even better rock pile (Figure 8.7*b*).

There are also many proprietary systems consisting of prefabricated units that can be used for this type of structure (Figure 8.8). An advantage of this structure is its ability to drain water from the back of the wall directly through the porous wall, avoiding a major problem for the solid concrete or masonry wall in terms of hydrostatic pressure behind the wall.

To reduce the potential of damage from an earthquake, designers could well consider the use of these "soft" structures for various site purposes, including walks and driveways.

8.3   TOWERS

The towerlike structure is defined not so much by height or overall size as by its proportions of height to width. This height-to-width ratio is the surest measure of the development of critical structural responses. The most notable concern is for overturn, or simply the maximum moment at the base of the vertical cantilever.

On this basis, towerlike actions can be ascribed to slender poles with buried bottom ends (see Section 8.5), freestanding walls used as fences, and very tall shear walls (see Section 8.4). In fact, any structure with an aspect ratio of height to base width of more than 3 or so will begin to demonstrate towerlike responses to lateral forces. When the ratio exceeds 5 or so, overturn may be expected to be a predominant concern.

As the height increases, however, lateral forces are affected by the dimension itself. The height will determine the nature of wind pressures and the general overall dimensions of a structure will relate to dynamic properties that will modify responses to earthquakes.

FIGURE 8.8   Another "loose" structure using proprietary cast concrete units to sustain a steep slope.

While the size dimensions of a tower establish responses to lateral loads, the greater concern may be for the ratio of the height to the width of the base. In the case of a free-standing wall, this may apply to the width of the footing, rather than simply to the dimensions at the bottom of the wall. If a wall is well anchored to its footing, the critical overturn may be that for the footing-to-soil interface.

A form commonly used to provide stability where overturn due to lateral effects is critical is one with a spread base. Examples include the tripod and the pyramid. Trussed towers often use this tapered form, as seen in the common form of support towers for electric power transmission lines (Figure 8.9). A famous example of this form is the Eiffel Tower in Paris.

Very tall high-rise buildings sometimes approach the aspect ratio of a towerlike structure. But individual tower-form shear walls, braced frame bents, or general core-bracing structures may occur in any building. In the trussed bent example in Section 13.2, for instance, the building as a whole is quite squat in form, with a height-width ratio of less than 0.5 in the short dimension of the plan. However, the individual trussed bents in the core bracing have a height-width ratio of about 4, which is beginning to approach a towerlike action dimension.

FIGURE 8.9 A highly familiar trussed tower form. Structural form here is derived almost purely from structural demands, including need for lateral stability.

The most frequently encountered towerlike bracing structure is the individual shear wall pier, which is discussed in the next section.

8.4   FOUNDATIONS FOR SHEAR WALLS

Shear walls typically function as vertical cantilevers, with the fixed end represented by the shear wall's foundation. Shear walls usually rest on shallow bearing footings in one of the following situations:

1. The individual shear wall is part of a continuous wall and is supported by a continuous wall footing that extends past the shear wall ends.
2. The shear wall is an isolated wall and is supported by its own foundation, in the manner of a freestanding tower.

Freestanding Wall and Foundation

For the freestanding wall, the basic behavior was illustrated in the discussion in Section 3.10. Design of such a foundation involves the following considerations.

Anchorage of the Shear Wall. The supported shear wall is anchored to the foundation to resist sliding and overturn.

Sliding of the Foundation. Some combination of sliding friction and passive soil pressure resists the horizontal movement of the foundation.

Overturn of the Foundation. Rotational toppling (overturn) of the foundation must be resisted by some combination of the restoring moment due to the dead weight of the structure (wall plus foundation) and soil pressures on the foundation.

Maximum Vertical Soil Pressure. Vertical load plus overturn must not produce a level of soil pressure beyond that permitted for the soil at the bottom of the footing.
    The process of investigating and designing shear wall foundations is illustrated in the following examples.

Example One: Small Freestanding Wall

The wall and its proposed foundation are shown in Figure 8.10a. Loading for the wall is as shown. The following criteria are assumed:

Maximum allowable vertical soil pressure: 1500 pounds per square foot (psf)
Permissible coefficient of soil friction: 0.25

The active and reactive forces on the structure are shown in Figure 8.10b. Assuming rotation for overturn to be about the toe of the footing, the investigation for overturn proceeds as described below.

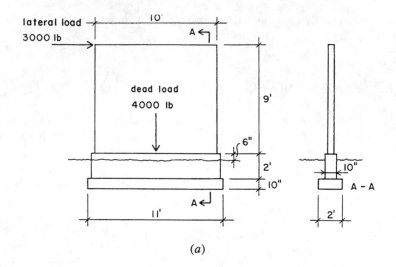

(*a*)

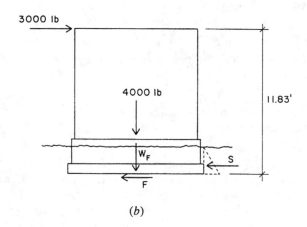

(*b*)

FIGURE 8.10   Investigation of the shear wall foundation.

Overturning moment of lateral force:

$$M = (3,000)(11.83) = 35,490 \text{ lb-ft}$$

Dead loads for restoring moment:

Foundation wall: (2)(10/12)(10.5)(150 pcf) = 2,625 lb
Footing: (10/12)(11)(2)(150) = 2750 lb
Soil over footing: (1.17)(1.5)(11)(80 pcf) = 1,544 lb
Total dead load including supported wall: 10,919 lb

Restoring moment of dead load:

$$M = (10,919)(5.5) = 60,055 \text{ lb-ft}$$

Safety factor against overturn:

$$SF = \frac{60,055}{35,490} = 1.69$$

For the investigation as performed, an acceptable safety factor is usually 1.5.
    For horizontal sliding resistance, the available force is

$$F = (0.25)(10,919) = 2,730 \text{ lb}$$

This is slightly less than the lateral force of 3,000 lb. However, there are two mitigating factors to consider. First is the existence of useable passive horizontal soil pressure on the end of the foundation wall and footing. The second factor relates to the duration of load—either wind or seismic—for which building codes ordinarily permit an increase in allowable stress. Use of the resisting horizontal soil pressure is demonstrated in the next example.
    The process for determining maximum soil pressure was discussed in Section 3.10. The equivalent eccentricity of the vertical load is first found as

$$e = \frac{\text{Overturning moment}}{\text{Normal force}} = \frac{35,490}{10,919} = 3.25 \text{ ft}$$

This is outside the kern limit of 11/6 = 1.83 ft, so the pressure wedge method is used to determine the maximum soil pressure (see Figure 3.64).
Distance of the eccentric load from the footing end is

$$5.5 - 3.25 = 2.25 \text{ ft}$$

Therefore, distance x, as shown in Figure 3.64, is

$$x = (3)(2.25) = 6.75 \text{ ft}$$

and the maximum soil pressure is found as

$$p = \frac{2N}{wx} = \frac{(2)(10,919)}{(2)(6.75)} = 1,618 \text{ psf}$$

This slightly exceeds the limit, but it may be acceptable if the code permits an increase for the lateral loading.

Example Two: Tall Shear Wall

The wall and proposed foundation for this example are shown in Figure 8.11*a*. Criteria are as follows:

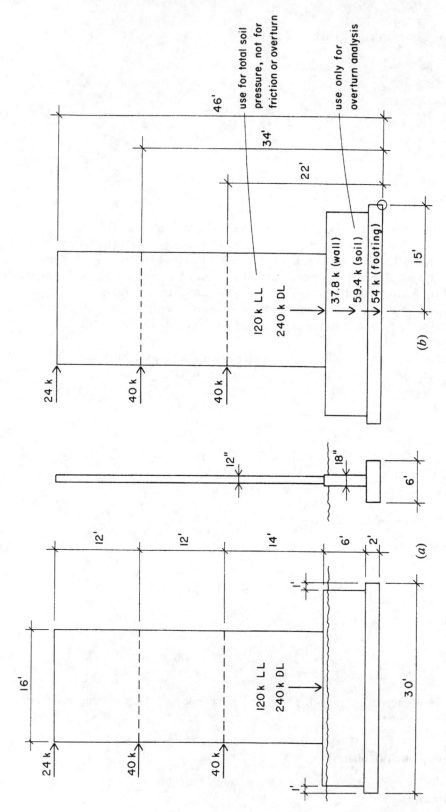

FIGURE 8.11 Investigation of the foundation for the freestanding multistory shear wall.

202

Allowable vertical soil pressure: 3000 psf
Coefficient of sliding friction: 0.25

The loads to be used for investigation are shown in Figure 8.11*b*. Note that the wall live load here is used for investigation of maximum soil pressure, but not for sliding or over-turn resistance. Also the weight of the soil on top of the footing is used to resist overturn, but not to develop sliding resistance or maximum vertical soil pressure. These refinements were not included in the preceding example.

Again, assuming rotation about the toe of the footing, overturning moment of the lateral forces is

$$M = (24)(46) + (40)(34) + (40)(22) = 1104 + 1360 + 880 = 3344 \text{ kip-ft}$$

Using the loads from the illustration, the total vertical load is

$$N = 240 + 37.8 + 54 + 59.4 = 391.2 \text{ kips}$$

And as the load is symmetrically placed, the restoring moment is

$$M = (391.2)(15) = 5868 \text{ kip-ft}$$

The safety factor against overturn is

$$SF = \frac{5868}{3344} = 1.75$$

which is greater than the usual minimum of 1.5.

Leaving out the live load and the soil weight, the useable soil friction is determined as

$$F = (0.25)(331.8) = 83 \text{ kips}$$

Since this is less than the total lateral load of 104 kips, it might be wise to determine the available horizontal passive soil pressure on the end of the foundation wall and footing. Permissible lateral soil pressures is determined from a soil analysis, but for the purpose of the illustration, assume a value of 150 psf per foot of depth below grade. On this basis, the soil pressure is represented by the wedge-shaped diagram in Figure 8.12. Using the given dimensions of the foundation, the total available force is determined as the sum of the two components S_1 and S_2. This produces a total force resistance of 15.1 kips. Adding this to the available friction the total resistance becomes $15.1 + 83 = 98.1$ kips, which is still a bit short of the total lateral force.

Unless an increase in allowable stresses is permitted for the loading, it may be neces-sary to increase the foundation dimensions to increase resistance to horizontal movement.

For the foundation as shown, the vertical soil pressure will be found to occur as shown in Figure 3.64, with the maximum value determined as

$$e = \frac{3344}{391.2} = 8.55 \text{ ft}$$

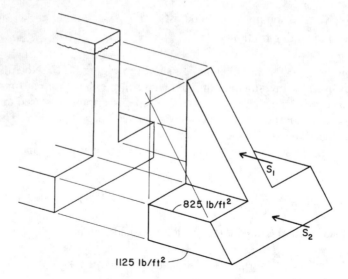

FIGURE 8.12　Investigation for horizontal soil pressure.

$$x = 3(15-8.55) = 19.35 \text{ ft}$$

$$p = \frac{2N}{wx} = \frac{(2)(391,200)}{(6)(19.35)} = 6,739 \text{ psf}$$

which exceeds the allowable pressure of 3,000 psf by a considerable amount, even allowing for the usual increase for loading duration.

All in all, it seems that this is not an adequate foundation for the loads and design criteria given.

Shear Walls with Upper-Level Constraint

In Example 2, the shear wall and its foundation were assumed to be completely independent of the building structure and to function as a freestanding tower. This is not always the case. One such differing case is shown in Figure 8.13, in which lateral constraint of the wall is provided at the first level above the foundation. This is quite a common situation, in which a first-floor framed structure exists and is itself constrained by basement walls at the building edge. If the floor structure is capable of transferring forces from the wall to the building perimeter construction, the shear wall foundation may actually be relieved of the usual sliding function.

As shown in Figure 8.13, when the upper-level constraint is present, the rotation point for overturn moves to this point. The forces that contribute to the resisting moment become the gravity load W, the sliding friction F, and the passive soil pressure S. The following example illustrates the analysis for such a structure.

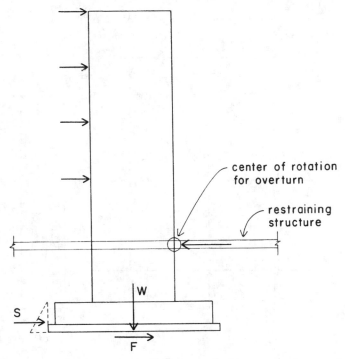

FIGURE 8.13   Behavior of a multistory retaining wall with upper-level constraint.

Example Three: Tall Wall with Upper-Level Constraint

Figure 8.14 shows a structure that is a modification of that used in Example 2. In this case, the shear wall is laterally constrained at the first floor level above the foundation. Construction and data are assumed to be the same as in Example 2.

A modification of the vertical load consists of the addition of the basement portion of the shear wall, which is assumed to increase the total load to the footing as shown in Figure 8.14b.

The overturning analysis in this case begins with a comparison of the overturning moment and the resisting dead load moment. For a traditional analysis, if this does not result in a safety factor of 1.5, some modification is necessary. (*UBC* load combinations may provide a different basis for this analysis in a real situation.)

Overturning moment:

$$M = (24)(38) + (40)(26) + (40)(14) = 2512 \text{ kip-ft}$$

Dead load restoring moment required:

$$M = 1.5(2512) = 3768 \text{ kip-ft}$$

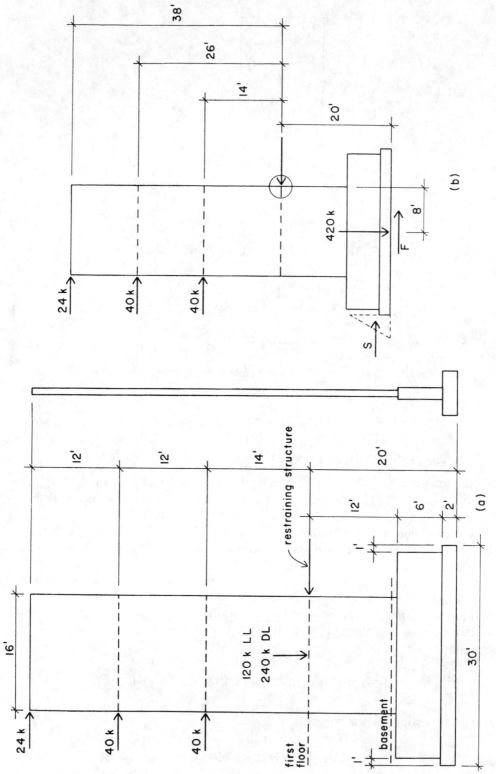

FIGURE 8.14 Investigation of the shear wall with upper-level constraint.

Actual dead load moment:

$$M = (420)(8) = 3360 \text{ kip-ft}$$

This is just a bit short of the requirement, but inclusion of a minor friction force and some passive soil pressure, as shown in Figure 8.14, probably will make up for this adequately. If not, some weight can be added by increasing dimensions of the wall or the footing.

If rotational stability of the wall is maintained in the manner assumed in the preceding computations, the vertical soil pressure on the footing is relieved from the overturning effect. Thus, the pressure is uniform due to the vertical loads and to the footing being designed as a conventional bearing footing.

Another relationship that commonly occurs between the shear wall structure and the rest of the building is that of some connection between the shear wall foundation and other adjacent foundations, tying the building foundations together in general. This situation calls for other investigations regarding the total effect on the shear wall foundation and the lateral stability of connected foundations.

Shear Walls on Continuous Foundations

Shear walls on the building perimeter often occur as individual wall segments (piers). In these situations, the foundation often consists of a continuous wall and footing or a grade beam that extends along the entire perimeter edge. The effect of the shear wall overturn on such a foundation is illustrated in Figure 8.15. The loading tends to develop shear and bending in the foundation, both of which are one-half the magnitude of that in the wall base.

The overturning effect just described must be added to other loadings for the continuous foundation structure. It is likely that such a structure also functions as a distributing member for the gravity loads.

8.5   POLE STRUCTURES

A type of construction used extensively in ancient times and still used in some regions is that which employs wood poles as vertical structural members. Although processed poles, cut to have a constant diameter, are available, most poles are simply tree trunks with the branches and soft outer layers of material stripped away.

There are three ways in which poles are commonly used: As timber piles, driven into the ground; as vertical building columns in a framed structure; or as buried-end poles, partly below ground and extending partly above it. The following discussion is limited to consideration of the buried-end pole.

The two chief means of using buried-end poles are for pole-frame buildings and pole-platform buildings. For a pole-frame building, the poles are extended above the ground to become building columns. Thus the pole is at once a column and its own foundation—and a laterally braced column at that. Altogether quite a useful structural element, if various living organisms and chemical processes can be prevented from devouring it.

For the pole-platform, the poles are cut off at some level above ground and a flat structure (platform) is built on them. The platform may be used as is, for a raised deck, or it may be made to support another construction, such as a building.

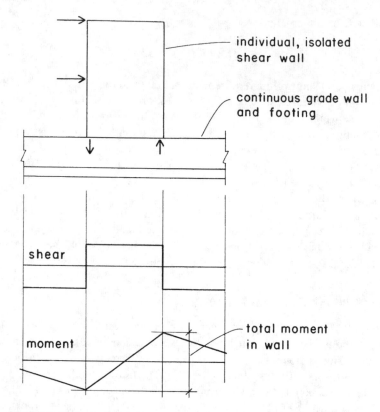

FIGURE 8.15   Isolated shear wall on a continuous foundation.

For vertical loads, the pole end simply functions in direct bearing. With the wide end of the pole placed in the hole, the bearing capacity is based on the area of the flattened wide end. The three common forms for buried-end pole foundations are shown in Figure 8.16. In Figure 8.16*a*, the bottom of the hole is filled with concrete to provide a footing—a preferred method in very soft soils. Another way of achieving a harder bottom is to fill the hole partly with gravel and compact the gravel before placing the pole.

In Figure 8.16*b*, the pole bears directly on the bottom of the hole, the hole is partly filled with soil, and a concrete collar is cast around the pole before filling of the hole is completed. The collar helps to increase vertical load capacity, but it is most useful for improving the lateral stability of the pole. (Of course, if a pavement is to be cast around the pole at ground surface level, the collar is not necessary.) Lag bolts are installed in the pole to anchor the pole to the concrete collar.

In Figure 8.16*c*, the hole is completely filled with concrete. This may be done to protect the pole or as a means for laterally stabilizing the pole because of very soft soil conditions.

Pole-building construction is quite regionally limited, although it is still widely used for service buildings in rural areas. Local codes and practices often determine details of the construction as well as load capacities for pole foundations. For vertical loads, capaci-

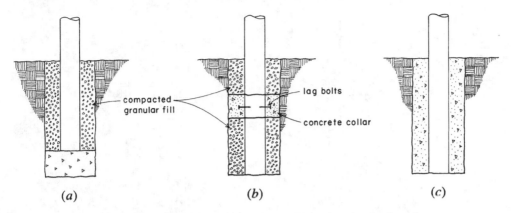

(a)   (b)   (c)

FIGURE 8.16   Methods for development of lateral constraint for poles.

ties of 6 to 10 kips per pole are common, depending on soil conditions and the wood species of the poles.

Pole-frame and pole-platform structures function somewhat differently for lateral loads. The pole-frame building may be held in considerable constraint above the ground, as shown in Figure 8.17a. This minimizes lateral movement of the pole in the hole, as the lower (usually stiffer) end of the pole works as a short cantilever.

For the pole-platform building, especially when the platform is quite close to ground level, there is less possibility to restrain the poles for rotation at their tops, and they thus will function as cantilevers upwards from the holes. Compared to the pole-frame building, this bending action takes place at the narrow and more pliable end of the poles. The narrower pole also gets less horizontal bearing resistance from the surrounding ground. Because of the concern for lateral movement, poles for platform structure buildings are usually buried slightly deeper in the ground (Figure 8.17b) than those for pole-frame buildings.

For the best lateral bracing, holes filled with soil should have the fill well compacted during placement. This may require use of some soil other than that removed during construction, preferably a well-graded sand or a sandy gravel.

For lateral forces, building code requirements generally deal with the pole structure in one of the two situations shown in Figure 8.18. If construction is at ground level, the later-

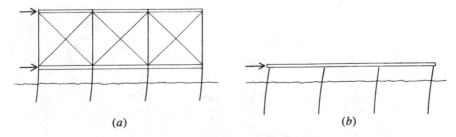

(a)   (b)

FIGURE 8.17   Basic forms of pole structures.

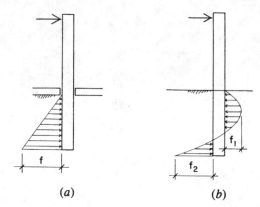

FIGURE 8.18 Development of lateral resistance for poles (*a*) with grade-level constraint and (*b*) without grade-level constraint.

al movement of the pole may be sufficiently resisted there. Thus, the rotation of the pole occurs at this point and the development of soil pressure resistance to lateral movement is as shown in Figure 8.18*a*. If ground-level constraint is minor or nonexistent, lateral resistance will be developed by opposing soil pressures as shown in Figure 8.18*b*.

The following example illustrates the use of design criteria for the unconstrained pole.

Example Four: Unconstrained Pole

A 12-in. diameter round wood pole is used, as shown in Figure 8.19. The site soil is a medium compacted silty sand. Is a 10-ft embedment adequate?

Solution.   Using criteria from the *City of Los Angeles Building Code*, a determination is made of the two critical soil stresses as shown in Figure 8.18*b*. These computed stresses are then compared to the allowable pressures. Using formulas from the code

$$f_2 = \frac{7.62P(2h + d)}{bd^2} = \frac{7.62(1000)(50)}{(1)(10)^2} = 3810 \text{ psf}$$

and

$$f_1 = \frac{2.85P}{bd} + \frac{f_2}{4} = \frac{(2.85)(1000)}{(1)(10)} + \frac{3810}{4} = 285 + 953 = 1238 \text{ psf}$$

From the code, the allowable lateral bearing pressure for the soil is 233 psf per foot of depth. For f_1, the depth is taken as one-third the total, and the allowable stress is thus

$$p = \frac{10}{3} \times 233 \times \frac{4}{3} = 1036 \text{ psf}$$

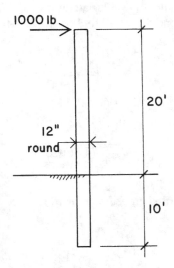

FIGURE 8.19   Form and loading for the pole structure.

(This assumes that the lateral force is due to wind or seismic effect, so a one-third increase is reasonable in the allowable stress.)

For f_2, the allowable pressure is

$$p = 10 \times 233 \times 4/3 = 3107 \text{ psf}$$

Both of the computed stresses exceed the allowable stress, indicating that some additional embedment length is required. Solving for the required depth is not very direct with the formulas from this code. On the other hand, the *UBC* provides a formula for direct determination of the depth of embedment as follows.

$$d = \frac{A}{2} \left(1 + \sqrt{1 + \frac{4.36h}{A}} \right)$$

For which

$$A = \frac{2.34P}{S_1 b}$$

and

b = diameter of the post in ft
d = depth of embedment in ft
h = distance from ground to point of application of P, in ft
P = applied lateral force in pounds
S_1 = allowable lateral soil pressure in psf, based on a depth of one-third the embedment

From the *UBC*, for silty sand, the allowable lateral pressure is 150 psf per ft of depth. Using this, with an increase of one-third for wind or seismic effect

$$S_1 = 150 \times \frac{10}{3} \times \frac{4}{3} = 667 \text{ psf}$$

$$A = \frac{(2.34)(1000)}{(667)(1)} = 3.51$$

$$d = \frac{3.51}{2} \left[1 + \sqrt{1 + \frac{(4.36)(20)}{3.51}} \right] = 14.24 \text{ ft}$$

This also indicates that the proposed embedment of 10 ft is not adequate.

9

Special Design Issues

Construction design, managing its progress, and ensuring that the completed design is properly executed during construction require both creativity and knowledge. This chapter treats some of the critical issues that relate to the general performance of design work as it progresses from concept to finished construction.

9.1 DETERMINING RISK

Major Concerns

Establishing the conditions of risk for potential earthquake damage is a major factor in seismic design. Major concerns include:

Location of the Site. Proximity to known faults, jurisdiction of building codes, and particular geological or ground surface form require consideration. The bottom line involves determining the degree of risk and the particular types of risk (for example, soil liquefaction).

Site Development. Existing conditions for the site may be determined by a thorough discovery process. Also of concern are modifications that will be made to the site as part of the construction process and how these cause new areas of risk. In other words, risk may be predetermined by existing site conditions, but then may be made better or worse by design decisions.

Building Design. Design decisions regarding construction, such as building form and choice of materials, may produce various forms of risk. All parts of the building are involved, including plumbing, lighting, decorative elements, and so on—in addition to the basic structure and construction.

In effect, design for seismic response begins with the establishment of the types and levels of risk, for otherwise, there is no basis for quantified evaluations of response. This makes the issue of risk quite possibly the biggest design decision of all. For the structural design, this is the first step, as we discussed in Chapter 3.

Whoever is responsible for the efficacy of the design work in establishing a desired level of safety and reduction of damage needs to understand thoroughly how risk is established. In many cases, determining risk is a matter of fitting the design within the constraints of the building code with jurisdiction. This is a good starting point of course, but it does not entirely cover all the issues of risk, especially ones involving damage to the construction, as we discussed in Chapter 4.

9.2   MANAGING DESIGN

Design of complex objects involves many people and requires careful management. Many designs bog down in the process due to bad management, in spite of the work of skilled and experienced designers. It behooves everyone involved—most notably, those in charge—to understand the process completely in order to anticipate some of the problems that might occur.

Design is essentially a continuing task of inquiry and decision. The inquiry and decision-making continue as long as questions can be brought up.

Final design solutions for complex systems, such as those for building structures, often contain many compromises and many relatively arbitrary choices. The most economical, fire resistive, quickly erected, handsome, or architecturally accommodating structure is only accidentally likely to be the optimal choice for the resistance of lateral loads.

Designing for Lateral Force

Design examples in this book do not reveal the complete design process, although considerations of factors other than lateral force actions are frequently mentioned. The design solutions developed here are thus unavoidably somewhat simplistic and myopic in their concentration on the lateral force problem.

In general, with regard to the lateral force-resistive system, the design process incorporates the following:

Determining the Basic Scheme.   This includes choosing general type, basic construction form, layout, and materials for the elements of the lateral resistive system.

Determining Loads.   This involves establishing criteria and standards, choosing investigative methods, and performing necessary computations.

Determining the Load Propagation.   This consists of tracing loads through the structure, from element to element of the system, until they are finally resolved into the supporting ground.

Design of Individual Elements.   Based on their functions and load-sharing roles, each separate element of the system must be investigated and designed in sufficient detail to permit unequivocal definition for the builder.

Design for Interactions.   Connections between elements of the bracing system, and between structural and nonstructural parts of the building, must be investigated, designed, and completely described.

Design Documentation.   Because the design as such is only an idea, all information necessary to thoroughly describe the construction for others must be documented—traditionally in construction drawings and specifications.

All of these aspects of the design process are given some consideration in the examples in Part Two.

Design Methods

The design of building structures includes a certain amount of mathematical, engineering-based, analytical work, but it also includes a lot of visualization, planning, and the development of construction plans and details. Typically, it also involves the efforts of more than a single person and, frequently, even more than a single design organization.

The most practical method used to achieve a single task—for example, designing a single reinforced concrete column—may be relatively easily determined. The best method for achieving a whole system design, however—subject to so many special considerations for each system—is quite elusive. This is the essence of design management and requires major management skills as well as basic design skills.

Whatever methods are used, they must account for some fundamental aspects of the work:

1. Complete investigation of the definable loading demands: What can happen that should be considered for an assurance of safety?
2. Reasonable consideration of all the feasible alternatives for solution of the problem: Final choices should be made after an effort to assess all the possibilities is made.
3. The design of each subsystem is integrated with all the other subsystems with which it interacts and within the predominant concerns for the whole system of which it is a part.
4. The final definition of the design is rendered in a communicable form for those who will perform the construction. In the end, that typically means written specifications and annotated graphics (working drawings).

Whatever works to get that done in a responsible, reliable manner, in reasonable time, at minimum cost, is a good method.

9.3   INFORMATION AND AIDS FOR DESIGN

All design work utilizes various aids in the execution of the work. Typically, the chief aids are records of previous designs of a similar nature that proved to be reasonably successful. As most design work is highly repetitive, and nothing shines as bright as demonstrated success, this is usually the first place to look for help.

Textbooks, handbooks, industry-supplied data, research reports, models, and computer-aided processes are all used when the occasion indicates they would be useful. Mostly, it is the designer's familiarity with the aids that is critical for their effective use. That starts with knowing they exist, then how to access them, and finally on to how to use them. The various industry organizations and professional organizations that relate to a specific area are good sources for determination of the availability of design aids.

Designers approach a particular design task armed with their individual collection of design experience, developed skills, and personal store of knowledge. Routine tasks may be performed out of hand, with no other references. However, for most design work, considerable use will be made of reference sources for assistance. Some of these references may provide direct information for individual design tasks. Other sources will provide basic information that establishes fundamental design criteria and standards for design requirements, without which measurement of design acceptability is impossible.

Potential Sources

Criteria and standards apply to all phases of the design work. Referring to the itemized list in Section 9.1, some of the potential sources that can be used for the various stages of design are discussed below.

Determining the Basic Scheme.   This is largely a matter of the designer's judgment. However, various sources of information may assist in the comparison of basic schemes in terms of their appropriateness. Thus, the degree of risk of windstorms or earthquakes, the size and form of a building, special site conditions, and other factors will define a particular situation. For that situation, the feasibility or effectiveness of various basic schemes may be evaluated.

Evaluations of this kind may be largely judgmental, or may be made with some reliable data from observed performances, research, or analysis of basic criteria and standards. Many studies of this kind have been made and are part of the technical literature. For common situations, these studies will probably be of some practical value. For unique situations, they will provide a starting point for a more precise design study of the situation at hand.

In the end, it may be necessary to carry design work for more than one scheme to some level of detail in order to make an evaluation for a particular design. Since the basic scheme for the lateral bracing system may be closely related to the basic architectural design, this kind of study may be required by others as well as the structural designer.

The reality here is that there is no one identifiable source with singular reliability for supporting this phase of the design work. Any borrowed information used here is subject to someone else's judgments or opinions.

Determining Loads.   The enforceable building code for a particular project is obviously a starting point for this and must be satisfied at a minimum. Is a minimal design acceptable for this work? If real optimization is desired, then a much deeper investigation must be made for design criteria and, in later stages of the design work, for design performance evaluation. This means either the designer making some educated judgments or doing some research into what the building codes themselves used as reference sources. A much *safer* design may begin simply with some increase in the loading as defined by the codes. If the rest of the design work is reliably performed, that will certainly provide a stronger structure.

Required loads provided in the building codes are not arbitrarily developed. If designers want to challenge them, they have to find out how the loads were determined and then make their own evaluations as those who wrote the codes did.

Determining the Load Propagation.   This consists of the structural investigation for the internal forces and deformations produced by the loads. Performing this reliably requires the designer use whatever analytical methods are available. For simple structural systems (such as most of those illustrated in this book), the work may be performed relatively easily. For a true dynamic load analysis of a highly indeterminate structure, using strength methods and deformation-limit criteria, the work may strain the capabilities of the most sophisticated computer-aided programs.

A fundamental question here is what is acceptable as an investigation. Building codes may sometimes stipulate the required method of investigation, but mostly it is a matter of judgement—by the designer and by anyone who has to review the design work. There is an existing body of knowledge that professional designers are expected to know, and be able to apply to design work. That situation changes over time, advancing with new research, theories, and experience. The best sources are usually the latest popular professional text and reference books on the topic.

For review of the design work as part of the general review for acceptability of the proposed construction, some documentation of the structural investigation will usually be required for anything other than very simple buildings. This means that the form of the investigation should be one that is generally familiar, or the reviewers will not be able to follow the work.

Design of Individual Elements.   Unless a unique invention is being contrived by the designer, this is probably the easiest task in terms of available references. Promotional work by the manufacturers of materials and products generally include reference data and recommended designs for just about anything that could be conceivably done with the materials and products. Industry organizations, such as the American Concrete Institute (ACI), American Institute for Steel Construction (AISC), and Brick Institute of America BIA provide standards that are widely accepted by building codes and whole libraries of design guides. Name a structural material or product and there is most likely at least one organization that provides reference materials.

For the most widely used materials, and the most widely used basic elements and systems, there are also basic reference textbooks, handbooks, and information available from individual manufacturers or suppliers.

Design for Interactions.   There are two levels to this category. The first level involves the interaction of the separate parts of the structural system, necessary to assure load transfers within the system and the overall performance of the system. For performance analysis, this is an extension of the third and fourth items above. For a final design development, it involves a thorough study of the necessary construction details to assure the necessary structural actions. This requires that the structural designer follow through with a review of the execution of the construction—all the way to the actual erection process, if necessary. It assumes, of course, that the designer has a considerable knowledge of construction work and can pass judgment on both its specification and graphic detailing as well as its actual execution by workers.

This is an area where a lot of problems occur. First of all, not all designers are knowledgeable about specifications, graphics, and construction work. This means that someone else (if anyone) must follow through beyond the stage of basic structural computations. The more people added to the chain—from structural investigation to final construction—the more opportunities for lack of follow-through.

A problem here is that reference sources do not often themselves follow through from basic structural investigation to final construction. Therefore, it behooves *somebody*— hopefully the structural designer—to do so.

Design Documentation. The principal purpose of the design documentation is to communicate the design to others. For structures, the basic components of the documentation are the structural computations, the structural specifications, and the parts of the building construction drawings that deal with the structure. That package is the definition of the final design and the total communication from designer to builder.

However individual the design or whatever the designer's style, the communication must be in common language, understandable by the builder as well as many others. Standard references in use by the construction industry must be used so as not to confuse the communication process. This means using whatever exists in the form of accepted common language, notation, symbols, and even writing and drafting styles. The single best source for this common language is the Construction Specifications Institute (CSI), which is both the author and a principal user of the standard materials.

The detailed illustrations of construction in this part (framing plans and construction section details) are done in a general form similar to the standards in use, but are developed here principally for illustration and in most cases are not complete.

It is a critical concern for the separate elements of the design documentation that all the parts say the same thing. This is not so easy to achieve when each element (computations, specifications, and drawings) is produced by different people—which is often the case in large design offices. This coordination needs to be assigned to someone in the design process, preferably the structural designer.

This book's Bibliography contains several useful references for the design of lateral bracing systems, but a complete list of all such references would possibly be the size of this entire book. A few very general references may be used by most designers, but for a specific project a relatively short, specialized list of useful references must be custom assembled.

9.4   CONTROL OF CONSTRUCTION

Recent studies, including those of damaged buildings following major windstorms and earthquakes, indicate that a considerable amount of what is designed and specified in the way of special construction for lateral bracing does not actually get installed during the building construction work. This applies especially to anchors and connectors for wood construction and to reinforcement for concrete and masonry structures—items not in view once the construction is completed.

Poor construction is often attributable to the lack of inspection of the builder's work at critical points during construction. The proper time for an inspection is often a short interval, and if the inspector is not present at the appropriate time, the work continues. It may also be that the inspector is incompetent, irresponsible, or in collusion with the builder to defraud the building owner.

Someone should ascertain that the designed and specified work for the building construction is properly done, and certainly no one knows what should be done better than the building designer. If the contracted services of the designer do not include that work, as it increasingly does not, some gap between design intentions and actual construction is likely to occur.

Responsible structural design firms provide inspection of the construction at critical points as part of their full consulting services. This is simply good business, both for the full service to the client and for the assurance to the design firm that the work for which they accept responsibility will not fail.

9.5   USE OF COMPUTERS

Computers can be used to aid the work in all phases of design. Their use is more critical for some tasks, particularly the investigation of very complex systems for multiple loading conditions. Increasingly, however, a significant use is in applying the steadily accumulating data of evaluations of performances of previously designed structures to new design. This use holds the promise of providing a much more intelligent basis for the work in early stages of design.

Computer programs for the investigation and design of most ordinary structures are readily available from commercial sources and industry and professional organizations.

PART 2

Example Design Cases

This part uses seven design situations as references for forcused discussion regarding seismic design. The buildings and sites are defined only to the extent necessary to provide a realistic background for the discussion. These are not real design cases, although they have been chosen to represent a range of common situations. Data, experiences, and even photographs from similar—but real—situations are incorporated.

The presentation first considers what might happen in an earthquake and then develops the design for improved response. To keep the presentation brief, reference to materials in Part One is cited to provide support regarding basic issues and problems that are discussed fully there. In order to avoid excessive repetition, the lengthy general discussions in the first examples are not repeated in later cases. As the chapters and cases proceed in sequence, discussion begins to focus on the unique conditions for each case.

10

Wood-Framed Residence

This building represents the class of small, conventional wood-framed buildings, which accounts for the vast majority of existing buildings in the United States.

10.1 DESCRIPTION

As American as Mom and Apple Pie, the 2 X 4 stud, joist and rafter, panel-sheathed wood structure still dominates the small building business. Adaptable as almost nothing else in the construction lexicon, it provides the basic structure for most of our buildings. Add stucco (or imitation stucco) to its exterior, and you can create *anything*! The example here is also an American icon: a single-family house (Figure 10.1).

Typical Construction

Derived originally from the timber frame structures of European buildings, the light wood frame developed mostly in the early nineteenth century as stands of timber were depleted and saw mills became capable of producing smaller dimension lumber. Much of the form and detail of present structures (Figure 10.2) was set by shared experience of carpenters before the twentieth century. Major changes in modern times include the use of panelized sheathing (versus boards) and formed sheet metal fasteners.

Not a small factor in its continued popularity in recent times is its ability to provide extensive void spaces for the stuffing of the steadily increasing items of building equipment and service. Piping, wiring, ducts, mounted fixtures, and all sorts of things can be absorbed with ease, and readily accessed for modification or repair.

The basic structure is little changed from region to region. Major differences have to do with exterior finish materials, roofing, and foundation construction. Because of its special vulnerabilities, the example case will be assumed to be built in a mild climate with no serious concern for frost.

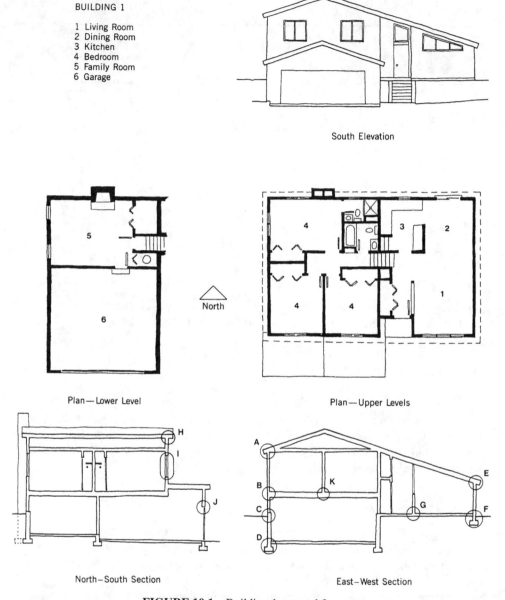

BUILDING 1

1 Living Room
2 Dining Room
3 Kitchen
4 Bedroom
5 Family Room
6 Garage

South Elevation

North

Plan—Lower Level

Plan—Upper Levels

North–South Section

East–West Section

FIGURE 10.1 Building 1, general form.

In discussing this class of construction, it must be borne in mind that design, construction, and code requirements are usually somewhat relaxed—that is, the level of complexity and sophistication of treatment is not in the same class with that encountered with larger buildings. This work does not get the attention of the highest paid engineering consultants, is often not performed by large construction companies with extensive technical capabilities, and is usually regulated by a simplified form of the building code. A higher percentage of the work here is left to the discretion of the designers, contractors, and workers. Inspec-

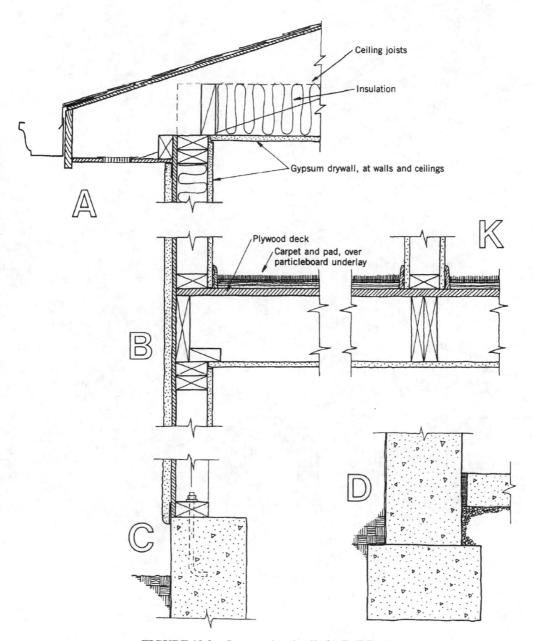

FIGURE 10.2   Construction details for Building 1.

tion of the construction for code compliance is frequently cursory at best. What you get is often not exactly what is on the construction drawings or in the specifications.

Structural Alternatives

The light wood frame (Figure 10.3) is still predominant in use for this type. The 2×4 stud, 2×6, 8, 10, or 12 joists and rafters, and the 4-ft by 8-ft panel size for sheathing and

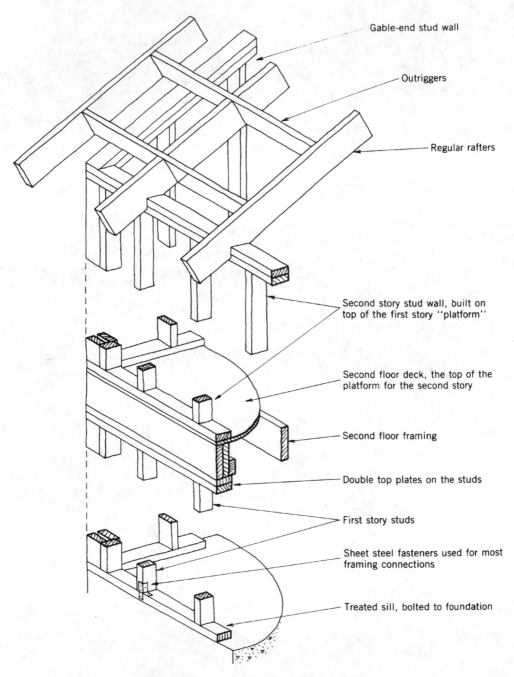

Gable-end stud wall

Outriggers

Regular rafters

Second story stud wall, built on top of the first story "platform"

Second floor deck, the top of the platform for the second story

Second floor framing

Double top plates on the studs

First story studs

Sheet steel fasteners used for most framing connections

Treated sill, bolted to foundation

FIGURE 10.3   Basic form of the light wood frame.

decking set a modular system of dimensions in place. Frame spacings of 12, 16, 24, 32, 48, and 96 in. are thus obvious and the 3.5-in.-wide void space in stud-framed walls is typical. Dimensions off the module are to be expected, but pressure to reduce waste makes use of the popular, readily available units of materials important. A major cost factor, as for all building construction, is the need to reduce to a minimum the need for on-site labor, particularly of the skilled crafts.

Despite the strong control of the modular dimensions of standard products, this structural system has immense potential for accommodating variations of building form, size, and detail. The materials are relatively easy to work with—on or off the site—and custom forming can be done virtually without limit. This adds considerably to the enduring popularity of this building type with designers and builders.

There are, of course, other possible structures for this type of building. The light wood frame can be emulated in steel, using light-gage elements. Use of steel offers the principal advantage of reducing the mass of combustible material in the building. This may be a desirable feature in some situations, or an actual building or zoning code requirement in others. In former times, it was hardly ever an economic advantage. With the present cost of lumber, however, there is some increase in the use of light-gage steel frames, although basic system forms still generally emulate the good old light wood frame (2×4 studs, etc.).

In times past, the wood structure was frequently developed as a heavy timber frame, often with infill utilizing elements of light wood framing. While the elegantly crafted, exposed wood frame can be very attractive and dramatic in appearance, usually it is not economically competitive for most ordinary buildings. The lack of available craft workers and difficulty of obtaining good timbers makes for difficulty even when cost is not a concern. There is, however, a resurgence of popularity for this system at present, in spite of its craft dependency and somewhat against-the-current nature in terms of trends for material and production use.

While the 2×4 is the workhorse of the light wood framing system, and the 3.5-in.-wide stud space most common, there are sometimes compelling reasons for variation of wall thickness. For tight planning situations, nonstructural walls of thinner dimension can be produced by using 2×3 studs or even 2×2 studs. More often, however, there is a need for thicker walls, or more specifically, for a wider void space. The two most common reasons for this are the need for more insulation in exterior walls and the need to accommodate large items, such as ducts or extensive plumbing.

The void spaces in walls, as well as those between joists and rafters, are utilized for many practical purposes, primarily to contain wiring, piping, ducts, and the various items for the electrical power, lighting, water and waste, doorbell, and security alarm systems. The hollow wall space can also contain columns for a heavier frame in some cases, without having the frame intrude in the building's occupied space.

Use of solid sawn wood pieces for the light wood frame requires control of the quality of the wood used in order to have economic usage with a minimum of dimensional and shape change due to shrinkage. There has been a general, steady reduction in the quality of lumber used for the light wood frame, mostly for economic reasons. Use of fabricated elements, such as laminated members, wood + plywood I or box sections, and light prefabricated trusses, is becoming more prevalent for floor and roof structures—especially for spans over 15 ft or so.

Wall sheathing and floor and roof decking were mostly achieved with solid sawn wood boards in the past. Early in this century, these were gradually replaced, with decking mostly done with plywood and wall sheathing with plywood and various wood fiber products in panel form. Now compressed-fiber products—particleboard, hardboard, and so on—are steadily replacing plywood for wall sheathing and roof decking. This is not so much the ascendancy of a superior product as it is the ability to utilize lower quality wood from smaller, fast-growing trees, conserving the increasingly scarce high-quality lumber from old-growth trees for applications where it is really needed.

It is possible, of course, to use any form of structure for a house. Steel frames, masonry, reinforced concrete, aluminum skins, and fabric have been used—as well as ice, mud, twigs, and animal skins. The homemade or highly crafted, custom-designed house offers endless possibilities and some notable, outstanding examples exist. For everyday consumption, however, the light wood frame still stands as the most widely used system.

Variations of the details of the construction and options for materials used for basic components derive from regional climate and construction practices. While the system used is similar throughout the United States, there is indeed a wide variation of details and construction form. Design for earthquakes begins with a general form and proceeds to investigations for improvement.

10.2   WHAT CAN HAPPEN IN AN EARTHQUAKE?

Consider some possible scenarios for this building in the event of a major earthquake. It is assumed that design and construction has been performed in accordance with the codes in general and that wind has been considered, although not a violent windstorm condition.

As with any building, when the earthquake occurs, anything not securely fastened in place will get tossed around. This includes the building occupants, furnishings, and some unsecured items of the building equipment. Any heavy items thus launched can do damage as missiles and may be responsible for significant damage to walls, windows, and other impact-vulnerable parts of the construction. This situation is largely outside the realm of control by the building designers, so there is not much that architects or engineers can do about it.

Conditions that Could Cause Collapse

For the basic structure, the first concern is for actual structural collapse. For the typical wood frame, with a lot of redundant lumber, and with some design for the lateral and vertical uplift effects of wind, full collapse is not likely, unless some really bad situations exist, such as those that follow.

Inadequate Foundation Anchorage.   The earthquake transmits its whole punch through the building base, and the building will be dislodged from its foundation supports if the attachment is not adequate (Figure 10.4). This is generally a horizontal force problem, but it could also be a vertical force problem. Rusted out anchor bolts, oversized holes in sills, missing nuts on anchor bolts, or unbraced piers or stilts may produce a failure. The lightly anchored, heavy building may not blow away in the wind, but it can be easily launched off its supports in an earthquake.

Bad Distribution of the Building Mass.   For horizontal force, building structures function as cantilevers with fixed bases. If a major part of the building weight is at the top (end

FIGURE 10.4 Classic base failures of wood structures. (*a*) Lateral collapse of the propped-up building (with a crawl space) by tilting the props or sliding from the foundation. (*b*) Fracture at the foundation top, between the wall sill and the foundation.

of the cantilever) or is off-center (horizontally) in the plan from the structural centroid, major overturning or twisting can be developed at the building base. Add these effects to uplift and horizontal force, and the combination can be disastrous. And, the building lateral-resistive structure is more heavily loaded. Heavy roof construction is not so smart in high-risk seismic zones (but, unfortunately, is popular).

Bad Distribution of the Lateral Bracing Structure.   The typical wood frame for a residence, plus the planar elements of roof, floor, and wall surfacing, usually constitute a significant amount of potential as shear walls and horizontal diaphragms. However, their placement in the building may not necessarily be optimal, or even *adequate* for some loading conditions. At a particularly strategic location, a wall may be fully glazed, rather than solidly surfaced. A roof may be constituted in complex folds or curves, rather than in single large planes. Floors may be multilevel or considerably pierced for stairs, atrium spaces, or installed equipment (for example, sunken tubs). In other words, there may be a lot of structure, but its arrangement and form does not necessarily add up to a functional lateral-resistive system.

Inadequate Resistance of Individual Elements.   For the basic lateral-resistive structure, it is not enough to have a majority of the structure succeed—every element has to work. If an individual, heavily-stressed, shear wall is not adequately sheathed (for example, with gypsum drywall instead of plywood), its failure may represent the first domino to fall, transferring load to other walls and triggering a progressive collapse of the whole system. Collapse might also be only on a local basis; but nevertheless, every individual part of the system needs to work.

Interaction Failure.   The system may be well-disposed and the individual elements adequate for their tasks, but the whole thing won't work unless the elements are capable of interacting—that is, they are properly and securely attached to each other. This is a major form of failure for buildings not deliberately designed for seismic resistance because a lot of special anchorage and fastening may be required. Ordinary carpenter practices fall down here. This and other concerns have promoted the use of sheet metal fastening devices, which are now largely designed to perform reasonable anchorage tasks. Still, some particularly vulnerable situations persist, among them are wall corners and wall intersections, where firm attachment of the walls to each other is not always accomplished.

Nonstructural Damage.   While the basic lateral-resistive structure is the first line of defense, and justifiably the prime concern for seismic resistance, *everything* in the build-

FIGURE 10.5   Damage to nonstructural elements. (*a*) Roof tiles are heavy and can be easily dislodged unless securely anchored. Installation may have been proper, but, with time, deterioration can cause loss of anchorage.

FIGURE 10.5 (*Continued*)   (*b*) Interior walls of rigid planar construction may be the stiffest elements in a building with flexible bracing. They have to fail before the structure can function. (*c*) Heavy rooftop equipment must be securely anchored for both vertical and horizontal forces.

ing construction should be resistive to seismic forces (Figure 10.5). Nonstructural walls, suspended ceilings, window frames, curtain walls, and decorative elements should be secure against movement during the shaking actions. Failure here may not lead to building collapse, but it will still constitute danger for occupants and cost for replacement or repair. Loss of stucco, masonry veneer, window glass, roof tiles, and suspended ceilings is classed as "cosmetic" failure by structural engineers, but it still adds to the bill for getting the building back in shape.

Damage to Service Systems.   Along for the ride, of course, is everything in the building, including the building's HVAC, piping, wiring, general plumbing, elevators, and other equipment (Figure 10.5*c*). A common failure is that of toilets, which become dislodged from their rusted-out anchor bolts and the water tanks that sit on them. Suspended lighting can fail by swinging or dropping. Furnaces, air conditioners, and water heaters not firmly braced can tilt over or slide sideways. Particularly dangerous are the gas appliances that get dislodged, leaving broken gas lines.

Broken Seals.   Water-sealing membranes and flashing may be ruptured or pulled loose as the building rocks and rolls. If everything else works, but the roof leaks or the curtain wall leaks, the building owner will not be happy. Violent back-and-forth jerking of any building is likely to produce tearing fractures of sealed and flashed joints. The greater the number of such joints (due, for example to complex roof geometries), the higher the statistical likelihood of leaks, whether caused by an earthquake or only aggravated by it. For the highly vulnerable flat roof, a major earthquake jolt is almost certain to produce some leaks, and the next rainstorm will prove it.

Chimneys.   Older residences in all regions often have masonry chimneys and fireplaces. This refers to *real* masonry, not something applied to make it appear to be a masonry structure. For a modest wood frame residence, a large masonry fireplace with a tall masonry chimney and a heavy masonry or concrete foundation may well represent a total weight greater than that of the whole rest of the residence construction. It is also a monolithic unit and will respond quite independently during an earthquake (Figure 10.6).

FIGURE 10.6   The heavy chimney can pull loose, and rupture water seals, even if it doesn't fall. Fire separation requirements make it hard to secure this anchorage.

All the possibilities described in Section 2.6 must be considered for the site. The wood frame structure itself is capable of some adjustment to deformations, but the same is likely not true for window glazing, stucco walls, masonry veneers, tile floors, and the many water seals in the exterior. Thus, excessive site movements may not cause structural failures but will certainly cause a lot of cosmetic damage.

Figure 10.7 shows a site plan and two sections through the building and site. The site slopes approximately 10 ft from the northwest to the southeast corner. The profile of the original grade is shown as the dashed line on the two sections. The lower-level floor is well below the original grade, so no significant settlement should occur in this part of the

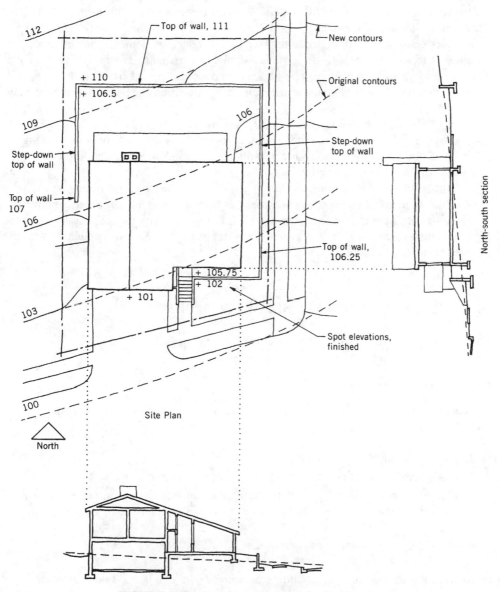

FIGURE 10.7   Site plan and section for Building 1.

house. The middle-level floor, however, is mostly at or above the original grade; in addition, its shallow foundations may well fall above the original grade unless some extension downward is provided.

Even if adequate provisions are made for gravity loads, some difference in settlement may occur during an earthquake, stressing the general connection between the one-story and two-story portions of the house. Any general consolidation of upper-level soil materials due to seismic actions will tend to drop the one-story portion more than the two-story portion.

In addition to the possible distress to the building, movements of the site surface and of any site structures generally supported near the surface level need to be considered. The backyard is placed at a level representing a cut below original grade, so little subsidence should be anticipated here. The site at the front of the house is mostly built up, however, and some consolidation of the fill materials—with corresponding subsidence of the finished grade—should be expected.

Another possible area of concern involves building service elements that are placed in the ground (for example, piping for water supply, sewers, and gas supply). If these are near the ground surface, and seismic actions produce downward movement of the soil without corresponding movement of the building, connections at the building edge may be broken.

Even when buildings are fully repaired following a major earthquake, the disturbance of soils may result in subsequent movement, both vertically and horizontally. Shaking of the ground and bouncing of the surface soils disturb long-standing equilibrium, and it takes a lot of time to regain stability.

On the building interior, common failures involve fracture of rigid piping and movement of heavy items of equipment, such as water heaters, furnaces, large fans, and refrigeration units. Refrigerators, stoves, washers, and driers are easily moved, possibly rupturing connecting electrical wiring or piping for water or gas. Fixtures or appliances that are not well fastened in place may dislodge.

10.3   DESIGN FOR IMPROVED SEISMIC RESPONSE

Careful design can reduce the effects described in Section 10.2.

General Design Approach

A general approach to building and site design for improved seismic response would include these goals:

1. Clearly defining the potential seismic risk
2. Understanding what constitutes a good response to earthquake effects
3. Defining design limits (acceptable risk, tolerable damage, degrees of failure related to levels of effect) and developing values to measure design proposals against
4. Understanding the intent of code limits

Seismic design requires that a building have *some kind* of a lateral bracing system.

Basic forms of lateral bracing have not changed much for a long time, although the specific form of construction used to produce them changes continuously. As we discussed in Section 3.2, the common ways to brace a building are with rigid shear planes called *diaphragms*, trussing, or rigid-frame action for frameworks. External struts, guys, or flying buttresses can also be used, but they are not common solutions.

Some types of structures may be inherently stable, such as the tripod, the buried fence-post, and the gravity dam or retaining wall. But most building assemblages need some modifications of their basic construction or added bracing elements.

The first requirement of bracing, of whatever form, is to keep the structure and the general construction of the building from collapsing. Life safety is fundamentally dependent on this performance aspect. However, two other performance goals are significant for the general building design:

Damage control—For the owner's sake, the bracing should permit very limited movement, or otherwise function in a way that reduces possible damage to the construction in general. The damage might not be life threatening, but it might be so costly that it ties up the building a long time for repairs or is too expensive to do at all.

Accommodation of planning—For the architect's sake, the bracing should accommodate intelligent planning of the building in general, allowing for clear spans and open, accessible spaces inside the building and reasonable development of entry and fenestration in the building exterior.

Beyond the fundamental bracing system, which may well need to be designed by the best structural designers available, the whole of the building construction is the architect's responsibility.

Site design is frequently the most difficult aspect of seismic design. Because the architect, structural engineer, civil engineer, landscape architect, geotechnical specialist, geologist, seismologist, building code administrator, foundation and site work contractor, and landscape contractor all have a piece of this action, orchestrating these professional's activity is a challenging assignment. What is most important is to ensure that the critical goals—including seismic response—do not get overlooked.

Help for the Wood Frame House

Design decisions involving the general building form, selection of finish materials and details, planning of vertical supports, locations of openings for doors and windows, and the overall configuration and detail of the construction affect seismic response. It is seldom possible to let seismic design predominate over all other concerns, but an effort at optimizing seismic response by reducing inherent vulnerabilities will surely improve matters.

For example, before trying to strengthen the lateral-resistive structure, a complete review of all the architectural decisions that relate to seismic response is in order. Start with the general building form and reconsider decisions such as the totally open building side that produces a three-sided building condition; the open first floor that sets up the possibility for a soft story in the multistory building; and the materials that result in excessive weight at the top of the building. In other words, give the structure a break before asking it to brace the building.

These considerations are within the scope of the architect's design work. However, the basic planning of the lateral bracing system also involves architectural design decisions, so it should be done in cooperation with the structural designer. Where to place a shear wall, and what exactly its dimensions should be, are both an architectural and a structural decision.

Decisions to use a relatively heavy timber roof structure, with a heavy timber deck, supporting either heavy built-up flat roofing or heavy clay tile, work toward increases in the weight at the top of the building and the maximizing of seismic force. Decisions to use masonry veneers, stucco, plaster, or other rigid, brittle, heavy wall materials have a double effect—increasing the building mass (and thus the seismic force) and using highly vulnerable construction in terms of potential damage.

Considerations such as these can be pushed to the point of generating a very limited palette of useable materials and a very limited set of highly simplistic architectural forms. Still, the seismic response consequences should be a part of every architectural design decision. The cost in necessary construction to obtain seismic resistance also should be considered. Seismic considerations cannot always be the major factor in design decisions, but they should not be ignored or overlooked.

The lateral bracing structure for the light wood-framed residence should be designed with the following considerations in mind:

General Form. Shear walls should be well dispersed, not all on one side of the building, not all in one direction and none in the other. A shear wall should have a reasonable aspect ratio (height-to-plan length). For limited shear deformation and better overturn resistance, the plan length preferably would exceed the height for a single-story wall. Horizontal diaphragms (roof and floor decks) should be single planes, have minimal piercing with openings, and have a reasonable aspect ratio (preferably not more than 2:1, length to width).

Continuity of the Frame. The wood frame—especially those members utilized as edges of the shear walls and horizontal diaphragms—should be developed with the least disruption. Top plates of walls should be made continuous with a lapping of the two parts of the double plate or should be spliced with bolting. In addition to serving as the edge chords of diaphragms, these function to transfer loads to all the bracing walls and to tie the whole wall system together at the top. Whatever else functions as the chords for the horizontal diaphragm should also have this type of continuity.

Anchorage and Interconnection of the Construction and Bracing. It is critical to trace the load paths through the structure. Start with every element that generates horizontal seismic force due to its impelled weight moving horizontally. As an example, how is a heavy suspended light fixture suspended? From what? What keeps it from swinging freely? How does its individual contribution to the horizontal load get to the end of the bracing chain (the ground)? Is its load contribution included in the loading for all the bracing elements involved: the fixture supports, the horizontal diaphragm, the shear walls, the shear wall supports? E*very* part of the building must be held in place, have its load added to the horizontal force on the bracing system, and, eventually, be resisted by the foundations and by the ground that supports the building. Tracing the path for just one construction item will reveal the many connections involved in this convoluted chain. If one connection fails, the chain is vulnerable.

The Individual Diaphragms.   The roof deck, floor deck, and shear wall surfacing must be adequate for the diaphragm actions required (basically in-plane shear). Board and plank decking doesn't work, unless it is placed diagonally to the supporting frame—and even then it has very limited capacity for shear resistance. It is more common to use sheets of paneling with a lot of edge nailing and field nailing (in the panel interior). The nails have to be of a type, size, and number appropriate to the paneling, to the framing, and to the seismic shear load demands. Plywood still makes the best diaphragm paneling, although it should be an industry-rated product and at least 5 ply for significant shear loading. Other materials are rated by some codes, but they are questionable for heavy seismic loading, even though the numbers may be sufficient if enough length of paneling is used. A large amount of weak material fails to produce the same resistance as a smaller amount of good structural paneling.

Building Foundations.   For seismic forces, the building base is a critical interface between the ground and the above-grade building. In reality, the ground is the source of the seismic effect on the building. Once impelled by the ground motion, however, the building is under the effect of its own momentum; and the ground—through the building base—is what may stop it from launching from the site. In any event, the anchorage of the building to its base, and the secure embedment of the base in the ground is a critical first concern. Then the foundation system must be made capable of anchoring the building; for example, it must be heavy enough and must hold itself together during the ground movement. Holding together may be relatively easy for a major below-grade basement of reinforced concrete, but isolated footings might need something extra to function as a tied-together unit, rather than having each separate footing go its own way.

The Building Site.   Individual houses sit mostly on small lots, so that site problems of a general geological nature tend to extend through more than one property. However, just about any individual building site receives some regrading, with some amount of cut and/or fill. Cuts may create some unstable slope conditions, but fills are typically the bigger problem, as is probably not considered for a single residence. Expect some movement of fills, with both vertical surface subsidence and some lateral shifting. To avoid this, a tough specification for the regrading work, inspection, and testing are needed. Even still, supported structures on fill *will* settle, unless the structures are separately supported on deep foundations that extend to undisturbed soils.

Seismic Design for Building One

Assuming the use of the general construction shown in Figure 10.2, there is good potential for developing an adequate lateral bracing system for this building. Using plywood for the roof and upper-floor surfaces and for the exterior walls is a good beginning. For major seismic resistance, however, 5-ply panels (at a minimum) should be used for the roof and wall plywood. And, of course, nailing should be provided for computed shear stresses; although minimum code-required nailing likely would be adequate for most situations. Design for these conditions is illustrated in the discussion for Building 2 in Chapter 11.

As in the simplest of buildings, however, it pays to study the structure completely to visualize all the force transfers. There are indeed some special problems here that deserve attention as the following discussions demonstrates.

Joint Between Building Masses.   Several considerations should be investigated for the connection between the two parts: the one-story living room and kitchen part and the two-level part. Foundations for the one-story part should be located well below the original grade, to assure a minimum of differential settlement between the two parts. In addition, some consideration should be given to using a supported concrete framed floor in the one-story part, instead of the usual slab on grade, as the fill will undoubtedly settle during an earthquake, taking the slab on grade with it.

Since the roof surface as shown in Figure 10.1 is continuous across the two building parts, any significant differential movement between the parts will show as a wrinkle at the connection. Therefore, it might be wise to consider a redesign of the roof, with a break in the construction, as shown in the alternative elevation in Figure 10.8. Differential settlement might still cause some cosmetic damage or rupture water seals, unless separation and flexibility is provided in the wall and roof finish construction.

Shear Walls at the South Side.   The building shown in Figure 10.1 does not provide for any useful shear walls. None of the front walls of the living room or the garage have any wide wall portions that extend to the roof. While the front wall of the upper level has a certain extent of unbroken wall surface, there is no wall in the garage beneath this wall. Furthermore, lateral resistance is not possible at the ends of the upper-level wall, as it is supported only by the short wall portions above the foundation walls.

Possible solutions here involve the use of stiff rigid frames of steel, built into the front walls of the garage or living room, or into both. Another possibility is to drag the load into the living room wall beneath the high windows. If the latter solution is chosen, care should be exercised in the design of the foundation for this wall, which ordinarily might be quite shallow and barely seated below original grade. What drags the lateral forces to the bracing wall must also be carefully designed, as routine construction probably will not perform this task.

Load Transfers in the Wood Frame.   With all the ingredients present for the parts of a lateral bracing system, ordinary light wood frame construction commonly lacks the connections that assure load transfers through the system. There is no shortcut for this in design, and all the load paths should be traced to assure this is adequately achieved. Consider the details for the two-story wall, as shown in Figure 10.2. How does the lateral load

FIGURE 10.8   Alternative roof form for Building 1.

from the roof plywood diaphragm get into the foundations? It has first to be transferred to a chord at the roof edge. Then to the second-level wall plywood. Then the first-level wall plywood must pick up the shear load from the second-level wall plus the upper-level floor. And finally, the load must be transferred from the lower-level wall into the concrete foundation wall. Ordinary connections may help with some of this, but the details as shown in Figure 10.2 simply do not provide anything at some transfer points. For example, where is the roof chord and edge collector, and how does the roof load get to the wall plywood?

Figure 10.9 shows the same wall as in Figure 10.2, stripped to its structural essentials, indicating special provisions for transfer of the shear loading from top to bottom of the wall. Variations are possible, but the load path is achieved with these details. Various metal fastening devices are also available to assist these connections.

10.4   RETROFIT OR REPAIR

Suppose that this building is date stamped with regard to codes and construction with a sufficient time gap to be way behind the current practices. We may now consider how to improve its seismic resistance. Worse yet, maybe it was *never* designed for seismic resistance, but a new owner wants to have some seismic resistance. What are the possibilities?

A first concern should be for improvement of the lateral force-resisting structure. Attention should also be given to everything else in the building that can be lost in an earthquake: water heaters, rooftop equipment, pendant light fixtures, and all of the nonstructural construction.

Generally, the small wood-framed residence has not been designed for the rigorous requirements of the full building code, no matter when it was built. Often a separate, much abbreviated code covers housing—and sometimes small buildings in general of ordinary Type V construction. Review for the building permit may be cursory and inspection during construction may be infrequent. Altogether, the integrity of the contractor and workers may be the only guarantee of correctness and quality of the work.

It is quite likely that little, if any, structural design for this particular building was performed by a highly experienced, qualified, registered structural engineer. And if it was, one day of the engineer's time probably would have used up the architect's budget for consultation.

For these reasons, assume that—unless the house was built fairly recently in a large metropolitan area in a high-risk seismic zone—it has few special provisions for earthquake resistance. What it needs first then is a comprehensive seismic bracing system. It needs shear walls. The horizontal diaphragms need to be adequately attached to the vertical bracing. If an entire side of the building is structurally open and glazed, something should be done to correct the three-sided building effect. More detailed improvements cannot be considered until the basic system is made to work.

Existing walls might work as shear walls, even though they were not considered as such when built. However, some features must either be present or must be added:

Adequate attachment of the surfacing materials (assumed to be in sheet-form)—
Minimal plywood nailing provides some resistance, but most serious plywood shear walls use bigger nails and more of them (or heavier and more extensive attachment in general, if something other than ordinary nails are used). To obtain

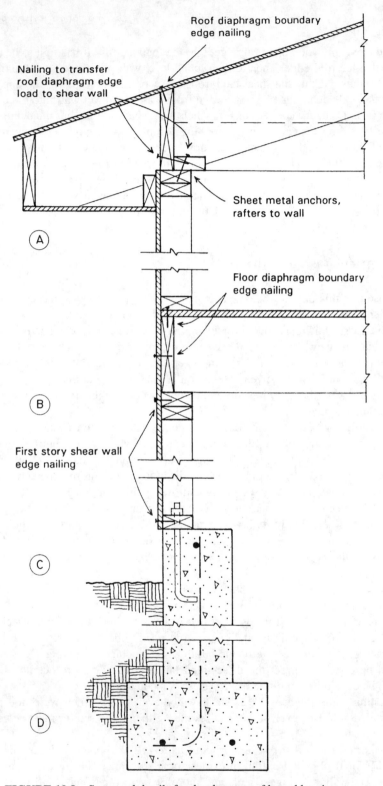

Roof diaphragm boundary
edge nailing

Nailing to transfer
roof diaphragm edge
load to shear wall

Sheet metal anchors,
rafters to wall

Ⓐ

Floor diaphragm boundary
edge nailing

Ⓑ

First story shear wall
edge nailing

Ⓒ

Ⓓ

FIGURE 10.9   Structural details for development of lateral bracing.

code-rated shear capacities, other materials—such as gypsum drywall, stucco, and wood fiber panels—must also be installed to special specifications. If existing attachment is not up to par, it will probably be necessary to replace the structural surfacing in order to qualify a wall as a shear wall.

Acceptable surfacing materials with code-rated capacity for shear wall use—Design for wind resistance may have required this consideration already. However, seismic requirements may be more stringent. Some recent experience indicates that good plywood is the only really acceptable material for a heavily loaded, wood-framed shear wall (a first-story wall in a multistory building, for example). "Good" in this regard means at least 5-ply panels.

Anchorage of shear walls for sliding and overturn at the base—Code minimum anchor bolting may resist sliding, but overturn of any significance should be resisted by load-rated tie-down anchors, bolted to the end framing of the walls and buried a lot deeper in the foundations than minimum anchor bolts. Of course, anchorage of upper-level walls in multistory construction must be achieved by other means, often by metal straps.

Aspect ratio (height-to-length) of the wall—Forget about turning an existing wall into a shear wall if it is not at least as long in plan length as it is tall. Overturn likely will be a problem and is hard for an existing wall to deal with.

Location of walls—An individual wall may otherwise be a good candidate for a shear wall, but it must be located where it is strategically useful. There needs to be a workable arrangement of walls in the building plan: some in each direction—not all on one side of the building— and not defining a three-sided condition, a soft story, or an irregular structure in general.

If a shear wall system can be developed, the availability of horizontal structures that can be utilized as horizontal diaphragms is the next concern. For two-story buildings, an upper-floor structure may be utilized if the deck material is adequate and attachments for shear transfer can be made to shear walls. With the relatively short spans of the average residential structure, the unit stresses in a floor diaphragm should be quite low, so that even a board deck may suffice. Nevertheless, after investigation, if a better deck is needed, a simple remedy is to nail plywood to the top of the old floor.

Anchorage of the horizontal diaphragms to the walls may require that the old construction be torn up to get to the floor-wall or roof-wall joints. If the exterior is to be resheathed with plywood or otherwise rebuilt, they may be attached from the outside.

Most older homes will have sloping roof surfaces, and even if existing sheathing can function for diaphragm purposes, it may be positioned at too steep an angle to be effective as a horizontal diaphragm. In this case, it may be necessary to develop a horizontal truss or other structure at the bottom-edge level of the roof—possibly above the ceiling or an attic floor. This is sometimes done with new construction when steep roofs or other conditions prevent the use of the roof surface as a diaphragm.

Existing masonry construction may well need to be replaced. Heavy veneers not properly anchored present a real problem, as do any unreinforced structural masonry walls or construction for fireplaces and chimneys. A lot of delicate rescue work has been undertaken for preservation of historic landmarks, but it is quite costly and largely unproven under earthquakes strikes. A compromise is to build a new supporting structure next to the existing masonry, and then use it to brace the old structure as well as support what the masonry used to. This is also costly, and no guarantee for the survival of the old masonry, but it probably will safeguard the rest of the building.

Foundations that are not tied sufficiently together to function as a unit during an earthquake present a tricky problem. If access is possible, this tying should be done, or the house supports may well go in different directions during an earthquake. And, even if they all move the same, the house may detach—totally or in parts.

A more difficult problem stems from the probability that the foundations were built with little or no steel reinforcement. This was quite common for the single-family house until quite recently (Figure 10.9). There is no simple retrofit solution for this situation. It may be possible to pick up the house and build a whole new foundation under it or even move it to a site with no soil liquefaction or nearby crumbling cliff.

All in all, it is relatively easy to figure out what ought to be done, but the tricky business of any remodeling work is to figure out how to get it done. Not being sure of what is actually there under the stucco and interior finishes adds a degree of speculation to the work.

One of the most difficult areas of consideration for improvement regards the vulnerability of site and foundation situations. Minor site problems, confined to the actual boundaries of the property, might be dealt with, but conditions involving the whole neighborhood can't be solved by an individual property owner. If a neighbor's house is perched on a fragile cliff directly above, it is hard to defend against. Any work done to the cliff from below may well precipitate a failure, and both properties could be lost. At the least, a cooperative solution must be developed involving both property owners and more likely, the whole neighborhood or community should be consulted.

Any building foundation is subject to so many possible failures that it is hard to know where to start improving. If the supporting ground is the problem, that must be addressed first with the help of a qualified geotechnical engineer. The best course may be to pursue some ground modification (see Section 6.5), which could result in a significant reduction of problems for the foundation construction. If the foundation is the essential problem, no simple, inexpensive solutions are generally available. Cost feasibility must be determined early on, before remedial design is carried very far. Jacking the house up and off the foundation and replacing the foundation completely is possible, but the owner has to want the house very much to pay for it.

10.5 OPTIMAL DESIGN

Ideally, the best design achievable avoids all the bad scenarios and eliminates any need for retrofit actions. As we discussed in Chapter 6, the first stage of such a design process should be a consideration of all the mitigation efforts that are possible, thus reducing the *need* for seismic response of any construction to a minimum. After that a clear set of realistic goals should be established for the design that is based on both the owner's and designer's aspirations and expectations.

The Site

Of course, a first consideration should be whether to use the site at all, if it presents an extreme case of seismic hazard. If the decision to build on the site is unshakeable, then the design should avoid aggravating any current risks, possibly developing both the site and the building to reduce risks that can be affected by design decisions.

A major goal is to avoid creating thick layers of fill on top of the site surface. This is often unavoidable because of the need to raise the site level in general, to replace undesirable soils, or for other reasons. Still, movement and general consolidation of fill is to be expected in a major seismic event, with unavoidable site surface failures—major or minor. At particular risk, structures placed on fill, including site walls, retaining walls, and pavements, are certain to move when the site surface is readjusted by the earthquake.

If precipitous slopes exist, it may be possible to improve the situation by regrading or by using of construction to retain them. The building itself may be used for this purpose in some situations. Above all, avoid creating new precipitous situations, either by cutting the present surface or by grading fill.

The design should not create situations in which a sequence of failures can be triggered by a relatively minor site fault (Figure 2.15). It might be advisable to create some redundancy in the site bracing systems, with backup elements capable of functioning if others fail.

Adopt a defensive position with regard to neighboring properties. The design should protect from the down-slope movements of up-slope neighbors by stabilizing the slope, if possible. The down-slope edge of the property should be secured from sliding onto a down-slope neighbor.

Be sure that the discovery process for information about the site is as complete as possible regarding seismic risk. This should be accomplished largely before any design work is done. It should also be an ongoing process, however, as both the design and construction work are sure to create or discover new considerations. A late design decision to use deep foundations, for instance, would probably require more information about deep soil deposits. Almost every construction project that involves deep excavation or major cuts of the site surface produces some surprises about true subgrade conditions.

For Building 1, some of these considerations affected the decisions for site development and placement of the building. Site edges have been somewhat protected by site wall construction. Whenever possible, site construction (except for some pavements) has been seated below the original site grade. Where they are placed on considerable fill, the concrete pavement slabs for building floors have been structurally supported. Not apparent in the drawings are provisions made in specifications or contracts for consolidation of fill materials on the site surface. Also, the paving floor slabs are frequently relied on to stabilize foundation walls that they join, and the details for tying them to the walls should be developed.

The Building

For the building, the designer should first consider the potential constraints indicated by site conditions. This includes many of the issues just mentioned for the site, as well as any potential for building-site interactions caused by the fundamental period of the site and any special conditions such as a liquefiable soil. These may affect the general planning of the building as well as the design of the lateral bracing system.

The building shown in Figure 10.1 is multimassed, and some consideration might be given to reducing the resulting interactions by rethinking the building's basic form. For this small building, it is probably quite feasible to avoid this problem by careful detailing of the construction to tie the separate masses together (mainly at the link between the one-story and two-story parts).

One modification that might be considered is dropping the level of the floor in the one-story part. This could eliminate the need for the structurally supported floor and reduce the extent of retaining structures at the front of the house. But to do so would mean lowering the level of the backyard and increasing the height of the retaining structures at the rear of the site.

Another design modification would be to improve the front shear wall by eliminating the living room windows at the front of the house.

11

Single-Story Commercial Building

Building 2 is a simple box: A single-story, flat roofed, rectangular building. Problems of this basic building form and usage, and construction with three alternative systems, are examined in this chapter.

11.1 SCHEME 1: WOOD FRAME STRUCTURE

The general configuration of the building and some details for an all-wood building are shown in Figures 11.1 and 11.2. As shown in Figure 11.2, the construction for Scheme 1 uses the same basic light wood frame as Building 1 in Chapter 10. Many of the comments made for Building 1 regarding the general nature, seismic response, and problems of design of the basic system also apply here. We will concentrate on the development of this basic building form and the two major elements of its lateral bracing system: the large, single roof diaphragm and the perimeter, exterior shear walls.

For the basic construction, the following is assumed:

Roofing: built-up, 6.5 psf.

Suspended ceiling: framing + finish, 10 psf.

Roof insulation, lights, ducts, and so on, 5 psf.

Exterior walls: stucco outside, drywall inside, 20 psf.

Interior nonstructural walls: drywall, 8 psf.

An all-air HVAC system is employed, using rooftop equipment with ducts and registers in the ceiling space. Roof drainage is accomplished by sloping the surface to the rear of the building (north side) and draining to scuppers in the wall parapet at the roof edge.

The structural surface of the roof is developed with plywood panels, which are also utilized as the horizontal diaphragm for the bracing system. Various roof spanning structures are possible, depending on the need for a clear span or whether interior supports are used.

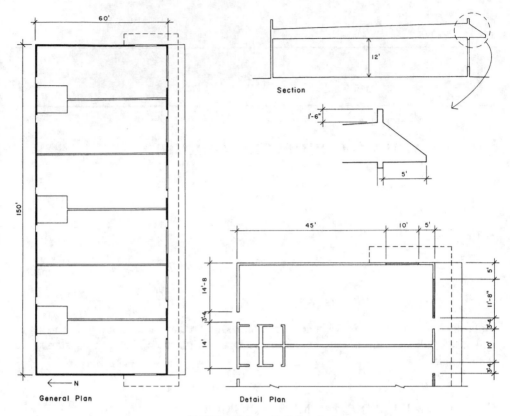

FIGURE 11.1   Building 2.

The 60-ft span in this case can easily be achieved as a clear span with steel open web joists or composite wood and steel joist/trusses. The interior walls are not necessarily permanent, although the building plan as shown suggests the logic of their use. The roof support system is shown in Figure 11.3, with two rows of interior columns placed at the locations of the separating partition walls.

11.2   SEISMIC RESPONSE OF THE WOOD STRUCTURE

As typically constituted, the light wood frame structure with structural surfacing on its roof and exterior walls has considerable natural potential for resistance to earthquake forces. The simple box in this example has only a few components in its lateral bracing structure, and their actions and interactions are quite direct and easy to visualize. However, failures can result from a number of shortcomings. We discuss these possibilities by considering the major areas relating to response.

The Roof Diaphragm

The major function of the roof for lateral bracing is to collect the combined lateral forces in the upper part of the building and distribute the load to the various elements of the vertical bracing system. This involves considerations for the following issues.

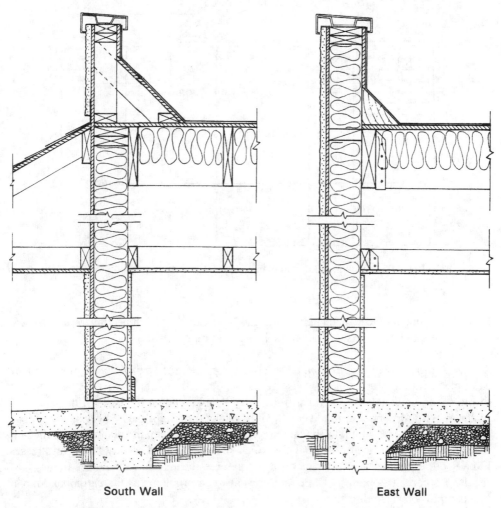

South Wall   East Wall

FIGURE 11.2   Building 2: Construction details for the wood structure.

Diaphragm Shear.   The beam action shear in the diaphragm surface must be resisted by the structural surfacing of the roof. The material of the units of the roof deck must be adequate for this, although a more critical concern often is the jointing of the units to achieve a continuous structural element for the diaphragm.

Diaphragm Chord.   Something at the diaphragm edge must serve as the moment-resisting flange or chord of the diaphragm. The chord must be capable of both compression and tension as the seismic forces reverse direction. Tension continuity is often a problem, as a single piece is seldom used for the entire length of a chord. In fact, the continuity of the chord may be difficult to achieve if the walls are not straight, roof levels change, openings exist at the roof edge, and so on.

Anchorage and Load Transfer.   The roof diaphragm must be adequately connected to the supporting walls in order to transfer the lateral loads to the shear walls and, possibly, to anchor the roof against separation from the walls. Ordinary details for the light wood

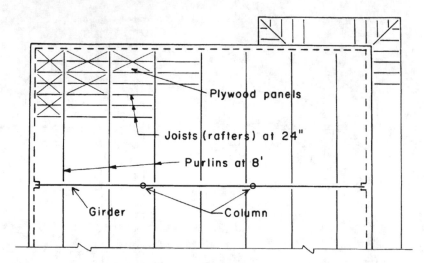

FIGURE 11.3   Building 2: Partial plan of roof framing for the wood roof structure.

frame may not provide adequately for these load transfers. Connecting rafters to wall plates with toenails is not adequate for seismic load transfer.

Aspect Ratio of the Diaphragm.   Generally, for a single-span diaphragm (as in this example, without interior shear walls), a reasonable stiffness must exist for development of the spanning action. A general stiffness may be assumed on the basis of the roof deck material (stiff if concrete; relatively flexible if wood or light gage sheet steel) and the aspect ratio (span-to-width) of the diaphragm. It is wise to keep the diaphragm in the general class of a deep beam, so the deflection will be generated mostly by shear stresses. Excess deflection may affect supporting structures during an earthquake. It may also result in a certain floppiness that could present extra problems as the earthquake movements rapidly reverse direction.

Horizontal Orientation of the Diaphragm.   In order to handle horizontal forces, the roof diaphragm should be in a reasonably flat (horizontal) plane. As the roof slope increases, the surface becomes increasingly less effective for action as a horizontal diaphragm, and other systems may be required to function for the horizontal structure of the bracing system. If these do not exist, there may be no real horizontal element in the bracing system.

Shear Walls

Shear walls are often utilized as bearing walls as well. In any event, they are building walls and have many architectural functions. For this discussion, however, their primary function is as members of the lateral bracing system; receiving lateral loads from above and transferring them to lower supports.

Orientation to Lateral Loads.   As relatively thin planar elements, shear walls function only to resist forces parallel to the wall surface. Out-of-plane forces may be resolved by other actions, but the shear wall function relates only to a set of forces in a single direction.

Orientation in Building Plan.   To resolve horizontal forces from any direction, the shear walls must have their planes aimed in differing directions. In addition, they must be dispersed in the building plan—not be on only one side of the building, for example.

Aspect Ratio.   As with the horizontal diaphragm, shear walls should be reasonably stiff. They must resist overturning (toppling) effects without requiring major development of resisting moments and uplift anchorage at their bases. These concerns relate to limiting ratios of height-to-plan length of the walls. If they are too tall and skinny, they may work as columns, but no longer work as walls. Codes usually provide upper limits for aspect ratios relating to the materials of the wall construction; however, at those limits, deflection is likely to be critical.

Chords.   At wall ends, there must be some elements that function as the moment-resisting chords. This may be achieved by strengthening the wall ends (for example, doubled studs or a post located in a wood wall), or by attaching the wall ends to a major vertical structure (for example, a building column). Resistance to overturn is usually developed by anchoring of the chord.

Shear Capacity.   As with the horizontal diaphragm, the wall surfacing material and the joints between separate surfacing units must resist the diaphragm shear. This includes the diagonal tension and diagonal compression effects. Tension produces X-shaped cracking in concrete, masonry, and stucco. Compression produces buckling in thin sheets of plywood. With very thin wall sheathing and widely spaced wall stud framing, this may well be a problem. Additionally, the usual 48 x 96-in. plywood panels must be adequately nailed at studs in the center portion of the sheets, not just at panel edges. Finally, the wood frame must help in transferring forces from wall panel to wall panel. Thin, low-grade studs, with a lot of closely spaced panel nails and extensive holes or notches cut for buried wiring or piping, may represent a weak link in the continuity of the shear wall surface.

Anchorage for Sliding and Overturn.   Shear walls are transfer devices, receiving loads from the structures attached to them and delivering them to wall supports. The total horizontal force on a wall must be transferred out by something that resists the horizontal sliding of the wall. Typically, in the wood frame, this is the attachment of the wall sill plate to its supports. Foundation supports require anchor bolts cast into the concrete or masonry. Overcutting the bolt holes in the sill (a common practice) can make this less than a firm attachment. For overturn resistance, tension anchorage is usually achieved between the wall ends and whatever serves as the diaphragm chord. Over time, bolts may loosen due to shrinkage of the wood or they may rust away if the bolt diameters are too small. Oversized holes can allow bolts to slip vertically, as the nut and washer sink into the sill hole.

Openings.   Openings reduce diaphragm strength. Size and placement of openings for windows or doors can seriously affect the development of shear walls as fracture of the wall can occur at opening edges or corners. For the wood framed wall, the articulation of framing may be critical for resistance to these effects. The wall can separate into units defined by the pattern of openings.

Intersecting Walls.   For all buildings, intersecting walls pose problems. This is mostly seen in their failure at outside building corners (Figure 10.5). Although walls have great lateral strength in their own planes they have very little in the perpendicular direction. When walls interact in the perpendicular, they can work on each other's weak aspect and the joint between them can fail. This is a more common problem with concrete and masonry walls, but wood framed walls might experience problems too.

Foundations

The total lateral force on the building must be transferred to the ground through the building foundation. However, the forces may be applied at isolated locations, being directly transferred by the vertical bracing elements. Thus, unless it is sufficiently tied together, the lateral force may not be shared well by the whole foundation system. Most critical are overturning effects of isolated shear walls, which tend to be highly concentrated. Of course, foundation failures may also originate from failures of the supporting site. Older foundations, mostly built without steel reinforcement, have little capacity to resist concentrated force effects or the movement of supporting soils.

General Building Form

As we discussed in Chapter 4, many aspects of a building's response to earthquakes may be derived from the form and dimensions of the building. The aspect ratios of the roof diaphragm and of the individual shear walls derive from this source.

Overturn of the Building.   For tall buildings, overturn of the building as a whole is a critical concern. This relates to the aspect ratio of the building, involving its total height (h) and its plan width (w) at the base. If the $h{:}w$ ratio is more than 2, and the building weight is relatively low, the overturn may require anchorage at the building edges. However, when a building is braced by individual vertical elements (shear walls or trussed towers), the $h{:}w$ ratio of the bracing elements is the concern.

As the building section drawing in Figure 11.1 reveals, Building 1 is quite low in its vertical profile and aspect ratio of $h{:}w$ (approximately 0.3), so the building as a whole is not at risk for overturn. However, the individual shear walls must be investigated for this problem, which is part of the routine design procedure illustrated in the next section.

Irregular Shape.   Of the many potential problems regarding irregular form (see the discussion in Section 4.3), the one most likely to be critical for this building is the case of the open side. If any of the exterior sides of the building are constructed to have little or no shear wall bracing, there may be any of several types of problems. Three common conditions are shown in Figure 11.4. For the plan shown in Figure 11.1, the most likely condition is that of the three-sided effect because of the large number of openings in the south side.

Possible failures resulting from the three-sided condition include in-plane shear failure of the open wall, twisting of the whole building with rupture of various points of connection between the walls and roof (Figures 11.5 and 11.6), or failure of other shear walls as they take up the resistance effort not developed by the south wall.

Of course, if the building is not of the simple box shape in this example, there may well be other problems, which we address in later chapters. Despite its simple form, the possibilities for failure of this type of structure are considerable. Precisely because of its simple construction, inspection of the construction work is likely to be somewhat relaxed, with greater reliance on the integrity of the contractors and workers.

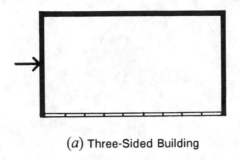

(*a*) Three-Sided Building

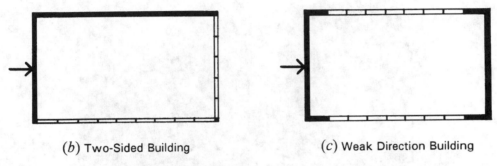

(*b*) Two-Sided Building   (*c*) Weak Direction Building

FIGURE 11.4   Effects of open sides on seismic design.

11.3   DESIGN OF THE WOOD STRUCTURE

Resisting seismic forces on Building 2 involves the following:

1 Design of the roof diaphragm for forces in both directions
2. Design of the shear walls
3. Design of the various construction details for transfer of forces from the roof to the shear walls and for transfer of the forces from the shear walls to the foundations
4. Design of the foundations for the various effects of the shear walls: horizontal force, uplift, and overturning
5. Concerns for the nonstructural parts of the construction and for the building service elements

Identifying the walls to be used as shear walls is a critical preliminary decision. Considered in this decision are the following:

1. The magnitude of total force in each direction that the resisting walls in that direction must respond to; a quick estimate of the required total wall length can be made based on the capacity of the chosen form of wall.
2. Identification of walls that lend themselves to being used as shear walls; this concerns their plan location, their orientation to the load direction, their aspect

FIGURE 11.5   A classic corner failure in masonry construction.

ratio (height:plan length), their construction, and the means for getting load to them from the roof diaphragm.

3. Type of structural surfacing (sheathing) to be used for the individual walls; this will affect their shear capacity, their limiting aspect ratio, and their relative stiffness.

Gypsum drywall will be used for all interior wall surfaces and stucco (cement plaster), for all exterior walls. For exterior walls, the stiffer stucco might be used to determine shear capacity. However, our example uses plywood sheathing under the stucco as the shear-resisting material. If interior walls are used as shear walls, and the sheathing is the same on both sides of the wall, the two surface resistances are added together. When the sheathing is different on the two sides, however, only the stiffer material is used for design capacity.

Figure 11.7 shows a proposed layout for the shear walls. For loads in the north-south direction, with no interior shear walls, the roof spans the building end to end, and is braced only by the two 45-ft-long end shear walls. For loads in the east-west direction, the shear wall system is asymmetrical, with five 10-ft-long walls on the south side and the

FIGURE 11.6 Extreme movement of the three-sided building can cause various damage to the building, including a lot of nonstructural damage. Here, the end bay of the roofing was collapsed by the movement

whole wall length minus only the narrow door openings on the north side (considered a net plan length of 130 ft).

Design of the Roof Diaphragm

The lateral seismic force that affects the roof diaphragm derives from the weight of the roof, plus everything attached to the roof (for example, the suspended ceiling and canopy), plus the upper portion of the walls. In each direction, the wall loads are only those of the walls perpendicular to the load direction. Walls parallel to the load direction are stiff enough to brace themselves.

Table 11.1 summarizes the computations for the seismic lateral load to the roof diaphragm. Weights are based on the construction described in Section 11.1. The spanning action of the exterior walls is shown in Figure 11.8, with lateral loads perpendicular to the wall. With the actions and dimensions shown in Figure 11.8, the load of the upper portion of exterior walls is based on 10.5 ft (7.5 + 3) of wall height. Although openings occur in the walls, they are mostly in the lower portions of the walls; thus, the upper portions are considered to be all solid for the load computation. Interior walls are assumed to span from the floor to the underside of the roof. Because of the difference of wall loads in each direction, separate tabulations are made for the north-south and the east-west direction loads.

In addition to the total direct force in each direction, there may be torsional twisting of the building because of the location of loads or the layout of the shear walls. For this building, the plans indicate a reasonable symmetry for both the shear walls and the general building construction with regard to force in the north-south direction. In the east-west direction, however, there is an asymmetrical shear wall layout and the canopy on the south side. The toilet rooms along the north wall represent asymmetrical construction elements. Some investigation should be made for the effects of torsion, although this will most affect the shear walls.

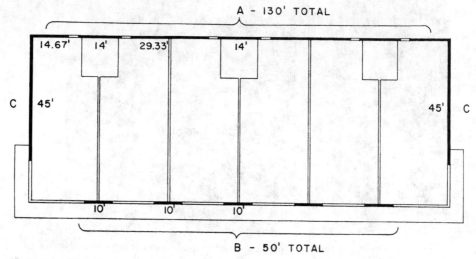

A - 130' TOTAL

14.67' | 14' | 29.33' | 14'

C | 45' | | | 45' | C

10' | 10' | 10'

B - 50' TOTAL

THE SHEAR WALL SYSTEM

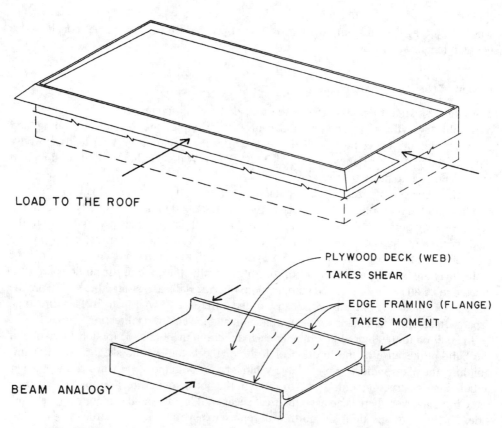

LOAD TO THE ROOF

PLYWOOD DECK (WEB)
TAKES SHEAR

EDGE FRAMING (FLANGE)
TAKES MOMENT

BEAM ANALOGY

FIGURE 11.7   Building 2: Development of the wood system for lateral resistance.

TABLE 11.1   Loads to the Roof Diaphragm

Load Source and Calculation	Loads (kips)	
	N-S	E-W
Roof dead load:	243.0	243.0
150 × 60 × 27 psf		
East and west exterior walls:	0.0	20.2
60 × 10.5 × 16 psf × 2		
North and south exterior walls:	50.4	0.0
150 × 10.5 × 16 × 2		
Interior dividing walls:	0.0	17.6
1/2 × 58 × 15 × 8 psf × 5		
Toilet walls:	12.0	12.0
1/2 × 200 × 15 × 8psf		
Canopy:	19.0	19.0
190 ft × 100 lb/ft		
Rooftop HVAC units (estimate)	5.0	5.0
Total load (W for seismic calculation)	329.4	316.6

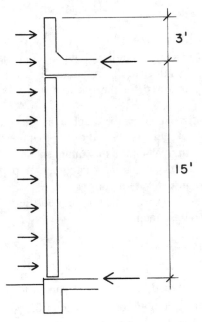

FIGURE 11.8   Assumed action of the exterior wall in resisting lateral force perpendicular to the wall plane.

Using the *UBC* equivalent static load method, the total lateral seismic force is determined as a percentage of the dead load of the building weight. Thus,

$$V = (x\%)(W)$$

The value of x is determined by using all the code-required variables based on seismic risk zones, building form, type of lateral bracing, and so on, as we discussed in Section

2.2. A full explanation of this process, even for this simple building, would require a whole book the size of this one. Such books are available, but the process and variables will change at least four times in the next ten years, so we have decided to bypass it and assume a reasonable value for x so that we can shortcut the process here and move on to illustrate the analysis. Assume x equals 0.14 (14%). Thus,

$$V = 0.14W$$

Using the loads from Table 11.1, the seismic loads to the roof diaphragm are determined as

$$V = 0.14(329.4) = 46.1 \text{ kips in the N-S direction}$$
$$V = 0.14(316.8) = 44.4 \text{ kips in the E-W direction}$$

Ignoring torsion, the maximum shear in the diaphragm at the east and west ends is one-half of 46.1, or 23.05 kips. Using the full diaphragm width of 60 ft, the unit shear in the plywood is

$$v = \frac{23,050}{60} = 384 \text{ lb/ft}$$

This value may be used for selection of the plywood and its nailing, although an investigation for torsion might add slightly to this required shear capacity. A minimum of 1/2-in.-thick plywood is usually required for the flat roof and this shear load is within that range.

If the load is uniformly distributed to the diaphragm, the shear diagram for the spanning diaphragm is as shown in Figure 11.9a, indicating that the shear decreases in value to zero at the center of the building. When the maximum shear at the end is high (as it often is with no interior shear walls), the nailing in the center portions of the roof can be decreased to the minimum required code nailing.

In addition to the thickness, there are many other considerations to determine the plywood deck's shear capacity. These include

1. Grade of the plywood panels
2. Layout of the plywood panels on the framing
3. Presence or lack of solid wood blocking at all panel joints
4. Grade and thickness of framing used for nailing of the panels
5. Type, size, and spacing of the nails

The example in Figure 11.9 uses values obtained from a table in the *UBC*. Values are shown for various nail spacings for different areas of the roof.

Of course, the plywood must also function adequately for gravity loading and for its construction functions. Choice of the plywood panels and their complete specification for installation must reflect all of these concerns.

The edge chords for the diaphragm must resist the simple beam bending moment, determined as

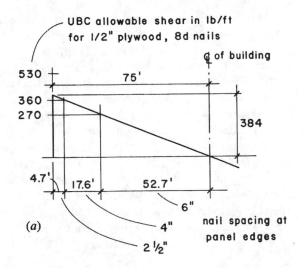

(a)

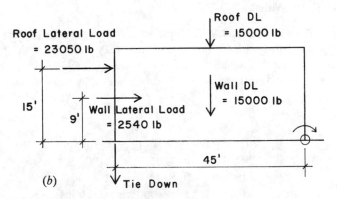

(b)

FIGURE 11.9 Investigation of the basic components of the lateral resistive system: (a) Zoned nailing for the roof diaphragm, (b) stability of the end shear wall.

$$M = \frac{WL}{8}$$

and the chord force is determined as

$$T \text{ or } C = \frac{M}{d}$$

where d is the diaphragm width.

Using the values determined for the example

$$M = \frac{(46,100)(150)}{8} = 864,375 \text{ ft-lb}$$

and

$$T = C = \frac{864,375}{60} = 14,400 \text{ lb}$$

This force is used as both a tension force and a compression force for design of whatever functions as the diaphragm chord. For tension, a concern might be for a net section reduced by bolt holes, if bolting is used to achieve continuity for the 150-ft-long member.

For compression, bracing for lateral buckling is a concern. Development of the entire roof-to-wall construction joint must be completed before a chord can be identified (or created, if the construction does not automatically present a candidate).

Shear stress in the diaphragm is much lower due to force in the east-west direction, so the roof plywood design is likely to be developed on the basis of the north-south load. A possible concern, however, is how the load is to be collected at the diaphragm edges and transferred to the shear walls. This is especially critical at the south wall, where only 50 ft of shear wall is present along the 150-ft-long edge. Some part of the wood framing at this location must be made to function as a collector and a drag-strut, collecting the roof edge nailing and pushing and pulling the shear walls. At the building ends, there must be a similar element over the windows, as only 45 ft of the 60-ft-long roof edge is engaged directly by the shear walls.

Design of the Shear Walls

The east and west shear walls carry the shear forces from the roof diaphragm—the maximum shear indicated in Figure 11.9a. In addition, they must resist the full force of the wall weight in the plane of the shear wall, which was not included in the diaphragm load (Table 11.1). So, the end walls resist the load of 23.05 kips from the roof—plus the following:

Wall weight:

$$20 \text{ psf} \times 17 \text{ ft} \times 45 \text{ ft} = 15,300 \text{ lb}$$
$$20 \text{ psf} \times 7 \text{ ft} \times 15 \text{ ft} = 2,100$$
$$5 \text{ psf} \times 10 \text{ ft} \times 15 \text{ ft} = 750$$
$$\text{Total} = 18,150 \text{ lb}$$

Lateral load:

$$0.14 \, W = 0.14(18,150) = 2,540 \text{ lb}$$

The loading of the end shear wall is as shown in Figure 11.9b. The total shear force is 25,590 lb and the unit shear force in the wall is

$$v = \frac{25,590}{45} = 569 \text{ lb/ft}$$

While the shear stress in the roof diaphragm varies, this stress is relatively constant from top of the wall to bottom. As with the roof, the choice of plywood relates to other wall functions. For regions of high seismic risk it is recommended that a minimum of 5-ply plywood be selected; this is ordinary for $1/2$-in. plywood, but requires special specification for $3/8$-in. plywood.

For overturn, the usual procedure is to investigate for the relationship between the overturning moment and the stabilizing moment produced by dead loads. In this case, dead load consists of the wall weight and whatever portion of the roof dead load is carried by the wall. The *UBC* requires that only 85% of this dead load be used for the overturn investigation. If the stabilizing moment does not produce an adequate safety factor (usually 1.5) against the wall tipping, some form of anchorage must be used.

In this example, there are two sources of anchorage at the wall ends created by the construction. At the building corner, the two abutting walls are connected through their nailing to the corner framing. Thus, neither wall can be lifted without lifting the other wall—which should provide adequate anchorage. At the other end of the wall, the header beam over the window is supported by a post in the shear wall end—which should provide considerable concentrated dead load.

Regardless of this natural anchorage of the wall, many designers prefer to provide foundation ties at the wall ends for such a heavily loaded shear wall. However, unless dead loads are ignored, there is no real basis for computations of required loads for any tie-down anchors.

Another concern is for the wall's horizontal sliding—that is, the sliding of the sill plate on top of the wall foundation. Ignoring friction, this requires that the anchor bolts for the sill resist the total horizontal force of 25,590 lb. This requires much heavier bolting than that required by the building code for minimum attachment of wood sills.

In the east-west direction, there is a lack of symmetry in the disposition of the shear walls (the north and south walls). There are two approaches to the analysis for the seismic forces on these walls—by peripheral distribution and by torsional effect.

Analysis by Peripheral Distribution   In this analysis, the roof acts as a simple beam and thus one-half of the total lateral load is delivered to each wall, regardless of the relative stiffnesses of the walls. Thus, the shear stresses in the walls are determined as the load (one-half of the total) divided by the total wall length for each wall.

For the north wall:

$$v = \frac{22,200}{130} = 171 \text{ lb/ft}$$

For the south wall:

$$v = \frac{22,200}{50} = 444 \text{ lb/ft}$$

This is the procedure that usually is used with the relatively flexible wood-framed diaphragm.

Analysis by Torsional Effect.   In this analysis, the walls are considered in terms of their relative stiffness, with the stiffness of the plywood walls considered proportionate to their plan lengths. Stress in a single wall is considered to be the combination of a direct stress (total lateral force divided by the sum of stiffnesses of all the walls parallel to the direction of the force) plus a torsional stress as determined by an analysis that includes the effects of all the building perimeter walls. The following procedure demonstrates this analysis for Building 2.

For the direct stress:

$$v = \frac{44,400}{180} = 247 \text{ lb/ft}$$

For the torsional analysis, it is necessary to determine the center of stiffness of the shear wall system (*c.s.* in Figure 11.10). This can be done by a static moment summation that uses each wall as a force proportionate to its length. Since the system is symmetrical on one axis, the problem is to find the location of the center of stiffness in the north-south direction. This involves only the north and south walls and the location may be computed in the following manner.

The sum of the moments of the walls about the north wall is

$$M = (\text{length of south walls}) \times (\text{distance of south wall from north wall})$$

$$M = (50)(60) = 3000 \text{ ft}^2$$

The location of *c.s.* is this moment divided by the sum of the north and south wall lengths:

$$y = \frac{3000}{180} = 16.67 \text{ ft}$$

as shown in Figure 11.10.

The torsional moment of inertia (*J*) is determined by multiplying each shear wall length by the square of its distance from the center of stiffness (*c.s.*). This computation is shown in Table 11.2 and torsional shear in each wall is determined from the torsional shear stress formula as

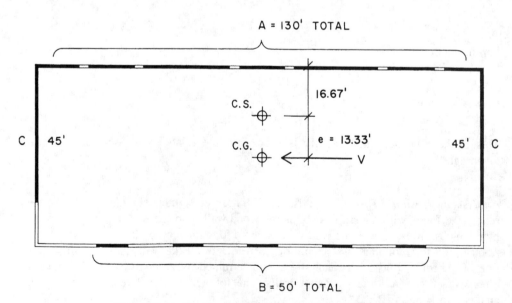

FIGURE 11.10   Torsion due to the east-west seismic load.

TABLE 11.2   Torsional Moment of Inertia of the Shear Walls

Wall	Length (Ft)	Distance from Center of Stiffness (ft)	$J = L(d)^2$
A	130	16.67	36,126
B	50	43.33	93,874
C	2(45)	75.00	506,250
Total J for the shear walls			636,250

$$v = \frac{Tc}{J}$$

in which:

T = the torsional moment, computed as the lateral force times the distance from the center of gravity to the center of stiffness of the walls
c = the distance from the wall for which the stress is being computed to c.s.
J = the torsional moment of inertia

For the south walls, the computation is

$$v = \frac{[44,400(13.33)](43.33)}{636,250} = 40 \text{ lb/ft}$$

and the total shear stress in the south walls is thus

$$v = 247 + 40 = 287 \text{ lb/ft}$$

In theory, the torsional shear stress is negative for the north walls; that is, the total stress is the direct shear minus the torsional shear. However, the usual practice is not to deduct but only to add torsional effects.

In fact, for a conservative design, the stress determined by peripheral distribution can be used for the south wall and the stress determined by torsional analysis used for the north wall. If this is done, the stresses for design are

$$v = 444 \text{ lb/ft for the south wall}$$
$$v = 247 \text{ lb/ft for the north wall}$$

These values are both within reason for the plywood walls with ordinary construction. Sliding and overturn should be investigated to determine the form of connection between the wall and its foundations. As with the end walls, minimum code-required anchor bolts are not adequate, so either heavier bolts or closer spacing is required. The investigation for overturn of the south wall is illustrated in Figure 11.11. The lateral force from the roof is applied at the level of the roof deck. The lateral force developed by the wall weight is applied at mid-height of the wall. The vertical dead load centered on the wall is a combi-

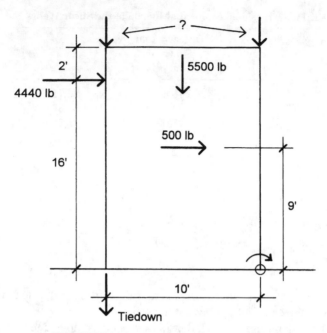

FIGURE 11.11   Overturn of the south shear walls.

nation of the wall weight and the weight of the portion of the canopy at the wall. Using these values, the overturn investigation follows.

Overturning moment, with a safety factor of 1.5:

$$M = 1.5[(4,440\ (16) + (500\ (9)] = 113,310 \text{ ft-lb}$$

Restoring moment due to dead loads (at 85% per the *UBC*):

$$M = 0.85(5,500 \times 5) = 23,375 \text{ ft-lb}$$

This leaves a discrepancy of $113,310 - 23,375 = 89,935$ ft-lb of moment that must be resisted by anchorage of the ends of the walls. If accomplished entirely by an end tie-down anchor, the required ultimate resistance of the anchor is

$$T = \frac{89,935}{10} = 8,994 \text{ lb}$$

However, the window headers are supported on the ends of these walls, which will supply some part of the anchoring force. Also, depending on the roof framing layout, some portion of the roof dead load will be carried by both the wall and the headers. So, it is possible that no anchorage is required. For this relatively tall and slender wall pier (aspect ratio of 1.6), however, some end anchorage is advisable, even if computations show otherwise.

An additional concern is the effect this relatively large force as a concentrated effect will have on the shear wall foundation. Assuming a continuous grade beam for the whole south wall, the issue is as we discussed in Sections 2.9 3.10 and 8.4. A relatively large-grade beam foundation may be adequate for shear, but top and bottom reinforcement for flexure is advised.

Effectiveness of the Bracing System

It should be noted that the bracing system described here is commonly used, but that it has some features that are currently not favored by the codes. One of these features has to do with the lack of redundancy in the system for north-south loading. Resistance to this loading depends on the two end shear walls. If one fails, there is no backup—that is, there is no redundancy in the system.

To comply with the requirements of the 1997 *UBC*, it might be necessary to use a magnification factor for this loading. The higher load required will create a different form of redundancy by building extra strength (redundant strength) into the single wall. The code prefers to have multiple elements in the load path, so that others can back up the failure of any single element. The use of a dual bracing system on the end walls (steel rigid frame plus the plywood shear wall, acting in tandem) would eliminate the required magnification factor for lack of redundancy. In fact, the design load would actually be *reduced*, since the code allows a reduced load with the dual system versus a shear wall system alone.

Construction Details for the Wood Structure

The drawings that follow show some details of the wood structure. These drawings show only the basic construction of the structure and so are not complete with regard to the entire building construction. Fairly equivalent alternatives exist for many of these details. Choosing among the alternatives requires an understanding of all the factors affecting the parts and the whole. Thus, the complete building design involving architectural finishes, lighting, HVAC, and sound control, for example, conditions decisions about the structure as well.

Structural Plans.   The details shown in Figures 11.12 and 11.13 illustrate a roof system with ordinary rafter framing and interior columns. A system using clear-spanning trusses for the roof would produce different details for the wall-to-roof connections. Foundation and roof-framing layouts are shown in the partial plans in Figure 11.3.

Detail A (Figure 11.12).   This shows the top of the shear wall and the edge of the roof at the south wall, together with the canopy and the parapet. Depending on the height of the parapet, the level of the roof, and the top of the canopy, there may be better alternatives. For instance, it might be advisable to extend the wall studs from below, all the way to the top of the parapet; this would allow the top of the canopy to extend above the roof level. As shown, the canopy is anchored to the roof edge and the parapet is a short stud wall built on top of the lower wall and the roof. If the parapet wall is more than a few feet high, it must be braced with external diagonal members carried back to the roof surface. As shown here, the diagonal braces are used to support the roof deck that makes the transition from the horizontal to the vertical for the roofing.

In the detail shown, both the roof deck and the wall sheathing are nailed to the top plate of the shear wall. This achieves a very smooth flow of forces from the horizontal

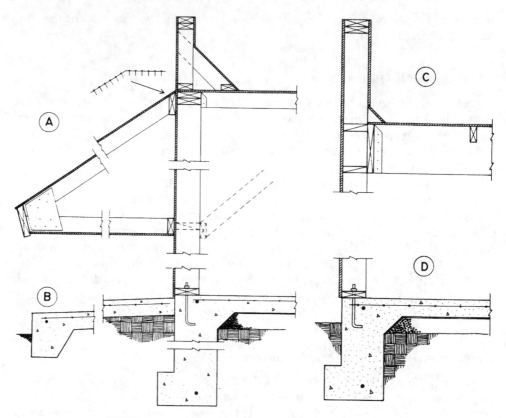

FIGURE 11.12   Construction details for the wood structure.

diaphragm (roof deck) to the shear wall. If the wall studs are continuous to the top of the parapet, a different load transfer situation occurs; this is described in Detail *C*.

The diagonal framing member for the canopy must be anchored for tension at the wall. Since this occurs at the same level as the roof deck, this can be done with strap anchors as shown in the drawing, but this requires aligning the canopy rafters and the building roof rafters. To avoid this, the anchor could be attached to the wall plates alone. Also, the lateral seismic load of the canopy parallel to the wall must be transferred to the wall at this point. The ledger must be nailed to the studs to accept this loading.

Another concern regarding the canopy involves the detail where the horizontal canopy -framing member attaches to the wall studs. This attachment—and the wall studs—must be designed for the gravity load cantilever force and the lateral load of the canopy perpendicular to the wall. As the drawing indicates, consideration might be given to the use of a kick-brace from the wall stud to the roof framing at this location to help brace the tall studs.

Detail B (Figure 11.12).   The details of the wall footing, grade wall, and floor slab are subject to considerable variation here. The detail as shown indicates a relatively shallow, single-piece member forming simultaneously (by a single concrete pour) the footing, grade wall, and floor slab edge. This member is then constituted as a grade beam with flexural reinforcement in its top and bottom. With the wall consisting of alternating shear wall piers and open areas for doors and windows, this continuous flexural member can

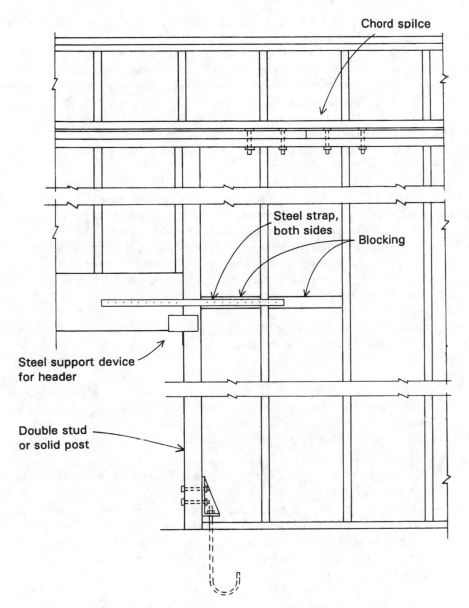

Chord spilce

Steel strap,
both sides

Blocking

Steel support device
for header

Double stud
or solid post

FIGURE 11.13   Partial elevation of the wall framing.

span across the openings and take the bending represented by the overturn on the shear walls. Although it is possible to pour the floor slab, foundation wall, and footing all at once, it is not common practice. The slab should be tied to the foundation wall to provide lateral support for the foundation.

Detail C (Figure 11.12).   This shows the condition at the east and west walls, where the level of the roof deck changes as the roof surface pitches toward the rear of the building. If the same detail as in *A* is used here, the top plates of the shear wall would have to be sloped and the studs all cut to different lengths. A simpler construction consists of running all the studs to the top of the parapet and supporting the roof edge on a ledger that is attached to the face of the wall studs.

The lateral forces must be transferred from the roof deck to the ledger and then from the ledger to the wall plywood sheathing. Since the wall sheathing is not directly attached to the ledger, some means must be established to connect the ledger to the studs and then to help the studs to drag the load into the plywood. One nail every 16 or 24 inches in a stud will not connect the studs and the wall sheathing for this load transfer. The horizontal blocking between studs provides a nailing edge for the plywood. If the ledger is then attached to both the studs and the blocks, the assembly works for the load transfer, albeit a little circuitously.

Detail D (Figure 11.12).   Essentially, this shows the same condition as *B*, except for the absence of the exterior paving slab. Depending on the level of the exterior grade, it may be necessary to use a curb to raise the wood sill plate above the exterior soil. Details for such a curb must be carefully developed to ensure the required strength for transfer of the considerable horizontal sliding force for this shear wall. This may be tough to achieve if the wall studs are 2×4, so that the curb is only 3.5 in. wide. The tall wall here is likely to use at least 2×6 studs, so the situation is not quite so bad, depending on the height of the curb.

Detail E (Figure 11.13).   This is a partial elevation of the south wall, showing the wood framing without the covering plywood sheathing. The drawing shows three details for special seismic load development.

1. The splice, using steel bolts, of the top plates of the shear wall at the roof edge. Because this member functions as the chord for the roof diaphragm, it carries the compression and tension force described for the chord. Conventional lapping and nailing of the double-member plate may be sufficient if the chord forces are expected to be low.

2. The anchorage of the end framing member of the shear wall to the foundation for development of resistance to uplift.

3. Use of construction at the support of the window header that achieves both a tension and compression transfer between the header and the shear wall. In this case, blocking is added between the wall studs with steel straps nailed to the header and the blocking. The intention is to drag the push-pull force into the wall, rather than attach only to the wall edge. In this example, the wall piers used as shear walls comprise only a third of the wall length in plan, so a considerable amount of the whole wall load is dragged in by the headers. For smaller openings, the attachment may be achieved with metal fastening members between the header and the wall end post.

The following scheme uses different materials to achieve the same basic building form.

11.4   SCHEME 2: MASONRY STRUCTURE

Figure 11.14 shows the plan layout for an alternate structure for Building 2 that uses exterior walls of CMU construction and a wood roof of heavy timber. The plan dimensions have been altered slightly to make 16-in. units for the CMU construction. The wood roof structure uses a single row of interior columns to support solid-sawn timber beams, which

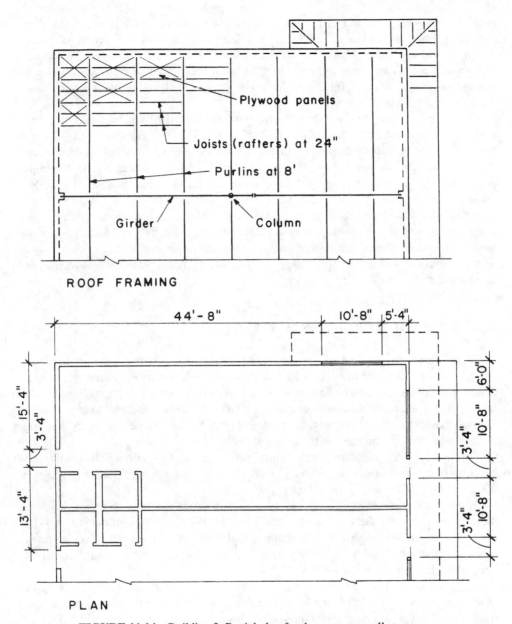

FIGURE 11.14   Building 2: Partial plan for the masonry wall structure.

in turn support timber purlins and a panel system consisting of light wood frames with plywood deck.

11.5   SEISMIC RESPONSE OF THE MASONRY STRUCTURE

The response of Building 2 to seismic effects derives essentially from its form, dimensions, and lateral resistive system. Although much of the discussion presented in Section 11.2 for the wood structure applies to this scheme, the masonry walls present two major concerns: the weight (dead load) of the construction—typically three to four times that of wood construction—and the relative stiffness of the walls in shear wall action.

The heavy walls add appreciably to the seismic force on the structure. The increased stiffness attracts more of the dynamic load. Both of these determine the seismic loading for the building—whether measured by true dynamic analysis or by the approximate equivalent static load method.

For seismic loadings in high-risk zones, the form described here is the only form of CMU construction used for lateral resistive structures. The base capacity of this system is established by the minimum code requirements for the construction and by the grades of the materials used for the masonry units, the mortar, and the reinforcing. Using higher-grade materials or grouting and reinforcing more of the block voids will give the building greater strength. These options are discussed in the next section.

As in all systems for lateral resistance, the connection between construction elements (roof to wall, in this case) must provide positive anchorage for the dynamic seismic movements. The effect of outward seismic force on the walls requires a well-developed connection between the wall and the roof edge—something not often provided by ordinary construction details.

11.6 DESIGN OF THE MASONRY STRUCTURE

The form of the lateral load-resistive system for this scheme is the same as that for the wood structure described in Section 11.3. The wood roof structure is different in its use of framing members, but similar in the use of a plywood diaphragm. The magnitude of the lateral load is increased, however, due to the increased stiffness and the greater weight of the walls. With the timber framing, the roof is slightly heavier. Table 11.3 gives the weight to determine the seismic load on the roof and shear walls.

The stiff masonry walls will increase the percentage of the building weight that must be considered for lateral force. Instead of the value of 14% assumed for the wood structure, a value of 18.33% is assumed here.

In the north-south direction, the load is symmetrically placed, the shear walls are symmetrical in plan, and the long diaphragm is reasonably flexible, resulting in very little potential torsion. Although the code requires that a minimum torsional effect be considered by placing the load off-center by 5% of the building long dimension, this will have very little effect on the shear walls.

Using the values for the building weight from Table 11.3, the total lateral force applied at the roof level can be determined for each direction. Design of the plywood diaphragm must satisfy the requirements for both the north-south and east-west loadings. At the east and west walls, the shear stress in the edge of the roof diaphragm due to the north-south load will be

$$\text{North-south force} = 0.1833(448) = 82 \text{ kips}$$
$$\text{Maximum shear force} = 82/2 = 41 \text{ kips, or } 41,000 \text{ lb}$$
$$\text{Maximum unit shear} = 41,000/60 = 683 \text{ lb/ft}$$

This is very high stress for the plywood diaphragm, so zoned nailing should be considered, along with using varying grades of plywood, to develop maximum strength at the building ends, but permit minimum construction for the center portion of the diaphragm. See the discussion of the roof diaphragm in Section 11.3.

TABLE 11.3   Loads to the Roof Diaphragm

	Loads (kips)	
Load Source and Calculation	N-S	E-W
Roof dead load:		
145 × 70 × 20 psf	174	
East and west exterior walls:		
50 × 11 × 70 psf × 2	0	77
10 × 6 × 70 psf × 2	0	9
10 × 6 × 10 psf × 2	0	1
North exterior wall:	126	0
150 × 12 × 70 psf		
South wall:		
65.3 × 10 × 70 psf	46	0
84 × 6 × 70 psf	35	0
84 × 6 × 10 psf	5	0
Interior dividing walls:	21	21
60 × 7 × 10 psf × 5		
Toilet walls:	17	17
250 × 7 × 10 psf		
Canopy:		
South: 150 ft × 100 lb/ft	15	15
East and west: 40 × 100 lb/ft	4	4
Rooftop HVAC units (estimate):	5	5
Total load (W for seismic calculation)	448	323

In the east-west direction the shear will be considerably less, so the deck construction will be determined by the requirements for the north-south loading.

> East-west force = (0.1833)(323) = 59 kips
> Maximum shear force = 59/2 = 29.5 kips, or 29,500 lb
> Maximum unit shear = 29,500/145 = 203 lb/ft

These calculations assume that the deck is nailed continuously at its boundaries, with collector elements of the wood framing serving to gather the deck load and push or drag it into the shear walls. Framing for gravity loads should be done with this requirement in mind, so that little extra framing is needed for the lateral loads. Framing elements involved in this dual action must be designed for the necessary load combinations. Framing members often need to be attached to establish the tension and/or compression continuity required for functioning as collectors or diaphragm chords. In this long building, the edge framing at the north and south sides is continuous for the 150-ft-long edge, but it will actually consist of several members butted end to end. True continuity of this string of elements will require splicing connections, which are not required for gravity loads alone.

Design of the Masonry Shear Walls

In the north-south direction, with no interior shear walls, the end shear forces will be resisted almost entirely by the long solid walls because of their relative stiffness. The shear force delivered to these walls is the sum of the end shear from the roof and the weight of the entire end wall. For the wall weight, the following is computed.

$$\text{Solid walls: 18 ft} \times \text{50 ft} \times \text{70 psf} = 63{,}000 \text{ lb}$$
$$\text{Solid wall at openings: 6 ft} \times \text{10.67 ft} \times \text{70 psf} = 4{,}481$$
$$\text{Glazed wall: 12 ft} \times \text{10.67 ft} \times \text{5 psf} = 640$$
$$\text{Total wall weight} = 68{,}121 \text{ lb}$$
$$\text{Lateral force} = 0.1833W = (0.1833)(68) = 12.5 \text{ kips}$$

The total force on the end wall is $12.5 + 41 = 53.5$ kips and the unit shear is

$$v = \frac{53{,}500}{44.67} = 1{,}198 \text{ lb/ft}$$

The code requires that this force be increased 50% for shear investigation of the masonry. Assuming a 60% solid wall, with nominal 8-in. blocks, the unit stress on the net area of the wall is

$$v = \frac{1{,}198(1.5)}{12(7.625)(0.60)} = 33 \text{ psi}$$

This is quite a low stress for the reinforced masonry wall, and can probably be developed adequately with minimum construction. The unit shear of 1,198 lb/ft, while low for a masonry wall, is near the top permitted for a very heavily nailed plywood wall. The capacity of masonry walls typically begins at the upper limit for plywood walls. Some additional stress will be placed on these walls as a result of torsion, so that it may be necessary to increase the reinforcement somewhat over the minimum required.

Overturn is not a problem for these walls because of their considerable dead weight and the natural tiedown provided by the dowelling of the vertical reinforcement at the ends of the walls. Vertical dowels also provide resistance to horizontal sliding of these walls.

In the east-west direction, the shear walls are not symmetrical in plan, which requires an investigation for torsion. The lateral load (building weight) is symmetrically placed, centered on the building. The individual wall piers are fixed at their bottoms by dowelling to the foundations and fixed at their tops by the wide continuous wall over the openings. Expansion or separation joints might alter this arrangement, but we will ignore them for now.

Individual pier stiffnesses are determined on the basis of the ratio of the pier height (h) to the plan length (d). Values for various $h{:}d$ ratios are found in references on masonry design such as Ref. 16. The stiffnesses of the individual walls, as well as the total stiffnesses of the four building walls, are determined in Figure 11.15. The location of the center of stiffness is determined as follows:

The torsional resistance (J) of the entire shear wall system is the sum of the products of the individual wall rigidities multiplied by the square of their distances from the center of stiffness. This summation is shown in Table 11.4. The torsional shear load for each wall is then found as

$$V_W = TcR = \frac{(V)(e)(c)(R \text{ for the wall})}{\text{sum of the } Rd^2 \text{ for all walls}}$$

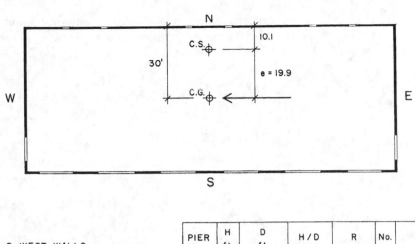

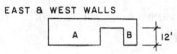

EAST & WEST WALLS

PIER	H ft.	D ft.	H/D	R	No.	ΣR
A	12	44.67	0.269	12.05	I	12.05
B	12	5.33	2.251	0.55	I	0.55

TOTAL WALL R = 12.60

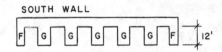

NORTH WALL

C	7	15.33	0.457	6.82	2	13.64
D	7	13.33	0.525	5.81	3	17.43
E	7	29.33	0.239	13.69	2	27.38

Σ = 58.45

SOUTH WALL

F	12	6	2	0.71	2	1.42
G	12	10.67	1.125	2.08	5	10.40

Σ = 11.82

FIGURE 11.15   Stiffness analysis of the masonry walls

TABLE 11.4   Torsional Resistance of the Masonry Shear Walls

Wall	Total Wall R	Distance from Center of Stiffness (ft)	$R(d)^2$
South	2.96	49.89	7,367
North	14.61	10.11	1,495
East	3.17	75.00	17,831
West	3.17	75.00	17,831
Torsional moment of inertia (J)			44,524

This investigation may be made for the required 5% eccentricity of the north-south load. However, we will demonstrate its use here only for the eccentric east-west load. Using the formula, the load for the end shear walls is

$$V_w = \frac{82(7.5)(75)(3.17)}{44,524} = 3.28 \text{ kips}$$

This is added to the direct shear of 53,500 lb.
For the north wall:

$$V_w = \frac{82(19.89)(10.11)(14.61)}{44,524} = 3.28 \text{ kips}$$

For this wall, this force is actually opposite in direction to the direct shear, but the code does not allow the reduction and, thus, the direct shear only is used.
For the south wall:

$$V_w = \frac{82(19.89)(49.89)(2.96)}{44,524} = 3.28 \text{ kips}$$

The total direct east-west shear will be distributed between the north and south walls in proportion to their stiffnesses.
For the north wall:

$$V_w = \frac{59(14.61)}{17.57} = 49.1 \text{ kips}$$

For the south wall:

$$V_w = \frac{59(2.96)}{17.57} = 9.94 \text{ kips}$$

The total shear loads on the walls are

North: $V = 49.1$ kips
South: $V = 3.89 + 9.94 = 13.83$ kips

The loads on the individual piers are distributed in proportion to the pier stiffnesses (R) as determined in Figure 11.15. The calculation for this distribution and the determination of the unit shear stresses per ft of wall length are shown in Table 11.5. A comparison with the previous calculations for the end walls shows that these stresses are not critical for the 8-in. block walls.

In most cases, the stabilizing dead loads plus the dowelling effect of the wall end reinforcement into the foundation will be sufficient to resist overturn effects. The heavy gravity loading on the header that is transferred to the ends of the walls provides another component of overturn resistance for most piers.

TABLE 11.5   Shear Stresses in the Masonry Walls

Wall	Shear Force on Wall (kips)	Wall R	Pier	Pier R	Shear Force on Pier (kips)	Pier Length (ft)	Shear Stress in Pier (lb/ft)
North	49.10	14.61	C	1.71	5.75	15.33	375.00
			D	1.45	4.87	13.33	365.00
			E	3.42	11.49	29.33	392.00
South	13.83	2.96	F	0.18	0.84	6.00	140.00
			G	0.52	2.43	10.67	228.00

Construction Plans and Details

The drawings that follow illustrate the construction of the timber and masonry structure for Building 2. These details are limited to illustration of the building structure and do not show the numerous details for finish materials, waterproofing, and so on.

Structural Plans.   Figure 11.16 shows partial plans for the roof structure and the foundation system. The basic components of the modular roof system are indicated. In addition to the plans, a nailing schedule or plan would be used to indicate variations in the nailing of the plywood diaphragm. The roof plans shows two variations for the major interior support for the roof. The first system uses a two-span girder with an interior column and pilasters at the masonry walls for supports. The second employs interior masonry bearing walls. The foundations for these variations are also shown. Locations of various details are indicated on the plans and are described as follows. These details are displayed in Figures 11.17 and 11.18.

Detail A (Figure 11.17).   This shows the typical condition at the front solid wall. The girder, pilaster, pilaster pier, and widened footing are shown in the background. A wood ledger is bolted to the face of the masonry wall to receive the edge of the plywood deck. To resist outward lateral force, positive anchorage of the wall must be developed with steel connectors embedded in the masonry and attached to framing members in the wood structure. Nailing the plywood deck to the ledger is not reliable for this anchorage.

Detail B (Figure 11.17).   This shows the foundation edge at the front (south) wall. Note the dowelling of the vertical wall reinforcement into the foundation. If the pilaster is used as shown, its form is extended as a cast pier below the masonry. The section shows the foundation between the widened footings for the wall piers.

Detail C (Figure 11.17).   This shows the roof edge at the building ends (east and west walls). The wood ledger performs the dual task of providing vertical support for the purlins and transferring the diaphragm edge loading to the shear wall. Because of the roof slope to the north side, the location of the top of the ledger varies along the wall length. The dimensions of this slope must be worked out to relate to the location of the filled and reinforced block courses in the wall in which the ledger bolts are embedded.

Detail D (Figure 11.17).   This detail is essentially the same as that at the front wall. If a footing is used instead of the grade beam shown, the center of the footing must be reason-

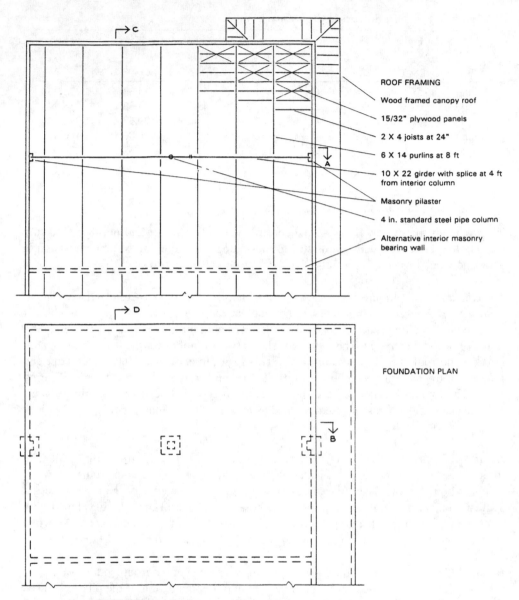

ROOF FRAMING

Wood framed canopy roof

15/32" plywood panels

2 X 4 joists at 24"

6 X 14 purlins at 8 ft

10 X 22 girder with splice at 4 ft
from interior column

Masonry pilaster

4 in. standard steel pipe column

Alternative interior masonry
bearing wall

FOUNDATION PLAN

FIGURE 11.16   Structural plans for the wood roof and foundation

ably aligned with the center of the wall, because the wall load is the major load on the footing.

Detail E (Figure 11.18).   This shows the typical form of the column-top support for a timber (or glued laminated) beam. While this type of joint can be developed to resist some bending moment, the requirement in this case is for vertical support only. If a beam joint occurs at this location, the support should be widened and at least two bolts used in the end of each beam to achieve a reasonable splice for continuity of the framing.

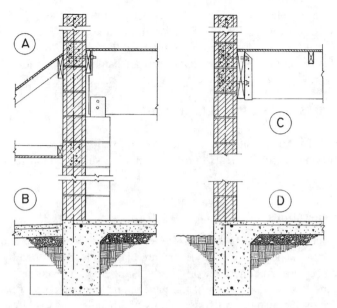

FIGURE 11.17   Construction details for the wood roof and masonry wall structure.

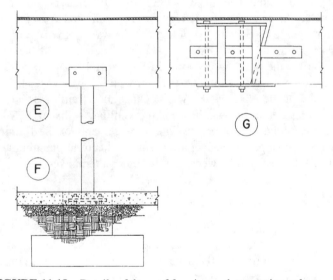

FIGURE 11.18   Details of the roof framing and supporting column.

Detail F (Figure 11.18).   This is an ordinary single column base. There is no lateral load transfer at this footing, so the only concern is to tie this footing adequately to the other building foundations. The details for this are not shown here, but may consist of simple cast ties between the footings.

Detail G (Figure 11.18).   As shown on the plan in Figure 11.16, the girder is spliced at a point off the column. This detail shows the use of a connecting device welded together from steel plates to achieve the necessary connector functions. For vertical support, the girder end on the left must support the girder end on the right. For horizontal continuity (probably required for collector functions in the roof diaphragm), the two ends are strapped and bolted. This is common, so proprietary hardware can be obtained for this connection.

11.7   SCHEME 3: TILT-UP WALL BUILDING

This scheme for Building 2 utilizes exterior bearing walls of precast concrete and a roof framed with wood or steel elements to make a building shape similar to the previous two buildings.

General Considerations

The precast concrete walls may be custom designed (original engineering design, construction details, and specifications), but they are likely to be developed by a contractor or company that does precast concrete work. In the latter case, the contractor is likely to provide engineering design, fabrication of the panels, and field erection. Except for specific dimensions, exposed finishes, and some details, the panels will likely conform to established practices of the supplier. In regions where use of this form of construction is widespread, such design/build contractors are generally available.

The roof structure, on the other hand, is likely to be of relatively conventional form and not much related to the concrete walls except where connected at points of support. Thus, the roof structure would be essentially the same if the walls were masonry or of some curtain wall (nonstructural) form with exterior supports developed with steel framing.

A wall section for the building is shown in Figure 11.19. The roof framing might use clear-spanning girders to achieve the 60-ft span, with a joist and deck system supported by the girders and at the edge by the walls. Other roof framing schemes are possible: Wood or steel joists could be used in a manner similar to that used with the masonry structure. If interior columns are permissible, arrangements of the framing with interior supports might be developed. Considerations for architectural planning and future use of the building affect the decision between these or other alternatives.

Columns for the Girder

The end reactions for short spanning joists or even for closely spaced long-span joists probably can be borne by the concrete wall panels. The magnitudes of the end reactions of the girders are likely too high for the same treatment. This requires consideration of the development of columns as end supports for the girders.

There are various solutions for the development of the whole wall construction. With the use of some form of column for the girders, the concrete panels are required to support only a short-span beam or the deck itself. However, the openings in the walls also must be developed, with various solutions. Header beams can be used, with support provided by the structural walls, or continuous framing at the walls can be used, eliminating the need for any bearing support by the wall panels.

An additional consideration in this regard is the development of the walls for shear wall functions. This requires that the walls and the roof deck (as the horizontal diaphragm) be attached somehow through the construction for transfer of the lateral forces.

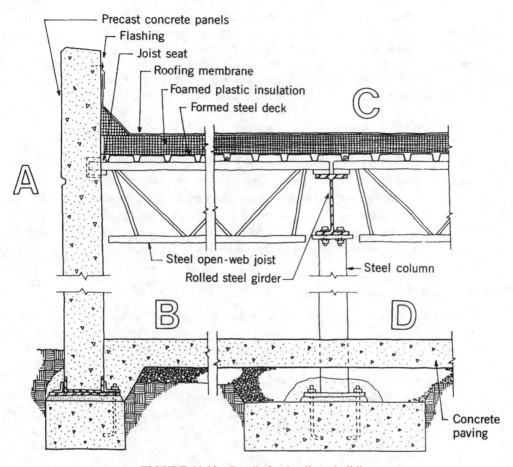

Precast concrete panels
Flashing
Joist seat
Roofing membrane
Foamed plastic insulation
Formed steel deck

Steel open-web joist
Rolled steel girder
Steel column
Concrete paving

FIGURE 11.19   Details for the tilt-up building.

For support of the girders, two general solutions are possible. The first is a reinforced concrete column, which might be sitecast in conjunction with the erection and attachment of the precast wall panels. This is likely to be done if the whole wall structure is developed independent of the roof framing.

The second possibility for the girders is to use a steel member that is attached to the wall panels for the purpose of column stability. This solution is likely to be used in conjunction with the development of a whole independent frame for the long walls. This is the case illustrated in the details in Figure 11.19. In those details, the use of a steel tubular column is shown. This column is considered to be laterally braced by the wall panels and is designed for half the girder load with a column effective length of zero. The result is a relatively small member, which can be easily incorporated into the interior construction finish of the walls.

Design of the Walls

For planning the concrete walls, the building designers obtain information directly from local suppliers. Structural details, materials, and construction joints are likely to conform to the supplier's standards, but finishes, panel dimensions, and some special details at openings or other locations may be custom fit to some of the building designers' preferences.

The details shown here are generally representative of common forms for this construction. Guidelines for design and construction detailing with this form of construction are available from various industry agencies, such as the ACI, the PCA, and the PCI.

Special concerns for the situation of this building include the following:

1. Use panels to support the ends of the joists; involves some bending induced by the eccentricity of the joist loads as applied through the steel ledger.
2. Develop walls to accommodate the openings shown in the plans; involves attaching window and door framing, headers over the openings, and so on.
3. Develop the interior wall surfaces; involves provision for attachment of additional interior construction.
4. Use the walls for shear wall functions; requires special attention to the design of the construction joints to develop the lateral force transfers required.

Design for Lateral Forces

The basic lateral-resistive structure for this building is similar to that in the previous schemes—using the roof deck as a horizontal diaphragm and the exterior structural walls as shear walls. The concrete panels have considerable potential for this use, depending on the aspect ratio (height-to-plan length) of the individual panels and the effects of any openings occurring within individual panels.

As usual, the deck must be attached to its supports and adjacent deck units joined for the development of the whole roof surface acting as an integral unit for the diaphragm action. The details shown here develop the continuity of the diaphragm and to transfer forces between the roof and the shear walls.

Construction Details

Figure 11.19 shows some details of the building's exterior walls. The exterior walls feature a parapet. The precast panels are single units extending from the ground to the top of the parapet. The roof structure thus runs into the back of the walls. These details reflect the particular concern for the enhancement of the interior sides of the walls. (For most industrial or utility buildings in mild climates, it is common to omit interior finish construction and expose the cast panels on the interior.)

12

Low-Rise MultiUnit Building

This chapter addresses a common form of building, consisting of a low-rise form (mostly two or three stories) with a considerable horizontal expanse. Such a building is frequently formed into multiple units of continuous construction in order to create a large plan area. Two common building types illustrate this construction; the first is an apartment complex and the second is a motel.

12.1 GENERAL CONSIDERATIONS FOR THE APARTMENT COMPLEX

As shown in Figure 12.1, Building 3 consists of a number of units of a repetitive form joined to form a continuous building. This single building is then grouped with other similar buildings to create large apartment complex. The wood frame construction used is essentially the same as that for Building 1 and for the wood structure for Building 2. The basic structure consists mostly of a light wood frame with rafters, joists, and wall studs of standard 2-in. nominal size lumber.

Without consideration for seismic forces, various economies can be achieved with this construction. While the widely used material for roof sheathing, floor decking, and exterior wall sheathing in the past was plywood, it now largely consists of various products using wood fibers, strands, and shavings, generally described as compressed wood fiber panels. One type of product used frequently for structural sheathing is *oriented strand board* (OSB). In some codes, this is given shear capacities equivalent to those for plywood. However, its lack of resistance to water limits its use in some applications.

For interior partitions, the most common material is the product consisting of a sandwich of paper and gypsum plaster, usually described as *gypsum drywall*. This is also used for ceilings that are usually attached directly to the undersides of rafters or joists.

The resulting construction is quite light in weight, with a low building mass for seismic shear force, an advantage for seismic effects. If either tiles or built-up roofing are used, however, the weight at the top of the building may be doubled. In addition, it is now common to use concrete fill on upper-floor decks, so that the ordinary dead weight of floor

FIGURE 12.1   Building 3: General form of the low-rise apartment building.

construction may be doubled. Add stucco (cement plaster) or brick veneer as an exterior finish material, and the building is no longer so light in weight.

Needless to say, this construction is universally developed with minimal, code-mandated materials, regardless of the neighborhood or the cost of individual units. Enhancement for any purpose—seismic, fire, acoustics—is only grudgingly introduced.

What Can Happen in an Earthquake?

What happens to buildings of this construction was thoroughly discussed for Buildings 1 and 2. Two issues not treated there are the cases of the multistory building and the multiunit building. This chapter focuses on these.

Although this is a low-rise building, at three stories there may be significant gradation in structure from top to bottom. A primary concern is the differential in structural requirements for the walls from the top story to the first story. This relates to concerns for both gravity and lateral forces. After investigation, it might be determined that 2 x 4 studs at 16-in. centers are adequate for the lower story. A more critical concern is to determine the wall covering for shear walls in the first story. Particleboard, OSB, and gypsum drywall are given rated shear capacities by building codes, but they may be questionable for first-story walls.

Another concern for the three-story building is the aspect ratio of individual shear wall piers. If window openings are large, it may be infeasible to consider exterior walls as pierced walls. However, there may also not be much plan length available for openings between vertical strips of windows; thus, a three-story-tall wall pier may be quite short in plan length.

Two major concerns for this building derive from issues that relate primarily to architectural planning. The first of these is the multimassed condition defined by the building plan. This problem is examined in Section 4.2, and the general remedies are illustrated there. The separate units either must be joined adequately to resist the tearing apart of the units, or some form of seismic separation must be provided. A frequent concern is how to prevent the grinding of connecting elements between the apartment block units—often consisting of the vital stair towers—which can leave upper-floor occupants stranded if the exits are damaged (Figure 4.10).

An advantage here is that the wood frame is usually the least susceptible of any construction to deformation caused by seismic actions. Plaster, stucco, masonry veneers, and window glazing may be lost, but the basic structure is often only mildly bruised. Thus, major structural damage is often less severe than with flexible or unstable steel frames or highly rigid concrete or masonry construction. If the cosmetic damage is economically feasible to repair, restoration of the building may be achieved, even though the post-quake appearance might be quite gruesome.

A particularly disastrous condition resulting from architectural planning is that of an open ground floor, which may produce a soft or weak story or a three-sided condition at the ground floor or all three at once (Figures 4.24 and 4.27). Need for on-site parking often results in ground floors used for parking. This often results in fewer walls, compared to the upper apartment stories—a setup for a soft story and/or a weak story. Large garage doors or a fully open side may well produce a three-sided condition.

Use of economical construction in general can result in a lack of tolerance for movement in gas or water piping. Movements that are tolerable for the wood structure may not extend to the vertical risers for piping. Gas piping is especially hazardous, and gas-fed explosions and fires often occur in earthquakes. Fractured electrical wiring or fixtures may also produce hazardous conditions. And, of course, the combination of leaking gas and electrical sparks are a sure bet for trouble.

Large apartment complexes quite often require considerable site development. If this is also done inexpensively, consolidation of fills may not be close to optimal, and serious site failures may occur. These may result in damage to site construction and to buried service elements. A minor site failure can trigger a domino effect, generating a large site failure or a building foundation failure (Figure 2.15).

12.2   DESIGN OF THE WOOD STRUCTURE

Most of the basic components of this structure are similar to those discussed for Buildings 1 and 2. The wood-framed horizontal diaphragm and the wood-framed shear wall are the same here. Major design concerns here have to do with determining load distributions and the manner of interactions between basic components of the lateral bracing system. In turn, those determinations have to do with aspects of the general building planning and decisions about using seismic separation joints.

If, for example, the units are separated due to extensive use of seismic separation joints, the design needs to account for individual smaller units. Each unit is designed essentially as a freestanding structure. For such units the actions of individual horizontal diaphragms and shear walls may be quite evident and yield to simple investigations for design.

If, on the other hand, units are strongly connected, the overall behavior of the complex structure may be quite difficult to predict. Simple spanning actions and distributions of total shear to individual shear walls may be virtually undeterminable. Symmetry or simplifications of form may reduce this problem, but the true behavior of the multimassed building is beyond simple investigation.

When perimeter walls are constituted as individual piers, they are often aligned in three-story-tall units between windows. The limits for aspect ratio for these units are determined using the full three-story height. Although the *UBC* allows higher ratios, after many apartment building failures in the 1994 Northridge earthquake, the City of Los Angeles enforced a limit of 2-to-1 for such piers to stiffen the wall structures against lateral deflections.

Seismic separation joints may be used, at least partly because they allow for rational determination of the structure's potential behavior. Otherwise, a highly complex, and costly, method of investigation must be used. The client may have to decide whether to spend money for engineering design time or for construction of expensive seismic separation joints.

Certainly anything done in architectural planning to improve seismic responses will be beneficial. If not, the structure must respond by compensating for the problems created by planning. This may be possible, and the highly favored architectural form may be preserved, but the price may have to be paid for both design and construction of a very special structure. For a building project in which economy of construction is a major concern, this is not a good scheme for design.

The popular building form using an open ground floor for parking was seriously questioned following the many failures in the 1994 Northridge earthquake. While the various techniques illustrated in Figure 4.27 might help retain the building form, the concept may be just too questionable for planning. One method that has been more succeessful is to use a half sunken parking level with a half story above grade. This structure is usually built entirely of reinforced concrete and becomes a platform for the wood-framed structure above.

Apartment buildings typically have many walls that can be chosen for shear walls. Thus, redundancy in the system is often quite high. However, if only a few walls are chosen for shear walls, redundancy may be low, and the new requirement of the 1997 *UBC* should be checked to ensure that the scheme is not critical for redundancy. (See the discussion in Section 2.2.)

12.3   GENERAL CONSIDERATIONS FOR THE MOTEL

The drawings in Figure 12.2 show the site plan and site section for Building 4, a two-story motel. Viewed from the exterior, this building does not seem to be an irregular or a multi-massed building. What creates this, though, is the change in interior form between the two motel room wings and the central lobby. This is not just a change in interior planning; the structures for the two types of areas are also different.

Figure 12.3 shows the general form of the motel room wings. As shown, the motel room wing uses a double-loaded interior corridor. On the elevations, this generates large solid wall portions on the end of the wing and alternating vertical strips of windows and solid wall on the long sides. The details shown in Figures 12.4 and 12.5 reveal the construction of the exterior walls, roof, and upper floor. Solid wall portions consist of structural CMU construction with exterior brick veneer. The window strips are constructed with light wood frame between the masonry piers. The roof and second floor are achieved with precast concrete plank units with hollow cores.

The structure for the room wings is illustrated further in Figure 12.6. Framing at the stairs involves using some elements of both precast and sitecast concrete. Concrete fill is

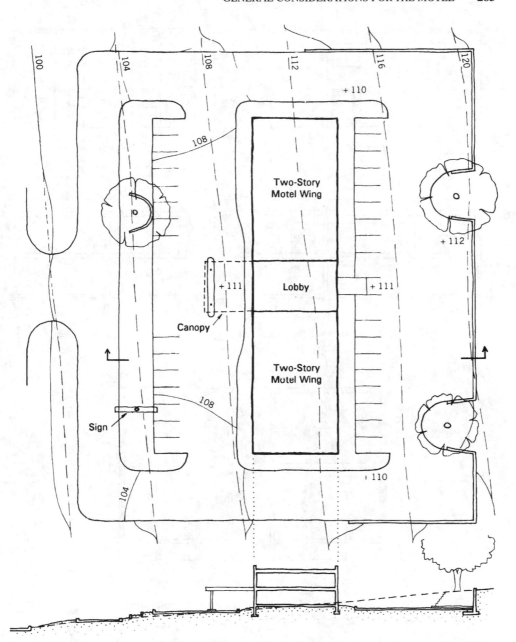

FIGURE 12.2   Building 4: Plan of the motel complex.

used in several ways. First, the CMU wall construction is developed as reinforced mason-ry, with reinforcement and concrete fill in selected voids. This fill is extended through the joints between the walls and the precast concrete plank units, and, together with extended reinforcement, achieves a connection between the vertical and horizontal construction. Development of the structure for lateral load resistance depends on this connection.

Concrete fill is also used on top of the precast planks to achieve a smooth top surface for flooring or roofing. The floor fill is of a structural grade, as a hard surface is required.

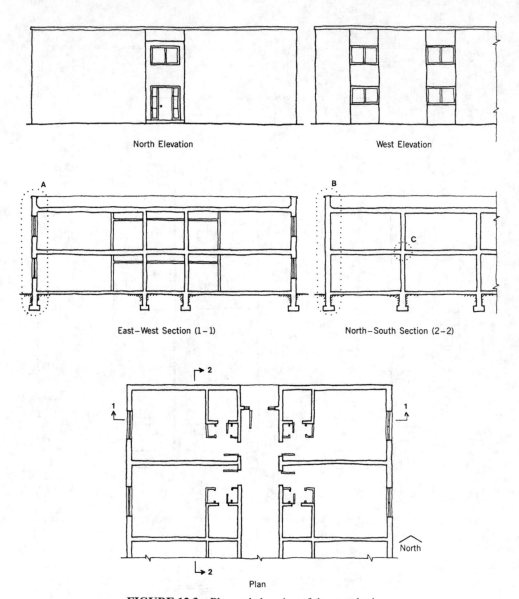

North Elevation

West Elevation

East–West Section (1–1)

North–South Section (2–2)

Plan

FIGURE 12.3 Plan and elevation of the motel wing.

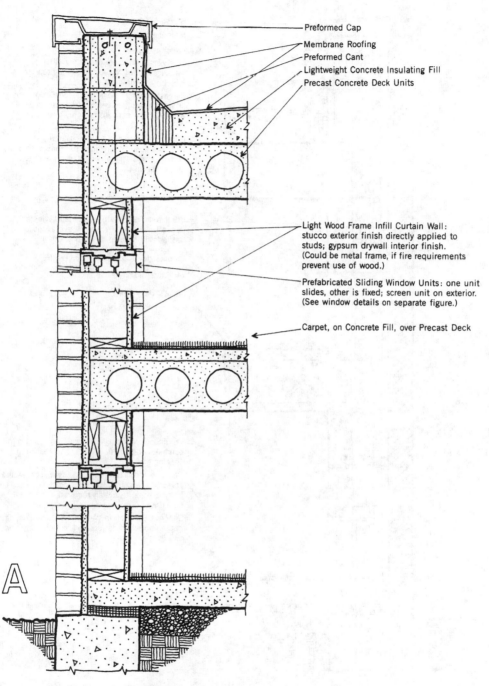

Preformed Cap

Membrane Roofing

Preformed Cant

Lightweight Concrete Insulating Fill

Precast Concrete Deck Units

Light Wood Frame Infill Curtain Wall:
stucco exterior finish directly applied to
studs; gypsum drywall interior finish.
(Could be metal frame, if fire requirements
prevent use of wood.)

Prefabricated Sliding Window Units: one unit
slides, other is fixed; screen unit on exterior.
(See window details on separate figure.)

Carpet, on Concrete Fill, over Precast Deck

A

FIGURE 12.4   Details of the motel construction.

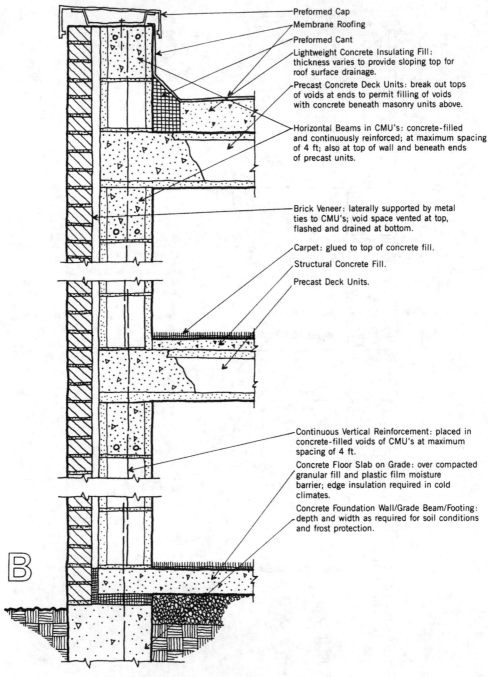

Preformed Cap

Membrane Roofing

Preformed Cant

Lightweight Concrete Insulating Fill: thickness varies to provide sloping top for roof surface drainage.

Precast Concrete Deck Units: break out tops of voids at ends to permit filling of voids with concrete beneath masonry units above.

Horizontal Beams in CMU's: concrete-filled and continuously reinforced; at maximum spacing of 4 ft; also at top of wall and beneath ends of precast units.

Brick Veneer: laterally supported by metal ties to CMU's; void space vented at top, flashed and drained at bottom.

Carpet: glued to top of concrete fill.

Structural Concrete Fill.

Precast Deck Units.

Continuous Vertical Reinforcement: placed in concrete-filled voids of CMU's at maximum spacing of 4 ft.

Concrete Floor Slab on Grade: over compacted granular fill and plastic film moisture barrier; edge insulation required in cold climates.

Concrete Foundation Wall/Grade Beam/Footing: depth and width as required for soil conditions and frost protection.

B

FIGURE 12.5 Details of the motel construction.

286

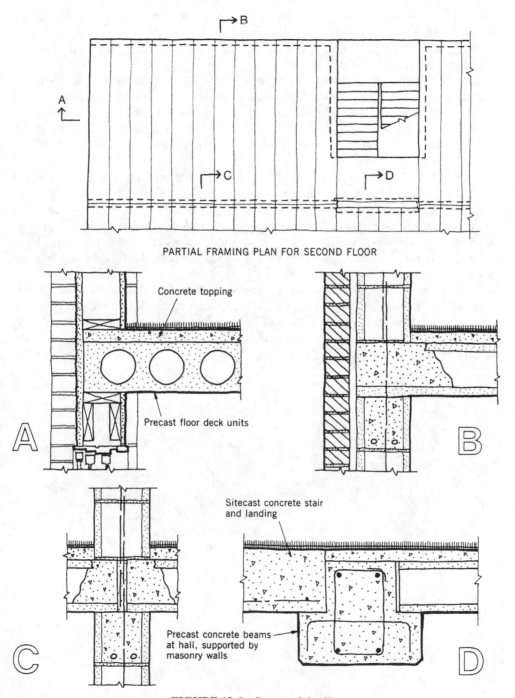

PARTIAL FRAMING PLAN FOR SECOND FLOOR

Concrete topping

Precast floor deck units

Sitecast concrete stair and landing

Precast concrete beams at hall, supported by masonry walls

FIGURE 12.6 Structural details.

This makes it possible to develop a composite action between the precast units and the fill, which increases the capacity of the spanning structure. If the concrete fill is at least 3 in. thick, it may be reinforced and used as the horizontal diaphragm, although it must be attached to the vertical bracing as well.

The roof fill, on the other hand, is usually a very lightweight material, which serves well as insulation and makes attaching roofing materials easier. For the roof, therefore, the precast units must serve alone for the spanning action. However, the live load is probably lower and the need to reduce bounce is less critical, so the same units might be used for both roof and floor. With the nonstructural fill, the roof units must be welded together to create a continuous diaphragm.

Construction of the center portion of the building between the two room wings is achieved with a conventional sitecast concrete frame structure. It is the difference between this rigid frame system and the shear wall bracing of the wings that creates a multimassed form of response here—not by geometry (form), but by difference in character of resistance. Thus, the response of this building to seismic forces perpendicular to its long axis will require consideration for the joint between the two distinct building structural masses.

One approach is to tie the two parts together at the joint. One method for achieving this is to use the masonry wall as an infill shear wall in the beam/column concrete frame at this location. In this case, the stiffness of this shear wall braced bent and the very stiff horizontal concrete slab diaphragm results in the two connecting bents carrying the entire lateral load for the central portion of the building.

13

Low-Rise Office Building

There is a considerable range of choice for the construction of Building 5, although in a particular place, at a particular time, a few favorite forms of construction tend to dominate the field. The plan and section in Figure 13.1 show a three-story building without a basement. The plan layout indicates the existence of an orderly placement of columns in 30-ft square bays. Building service elements (stairs, restrooms, duct risers, etc.) are grouped at the building center, leaving as much exterior wall space as possible for rental. This plan makes development of a steel- or concrete-framed structure relatively easy, although other options are possible.

13.1 GENERAL CONSIDERATIONS FOR THE BUILDING

Some modular planning is usually required for this type of building, involving the coordination of dimensions for spacing of columns, window mullions, and interior partitions in the building plan. This modular coordination may also be extended to development of ceiling construction, lighting, ceiling HVAC elements, and the systems for access to electric power, phones, and other signal wiring systems.

For buildings built as investment properties, with speculative occupancies that may vary over the life of the building, it is usually desirable to accommodate future redevelopment of the building interior. For the basic construction, this means a design with as few permanent structural elements as possible. At a bare minimum, this usually requires use of permanent construction only for the major structure (columns, floors, and roof), exterior walls, and the interior walls enclosing stairs, elevators, rest rooms, and risers for building services. Everything else should be nonstructural or demountable in nature, if possible.

Spacing of columns on the building interior should be as wide as possible, basically to reduce the number of freestanding columns in the rentable portion of the building plan. A column-free interior may be possible if the distance from a central core (grouped permanent elements) to the outside walls is not too far for a single span. Spacing of columns at the building perimeter does not affect this issue, so additional columns are sometimes

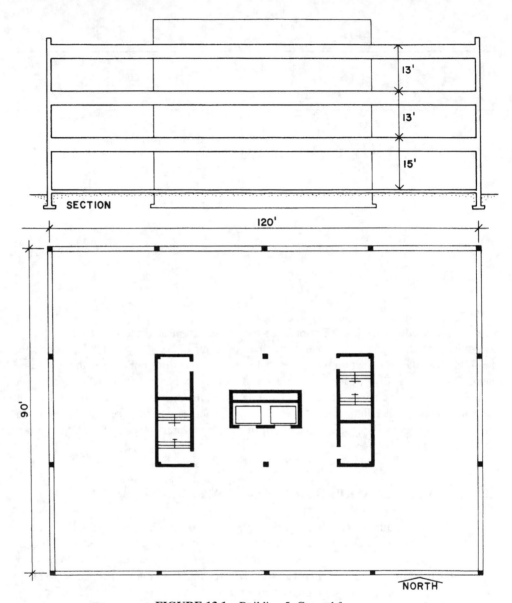

FIGURE 13.1 Building 5: General form.

used at this location to reduce their size for gravity loading or to develop a better perimeter rigid-frame system for lateral loads (Figure 3.45).

The space between suspended ceilings and floor or roof structures generally contains many elements besides those of the basic construction. This usually represents a situation requiring major coordination for the integration of the space. Optimization for structural requirements may be compromised by need for elements of the HVAC, electrical, communication, lighting, and fire-fighting systems.

The overall dimension of the space required for this collection of elements is a major decision that often must be made very early in the design process. Depth permitted for the spanning structure and the general level-to-level vertical building height will be established, and it will not be easy to change later, if the detailed design of any of the enclosed systems indicates a need for more space.

Generous provision of the space for building elements will make the work of the designers of the various subsystems easier, but the overall effect on the building must be considered. Extra height for the exterior walls, stairs, elevators, and service risers result in additional cost, making tight control of the level-to-level distance very important.

A major architectural design issue for this building is the choice of basic form of the construction of the exterior walls. The basic form of the construction as shown in Figures 13.2 and 13.3 involves the incorporation of the columns into the wall, with windows developed in horizontal strips between the columns.

Detailing of the wall construction (see detail A) results in a considerable interstitial void space. Although taken up partly with insulation materials, this space can be used to contain elements for the electrical system or other services. In very cold climates, a perimeter hot water heating system likely would be used, and it could be incorporated in the wall space shown here.

Structural Alternatives

There are many structural options for this example, including use of a light wood frame if the total floor area and zoning requirements permit. Certainly, the steel frame, concrete frame, and masonry bearing wall systems are feasible. Choice of the structural elements will depend mostly on the desired plan form, type of window arrangements, and clear spans required for the building interior. At this height and taller, the basic structure is often of steel or reinforced concrete.

Design of the structural system must take into account both gravity and lateral forces. Gravity requires the development of horizontal spanning systems for the roof and floors and the stacking of vertical supporting elements. The most common choices for the lateral bracing system follow (Figure 13.4).

Core Shear Wall System (Figure 13.4a).   Use of solid walls around core elements (stairs, elevators, rest rooms, and duct shafts) often produces a very rigid, towerlike structure; the rest of the building can lean on this rigid core.

Truss-Braced Core.   This is similar to the shear wall core, with trussed bents placed at the locations of some of the solid walls.

Perimeter Shear Wall (Figure 13.4b).   This turns the building into a tubelike structure; walls may be structurally continuous and pierced by holes for windows and doors, or they may be built as a series of individual, linked piers between vertically aligned openings.

Mixed Exterior and Interior Shear Walls or Trussed Bents.   For some building plans, the perimeter or core systems may be infeasible, requiring use of a mixture of walls and/or trussed bents.

Full Rigid-Frame System (Figure 13.4c).   This system uses the vertical planes of columns and beams in both directions as a series of rigid bents. For this building there would be four bents for bracing in one direction and five for bracing in the other direction.

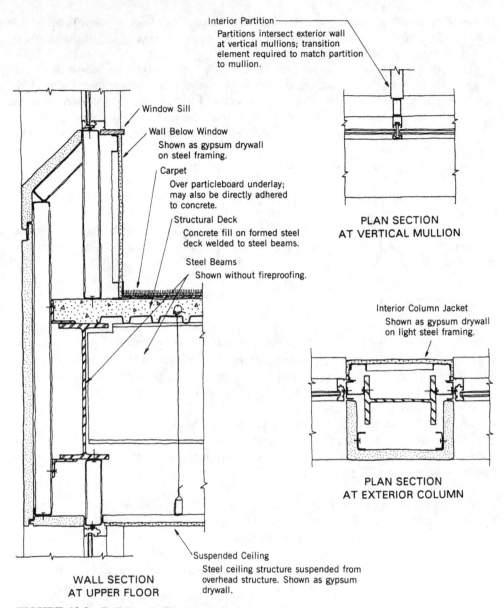

Interior Partition

Partitions intersect exterior wall at vertical mullions; transition element required to match partition to mullion.

Window Sill

Wall Below Window

Shown as gypsum drywall on steel framing.

Carpet

Over particleboard underlay; may also be directly adhered to concrete.

Structural Deck

Concrete fill on formed steel deck welded to steel beams.

Steel Beams

Shown without fireproofing.

**PLAN SECTION
AT VERTICAL MULLION**

Interior Column Jacket

Shown as gypsum drywall on light steel framing.

**PLAN SECTION
AT EXTERIOR COLUMN**

Suspended Ceiling

Steel ceiling structure suspended from overhead structure. Shown as gypsum drywall.

**WALL SECTION
AT UPPER FLOOR**

FIGURE 13.2   Building 5: Exterior wall, floor, ceiling, and column construction at the upper floor levels.

Perimeter Rigid-Frame System (Figure 13.4d).   This system uses only the columns and beams in the exterior wall planes, resulting in two bracing bents in each direction.

In the right circumstances, any of these systems may be acceptable. Each has advantages and disadvantages from both structural design and architectural planning points of view.

The core-braced schemes were once very popular, which evolved with the early development of tall buildings in regions where wind was the predominant concern. The core systems allow for the greatest freedom of planning of the exterior wall construction.

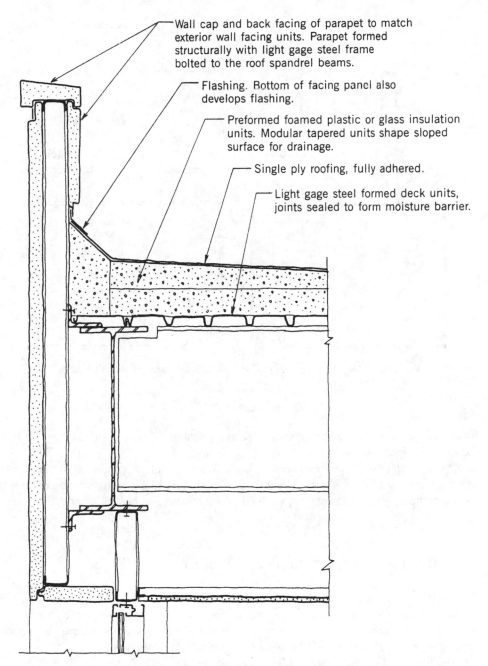

Wall cap and back facing of parapet to match exterior wall facing units. Parapet formed structurally with light gage steel frame bolted to the roof spandrel beams.

Flashing. Bottom of facing panel also develops flashing.

Preformed foamed plastic or glass insulation units. Modular tapered units shape sloped surface for drainage.

Single ply roofing, fully adhered.

Light gage steel formed deck units, joints sealed to form moisture barrier.

FIGURE 13.3   Building 5: Construction at the roof.

The perimeter systems produce the most torsionally stiff buildings which is an advantage for seismic resistance. They also allow for the greatest freedom of architectural planning of the building interior space. The full rigid frame systems allow for some degree of planning freedom, but require a regimented order for the interior column and beam layouts. Even when this order is preserved, the interior columns may be made considerably

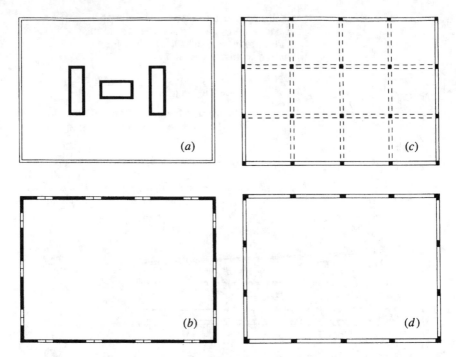

FIGURE 13.4   Options for development of lateral bracing for tall buildings.

smaller (and thus less intrusive for architectural planning) if rigid frame actions are limited to the perimeter bents.

In this chapter we examine schemes for the following lateral bracing systems: A truss-braced core and a full rigid-frame bent, both using vertical supports consisting of steel W-shape columns and schemes using a concrete rigid frame and both masonry and concrete structural walls.

13.2   DESIGN OF THE STEEL TRUSSED BENTS

This scheme uses vertical trussed bents placed at the building core. These bents are developed primarily with building columns and beams which serve dual purpose as members of the general structure for gravity loads. Addition of diagonal members turns the selected bents into vertically cantilevered trusses for resistance of lateral loads.

The following weights are used for the design work:

Floor finish: 5 psf

Ceilings, lights, ducts: 15 psf

Walls (average surface weight):

   Interior, permanent: 15 psf

   Exterior curtain wall: 25 psf

The Beam and Girder Floor Structure

Figure 13.5 shows a framing system for the typical upper floor that uses rolled steel beams spaced at a module related to the column spacing. As shown, the beams are 7.5 ft on center and the beams that are not on the column lines are supported by column line girders. Thus, three-fourths of the beams are supported by the girders and the remainder are supported directly by the columns. The beams in turn support a one-way spanning deck. This basic system offers a number of variables:

The Beam Spacing. Affects the deck span and the beam loading.

The Deck. A variety are available, as we discuss later.

Beam/Column Relationship in Plan. As shown, permits development of vertical bents in both directions.

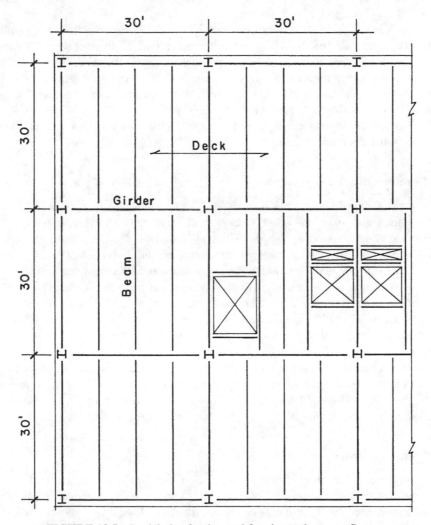

FIGURE 13.5   Partial plan for the steel framing at the upper floors.

Column Orientation. The W shape has a strong axis and accommodates framing differently in different directions.

The Structural Deck

Several options are possible for the floor deck. In addition to structural concerns, which include gravity loading and diaphragm action for lateral loads, consideration must be given to fire protection for the steel; to the accommodation of wiring, piping, and ducts; and to attachment of finish floor, roofing, and ceiling constructions. For office buildings, networks for electrical power and communication often must be built into the wall and floor constructions.

If the structural floor deck is a concrete slab, either sitecast or precast, a nonstructural fill usually is placed on top of the structural slab; power and communication networks may be buried in this fill. If a steel deck is used, closed cells of the formed sheet steel deck units may be used for some wiring.

The deck in this example is a formed steel deck with 1.5-in. deep ribs, on top of which a lightweight concrete fill is cast with a minimum depth of 2.5 in. over the steel units. The average dead weight of this deck depends on the thickness of the sheet steel, the profile of the deck folds, and the unit density of the concrete fill. For this example, the average weight is 30 psf. Adding to this the assumed weight of the floor finish and suspended items, the total dead load for the deck design is 50 psf.

While industrywide standards exist for these decks, data for deck design should be obtained from deck manufacturers.

The Common Beam

As shown in Figure 13.5, this beam spans 30 ft and carries a load strip that is 7.5 ft wide. For this load and span, tabulated sources will yield the following possible choices: W 16 × 45, W 18 × 46, or W 21 × 44. The choice may be affected by various considerations. For example, the deeper shape will obviously produce the least deflection, although in this case the live load deflection for the 16-in. shape is within the usual limit.

For these beams, the deck likely will provide virtually continuous lateral bracing of the top (compression) flange. Other concerns may involve developing connections and accommodating nonstructural elements in the construction. For deflection control, these beams are likely to be designed for composite action with the structural concrete fill on the deck.

This beam becomes the typical member, with other beams designed for special circumstances, including the column-line beams, the spandrels, and so on. Column-line beams will be considered if a rigid frame is developed for lateral bracing. Otherwise, ordinary beam/column framing connections will produce simple span behavior.

The Common Girder

Girders occur only on column lines. Their principal loading for gravity consists of the end reactions of supported beams at 7.5-ft intervals. A minor effect comes from the uniform loading represented by the girder weight, but the critical loading is as shown in Figure 13.6. This may be considered as a simple beam loading condition, unless end restraint is sufficient to develop significant negative moments at the columns. Ordinary framing con-

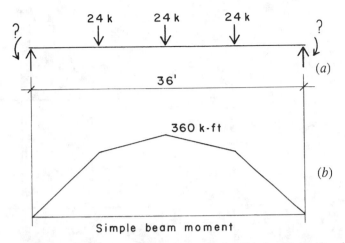

FIGURE 13.6   Approximation of the gravity loading for the interior girder.

nections, attaching girder webs to the supports, produce negligible restraint. Fully welded or bolted, moment-resistive connections for rigid frame development generally will provide complete restraint.

For consideration of gravity loads only, the lightest choices are a W 24 × 84 or a W 27 × 84. Within the range of consideration, depending on other concerns, are a W 21 × 93 and a W 30 × 90. The deeper members will have less deflection, but the shallower ones will allow greater room for building service elements in the floor/ceiling enclosed space.

Column Design for Gravity Loads

Design of the steel columns must include considerations for both gravity and lateral loads. If beams are rigidly attached to columns with moment-resistive connections—as is done in development of rigid frame bents—then gravity loads will cause bending moments and shears in the columns as well. Otherwise, the gravity loads are considered as axial compressive loads only.

Involvement of the columns in development of resistance to lateral loads depends on the form of the lateral bracing system. If trussed bents are used, some columns will function as chords in the vertically cantilevered trussed bents, which will add some compressive forces and possibly cause some reversals with net tension in the columns. If the columns are parts of rigid frame bents, the same chord actions will be involved, but the columns also will be subject to bending moments and shears from the rigid frame lateral actions.

Whatever the lateral force actions may do, the columns must also work for gravity load effects alone. And, of course, code-required load combinations and factors must be used for design.

Design of the Trussed Bents

Figure 13.7 shows a partial framing plan for the core area, indicating the placement of additional columns off the 30-ft grid. These columns are used together with the regular

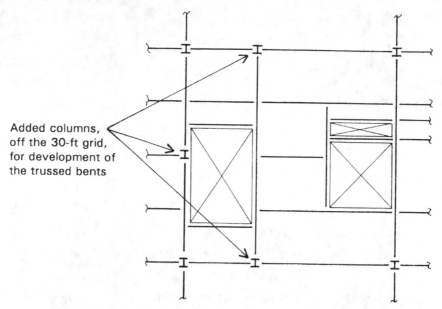

Added columns,
off the 30-ft grid,
for development of
the trussed bents

FIGURE 13.7   Modified steel framing for development of the trussed bents.

columns and some of the horizontal framing to define a series of vertical bents for the development of the trussed bracing system shown in Figure 13.8. With relatively slender diagonal members, the X bracing behaves as described in Section 3.6, with the tension diagonals functioning alone. Thus, four vertical, cantilevered, determinate trusses brace the building in each direction.

With the symmetrical building exterior form and the symmetrically placed core bracing, this is a reasonable system for use in conjunction with the horizontal roof and upper-floor structures in order to develop resistance to horizontal forces due to wind. The core-braced system is less effective for seismic resistance because of its low capacity for torsional resistance. In this example, the building symmetry produces little torsion, so the system may be possible, but it is not a typical solution. The work that follows illustrates the analytic process for seismic loading.

Table 13.1 summarizes the computation of building weight for determination of the total seismic shear. Assuming a factor of 0.15 (15%) for the seismic base shear, the total force is

$$V = 0.15(1827) = 274 \text{ kips}$$

This total force is distributed to the upper building levels using the criteria described in Section 3.11; the computation of this redistribution is summarized in Table 13.2. The forces from Table 13.2 are shown applied to one of the vertical trussed bents in Figure 13.8a. For one of the east-west bents, using the data from Table 13.2, the loads are determined by dividing by the number of bents. In the bent system shown in Figure 13.8 there are four bents for bracing in the east-west direction, and the values for the total load per level (from Table 13.2) are divided by 4 for the loading (Figure 13.9a).

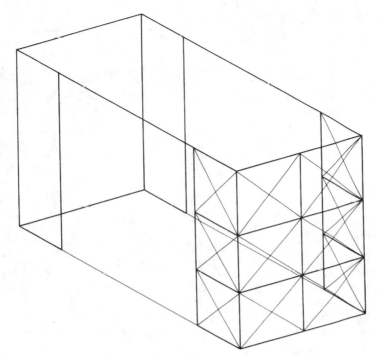

FIGURE 13.8   General form of the trussed bent bracing system at the building core.

The truss loading, together with the reaction forces at the supports, are shown in Figure 13.9*b*. The internal forces in the truss members resulting from this loading are shown in Figure 13.8*c*, with force values in pounds and sense indicated by C for compression and T for tension.

The forces in the diagonals may be used to design tension members, using the usual increase of allowable stress for the ASD method or the appropriate load factors and load combinations for the LRFD method. The compression forces in the columns may be added to the gravity loads to see if this load combination is critical for the column design. The uplift tension force at the windward column should be compared with the dead load to see if the column base needs to be designed for a tension anchorage force.

The horizontal forces should be added to the beams in the core framing and an investigation should be done for the combined bending and compression. Since beams are often weak on their minor axes (*y*-axis), it may be practical to add some framing members at right angles to these beams to brace them against lateral buckling.

Design of the diagonals and their connections to the beam and column frame must consider the form of the elements and the wall construction in which they are imbedded. Figure 13.10 shows some possible details for the diagonals and the connections. A problem that must be solved is that of the crossing of the two diagonals at the middle of the bent. If double angles are used for the diagonals (a common truss form), the splice joint shown in Figure 13.10 is necessary. One option is to use either single angles or channel shapes for the diagonals, allowing the members to pass each other back-to-back at the center. This involves a degree of eccentricity in the members and connections and a single shear load on the bolts, so if load magnitudes are high it is not advisable.

TABLE 13.1　Building Weight for the Seismic Load

Level	Source of Load	Unit Load (psf)		Load (kips)
Roof	Roof and ceiling	25	$120 \times 90 \times 25 =$	270
	Window walls	15	$420 \times 9.5 \times 15 =$	60
	Interior walls	10	$200 \times 5 \times 10 =$	10
	$1/2$-story columns			12
	Penthouse + equipment (estimate total) =			25
	Subtotal			377
Third Floor	Floor	55	$120 \times 90 \times 55 =$	594
	Window walls	15	$420 \times 13 \times 15 =$	82
	Story columns			24
	Interior walls	10	$200 \times 9 \times 10 =$	18
	Subtotal			718
Second Floor	Floor	55	$120 \times 90 \times 55 =$	594
	Window walls	15	$420 \times 14 \times 15 =$	88
	Story columns			30
	Interior walls	10	$200 \times 10 \times 10 =$	20
	Subtotal			732
Total dead load for the seismic base shear				1827

TABLE 13.2　Distribution of the Seismic Load

Level	w_x (kips)	h_x (ft)	$w_x \times h_x$	F_x (kips)
Roof	377	41	15,457	91
Third Floor	718	28	20,104	118
Second Floor	732	15	10,980	65
Total			46,541	

$$F_x = \frac{274}{46,541} \, (w_x h_x)$$

13.3　DESIGN OF THE STEEL RIGID FRAME

The general nature of rigid frames is discussed in Section 3.7. The lateral strength and stiffness of columns is a critical concern for multistory, multiple-bay frames. As the building must be developed to resist lateral forces in all directions, it is necessary in many cases to consider the shear and bending resistance of columns in two directions (north-south and east-west, for example). This presents a problem for W-shape columns, as they have considerably greater resistance on their major (x-x) axis versus their minor (y-y) axis. Thus, orientation of W-shape columns in plan sometimes becomes a major consideration in structural planning.

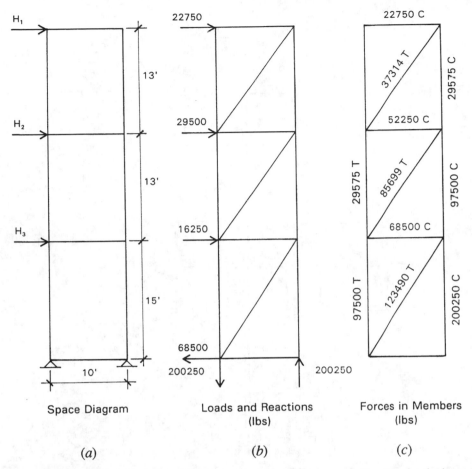

FIGURE 13.9 Investigation of an east-west trussed bent. (a) Layout and loading for the bent. (b) Resolution of external forces (loads and reactions) on the bent. (c) Internal forces in the bent members.

Figure 13.11*a* shows a possible plan arrangement for column orientation for Building 5, with two major bracing bents in the east-west direction and five shorter and less stiff bents in the north-south direction. The two stiff bents may well be approximately equal in resistance to the five shorter bents, giving the building a reasonably symmetrical response in the two directions.

Figure 13.11*b* shows a plan arrangement for columns designed to produce approximately symmetrical bents on the building perimeter. The form of such perimeter bracing is shown in Figure 13.12.

One advantage of perimeter bracing is the potential for using deeper (and thus stiffer) spandrel beams, as the restriction on depth that applies for interior beams does not apply at the exterior wall plane. Another possibility is to increase the number of columns at the exterior, as shown in Figure 13.11*c*; this does not compromise the building interior space. With deeper spandrels and closely spaced exterior columns, a very stiff perimeter bent is possible. In fact, such a bent may have very little flexing in the members, and its behavior approaches that of a pierced wall, rather than a flexible frame.

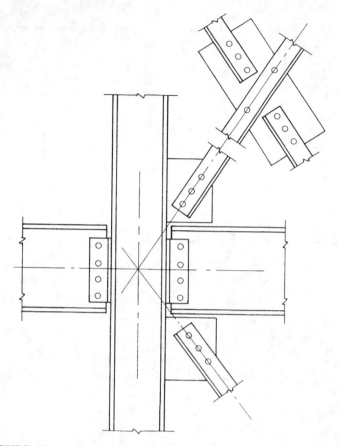

FIGURE 13.10   Details of the trussed bent construction with bolted joints.

At the expense of requiring much stronger (and thus heavier and/or larger) columns and expensive moment-resistive connections, rigid frame bracing offers architectural planning advantages by eliminating solid shear walls or truss diagonals in the walls. However, the lateral deflection of the frames must be carefully controlled, especially with regard to damage to nonstructural parts of the construction.

The various design problems of steel rigid frames are discussed in Section 3.7. General considerations for design of multistory rigid frames are more fully illustrated in Section 13.4.

13.4   DESIGN OF THE CONCRETE RIGID FRAME

A structural framing plan for the upper floors in Building 5 is presented in Figure 13.13, showing the use of a sitecast concrete slab and beam system. Support for the spanning structure is provided by concrete columns. The system for lateral bracing is that shown in Figure 13.4d, which uses the exterior columns and spandrel beams as rigid frame bents at the building perimeter. This is a highly indeterminate structure for both gravity and lateral loads, and its precise engineering design would undoubtedly be done with a computer-

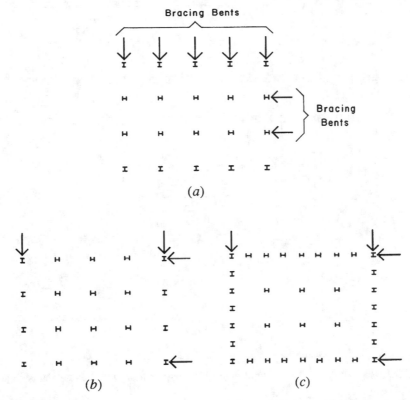

FIGURE 13.11 Optional schemes for orientation of the steel W-shape columns for development of rigid frame bents.

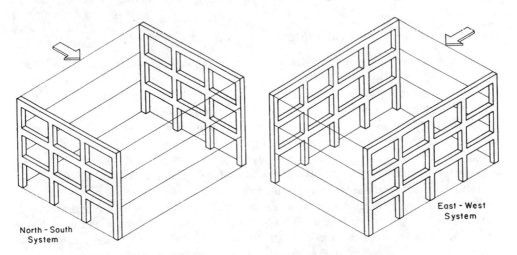

FIGURE 13.12 Form of the perimeter bent bracing system.

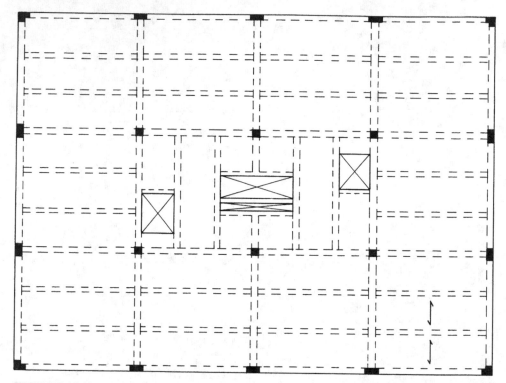

FIGURE 13.13   Building 5: Structural plan of the upper floor with the concrete slab-and-beam system.

aided design process. The presentation here discusses the major issues and illustrates an approximate investigation of the rigid frame using highly simplified methods.

The Slab-and-Beam Floor Structure

As shown in Figure 13.13, the floor framing system consists of a series of parallel beams at 10-ft centers that support a continuous, one-way spanning slab and are in turn supported by column-line girders or directly by columns. Although there are special beams required for the core framing, the system is made up largely of repeated elements.

Figure 13.14 shows a section of the exterior wall that illustrates the general form of the construction. The exterior columns and the spandrel beams are exposed to view. Using the full available depth of the spandrel beams results in a much stiffened bent on the building exterior. This is combined with the use of oblong-shaped columns at the exterior to create perimeter bents that will absorb most of the lateral force on the structure.

The use of the 5-in. slab is based on assumed minimum requirements for fire protection. If a thinner slab is possible, the 9-ft clear span would not require this thickness based on limiting bending or shear conditions or recommendations for deflection control. If the 5-in. slab is used, however, the result will be a slab with a low percentage of steel bar weight per square foot—usually resulting in lower cost for the structure.

The framing plan in Figure 13.13 shows that the girders on the north-south columns lines carry the ends of the beams as concentrated loads at their third points (10 ft from

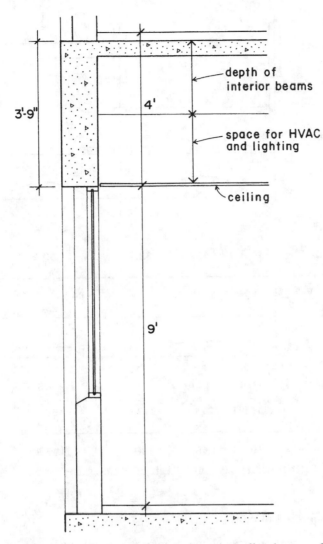

FIGURE 13.14 Section of the typical exterior wall at the upper floors.

each support). The spandrel girders at the building ends carry the outer ends of the beams plus their own dead weight. In addition, all the spandrel beams support the weight of the exterior curtain walls. The form of the spandrels and the wall construction is shown in Figure 13.14.

The spandrel beams that are components of the perimeter bracing bents carry a combination of uniformly distributed loads (spandrel weight plus wall) and concentrated loads (the beam ends).

Figure 13.15 presents a summary of the approximate moments for the spandrel girder. This is only the gravity loading, which must be combined with effects of lateral loads for complete design of the bents. A full analysis of the spandrel girder is therefore deferred until after the discussion of lateral loads later in this section.

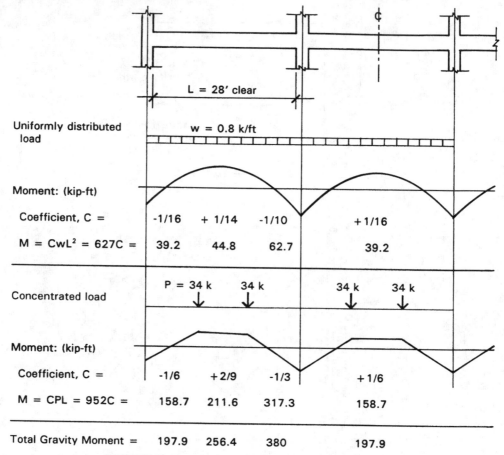

FIGURE 13.15 Gravity load effect on the spandrel beam.

Design of the Concrete Columns

The general cases for the concrete columns (Figure 13.16) follow:

1. The interior column primarily carries only gravity loads due to the stiffened perimeter bents.
2. The corner columns carry the ends of the spandrel beams and function as the ends of the perimeter bents in both directions.
3. The intermediate columns on the north and south sides carry the ends of the interior girders and function as members of the perimeter bents.
4. The intermediate columns on the east and west sides carry the ends of the column-line beams and function as members of the perimeter bents.

As all columns will be subjected to combinations of axial load and bending moments, gravity loads only represent the axial compression action. Gravity bending moments will be relatively low in magnitude on interior columns, since they are framed into by beams on all sides. As all reinforced concrete columns are designed for a minimum amount of

FIGURE 13.16   Relations between the columns and beams.

bending, routine design—even when done for axial load alone—provides for some residual moment capacity. For an approximate design, therefore, it is reasonable to consider the interior columns for axial gravity loads only.

A general cost-savings factor is the use of relatively low percentages of steel reinforcement. An economical column is therefore one with a minimum percentage (usually a threshold of 1% of the gross section) of reinforcement. However, other factors often effect design choices for columns, including:

1. Architectural planning of building interiors: Large columns often are difficult to plan around in developing of interior rooms, corridors, stair openings, and so on. Thus the *smallest* feasible column sizes—obtained with maximum percentages of steel—are often desired.

2. The ultimate load response of lightly reinforced columns borders on brittle fracture failure, whereas heavily reinforced columns tend to have a yield-form of ultimate failure. The yield character is especially desirable for rigid frame actions in general, and for seismic loading conditions particularly.

3. A general rule of practice in rigid-frame design for lateral loadings (wind or earthquakes) is to prefer a ratio of nature of ultimate response described as *strong column/weak beam failure*. In this example, this relates more to the columns in the perimeter bents, but it may also condition design choices for the interior columns, since they will take *some* lateral loads when the building as a whole deflects sideways.

Column form may also be an issue that relates to architectural planning or to structural concerns. Round columns work well for some structural actions and may be quite economical for forming, but unless they are totally freestanding, they do not fit so well for planning of the rest of the building construction. Even large square columns may be difficult to plan around in some cases—at the corners of stair wells and elevator shafts, for example. T-shaped or angle-shaped columns may be used in special situations.

Large bending moments in proportion to axial compression may also dictate adjustment of column form or the arrangement of reinforcement. When a column becomes essentially beamlike in its action, some of the practical considerations for beam design come into play. In this example, these concerns apply to the exterior columns to some degree.

For the intermediate exterior columns, there are four actions to consider:

1. The vertical compression due to gravity.
2. Bending moment induced by the interior framing that intersects the wall; these columns provide the end-resisting moments shown in Figure 13.15.
3. Bending moments in the plane of the wall bent, induced by unbalanced gravity load conditions (moveable live loads) on the spandrels.
4. Bending moments in the plane of the wall bents due to lateral loads.

For the corner columns, the situation is similar to that for the intermediate exterior columns; that is, there is bending on both axes. Gravity loads will produce simultaneous bending on both axes, resulting in a net moment that is diagonal to the column. Lateral loads can cause the same effect, since neither wind nor earthquakes will work neatly on the building's major axes, even though this is how design investigation is performed.

The exterior columns are discussed in the following considerations for lateral load effects.

Design for Lateral Forces

The major lateral force-resisting systems for this structure are the perimeter column/beam bents. The general form of this system is shown in Figure 13.12. Other elements of the construction will also resist lateral distortion of the structure, but by widening the exterior columns in the wall plane and using the very deep spandrel girders, the stiffness of these bents becomes considerable.

When lateral deformation occurs, the stiffer elements will attract the force first. Of course, the stiffest elements may not have the necessary strength, and thus may fail structurally, passing the resistance off to other resisting elements. Therefore, glass tightly held in flexible window frames, stucco on light wood structural frames, lightweight concrete block walls, or plastered partitions on light metal frames might be fractured first in lateral movements (and often are). For the successful design of this building, the detailing of the construction should be done carefully to ensure that these events do not occur, in spite of the relative stiffness of the perimeter bents. In any event, the bents shown in Figure 13.12 will be designed for the entire lateral load. Thus, they represent the safety assurance for the structure, if not a guarantee against loss of construction.

Determination of the building weight is presented in Table 13.3. Using these weights, the distribution of forces is determined in Table 13.4. Again shortcutting the process for its determination, a value of 0.06875 (6.875%) is assumed for the seismic force factor, and the base shear is determined as

$$V = 0.06875(5106) = 351 \text{ kips}$$

TABLE 13.3 Building Weight for the Seismic Load

Level	Source of Load	Unit Load (psf)		Load (kips)
Roof	Roof and ceiling	140	$120 \times 90 \times 140 =$	1512
	Window walls	15	$400 \times 4.5 \times 15 =$	27
	Interior walls	10	$200 \times 5 \times 10 =$	10
	$1/2$-story columns			72
	Penthouse + equipment (estimate total) =			25
	Subtotal			1646
Third Floor	Floor	140	$120 \times 90 \times 140 =$	1512
	Window walls	15	$420 \times 9 \times 15 =$	54
	Story columns			132
	Interior walls	10	$200 \times 9 \times 10 =$	18
	Subtotal			1716
Second Floor	Floor	140	$120 \times 90 \times 140 =$	1512
	Window walls	15	$400 \times 11 \times 15 =$	66
	Story columns			144
	Interior walls	10	$200 \times 11 \times 10 =$	22
	Subtotal			1744
Total dead load for the seismic base shear				5106

TABLE 13.4 Distribution of the Seismic Load

Level	w_x (kips)	h_x (ft)	$w_x \times h_x$	F_x (kips)
Roof	1,646	41	67,486	167
Third Floor	1,716	28	48,048	119
Second Floor	1,744	15	26,160	65
Total			141,694	

$$F_x = \frac{351}{141,694} (w_x h_x)$$

With two perimeter bents in each direction, the load for each bent is one-half of the forces determined in Table 13.4. Figure 13.17a shows a profile of the north-south bent with these loads applied.

For an approximate analysis, we consider the individual stories of the bent to behave as shown in Figure 13.17b, with the columns developing an inflection point at their mid-height points. Because the columns are all deflected the same sideways distance, the shear force in a single column may be assumed to be proportional to the relative stiffness of the column. If the columns all have the same stiffness, the total load at each story for this bent would simply be divided by 4 to obtain the column shear forces.

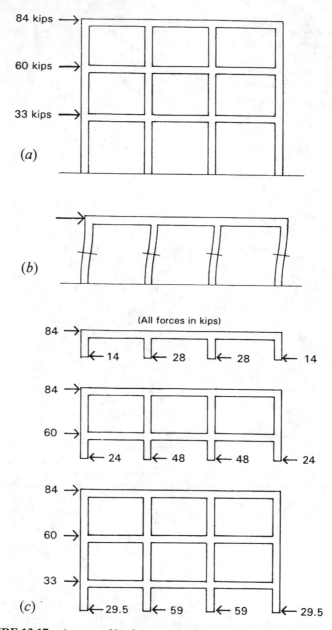

FIGURE 13.17   Aspects of load response of the north-south perimeter bents.

Even if the columns are all the same size, however, they may not all have the same resistance to lateral deflection. The end columns in the bent are slightly less restrained at their ends (top and bottom) because they are framed on only one side by a beam. For this approximation, therefore, it is assumed that the relative stiffness of the end columns is one-half that of the intermediate columns. Thus, the shear force in the end columns is one-sixth of the total story shear force and that in the intermediate column is one-third of the total force. The column shears for each of the three stories is shown in Figure 13.17c.

The column shear forces produce bending moments in the columns. With the column inflection points (points of zero moment) at mid-height, the moment produced by a single shear force is simply the product of the force and half the column height. These column moments must be resisted by the end moments in the rigidly attached beams, and the actions are as shown in Figure 13.18. At each column/beam intersection the sum of the column and beam moments must be balanced. Thus, the total of the beam moments may be equated to the total of the column moments, and the beam moments can be determined once the column moments are known. For example, at the second-floor level of the intermediate column, the sum of the column moments from Figure 13.18 is

$$M = 312 + 442.5 = 754.5 \text{ kip-ft}$$

Assuming the two beams framing the column to have equal stiffness at their ends, the beams will share this moment equally, and the end moment in each beam is

$$M = 754.5/2 = 377.25 \text{ kip-ft}$$

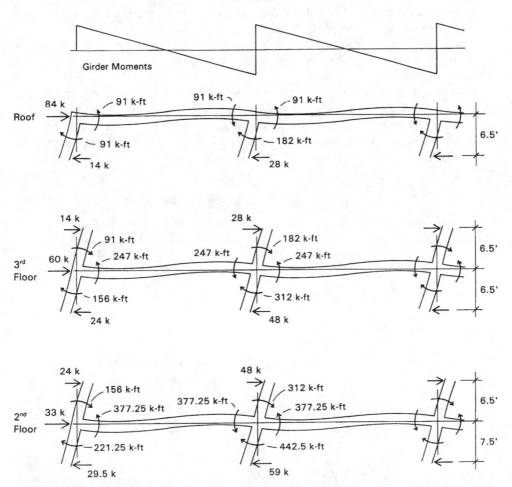

FIGURE 13.18 Investigation for column and girder bending moments in the north-south perimeter bent.

as shown in the figure. The data displayed in Figure 13.18 is now combined with that obtained from the gravity load analyses for a combined load investigation and final design of the bent members.

Design of the Bent Columns

The bent columns must be designed for the following loadings:

1. Vertical compression due to gravity
2. Vertical load due to lateral force action (overturning)
3. Bending due to gravity loads on both column axes
4. Bending due to lateral loads on the column axis perpendicular to the bent plane

The bent columns can be considered first for gravity loads alone to obtain some preliminary sizes. Approximate bending moments due to gravity produce the column moments shown in Figure 13.19. The moments for this analysis can be taken from the girder investigations. For some columns, it is common that the gravity-only design condition will prevail; this is most likely for the upper-story columns.

Bending moments for lateral load may be taken from Figure 13.18. These must be combined with the gravity-induced actions for a complete analysis, using the required load combinations.

When vertical compression prevails for the column design, reinforcement can be placed symmetrically in the columns. The bent columns are not square, however, and the predominant moment is on the axis perpendicular to the bent. For the columns with exceptionally high bending on this axis, the majority of the column bars may be placed at

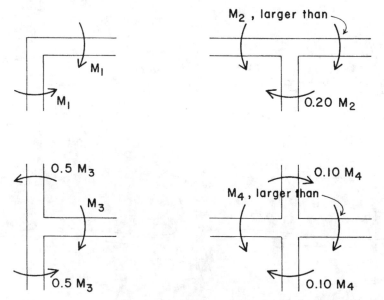

FIGURE 13.19 Approximations of the distribution of bending moments in the bent columns due to gravity loads.

the two narrow faces of the column. To work out the limits for these bars, spacing limitations and placement of the girder reinforcement must be considered.

Special detailing, as required by the *UBC*, for these bents determines the placement of both column and girder reinforcement. Column ties ordinarily required for bracing the bars and stirrups ordinarily required for girder shears may be modified for use as containment reinforcement in the region of the column/girder joints.

The corner column at the end of the bent is especially vulnerable. These columns do double service in both bents that meet at the corner. They are also end members, and thus have a large bending moment on both axes due to gravity forces. They might be the most critical elements of the bent and should be carefully designed.

The summary of design conditions for the corner and intermediate columns is given in Table 13.5. When bending moment is very high in comparison to the axial load (very large eccentricity), an effective approximate column design can be determined by designing a section simply as a beam with tension reinforcement; the reinforcement is then duplicated on both sides of the column.

Design of the Bent Girders

The spandrel girders must be designed for the same two basic load conditions as discussed for the columns. The summary of bending moments for the third-floor spandrel girder is shown in Figure 13.20. The construction assumed here is that shown in Figure 13.14, with the very deep, exposed girder. Some attention should be given to the relative stiffnesses of the columns and girders, as discussed later in this section. Since the girder is almost three times as long as the column, it may have a considerably stiffer section without causing a disproportionate relationship to occur. The deep and thin spandrel should be treated somewhat as a wall, with some additional horizontal bars at mid-height points.

It is advisable to use continuous top and bottom reinforcement in spandrels. This relates to some of the following considerations:

TABLE 13.5   Summary of Design Data for the Bent Columns

	Column	
	Intermediate	Corner
Axial Gravity Design Load (kips):		
Third Story	90.0	55.0
Second Story	179.0	117.0
First Story	277.0	176.0
Assumed Gravity Moment—from Analysis (kip-ft):		
Third Story	60.0	120.0
Second Story	39.0	100.0
First Story	39.0	100.0
Moment from Lateral Force Analysis (kip-ft):		
Third Story	182.0	91.0
Second Story	312.0	156.0
First Story	442.5	221.2

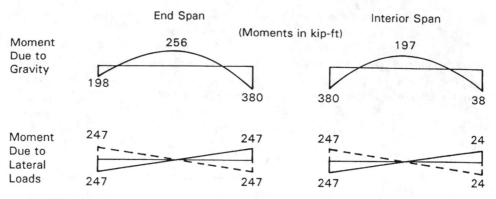

FIGURE 13.20   Combined lateral and gravity bending moments in the spandrel girder.

1. Miscalculation of lateral effects, giving some reserved reversal bending capacity to the girders
2. A general capability for torsional resistance throughout the beam length (intersecting beams produce this effect)
3. A device to hold up the continuous stirrups
4. Some reduction of long-term creep deflection with all sections doubly reinforced to help keep load off the window mullions and glazing

Relative Stiffness of Bent Members

Within a single bent, the behavior of the bent and the forces in individual members will be strongly affected by the relative stiffness of bent members. If story heights vary and beam spans vary, some very complex and unusual behaviors can be involved. Variations of column and beam stiffnesses may also be a significant factor.

A particular concern is the relative stiffnesses of all the columns in a single story of the bent. In many cases, the portion of lateral shear in the columns will be distributed on this basis. Thus, the stiffer columns may carry a major part of the lateral force.

The relative stiffnesses of columns in comparison to beams is another concern. Most bent analyses assume the column stiffness to be more-or-less equal to the beam stiffness, producing the classic form of lateral deformation shown in Figure 3.41a. Individual bent

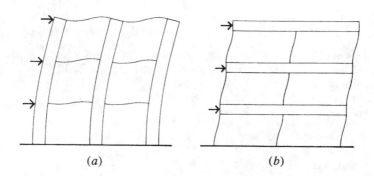

(a)   *(b)*

FIGURE 13.21   Proportionate stiffness in rigid bents.

members are assumed to take an S-shaped, inflected form. However, if the columns are exceptionally stiff in relation to the beams, the form of bent deformation may be more like that shown in Figure 13.21a, with virtually no inflection in the columns and an excessive deformation in upper beams. In tall frames, this is often the case in lower stories where gravity loads produce large columns.

Conversely, if the beams are exceptionally stiff in comparison to the columns, the form of bent deformation may be more like that shown in Figure 13.21b, with columns behaving as if fully fixed at their ends. Deep spandrel beams with relatively small columns commonly produce this situation.

The cases shown in Figure 13.21 can be dealt with in design, although it is important to understand which form of deformation is most likely to occur.

The Captive Frame

In Section 3.8 we examined the problem of interaction of parallel bents and walls. A special problem is that of the partially restrained column or beam, with inserted construction altering the form of deformation of bent members. An example of this, shown in Figures 13.22 and 13.23, is the *captive column*. In the example, a partial height wall is placed between columns. If this wall has sufficient stiffness and strength and is tightly wedged between columns, the laterally unbraced height of the column is drastically altered. As a result, the shear and bending in the column will be considerably different from that of the free column. In addition, the distribution of forces in the bent containing the captive columns may also be affected. Finally, the bent can be significantly stiffened and its share of the load in relation to other parallel bents made much higher.

This has been a major source of problems for concrete frames affected by seismic forces. It is an issue for the structural designer of the bents, but it must be considered in cooperation with whoever is doing the construction detailing for the wall construction.

13.5   DESIGN OF THE MASONRY WALL STRUCTURE

A structural framing plan for one of the upper floors of Building 5 is shown in Figure 13.24. The plan indicates bearing walls are the major supports for the floor framing. The

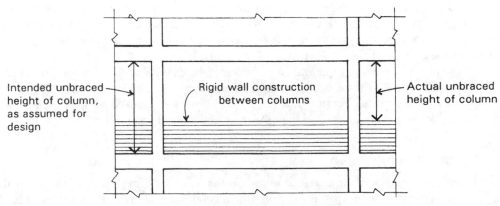

FIGURE 13.22   The captive column.

FIGURE 13.23   Columns captured by an infill balcony wall.

walls will constitute the lateral bracing system too, with a combination of perimeter and core-braced systems.

For the office building, elements for wiring, piping, heating and cooling, ventilating, controlling fire, and lighting must be incorporated. There are many options for the floor framing, depending on fire code requirements and the competitive pricing of local suppliers. Options for consideration include wood, steel, sitecast concrete, and precast concrete. For this example, the system consists of a plywood deck, light nailable prefabricated joists or trusses, and steel beams, as shown in Figure 13.25.

Figure 13.26 shows the general construction of the exterior walls, which use reinforced CMU construction for the wall structure. A multilayered exterior insulation (EFI) system is used on the outside surface and furring strips with gypsum drywall is used on the inside. We now examine the design of the structural masonry walls.

Design for Gravity Forces

There are two general structural concerns for the walls for gravity loading: first, for the general compressive bearing in the walls and, second, for the effects of concentrated loads

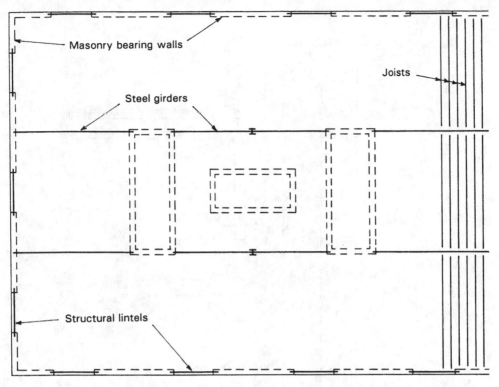

FIGURE 13.24 Building 5: Framing plan for upper floor, masonry wall structure.

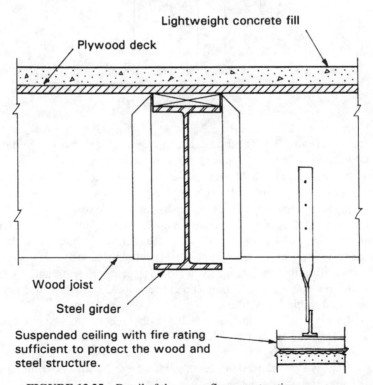

FIGURE 13.25 Detail of the upper floor construction.

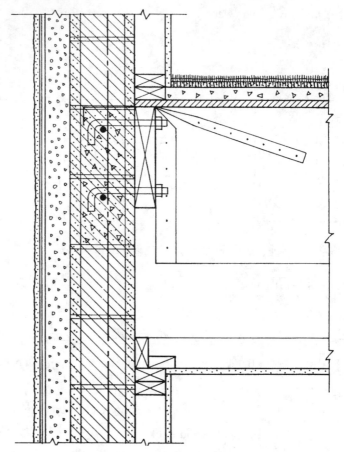

FIGURE 13.26   Construction of the masonry wall at the upper floors.

from supported beams. For general bearing, the greatest load will be in the first story, and this maximum load determines the required wall construction. From this maximum, the wall may be graded down in strength capacity in upper stories. Gradation of capacity can be achieved by changing the wall thickness (larger CMUs in lower stories), but it can also be done by making changes within the construction while maintaining a single thickness.

A minimum reinforced CMU construction is established by code requirements. With standard 16-in.-long, two-void units, voids are 8 in. on center. With the code-required minimum of reinforced voids every 4 ft, this means that only every sixth void is reinforced. From that minimum, it is possible to upgrade the wall strength by filling additional voids, up to a maximum of filling the entire wall. (Foundation walls and major shear walls are usually completely filled.)

As the framing plan in Figure 13.24 shows, the interior steel beams and the lintels are supported at the ends or corners of the bearing walls. With ordinary reinforced CMU construction, ends or corners have a filled and reinforced void, which likely will have a considerable capacity for compression bearing. However, it is also possible to create enlarged elements (pilasters) at these locations.

While design for gravity must be individually considered, the walls must eventually sustain the combination of gravity and lateral loads. Development of the CMU wall system for lateral loads is considered next.

Design for Lateral Forces

With the heavy masonry walls, the total weight of this building should be approximately the same as the concrete building's. However, the stiffness of the masonry shear walls results in a seismic shear of twice that for a concrete rigid frame. For investigation, we use the load distribution determined in Table 13.4 but double the values for the loads.

$$H_1 = 2(167) = 334 \text{ kips (at the roof)}$$
$$H_2 = 2(119) = 238 \text{ kips (at the 3rd floor)}$$
$$H_3 = 2(65) = 130 \text{ kips (at the 2nd floor)}$$

Figure 13.27 shows the plan indicating the masonry walls that offer potential as shear walls for resistance to wind in the north-south direction. The numbers in Figure 13.27a are the approximate plan lengths of the walls. Note that, although the core construction actually produces tubular-shaped elements, the walls have been considered to act only in resistance to forces parallel to the wall direction in plan. This is a conservative assumption, based on the questionable strength of the wall corners in typical CMU construction.

The walls shown in Figure 13.27 share the total loads delivered by the horizontal diaphragms. The manner of sharing depends to a degree on the relative stiffness of the horizontal diaphragm (roof or floor deck):

1. If the horizontal diaphragm is quite stiff (as for a sitecast concrete deck), it will deform very little, and distribution will be in proportion to the stiffness of individual walls.
2. If the horizontal diaphragm is reasonably deformable (as for a wood or steel deck), it will span horizontally like a simple beam between vertical elements, and distribution will be on a peripheral basis (using zones defined by one-half the distances between vertical elements).

The plan in Figure 13.27b illustrates distribution of the total wind load to the groups of end walls and core walls on the basis of peripheral distribution by a wood deck. The load thus determined puts a slightly higher stress on the core walls.

Although the distribution of shared loads to a set of masonry walls is usually done on the basis of relative stiffness, if the walls are stiff in proportion to their plan lengths (as is common for plywood walls), an approximate average shear stress can be obtained by dividing the shared total load by the sum of the wall lengths. On this basis, the average maximum shear stress at the first story is

$$v = \frac{702,000}{260} = 2,700 \text{ lb/ft of wall length}$$

This is quite a tolerable stress for a reinforced CMU wall. Even though the actual stress will be somewhat higher in the stiffer walls (notably, the 30-ft-long core walls), this

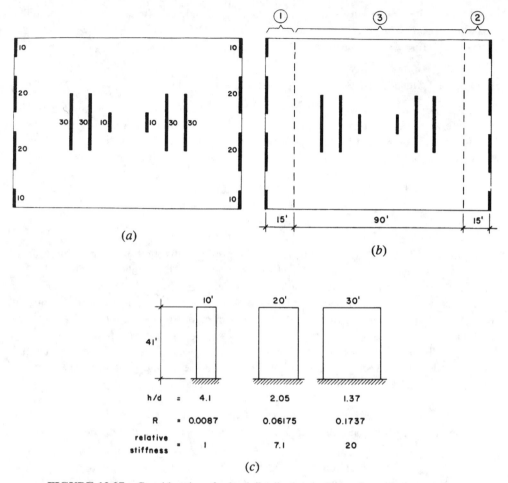

FIGURE 13.27 Considerations for load distribution to the north-south shear walls.

approximate computation establishes that there is a potential for adequate strength in the construction for the seismic loads.

If the individual wall elements shown in Figure 13.27*a* act as individual piers, they must be considered individually for overturn effects. For the building height shown, the 10-ft walls will be too slender if they have to work for all three stories. However, they really are not *needed* for the lower total shear force in the upper stories, so they can be considered for the first story only.

If the perimeter walls are developed as continuous walls with punched holes, rather than as linked sets of individual piers, their true lengths in Figure 13.27*a* should be shown as single 92-ft-long walls. In this case, the load to the core would be almost negligible because of the relative stiffness of the end walls.

With the building almost twice as wide as it is high in the narrow direction, there is no concern for general overturn of the structure. This is a major concern for very tall, tower-like buildings, but not critical for low-rise structures.

A truly critical issue of concern for this construction is the connection of the horizontal framing to the walls. If the major transfer of forces is through the wall faces with anchor bolts, as shown in Figure 13.26, this bolting must be carefully investigated for all the load combinations and carefully detailed for construction. There is a three-way force action here, involving vertical gravity force, lateral shear parallel to the wall, and a pull-away effect due to outward force on the wall (wind suction or seismic effect). Participation of all the structural elements in these actions (wall, anchor bolts, deck, joists, beams, ledgers) must be studied and appropriate connections developed.

Referring to Figure 13.27b, if we consider the group of core walls in peripheral zone 3, their total combined stiffness is

$$(4 \times 0.1737 = 0.6948) + (2 \times 0.0087 = 0.0174) = 0.7122$$

Thus, by proportionate stiffness, the portion of the load in this zone that is carried by a single 10-ft-long wall is

$$0.0087/0.7122 = 0.0122, \text{ or barely more than } 1\%$$

It is therefore reasonable to assume that the 30-ft walls carry the entire load to the building core zone. For a single pair of walls constituting one stair plus a rest room tower, the portion of the full lateral load is thus

$$\tfrac{1}{2} \times \tfrac{3}{4} \times F_x = 0.375 \, F_x$$

Referring to Table 13.4 and Figure 13.28, the loads for a single tower are

$$H_1 = 0.375(167) = 63 \text{ kips}$$
$$H_2 = 0.375(119) = 45 \text{ kips}$$
$$H_2 = 0.375(65) = 24 \text{ kips}$$

The overturning moments of these forces are

$$H_1 \times 41 = 63 \times 41 = 2583 \text{ kip-ft}$$
$$H_2 \times 28 = 45 \times 28 = 1260 \text{ kip-ft}$$
$$H_3 \times 15 = 24 \times 15 = 360 \text{ kip-ft}$$

and the total overturning moment at the first-floor level is

$$2583 + 1260 + 360 = 4203 \text{ kip-ft}$$

For the dead-load restoring moment that resists this overturn effect the following assumptions are made:

1. The walls are 8-in. concrete blocks that produce a wall weight of 60 psf of wall surface. Thus, the wall weight for the entire tower is approximately

$$(80 \text{ ft} \times 41 \text{ ft}) \times 60 \text{ psf} = 196.8 \text{ kips}$$

2. As bearing walls, the tower walls carry approximately 1800 ft^2 of roof or floor periphery, which results in a supported dead load of

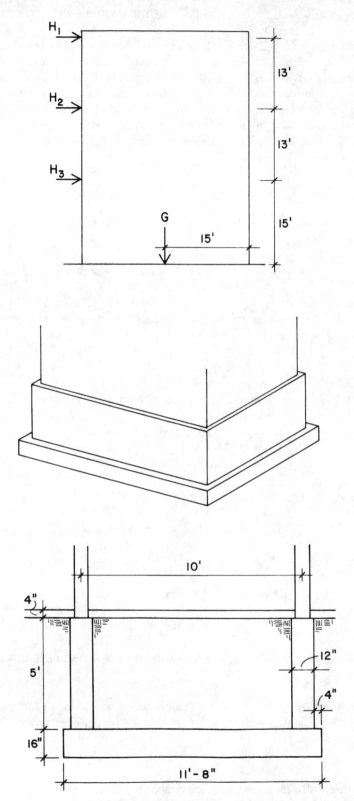

FIGURE 13.28   The stair tower.

55 psf × 1800 = 99 kips/floor, or 198 kips total
25 psf × 1800 = 45 kips of roof load

which results in a total dead load of 439.8 kips (G, as shown in Figure 13.28).

Using the *UBC* requirement for reducing this by 15%, the usable restoring moment is thus

$$M = 0.85(439.8 \times 15) = 5608 \text{ kip-ft}$$

The safety factor against overturn is thus

$$5608/4203 = 1.33$$

This is slightly less than the desired factor of 1.5, so some additional restraint is required. Two restraints are provided by the building construction. The first results from tying the walls to the foundation through the vertical reinforcement that is extended across the joint, thus adding the weight of the heavy foundation as a restoring force. In addition, besides its dead weight, the construction at the roof and floor levels will prevent movement of the tower. Thus, it would seem that this tower is not in real danger of overturning.

Of course, overturn should also be investigated at the bottom of the foundation, as discussed in Section 8.4.

Because of their relative stiffness, the core walls carry the major portion of the lateral force in this building. If the building were designed for wind force only, the core could be used alone for bracing, eliminating the need for exterior shear walls. For seismic effects, however, the exterior walls add significantly to the torsional resistance, making core bracing alone less desirable.

Figure 13.29 shows an elevation of the east and west walls for Building 4 with the structural masonry pierced with rows of windows aligned both vertically and horizontally.

Depending on details of the wall construction—notably, the locations of control joints in the masonry—the wall could be made to behave either as a continuous pierced wall or as a series of vertical piers consisting of the solid strips between the windows. In this case, the solid strips between the windows are 44 ft high and only 9 ft wide; an aspect ratio of height to width that is not very feasible for isolated shear walls.

If the wall is treated as a single, solid piece, 44 ft high and 92 ft long, it is extremely stiff as a vertical cantilever. Flexural action would be insignificant and the wall would be designed only for lateral shear plus vertical compression. This process has been illustrated in previous examples, so we will limit this example to examining a few special problems.

For the one-piece pierced wall, the critical design elements are the small panels between the windows—both horizontally and vertically. As shown in Fig. 13.29, there are two basic elements. The solid portion between windows in the horizontal row is called a *wall pier* and is subjected to horizontal shearing force. As a flexural member, it is fixed at its top and bottom and functions as a doubly fixed beam. This action is not significant because of the pier's extreme stiffness. Therefore, it is designed for the portion of the horizontal force that it carries in shearing action. Determining that portion, however, is accomplished by considering the wall stiffness due to its dimensions and aspect ratio, as illustrated in the previous examples in this section.

The solid portion of wall between windows in the vertical row is described in architectural terms as the *spandrel*. In the pierced wall, the spandrel panels function as *wall*

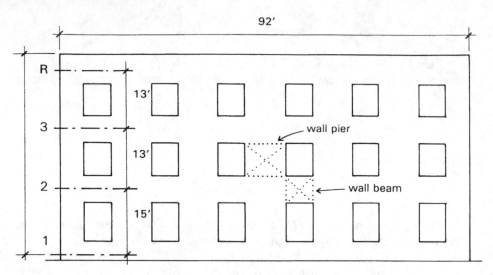

FIGURE 13.29 The pierced wall.

beams, spanning across the window openings. For vertical gravity loads, they may truly function as reinforced beams and be designed as such. Under lateral loads, they will be subjected to a vertical shearing action. The general effect of this shearing action is similar to that for the wall piers.

In tension-weak materials, such as concrete, masonry, and plaster, a critical shear action typically results in diagonal tension cracking. Under lateral load from a single direction, the wall piers and spandrels tend to develop these diagonal cracks. During an earthquake, as the load direction rapidly reverses, the typical form of cracking is an X shape. This is illustrated in the drawing in Figure 13.29 and in the photo in Figure 13.30.

With a nonstructural wall cladding of stucco or masonry veneer, the best means of preventing X cracks is to use control joints in the cladding and cushion the cladding in some way from the movements of the structure. If the wall is to truly work as a single-piece pierced shear wall, however, it will have to be adequately reinforced for the critical shear actions. Figure 13.31 shows two kinds of reinforcement.

The individual piers and spandrels also must be reinforced for the diagonal tension forces. Since this reinforcement usually can only be placed vertically and horizontally in the masonry, the practical solution is to place identical vertical and horizontal reinforcement amounts. This reinforcement must be fully developed within the boundaries of the piers and spandrels, which requires either extending into the adjacent wall or hooking the ends of the bars, as shown in Fig. 13.31. Some of the vertical bars in the piers and some of the horizontal bars in the spandrels will undoubtedly be continuous throughout the wall construction.

To reinforce the wall piers and spandrels most effectively, it would be desirable to place reinforcement in an X-shape pattern in direct resistance of the diagonal tension forces. While not generally feasible in masonry walls, this is possible in cast concrete walls.

If this wall is developed as a shear wall, it will function as a vertical support for the floor and roof structures as well. This involves attaching the wall to those constructions

FIGURE 13.30   Failure of wall piers and spandrels in a pierced concrete wall.

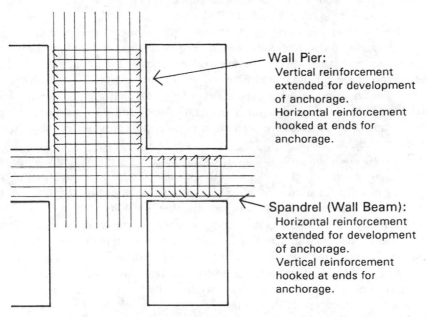

Wall Pier:
Vertical reinforcement
extended for development
of anchorage.
Horizontal reinforcement
hooked at ends for
anchorage.

Spandrel (Wall Beam):
Horizontal reinforcement
extended for development
of anchorage.
Vertical reinforcement
hooked at ends for
anchorage.

FIGURE 13.31   Development of reinforcement for the pierced wall.

for transfer of the loads to the wall. In developing the construction details for such inter-sections of it is desirable to achieve three goals.

1. No bending in the wall due to the gravity loads; that is, the supported loads should be placed axially on the wall.
2. Attachment of the horizontal construction to achieve the lateral force transmission to the shear wall.

3. Attachment of the horizontal construction to achieve an anchorage of the wall against outward movement (*horizontal anchorage*).

These goals must be achieved by means that are compatible with the many other requirements of the wall construction, including interior and exterior finishes, water control, fire resistance, and ordinary requirements for the particular form of masonry.

13.6 DESIGN OF THE CONCRETE WALL STRUCTURE

Concrete shear walls represent the single strongest element for resistance to lateral shear force. When used for subgrade construction (basement walls) or for extensive walls in low-rise buildings, they provide great stiffness and strength for the shear wall tasks. They are strongest when developed with sitecast construction (concrete poured in forms at the site in the desired position). However, large precast walls are also capable of considerable bracing.

Of critical concern for concrete walls—and all reinforced concrete, for that matter—is the proper detailing of the steel reinforcement. Recommended details for this are specified in building codes and in the publications of the various organizations in the concrete industry, including the ACI, PCA, and CRSI.

Much of what has been said about masonry construction in the preceding section also generally applies to concrete construction. The structures produced are heavy and stiff and weak in tension resistance. Maximum seismic shear forces are required due to the combination of weight and overall stiffness of the structures. For earthquakes, concrete shear walls can work well, but proper detailing of the construction is very important. When used in combination with other structures (wood and steel framing, for example), adequate anchorage or effective separation is needed to provide for the differences in seismic movements.

The heavy, solid, stiff structure (concrete or masonry) is often an advantage for wind, providing an anchor for lighter elements of the construction. Excessive weight is not the concern, generally, for wind as it is for seismic effects. Typically, concrete and masonry foundation walls are the direct anchors for structures of wood and steel.

An advantage of reinforced concrete over reinforced masonry (particularly concrete block construction) is the greater flexibility allowed in locating the steel reinforcing bars. These can be placed only in the modular voids and mortar joints of masonry walls, but they can be placed with more freedom in the concrete mass. Furthermore, the steel rods must be vertical or horizontal in masonry, while the bars can take any direction in the concrete mass. In Figure 13.31, for example, the bars can only be in the vertical/horizontal grid shown in the masonry construction. In a concrete wall, however, additional diagonal bars could be used adding strength in direct resistance to the diagonal tension stresses.

Most of the example buildings shown with masonry walls in this book could be developed with concrete shear walls, either sitecast or precast. Dimensions, of course, might differ, but the materials are essentially the same—heavy, stiff, and tension-weak—and many of the structural behaviors would be the same.

14

Multistory Apartment Building

This chapter examines the design of lateral bracing for a twelve-story apartment building. This building height is beyond the range of wood construction, but otherwise it is open to a range of possibilities in terms of types of steel or concrete structures. The presentation here considers four options: a truss-braced steel frame, a concrete rigid frame, concrete shear walls, and masonry shear walls. The general form of Building 6 is shown in the plan and section in Figure 14.1.

14.1 DESIGN WITH SHEAR WALL BRACING

Figure 14.1a shows a typical plan for the upper floor of the multistory apartment building that utilizes shear walls as the bracing system in both directions. In the north-south direction, the interior walls between the apartment units are used together with the two end walls at the stairs, giving a total of 14 walls, all approximately 20-ft long in plan.

In the east-west direction, the vertical bracing consists of the two interior corridor walls. While it is sometimes desirable to have a minimum of permanent interior wall construction for occupancies such as office buildings and stores, corridor walls are generally considered permanent construction for apartments, hotels, dormitories, jails, and hospitals. These long shear walls may be designed as pierced walls, as discussed in Section 13.5.

The long exterior walls consist of column and beam structures, with the ends of the shear walls serving as columns. Floor structures might be flat slabs or conventional slab and beam construction. The shear walls will serve as bearing walls too, so the whole heavy concrete structure can be used to anchor the walls against overturn.

There is a limit to the height or number of stories for the shear wall-braced building. The critical concern is for the aspect ratio of height to plan length; if the ratio is too high, overturn and lateral drift may become hazardous. As shown in Figure 14.1b, the apartment separating walls have an aspect ratio of 6:1, which is sometimes considered as a practical limit.

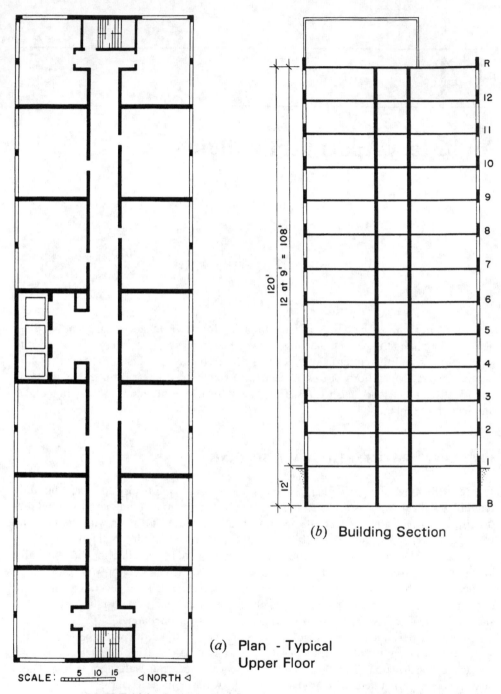

SCALE: 5 10 15 ◁ NORTH ◁

(a) Plan - Typical
Upper Floor

120'
12 at 9' = 108'

12'

R
12
11
10
9
8
7
6
5
4
3
2
1
B

(b) Building Section

FIGURE 14.1 Building 6: Plan and section of the apartment building.

328

The east-west corridor wall at the elevator consists of two shear walls, separated at the elevator lobby. Even so, the aspect ratio of these walls is less than 2:1, so overturn is surely not a problem. Careful detailing of special reinforcing of these walls is needed around the openings for the elevator entry doors.

The concrete shear wall structure is successful for resisting wind, but less successful for tall buildings in zones of high seismic risk. The combination of wall stiffness and very heavy construction generates a major lateral seismic force, whereas the weight is actually useful for overturn and uplift resistance against wind. For a building half this height, however, concrete or masonry shear walls may be equally practical for resistance of wind or seismic loads.

The change in this building's vertical structure at the first story might create a special problem. If this level is developed with a relatively open plan, a soft story may be created. If this level is very heavily braced, a weak story condition might be developed at the second story. All changes in the vertical structure must be studied for these conditions.

14.2   DESIGN WITH BRACED STEEL FRAME

If steel construction is a feasible solution for the apartment building, lateral resistance can be developed with either a braced frame or a rigid frame. Some options for development of north-south trussing are shown in Figure 14.2. The schemes shown in Figures 14.2*a*, *b*, and *c* utilize various forms of bracing in the same walls that were used for shear walls in Section 14.1. Thus, architectural planning for the braced frame is somewhat similar to planning for solid shear walls.

In this case, however, it is doubtful that it would be necessary to use bracing in every wall for the full height of the building. Figures 14.3 and 14.4 show the use of staggered or stepped bracing, in which some bays of bracing are reduced in upper floors. This corresponds to the variation of magnitude of horizontal shear and bending in the vertically cantilevered structure.

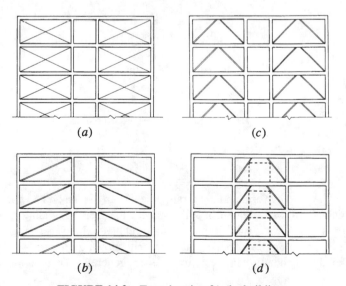

(*a*)   (*c*)

(*b*)   (*d*)

FIGURE 14.2   Truss bracing for the building.

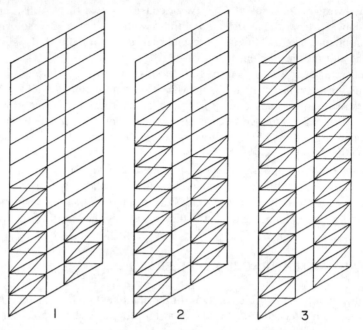

FIGURE 14.3   Isometric of the stepped bracing.

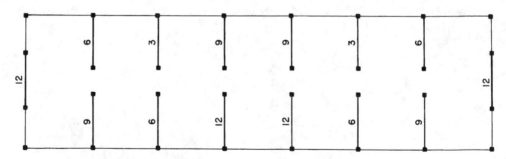

FIGURE 14.4   Plan of the stepped bracing.

Selection of the bracing form and the arrangement both in plan and profile depends part-ly on the magnitude of loads. For seismic resistance, an eccentric bracing system may pro-vide the energy capacity of a rigid frame with the relatively high resistance to drift of the trussed frame (see Section 3.6). The K-braced system shown in Figure 14.2*d* is such a sys-tem, although inducing bending in the columns is not generally accepted for seismic load.

14.3 DESIGN WITH CONCRETE FRAME

The plan in Figure 14.5 shows a scheme for the development of a concrete framed structure for the apartment building. East-west bracing is provided by the two perimeter bents on the long exterior walls. While more columns at closer spacing might be used to strengthen and stiffen this frame, the scheme shown is probably adequate for the height of this building. Columns are individually stiffened by taking an oblong plan form with the long dimension in the plane of the bent.

For the north-south bracing, it is not feasible to expect the horizontal diaphragm to span from end to end. In addition, the north-south bents are much shorter in plan length. Therefore the scheme shown uses the two column bents on either side of the elevator core, with closely spaced columns emulating the two end perimeter bents.

Of course, there would be additional vertical structure for the support of the floors and the roof. The plan as shown in Figure 14.5 indicates only the structure involved in the lateral bracing.

As with any building, the choice of the lateral bracing system has implications for architectural planning. In this example, if the scheme shown in Figure 14.5 is used, the layout of rooms would be less constrained than it would be with the shear wall or braced frame schemes. It might be favored, for example, if apartments of differing sizes were to be placed on the same floor.

A special problem to consider with the rigid frame is the potential for modification of the frame behavior by nonstructural elements of the construction. Wall construction installed between the columns in the interior bents must be very carefully detailed to avoid restricting normal rigid frame deformations of the structure. The exterior walls must be carefully developed as well. This is two-way protection: permitting the structure to flex normally and preventing structural deformations from damaging nonstructural elements.

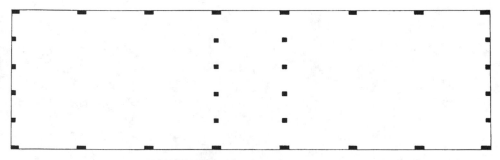

FIGURE 14.5 Plan for the concrete bents.

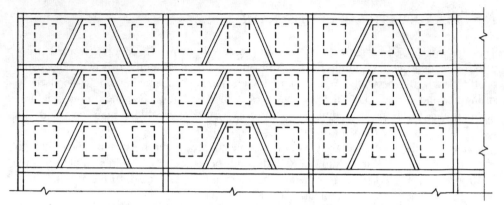

FIGURE 14.6   Eccentric bracing for the perimeter walls.

14.4   STEEL FRAME WITH ECCENTRIC BRACING

Figure 14.6 shows a scheme for the steel-framed apartment building, using fully eccentric bracing that dodges the window openings in the exterior walls. Properly designed, this scheme produces the highly energy-absorbing qualities of the rigid frame with its many plastic hinges while having much of the stiffness of the braced (trussed) frame with less lateral deflection.

Another property this type of structure offers is its relatively rapid damping of the vibration movements, an asset for building occupants, as opposed to the pure rigid frame with column/beam rigid connections, whose smooth flexing can leave tall structures swaying for some time after a major jolt. Of course, damping can also be provided with in-line shock absorbers, which could be used for some of the tilted members in the scheme in Figure 14.6.

15

Single-Story Warehouse

The general use of trussing for horizontal bracing elements is discussed in Section 3.6. A common reason for using horizontal trussing is the absence of an adequate horizontal decking that can be used for diaphragm action. Building 7, as described in this chapter, has a roof of a form that precludes diaphragm development, requiring some other form of horizontal bracing structure at the roof level.

15.1 DESCRIPTION

Figure 15.1 shows a large one-story building with a complex roof that consists of a regularly spaced series of sky windows. The roof structure consists of a series of clear-spanning trusses that define the planes for the windows. The remainder of the roof consists of sloped portions of decking that are supported by the top of one truss and the bottom of the next truss. This system is commonly called a *sawtooth roof*, and it has been widely used for large industrial facilities that are able to use the advantage of the potential daylighting and natural ventilation provided by the expanse of windows.

Due both to its steep slope and its lack of continuity, the roof decking can not perform diaphragm actions for the building as a whole. It can, however, contribute to the lateral bracing of the spanning trusses. The usual diaphragm action in the general plane of the roof structure is provided by the X bracing in the structural bays adjacent to the outside walls (Figure 15.1). This diagonal framing combines with the bottom chords of the spanning trusses and the horizontal framing in the wall structures to constitute a series of trusses at the building edges.

Because of the length of the building, the plan indicates the use of a center row of columns that are used to develop a three-span trussed bent, which serves to break the 240-ft-long roof into two units for the span of the horizontal trusses. Similar trussed bents are used at the building ends. Trussed bents also could be used along the long exterior walls, and the entire building lateral force resistive system would be developed with trussing. However, the exterior walls might also be developed with construction capable of the necessary shear wall actions.

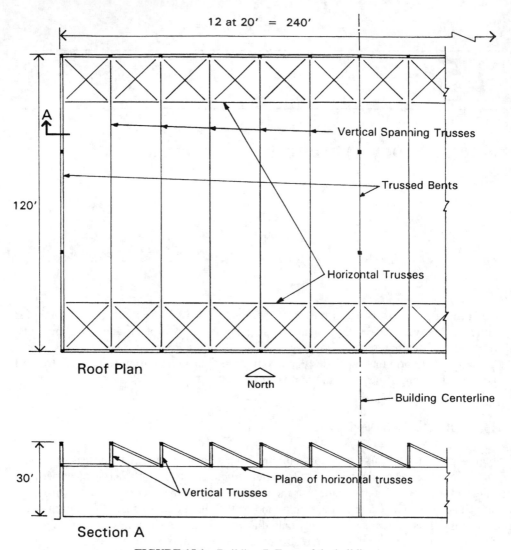

12 at 20′ = 240′

A

Vertical Spanning Trusses

Trussed Bents

120′

Horizontal Trusses

Roof Plan

North

Building Centerline

30′

Plane of horizontal trusses

Vertical Trusses

Section A

FIGURE 15.1 Building 7: Form of the building.

15.2 DESIGN OF THE HORIZONTAL TRUSSES

We will illustrate here the development of the horizontal X bracing along the long walls for resistance to lateral load in the north-south direction. Figure 15.2 illustrates a unit edge loading that is generated by the weight of the roof construction plus the upper portion of the north and south walls. The investigation of one of the X-braced trusses for this loading is shown in Figure 15.3.

The member forces shown in Figure 15.3 are relatively small for structural steel, and the X members could be quite small with regard to the required tension resistance. However, several considerations must be made in selecting the X bracing:

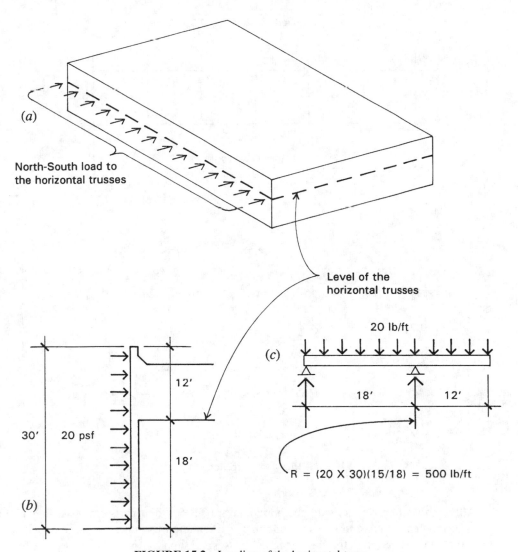

FIGURE 15.2   Loading of the horizontal truss.

1. The general form of the construction of the spanning trusses, regarding member shapes and joint details.
2. The need to reduce lateral movements by lowering the tension stress in the X members. Slightly larger members might be used to reduce strain and the elongation and deflection of the X-braced trusses.
3. The problem of sag, since the X members are quite long (approximately 28 ft), and, if essentially designed for tension, typically they will have low bending resistance on the horizontal span. This might be alleviated by using some suspension hangers from the roof construction above the centers of the X-braced bays.

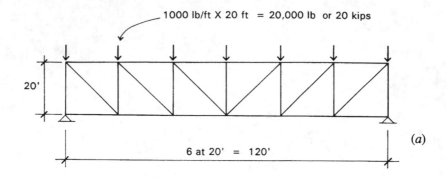

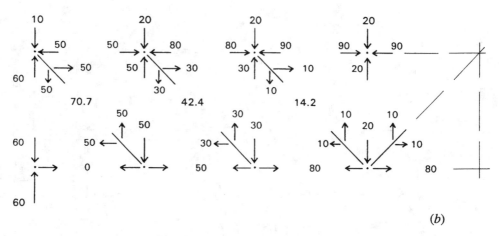

FIGURE 15.3   Investigation of the truss.

Although we have investigated the horizontal trusses for their particular task, they are parts of the general structural system and their participation for other purposes—such as providing lateral bracing for the spanning trusses or support for lighting—will affect selection of members and development of construction details.

As shown in the building roof plan in Figure 15.1, the X-bracing system is also used along the short exterior walls. In this example, with the use of the center trussed bents, the loading and span conditions for these trusses are actually the same as for the two-span trusses on the long sides. Even if the span conditions were different from those described here, the general construction used for the trusses on the longer side would likely be the same.

As the size of trusses increases, considerable deflection might be experienced under loading. The two primary components of this deformation are the elongation of long tension members and the multiple deformations that can occur in truss joints. While members sustaining pure tension can be quite slender and highly stressed, tension members in bracing trusses should be chosen so that they will not be highly stressed, thus reducing tension elongation. Joints should also be studied for reduction of deformation within the joints themselves. The objective is to stiffen the bracing with regard to its overall deformation (deflection), especially when the movement is back and forth, as occurs in an earthquake.

16

Sloping Sites

Buildings are frequently built on sites that are part of a large slope, often the side of a hill or the foothill area of a mountain. What happens to a site, or to buildings placed on it, in this situation depends on several factors, including the type of site development that is achieved. This chapter presents three cases: The transition site (leveled out), the unchanged slope, and the cliff edge.

16.1 THE TRANSITION SITE

Although it is possible to leave the sloping site essentially unchanged, and to conform the building to the slope (Figure 16.1), development of a *transition site* is common. Typically,

FIGURE 16.1 Building developed to conform to the unaltered slope.

the transition site combines a cut into the up-slope side of the site and a build-up of fill on the down-slope side, rendering the site reasonably flat. The flat site is sometimes needed for functional reasons, such as the layout of a large parking lot (Figure 16.2).

There are a number of potential problems with this type of site development, one of which is its behavior in an earthquake. As with many site failures that occur with an earthquake, the basic causes of the failure are usually in place before the earthquake. The earthquake is just a big push into the failure condition.

Description

Figure 16.3 shows a profile section through a building and its site. The site was originally part of a slope, and the original ground surface contour is shown in a dashed line in the section. To create the flat site for the building, the site has been cut to a depth of 12 ft on the up-slope side and built up 8 ft on the downslope side. The house is formed essentially as it would be on an originally flat site, with shallow bearing foundations of normal depth.

What Can Happen?

There are a lot of potential problems with this situation without considering the possibility of a major earthquake. Some major ones are:

Settlement of the Footings on Fill. No building designer or builder with any sense would place the house foundations as shown in Figure 16.3. The footings on the down-slope side at least should be dropped to the level of the original grade. Otherwise, there will be a major differential in settlements of the footings placed on the cut and the footings on the fill—no matter how well the fill is compacted.

Loss of the Down-Slope Edge. Erosion, settlement, and, possibly, rotational slope failure will chew away at the site edge. Some effort must be made to retain the edge. If a larger development of the slope is in progress, there may be neighbors on each side—uphill and down. Thus, the true site edges might look as shown in Figure 16.4, which only increases the problems at the edges. Loss of the down-slope edge is a double problem

FIGURE 16.2 Transition site for a parking lot.

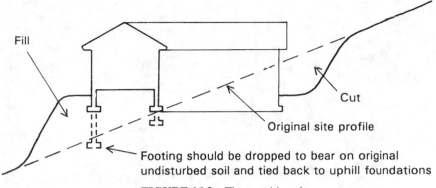

Fill

Cut

Original site profile

Footing should be dropped to bear on original undisturbed soil and tied back to uphill foundations

FIGURE 16.3   The transition site.

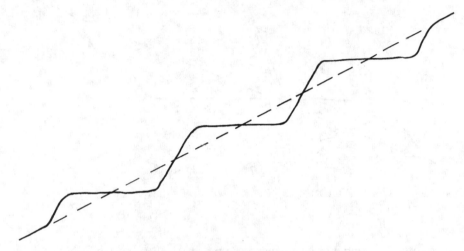

FIGURE 16.4   Stepped transition sites.

involving both neighbors—loss of site soil for the upper neighbor and a landslide for the down-slope neighbor.

Slope Failure at the Cut Edge of the Site.   Even without an up-slope neighbor, this cut slope may fail, pouring a mass of soil onto the site.

Failure of the Original Slope.   If the angle of the original slope is approaching a critical condition, or if existing subgrade soil strata are not horizontal, the piling up of the soil at the down-slope edge plus the weight of the house may cause a general failure of the slope, as shown in Figure 16.5.

Exposure of Sensitive or Unstable Soils by the Cut.   Any deep cut has the potential of exposing soil layers to new conditions that may cause some reaction. With the containment of the original soil removed and the formerly buried soil now exposed to sun, air, and rain (and maybe irrigation), there may be some structural changes in the newly exposed soils.

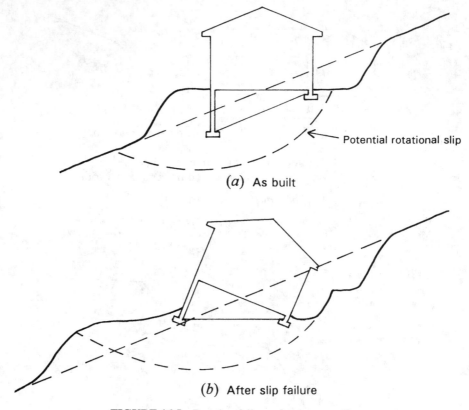

(a) As built

(b) After slip failure

FIGURE 16.5   Rotation failure of a site on a slope.

A lot of this potential trouble depends on the angle of the original slope. The cut and fill depths and the potential for slope failures will be minimized for a gradual slope, say 10 degrees or so. Problems become increasingly likely as the slope angle gets steeper. Typically, building codes or local enforcing agencies limit slopes based on local soils and experience. As slopes approach as much as 30 degrees or so, it is usually necessary to provide a form of positive slope retention.

However, for a large site—say 200 ft deep into the slope—to create a flat condition in a ten-degree slope requires a cut and fill adding up to about 17 ft. So, with an 8- to 10-ft cut or fill at each site edge, the edges become problematic, especially if a building is placed close to either edge.

Seismic Response

During an earthquake, most transition site failures that occur were in progress before the earthquake. That is to say, a slope failure or a massive consolidation of fill was developing, and the violent action of the earthquake simply aggravated things. Thus these actions might happen during an earthquake, but they were predictable from other causes earlier.

The remedies for seismic effects are similar to those for the general situation. Efforts to protect the site from failures due to gravity, soil consolidation, and other causes will also

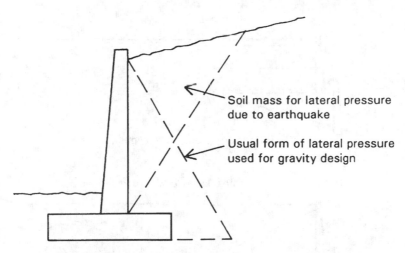

FIGURE 16.6   Seismic effect on retaining walls.

help retain it during an earthquake. However, there are some special considerations that might be appropriate when seismic risk is high. These include the following:

1. Extra provision for lateral force on a retaining structure. As shown in Figure 16.6, the lateral force that creates overturning for a retaining structure comes from the mass of retained soil on the high side of the structure. Ordinarily, lateral soil pressure is due to the gravity action of this retained mass, which acts like an equivalent fluid. During an earthquake, there is a potential for an additional pressure, caused by the horizontal movement of the impelled (horizontally thrown) soil mass. This calls for use of a higher lateral pressure for design of the retaining structure.

2. Reconstitution of the structure of supporting soils. Violent shaking of a soil mass can cause various forms of change in the soil. Especially vulnerable are those soils whose structure includes a lot of bonding of otherwise loose soil particles. Fracturing of these bonds can dramatically change the structural character of the soil. Settlements can occur instantly, or may be long term in nature, occurring only with seasonal cycles or fluctuations in water content. Where soils with this form of sensitivity exist, a new discovery program should be undertaken after any major earthquake, even if no problems are evident during post-quake inspections.

One technique for stabilizing the filled portion of the transition site is to tie it to the original slope, as shown in Figure 16.7. As shown in Figures 16.7*a* and *b*, this may be done incrementally which is probably best done when the horizontal length of the transition site down the slope is great. The slope is retained in portions, with tied-back layers or individually anchored retaining structures.

Another way of tying the filled portion is shown in Figure 16.7*c*. This consists of using a *downhill frame*—a frame laid on the original slope and anchored by deep foundation elements (driven piles or drilled piers). The frame serves as a transition device secured to

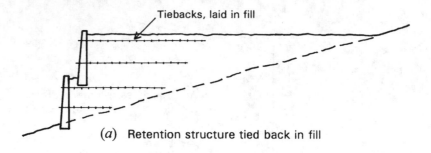

(*a*) Retention structure tied back in fill

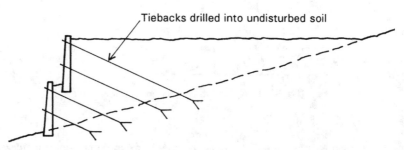

(*b*) Retention structure tied back to undisturbed soil

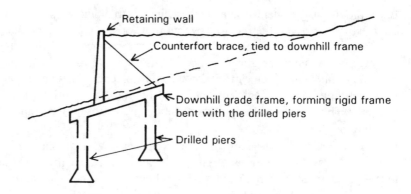

(*c*) Retaining wall supported and braced by downhill frame

FIGURE 16.7   Effectiveness of a retaining wall in sustaining a sloped site.

the slope, and then it serves as a base for retention of the fill above it. This method is appropriate for short, steep slopes. This method can also be used for a structure placed on an unaltered slope, as described in the next section.

16.2 THE UNCHANGED SLOPE

Buildings may sometimes be placed on a slope with the general form of the slope unaltered. A minor cut or transition may be made for access, but the major portion of the site that provides support for the building is unchanged, as shown in Figure 16.1.

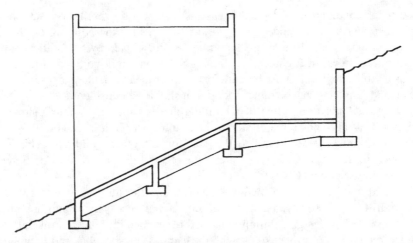

FIGURE 16.8   Framed foundation structure laid on the slope.

There is a natural tendency for anything placed on a slope to roll or slip down the slope. It doesn't take an earthquake to make that happen, so anchorage to the slope is a normal requirement. For a shallow slope, this can be achieved by burying the foundation some distance below the ground surface (Figure 16.8). Indeed, this also may be sufficient for resistance to additional lateral effects from an earthquake.

The issue in this case, as compared to the transition site in Section 16.1, is that the building is at risk, whereas it is the site itself that is at risk in the transition situation. Thus, the use of a downhill frame for the down-slope fill on the transition site also works to protect the building. Here, the frame would be used directly as a foundation for the building, as shown in Figure 16.9.

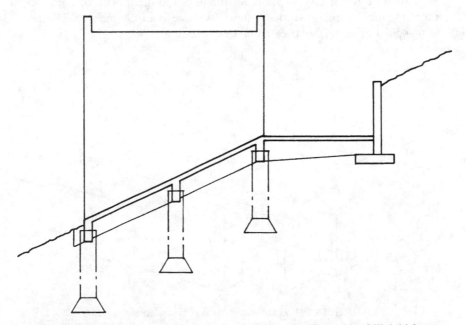

FIGURE 16.9   Foundation with deep elements, developed as a downhill rigid frame.

Another condition of risk in this case is that of a downhill slope failure that might remove supporting soils and undermine the footings for the building on the down-slope edge. A progressive failure of this type may be precipitated by a condition downhill. (See the example shown in Figure 2.15.) Such a situation might be beyond the control of the owner of this site, but it must be anticipated nevertheless. If the slope goes, the building goes, and if anything can be done to stop it, it should be considered.

An unusual situation is that of a building that is built deeply into a slope, so that the building itself becomes a major slope-retaining device. In a large complex, the retaining building would serve to stabilize the site for the other buildings. This method was employed in developing the large site of the central campus of the Air Force Academy near Colorado Springs, Colorado.

Located in the foothills of the Rocky Mountains, the site was nowhere flat. To provide a large drill field in the center of the campus, it was necessary to build retained edges as high as 35 ft. The design solution consisted of surrounding the central flat campus with multistory buildings on three sides, with the campus entry level at mid-height of the buildings (Figure 16.10). Lower stories constitute a retaining structure for the down-slope edges of the large transition site.

Another example is shown in Figure 16.11, in which a building is placed at the edge of a lower street, with a cliff looming over it. The retaining function provided by the building permits its being located here at all, and it also adds an assurance of stability for the buildings above on the cliff edge (Figure 16.12).

16.3   THE CLIFF EDGE

Is there a more dramatic site? At the edge of a high cliff, overlooking a valley or a body of water (Figure 16.13). But how can you keep the cliff edge, and any structure near to it, in place—especially in an earthquake?

Many cliffs were formed by a major slope failure, and the processes that precipitated that failure might be ongoing, so that a new cliff edge is in the making. The new edge could be at a point much farther back from the current edge.

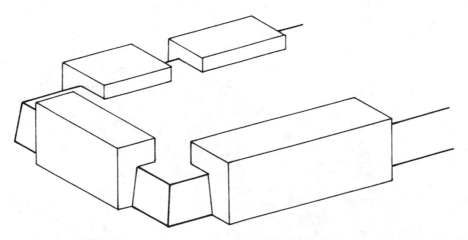

FIGURE 16.10   Form of the Air Force Academy campus.

FIGURE 16.11   A building used as a retaining wall.

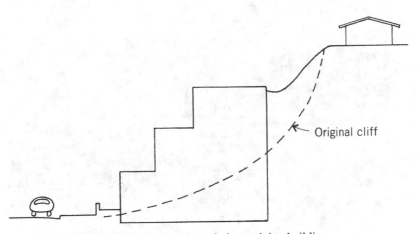

Original cliff

FIGURE 16.12   Section through the retaining building.

Remedies here often hinge on treating the conditions beneath the cliff. If major retention can be achieved at the base of the cliff, natural processes—including earthquakes—might be subverted. See the examples in Figures 16.10 and 16.11. Otherwise, the only real remedy is to stay back from the cliff edge by some conservative distance. Let a geotechnical expert do a slope failure analysis and use it to figure out where to build.

A special problem with cliff edges and ridges is the possibility of a *ridge effect* occurring during an earthquake (Figure 16.14). The upward movements are magnified as shock waves travel along the ground surface. Design of structures on the top of a ridge or cliff edge should account for magnified upward directed seismic movements.

FIGURE 16.13 Living on the edge.

FIGURE 16.14 What goes up doesn't always come down. This cliff-edge house didn't quite come back down on its braces, defying gravity.

Glossary

Abutment. Originally, the end support of an arch or vault. Now, any support that receives both vertical and lateral loading.

Acceleration. The rate of change of the velocity, expressed as the first derivative of the velocity (dv/dt) or as the second derivative of the displacement (d^2s/dt^2). Acceleration of the ground surface is more significant than its displacement during an earthquake as it relates more directly to the force effect. $F = ma$ as a dynamic force.

Accidental torsion. Minimum torsional effect on buildings required by the *UBC* in some instances, even when there is no actual computed torsional effect. See *Torsion*.

Active Lateral Pressure. See *Lateral Pressure*.

Adequate. Just enough; sufficient. Indicates a quality of bracketed acceptability—on the one hand not insufficient, on the other hand, not superlative or excessive.

Amplitude. See *Vibration*.

Anchorage. Refers to attachment for resistance to movement usually caused by uplift, overturn, sliding, or horizontal separation. Tie-down, or hold-down, refers to anchorage against uplift or overturn. Positive anchorage generally refers to direct fastening that does not loosen easily.

Aseismic. Describes resistance to seismic effects. Building design is actually *aseismic* design, therefore, although the term *seismic design* is more commonly used.

Aspect Ratio. The proportionate ratio of the dimensions of an object, such as the height-to-width ratio of a shear wall panel or a tower, the length-to-width ratio of a rectangular building plan, or the span-to-depth ratio of a beam, slab, or truss.

Base. The level at which earthquake motions are considered to be delivered to the building structure.

Base Shear. The total design lateral force (horizontal shear) at the building base.

Battering. Describes the effect that occurs when two elements in separate motion bump into each other repeatedly, such as two adjacent parts of a structure during an earthquake. Also called *hammering* or *pounding*.

Bent. A planar framework, or a portion of one, designed to resist both vertical and horizontal forces in the plane of the frame. May be achieved as a *rigid frame* with moment-resisting joints or as a *braced frame* with trussing.

Box System. A structural system in which lateral loads are not resisted by a vertical load-bearing space frame but rather by shear walls or a braced frame.

Braced Frame. Literally, any framework braced against lateral forces. Building codes use the term to describe a frame braced by trussing (triangulation).

Brittle Fracture. Sudden ultimate failure in tension or shear. The basic structural behavior of brittle materials.

Centroid. The geometric center of an object, usually analogous to the center of gravity. The point at which the entire mass of the object may be considered to be concentrated when moment of the mass is considered.

Collector. A force-transfer element that functions to collect loads from a horizontal diaphragm and distribute them to the vertical elements of the lateral resistive system.

Confined Concrete. Concrete mass that is wrapped by constraints (ties, spirals, stirrups, etc.) in order to resist three-dimensional stress conditions.

Continuity. Most often used to describe structures or parts of structures that have behavioral characteristics influenced by the monolithic, continuous nature of adjacent elements, such as continuous, vertical, multistory columns; continuous, multispan beams; and rigid frames.

Core Bracing. Vertical elements of a lateral-bracing system developed at the location of permanent interior walls for stairs, elevators, duct shafts, or rest rooms.

Critical Damping. The amount of damping that will result in a return from initial deformation to the neutral position without reversal.

Damping. See *Vibration*.

Degree of Freedom. See *Freedom*.

Determinate. Having defined limits; definite. In structures, the condition of having the exact sufficiency of stability externally and internally, therefore being determinable by the resolution of forces alone. An excess of stability conditions produces a structure characterized as *indeterminate*.

Diaphragm. A surface element (deck, wall, etc.) used to resist forces in its own plane by spanning or cantilevering. See also *Horizontal diaphragm* and *Shear wall*.

Displacement. Movement away from some fixed reference point. Motion is described mathematically as a displacement-time function. See also *Acceleration* and *Velocity*.

Drag. Generally refers to wind effects on surfaces parallel to the wind direction. Ground drag refers to the effect of the ground surface in slowing the wind velocity near ground level.

Drag Strut. A structural member used to transfer lateral load across the building and into some part of the vertical system. See also *Collector*.

Drift. Generally refers to lateral deflection. *Story drift* refers to lateral movement of one level of a structure with respect to another.

Dual Bracing System. Combination of a moment-resisting space frame and shear walls or braced frames, with the combined systems designed to share the lateral loads.

Ductile. Describes the load-strain behavior that results from the plastic yielding of materials or connections. To be significant, the plastic strain prior to failure should be considerably more than the elastic strain up to the point of plastic yield.

Ductile Moment-Resisting Space Frame. Rigid frame structure that complies with code requirements intended to assure a ductile yielding form of response to seismic forces.

Dynamic. Usually used to characterize load effects or structural behaviors that are not static in nature. That is, they involve time-related considerations such as vibrations, energy effects versus simple force, and so on.

Earthquake. The common term used to describe sensed ground movements, usually caused by subterranean faults or explosions. The point on the ground surface immediately above the subterranean shock is called the *epicenter*. The magnitude of the energy released at the location of the shock is the basis for the rating of the shock on the *Richter scale*.

Eccentric Braced Flame. Braced frame in which the bracing members do not connect to the joints of the beam-and-column frame, thus resulting in axial force in the braces, but bending and shear in the frame members. Forms include: knee brace, K brace, chevron brace (two forms: V brace and inverted V brace).

Elastic. Used to describe two aspects of stress-strain behavior. The first is a constant stress-strain proportionality, or constant modulus of elasticity, as represented by a straight line form of the stress-strain graph. The second is the limit within which all the strain is recoverable; that is, there is no permanent deformation. The latter phenomenon may occur even though the stress-strain relationship is nonlinear.

Element. A component or constituent part of a whole. Usually a distinct, separate entity.

Energy. Capacity for doing work; what is used up when work is done. Occurs in various forms: mechanical, heat, chemical, electrical, and so on.

Epicenter. See *Earthquake*.

Equivalent Static Force Analysis. The technique by which a dynamic effect is translated into a hypothetical (equivalent) static effect that produces a similar result.

Essential Facilities. Building code term for a building that should remain functional after a disaster such as a windstorm or major earthquake; affects establishment of the *I* factor for base shear or design wind pressure.

Factored Load. A percentage of the actual service load (usually an increase) used for strength design. See also *Load*.

Failure. Becoming incapable of a particular function. May have partial as well as total connotations in structures. For example, a single connection may fail, but the structure might not collapse because of its ability to redistribute the load.

Fatigue. A structural failure that occurs as the result of a load applied and removed (or reversed) repeatedly through a large number of cycles.

Fault. The subterranean effect that produces an earthquake. Usually a slippage, cracking, sudden strain release, and so on.

Feasible. Capable of being or likely to be accomplished.

Force. An effort that tends to change the shape or the state of motion of an object.

Fracture. A break, usually resulting in actual separation of the material. A characteristic result of tension failure.

Freedom. In structures, usually refers to the lack of any type of resistance or constraint. In static analysis, the connections between members and the supports of the structure are qualified as to type, or degree, of freedom. Thus, the terms *fixed support, pinned support*, and *sliding support* are used to qualify the types of movement resisted. In dynamic analysis, the degree of freedom is an important factor in determining the dynamic response of a structure.

Frequency. In harmonic motion (bouncing springs, vibrating strings, and swinging pendulums, etc.), the number of complete cycles of motion per unit of time. See also *Vibration*.

Fundamental Period. See *Period*.

Geophysical. Refers to the physical behavior characteristics of the ground surface and of subterranean masses.

Geotechnical. General term that refers to the engineering field dealing with soils and the behavior of structures in and on the ground.

Grain. 1. A discrete particle of the material that constitutes a loose material, such as soil. 2. The fibrous orientation of wood.

Hammering. See *Battering*.

Hertz. Cycles per second.

Hold-Down. See *Anchorage*.

Horizontal Bracing System. Truss system in a horizontal plane that functions as a horizontal diaphragm.

Horizontal Diaphragm. See *Diaphragm*. Usually a roof or floor deck used as part of the lateral bracing system.

Impact. Action of striking or hitting.

Impulse. An impelling force action, characterized by rapid acceleration or deceleration. Examples: gust of wind; violent thrust from an earthquake.

Indeterminate. See *Determinate*.

Inelastic. See *Stress-Strain Behavior*.

Inertia. See *Mass*.

Interrupted Shear Wall. A shear wall that is not continuous from its top to its foundation.

Irregular Structure. See *Regular Structure*.

Lateral. Literally means to the side or from the side. Often used to refer to something that is perpendicular to a major axis or direction. With reference to the vertical direction gravity forces, wind, earthquakes, and horizontally directed soil pressures are called *lateral effects*.

Lateral Force Resistive System. The combination of elements of the building construction that contributes directly to the general bracing of the building against lateral forces. Also called the *lateral bracing system* or simply the *bracing system*.

Lateral Pressure. Horizontal soil pressure of two kinds: 1. *Active* lateral pressure is that exerted by a retained soil upon the retaining structure. 2. *Passive* lateral pressure is that exerted by soil against an object that is attempting to move in a horizontal direction.

Liquefaction. Action in which a soil deposit temporarily loses its shear resistance and takes on the character of a liquid with low resistance to lateral movement; usually resulting from some dynamic vibration, such as that occuring during an earthquake.

Load. The active force (or combination of forces) exerted on a structure. *Dead load* is permanent load due to gravity, which includes the weight of the structure itself. *Live load* is any load component that is not permanent—including those due to wind, seismic effects, temperature changes, or shrinkage—but the term is most often used for gravity loads that are not permanent. *Service load* is the total load combination that the structure is expected to experience in use. *Factored load* is the service load multiplied by some factor (usually for increase) for use in strength design.

Load Path. The means by which applied forces (loads) flow through a structure and are resolved by its supports. *Multiple load paths* refers to structures with redundancy in the form of backup load resistance paths that can take over when the initial load path elements fail.

Mass. The dynamic property of an object that causes it to resist changes in its state of motion. This resistance is called *inertia*. The magnitude of the mass per unit volume of the object is called its *density*. Dynamic force is defined by $F = ma$ or force equals mass times acceleration. Weight is defined as the force produced by the acceleration of gravity—thus, $W = mg$.

Mat Foundation. A very large bearing-type foundation. When the entire bottom of a building is constituted as a single mat, it is also called a *raft foundation*.

Maximum Density. The theoretical density of a soil mass achieved when the void is reduced to the minimum possible.

Member. One of the distinct elements of an assemblage.

Mercalli Scale. System used to determine the location of the epicenter of an earthquake on the basis of defining zones of relative intensity of observed damage and experiences of persons during the quake. This is essentially the basis for the determination of the zones of intensity of risk in the *UBC*.

Modified Mercalli Scale. See *Mercalli Scale*. Present version of the system.

Moment-Resisting Space Frame. A vertical load-bearing framework in which members are capable of resisting forces primarily by flexure (*UBC* definition). See also *Rigid Frame*.

Natural Period. See *Period*.

Normal. 1. The ordinary, usual, unmodified state of something. 2. Perpendicular, such as pressure normal to a surface, stress normal to a cross section, and so on.

Occupancy Importance Factor (I). *UBC* term used in the basic equation for seismic force. Expresses potential for increased concern for certain occupancies.

Optimal. Best; most satisfying. The best solution to a set of design criteria is the optimal one. When criteria have opposed values, there may be no optimal solution, except for the superiority of a single criterion (e.g., the lightest, the strongest, the cheapest, and so on).

Overturn. The toppling, or tipping over, effect of lateral loads.

Passive Soil Pressure. See *Lateral Pressure*.

P-delta Effect. Secondary effect on members of a frame, induced by the vertical loads acting on the laterally displaced frame.

Period (of Vibration). The total elapsed time for one full cycle of vibration. For an elastic structure in simple, single-mode vibration, the period is a constant (called the *natural* or *fundamental period*) and is independent of the magnitude of the amplitude, of the number of cycles, and of most damping or resonance effects. See also *Vibration*.

Perimeter Bracing. Vertical elements of a lateral bracing system located at the building perimeter (outer walls).

Pier. 1. A short, stocky column with a height not greater than three times its least lateral dimension. The *UBC* defines a masonry wall as a pier if its plan length is less than three times the wall thickness. 2. A deep foundation element that is placed in an excavation rather than being driven as a pile. Although it actually refers to a particular method of excavation, the term *caisson* is also used to describe a pier foundation.

Plastic. 1. Usually, a synthetic material or organic origin, including many types of resins, polymers, cellulose derivatives, and casein materials. 2. In structural investigation, the type of stress response that occurs in ductile behavior, usually resulting in considerable permanent deformation.

Plastic Hinge. Region where the ultimate moment strength of a ductile member may be developed and maintained with corresponding significant rotation as a result of the local yielding of the material.

Polar Moment of Inertia. The second moment of an area about a line that is perpendicular to the plane of the area. Of significance in investigation of response to torsion.

Positive Anchorage. See *Anchorage.*

Pounding. See *Battering.*

Preconsolidation. The condition of a highly compressed soil, usually referring to a condition produced by the weight of soil above on some lower soil strata. May also refer to a condition produced by other than natural causes—piling up of soil on the ground surface, vibration, or saturation that dissolves soil bonding, for example.

Presumptive Soil Pressure. A value for the allowable vertical bearing pressure that is used in the absence of extensive investigation and testing. Requires a minimum of soil identification and is usually quite conservative.

Quick Soil. Soil deposit that is reasonably stable if undisturbed, but becomes suddenly quite loose and fluidlike when disturbed.

Raft Foundation. See *Mat Foundation.*

Redundancy. For structures, refers to the existence of multiple load paths or to multi-stage load response in general.

Reentrant Corner. An exterior corner in a building plan having a form such as that at the junction of the web and flange of a T.

Regular Structure. Building having no significant discontinuities in plan, in vertical configuration, or in its lateral force-resisting systems such as those described for irregular structures in *UBC* tables.

Reinforce. To strengthen, usually by adding something.

Relative Stiffness. See *Stiffness.*

Reserve Energy. Energy that a ductile system is capable of absorbing by plastic strains.

Resilience. The measurement of the absorption of energy by a structure without incurring permanent deformation or fracture. See *Toughness.*

Resonance. See *Vibration.*

Restoring Moment. The resistance to overturn due to the weight of the affected object.

Retrofit. Usually refers to the task of bringing an existing object (building, etc.) into conformance with recent, typically more stringent, standards.

Richter Scale. A log-based measuring system for evaluation of the relative energy level of an earthquake at its center of origin.

Rigid Bent. See *Rigid Frame.*

Rigid Frame. Framed structure in which the joints between the members are made to transmit moments between the ends of the members. Called a *bent* when the frame is planar.

Rigidity. Quality of resistance to deformation. Structures that are not rigid are called *flexible.*

Risk. The degree of probability of loss due to some potential hazard. The risk of an earthquake in a particular location is the basis for the Z factor in the *UBC* equation for seismic base shear.

Rotation. Motion in a circular path. Also used to describe twisting, or torsional, effect. See *Torsion.*

Safety. Relative unlikelihood of failure, absence of danger. The *safety factor* is the ratio of the resisting capacity of a structure to the actual demand on the structure.

Saturation. The condition that exists when the soil void is completely filled with water. A condition of *partial saturation* exists when the void is partly filled with water. *Oversaturation,* or *supersaturation,* occurs when the soil contains water in excess of the normal volume of the void, resulting in some flotation or suspension of the solid soil particles.

Seismic. Pertaining to ground shock. See also *Aseismic.*

Separation Joint. A connection between adjacent parts of a building that allows for some controlled movement of the separate parts; may allow for thermal effects, differential settlement, seismic motion, and so on.

Shear Wall. A vertical diaphragm.

Site Coefficient (S). A *UBC* term used in the basic equations for base shear to account for the effect of the period of the ground mass under the building.

Soft Story. In a multistory structure, a story level whose lateral stiffness is significantly less than that of stories above it.

Space Frame. An ambiguous term used variously to describe three-dimensional structures. The *UBC* gives a particular definition used in classifying structures for response to seismic effects.

Specific Gravity. A relative indication of density, using the weight of water as a reference. A specific gravity of 2 indicates a density (weight) twice that of water.

Spectrum. In seismic analysis, generally refers to the curve that describes the actual dynamic force effect on a structure as a function of variation in its fundamental period. Response spectra are the family of curves produced by various degrees of damping. This represents the basis for determining the building's general response to seismic force.

Stability. Refers to the inherent capability of a structure to develop force resistance as a property of its form, orientation, articulation of its parts, type of connections, methods of support, and so on. It is not directly related to quantified strength or stiffness, except when the actions involve the buckling of elements of the structure.

Static. The state that occurs when velocity is zero; thus, no motion is occurring. Generally refers to situations in which no change is occurring.

Stiffness. In structures, refers to resistance to deformation, as opposed to *strength*, which refers to resistance to force. A lack of stiffness indicates a flexible structure. Relative stiffness usually refers to the comparative deformation of two or more structural elements that share a load.

Story Drift. The total lateral displacement occurring in a single story of a multistory structure.

Strain. Deformation resulting from stress. It is usually measured as a percentage of deformation, called *unit strain* or *unit deformation,* and is dimensionless.

Strength. 1. In statics: Capacity to resist force. 2. In dynamics: Energy-absorbing capacity.

Strength Design. One of the two design techniques for ensuring safety for a structure. *Stress design,* also called *working stress design,* is performed by analyzing stresses produced by the estimated actual usage loads and assigning limits for the stresses that are below the ultimate capacity of the materials by some margin. *Strength design,* also called *ultimate strength design,* is performed by multiplying the actual loads by the desired factor of safety and designing a structure that will have the product of that process as its ultimate failure load.

Strengthening. Adding strength to a structure in one of two ways: (1) by reinforcing an existing structure, or (2) by adding elements to a structure designed for other loads. An existing building may be strengthened with added bracing for earthquakes, or a designed structure may be modified for additional strength.

Stress. The mechanism of force within the material of a structure; visualized as a pressure effect (tension or compression) or a shear effect on the surface of a cut section and quantified as force per unit area. *Allowable* stress refers to a limit used in stress design methods. *Ultimate* stress refers to the maximum stress that is developed just prior to failure of the material.

Stress Design. See *Strength Design.*

Stress-Strain Behavior. The relation of stress to strain in a material or a structure. It is usually visually represented by a stress-strain graph covering the range from no load to failure. Various forms of the graph define particular behavioral properties. A straight line indicates an elastic relationship; a bend or curve indicates inelastic behavior. A sudden bend in the graph usually indicates a plastic strain or yield that can result in permanent deformation. The slope of the graph (or of a tangent to the curve) is defined as the modulus of elasticity of the material.

Tie-Down. See *Anchorage.*

Torsion. Moment effect involving twisting or rotation in a plane perpendicular to the major axis of an element. Lateral loads produce torsion on a building when they tend to twist it about its vertical axis. This occurs when the centroid of the load does not coincide with the center of stiffness of the vertical elements of the lateral load-resisting structural system.

Toughness. The measurement of the total dynamic energy capacity of a structure, up to the point of complete failure. See also *Resilience.*

Ultimate Strength. Usually used to refer to the maximum static force resistance of a structure at the time of failure. This limit is the basis for the so-called strength design methods, as compared to the stress design methods that use an established stress limit, called the design stress, working stress, permissible stress, and so on.

Underpinning. Propping up a structure that is in danger of, or has already experienced some support failure due to excessive settlement, undermining, erosion, and so on.

Upheaval. Pushing upward of a soil mass.

Uplift. Net upward force effect due to wind, to overturning moment, or to upward seismic acceleration.

Velocity. The time rate of a motion. Also commonly called *speed.*

Vertical Diaphragm. See *Diaphragm.* Also called a *shear wall.*

Vibration. The cyclic, rhythmic motion of a body. Occurs when the body is displaced from some neutral position and seeks to restore itself to a state of equilibrium when released. In its pure form it occurs as a harmonic motion with a characteristic behavior described by the cosine form of the displacement-time graph of the motion. The magnitude of linear displacement from the neutral position is called the *amplitude*. The time elapsed for one full cycle of motion is called the *period*. The number of cycles occurring in one second is called the *frequency*. Effects that tend to reduce the amplitude of succeeding cycles are called *damping*. The increase of amplitude in successive cycles is called a *resonant effect*.

Viscosity. The general measurement of the mobility, or free-flowing character, of a fluid or semifluid mass. Heavy oil is viscous (has high viscosity); water has low viscosity.

Void. The open space within an object. In soils, refers to the portion of the volume not occupied by the solid materials, but filled partly with gas (air, etc.) and partly with liquid (water, oil, etc.).

Void Ratio. The term commonly used to indicate the amount of void in a soil mass, expressed at the ratio of volume of the void to the volume of the solids.

Wall (Structural). A vertical, planar building element. *Foundation walls* are those that are partly or totally below ground. *Bearing walls* are used to carry vertical loads in direct compression. *Grade walls* are those that are used to achieve the transition between the building that is above the ground and the foundation below it, (grade refers to the level of the ground surface at the edge of the building). *Shear walls* are those used to brace the building against horizontal forces due to wind or seismic shock. *Freestanding walls* are walls whose tops are not laterally braced. *Retaining walls* are walls that resist horizontal soil pressure.

Weak Story. In a multistory structure, a story level whose lateral strength is significantly less than that of stories above.

Zone. Usually refers to a bounded area on a surface, such as the ground surface or the plan of a level of a building. Building codes define geographic zones for assignment of risk.

Bibliography

The following list contains materials that have been used as references in the development of various portions of the text. Also included are some widely used publications that serve as general references for seismic design and for general design of building structures, although no direct use of materials from them has been made in this book. The numbering system is random and merely serves to simplify referencing by text notation.

EARTHQUAKES AND BUILDINGS

1. *Uniform Building Code, Vol. 2: Structural Engineering Design Provisions*, 1997 International Conference of Building Officials, 5360 South Workmanmill Road, Whittier, CA 90601, 1997. (Called the *UBC*.)
2. *Minimum Design Loads for Buildings and Other Structures* (ANSI/ASCE 7- 88), American Society of Civil Engineers (ASCE), (Revision of ANSI A58.1-1982.) 1995.
3. *Recommended Lateral Force Requirements and Commentary*, Seismology Committee, Structural Engineers Association of California (SEACA), 1990. (Known as the *SEACA Bluebook*.)
4. *Building Configuration and Design*, Chris Arnold and Robert Reitherman, Wiley, New York, 1982.
5. Henry J. Lagorio, *Earthquakes: An Architect's Guide to Nonstructural Seismic Hazards*, Wiley, New York, 1990.
6. Ellis L. Krinitzsky, James P. Gould, and Peter H. Edinger, *Fundamentals of Earthquake Resistant Construction*, Wiley, New York, 1993.
7. *Introduction to Earthquake Retrofitting: Tools and Techniques*, Building Education Center, 812 Page Street, Berkeley, CA, 94710, 1994.
8. *Strengthening Wood Frame Houses for Earthquake Safety*, Bay Area Regional Earthquake Preparedness Project, Office of Emergency Services, State of California, Oakland, CA.

BUILDING CONSTRUCTION AND STRUCTURES

9. Charles G. Ramsey and Harold R. Sleeper, *Architectural Graphic Standards*, 9th ed. Wiley, New York, 1994.

10. Edward Allen, *Fundamentals of Building Construction: Materials and Methods*, 2d ed., Wiley, New York, 1990.

11. *Manual of Steel Construction*, 8th ed., American Institute of Steel Construction (AISC), Chicago, IL, 1980. (Called the *AISC Manual*.)

12. *National Design Specification for Wood Construction*, National Forest Products Association, Washington D. C., 1991.

13. *Timber Construction Manual*, 3rd ed., American Institute of Timber Construction, Wiley, New York, 1985.

14. *Building Code Requirements for Reinforced Concrete*, ACI 318-89, American Concrete Institute, Detroit, MI, 1989. (Called the *ACI Code*.)

15. *CRSI Handbook*, 4th ed., Concrete Reinforcing Steel Institute, Schaumburg, IL, 1982.

16. *Masonry Design Manual*, 3d ed., Masonry Institute of America, 2550 Beverly Boulevard, Los Angeles, CA 90057, 1979.

17. R. R. Schneider and W. L. Dickey, *Reinforced Masonry Design*, 3d ed., Prentice-Hall, Englewood Cliffs, NJ, 1987.

18. *Steel Deck Institute Design Manual for Composite Decks, Form Decks, and Roof Decks*, Steel Deck Institute, P. O. Box 3812, St. Louis, MO 63122.

19. Jack C. McCormac, *Structural Analysis*, 4th ed., Harper & Row, New York, 1984.

20. Stan W. Crawley and Robert M. Dillon, *Steel Buildings: Analysis and Design*, 4th ed., Wiley, New York, 1993.

21. Donald E. Breyer, *Design of Wood Structures*, 3d ed., McGraw-Hill, New York, 1993.

22. Leonard Spiegel and George F. Limbrunner, *Reinforced Concrete Design,* 3d ed., Prentice-Hall, Englewood Cliffs, NJ, 1992.

23. James Ambrose, *Simplified Design of Building Foundations*, 2d ed., Wiley, New York, 1988.

INDEX